# Weight Watchers 1•2•3 Success Food List (continued)

| Food List | Serving | Points |
|---|---|---|
| *Desserts (continued)* | | |
| Cookies, any type | 2 small | 3 |
| Ice cream, nonfat, no sugar added | 1 scoop | 2 |
| Pudding, reduced-calorie (made w/skim, nonfat or low-fat {1%} milk) | 1 cup | 2 |
| Yogurt, frozen, nonfat, no sugar added | 1 scoop | 2 |
| *Eggs* | | |
| Egg | 1 | 2 |
| Egg substitute, fat-free | 1/4 cup | 1 |
| Egg whites | 3 | 1 |
| *Fats* | | |
| Margarine, fat-free | 4 Tbsp | 1 |
| Margarine, reduced-calorie | 2 tsp | 1 |
| Mayonnaise, fat-free | 4 Tbsp | 1 |
| Mayonnaise, reduced-calorie | 2 tsp | 1 |
| Vegetable oil | 1 tsp | 1 |
| *Fish & Shellfish (cooked w/o added fat)* | | |
| Fish, (except those listed below) | 1 fillet | 4 |
| Fish, fresh, flaked (except those listed below) | 1/2 cup | 1 |
| Fish, anchovies | 6 | 1 |
| Fish, salmon | 1 fillet | 7 |
| Shellfish, fresh (clams, crab, crayfish, lobster, mussels, oysters, scallops, shrimp) | 1/2 cup | 1 |
| Tuna, canned in water, drained | 1/2 cup | 3 |
| *Fruits & Fruit Juices* | | |
| Apple | 1 | 1 |
| Applesauce, unsweetened | 1 cup | 1 |
| Apricots | 3 | 1 |
| Banana | 1 | 2 |
| Berries: blackberries, blueberries, cranberries, raspberries, strawberries | 1 cup each | 1 pt. each |
| Cantaloupe | 1/4 melon or 1 cup | 1 |
| Cherries | 1 cup | 1 |
| Cranberry juice cocktail, low-calorie | 1 cup | 1 |
| Fruit salad | 1 cup | 2 |
| Grapefruit juice | 1/2 cup | 1 |
| Grapefruit sections | 1 cup | 1 |
| Grapes | 1 cup | 1 |
| Honeydew melon | 1/8 melon or 1 cup | 1 |
| Kiwi fruit | 1 | 1 |
| Mandarin orange | 1 | 1 |
| Olives | 10 small or 6 large | 1 |
| Orange | 1 | 1 |
| Orange juice | 1/2 cup | 1 |
| Peach | 1 | 1 |
| Pear | 1 | 1 |
| Pineapple | 1/4 or 1 cup | 2 |
| Prune juice | 1/2 cup | 1 |
| Watermelon | 2" slice or 1 cup | 1 |
| *Grains* | | |
| Barley, cooked | 1 cup | 2 |
| Brown rice, cooked | 1 cup | 4 |
| Couscous (semolina), cooked | 1 cup | 2 |

| Food List | Serving | Points |
|---|---|---|
| *Grains (continued)* | | |
| Wheat germ | 3 Tbsp | 1 |
| White rice, cooked | 1 cup | 5 |
| *Legumes (cooked)* | | |
| Dry beans and peas | 1/3 cup | 1 |
| Lentils | 1/3 cup | 1 |
| *Meat & Meat Products (cooked w/o added fat)* | | |
| Beef, lean | 1 slice or 1/2 cup cubed or shredded | 3 |
| Lamb, lean | 1 slice, 1 chop or 1/2 cup cubed or shredded | 3 |
| Luncheon meat, lean | 1 slice, less than 2 grams fat per oz | 1 |
| Steak, lean | 1 small | 5 |
| Veal, lean | 1 slice, 1 chop or 1/2 cup cubed or shredded | 3 |
| *Meat Substitutes, Dishes & Products* | | |
| Vegetarian breakfast patty (sausage-type) | 1 | 1 |
| Vegetarian burger | 1 | 2 |
| *Milk Products* | | |
| Milk: buttermilk, nonfat, 1%, 1.5%, or 2% | 1 cup | 2 |
| Milk: evaporated, skimmed or low-fat | 1/2 cup | 2 |
| Milk: skim, nonfat, or fat-free | 1 cup | 2 |
| *Pasta & Noodles (cooked)* | | |
| Noodles, egg | 1 cup | 3 |
| *Salad Dressings* | | |
| Fat-free, salad dressing (except Italian) | 2 Tbsp | 1 |
| Fat-free, salad dressing, Italian | 2 Tbsp | 0 |
| *Salads* | | |
| Salad, mixed greens | 1 cup | 0 |
| *Sauces* | | |
| Chili sauce | 1 Tbsp | 0 |
| Cocktail sauce | 1/4 cup | 1 |
| Ketchup | 1/4 cup | 1 |
| Spaghetti sauce, bottled, any type | 1/2 cup | 2 |
| Taco sauce | 1 Tbsp | 0 |
| Tomato sauce | 1/2 cup | 0 |
| *Snacks* | | |
| Cereal bar, fat-free | 1 | 2 |
| Peanut butter | 1 Tbsp | 2 |
| Popcorn, hot-air or light microwave-popped | 3 cups | 1 |
| *Soups* | | |
| Broth, any type | 1 cup | 0 |
| Chicken noodle soup, canned | 1 cup | 1 |
| Lentil soup, canned | 1 cup | 2 |
| Vegetable soup, canned | 1 cup | 2 |
| *Spreads* | | |
| Jam, jelly, or preserves | 1 Tbsp | 1 |
| *Yogurt* | | |
| Fruit-flavored, nonfat, sweetened w/sugar | 1 cup | 4 |

# Weight Watchers

# New Complete Cookbook

# Weight Watchers®
# New
# Complete
# Cookbook

*Macmillan • USA*

**MACMILLAN**

A Simon & Schuster Macmillan Company

1633 Broadway

New York, NY 10019-6785

Macmillan Publishing books may be purchased for business or sales promotional use. For information please write: Special Markets Department, Macmillan Publishing USA, 1633 Broadway, New York, NY 10019.

## A Word About Weight Watchers

Since 1963, Weight Watchers has grown from a handful of people to millions of enrollees annually. Today, Weight Watchers is recognized as the leading name in safe and sensible weight control. Weight Watchers members form a diverse group, from youths to senior citizens, attending meetings virtually around the globe.

Weight-loss and weight-management results vary by individual, but we recommend that you attend Weight Watchers meetings, follow the Weight Watchers food plan and participate in regular physical activity. For the Weight Watchers meeting nearest you, call 1-800-651-6000.

### WEIGHT WATCHERS PUBLISHING GROUP

Editorial Director: Nancy Gagliardi

Senior Editor: Martha Schueneman

Associate Editor: Christine Senft, M.S.

General Manager of Program Development, Weight Watchers International, Inc.: Karen Miller-Kovach

Recipe Developers: Beth Allen, Catherine Chatham, Jean Galton, Catherine Garvey, Sandra Gluck, Luli Gray, Joyce Hendley, Tamara Holt, Joel Jason, Phyllis Kohn, Kristine Napier, M. P. H.; R.D., Linda Ann Rosensweig and Marianne Zanzarella

Nutrition Consultants: Mindy Hermann, M.B.A., R.D. and Lynne S. Hill, M.S., R.D., L.D.

Photographer: Rita Maas

Food Stylist: Mariann Sauvion

Prop Stylist: Cathy Cook

Cover Design by Michael J. Freeland and Paul Costello

Book Design by Paul Costello and Carol Shufro

Frontispiece: Fettuccine with Chicken and Broccoli Rabe (page 269)

ISBN 0-02-862449-1

Manufactured in China

# Contents

Contents

# Introduction

## A Weighty Reason

Although many of us want to lose weight simply to look better in a bathing suit, at a class reunion or to get back into that favorite outfit, reasons for losing weight can be far more serious—especially as we get older. With a full one-third of the population of the United States currently overweight and the numbers seemingly on the rise, obesity has become one of the most widespread health problems in the country. In fact, being overweight has been linked to an increased risk of heart disease, diabetes, high blood pressure, stroke, gallbladder disease and some types of cancer. Fortunately, even a moderate weight loss of ten to fifteen pounds can help to reduce these health risks.

Since 1963, Weight Watchers has been recognized as a leader in the weight-management field. Developed with the guidance and supervision of respected medical, nutrition, exercise physiology and psychology professionals, the Weight Watchers Program represents the most current and scientifically designed approach to weight loss and control available today. With the basic principles of good nutrition as its backbone, Weight Watchers continues to provide a thoroughly comprehensive approach to weight loss.

## What Is Good Nutrition?

Lately, it seems that you can't go anywhere without hearing about the importance of good nutrition. But what is good nutrition, really? While the foods you choose cannot themselves guarantee good health or weight loss, eating the right kinds of foods in appropriate amounts *can* improve your health and help you to lose weight. In other words, you need to strike a healthy balance when it comes to eating.

In order to strike that balance, variety is key. Not only does eating a variety of foods keep your meals interesting, it also helps to expand your food repertoire while supplying your body with all the nutrients it requires. The Weight Watchers Program, which meets the nutritional recommendations of many health organizations in North America, including the USDA Food Guide Pyramid and Canada's Food Guide to Healthy Eating (also known as Rainbow), is designed to help you eat a wide variety of foods in amounts appropriate for a safe rate of weight loss (up to two pounds per week after the first few weeks).

## The Key Players

### The Macronutrients

An important part of eating a healthful variety of foods is an appropriate balance of the macronutrients: carbohydrates, proteins and fats. The Weight Watchers Program stresses a diet that's high in complex carbohydrates, moderate in protein and low in fat.

## CLEARING UP CARBOHYDRATE CONFUSION

**Carbohydrates**, which come mostly from fruits, vegetables, breads, cereals and whole grains, are the major source of energy on the Plan. Unfortunately, misinformation about carbohydrates abounds—eating bread and pasta will make you fat, for example. The truth is, eating too many calories from any food, whether it's a carbohydrate, fat or protein, can cause weight gain. For most people, though, a diet higher in carbohydrates and lower in fat can actually lead to weight *loss*.

In addition to providing energy, complex carbohydrates are the major source of dietary fiber in the diet, adding bulk for a feeling of fullness and playing a part in the prevention of certain diseases (see page xi). **Weight Watchers suggests that 50–60 percent of your daily calories should come from carbohydrates.**

## FAT: FRIEND OR FOE?

As the most concentrated source of calories in the diet (nine calories per gram of fat versus four calories per gram of both carbohydrates and proteins), **fat** has gained a bad reputation of late, and that has given rise to a myriad of fat-free and low-fat products. However, some dietary fat is necessary to provide essential fatty acids and to act as a carrier for certain fat-soluble vitamins (A, D, E and K). In addition, fat takes a longer time to be digested and absorbed into the bloodstream, which can actually *help* you to feel full and satisfied after eating. The goal, then, is not to eliminate fat entirely but to consume the right amount and type.

There are three kinds of fat: saturated, monounsaturated and polyunsaturated, all of which contain the same number of calories. Saturated fats (linked to a greater risk of heart disease), such as butter, are solid at room temperature.

Unsaturated fats, which include monounsaturated and polyunsaturated fat, are generally considered to be healthier than saturated and are found primarily in liquid vegetable oils and most margarines. **Weight Watchers suggests a total fat intake per day of less than 30 percent of calories and a saturated fat intake per day of less than 10 percent of calories.**

## THE POWER OF PROTEIN

You probably remember Mom's advice to eat your steak to build muscles. She was referring to the body-building power of **proteins**. Proteins help to maintain and build body tissues.

Protein-rich foods (such as meat, eggs and cheese), however, are often a significant source of fat and the major source of saturated fat in the foods we eat. Therefore, **Weight Watchers recommends that, after carbohydrates and fats, remaining calories per day come from proteins,** emphasizing protein choices that are lower in fat, such as lean meats, low-fat dairy products and legumes (dried beans).

# *The Micronutrients*

The micronutrients, which include vitamins and minerals, are also an important part of a balanced, healthy diet. **Vitamins** are natural organic substances (from both plant and animal sources) required in small amounts by the human body. Thirteen vitamins are essential for normal body growth and maintenance. These are categorized as fat-soluble or water-soluble. The fat-soluble vitamins, A, D, E and K, can be stored by the body. The water-solubles, C and the eight B vitamins, cannot be readily stored, so they must be consumed more frequently. The following chart provides the primary functions of each of these vitamins, as well as good food sources for working them into your diet.

| VITAMIN | WHY YOU NEED IT | WHERE TO GET IT |
|---|---|---|
| *Vitamin A* | *Maintains healthy skin, hair and gums; prevents night blindness; as a precursor to Vitamin A, beta carotene may help prevent some types of cancer.* | *Carrots, dark green leafy vegetables, tomatoes, pumpkins, apricots, cantaloupes, mangoes, sweet potatoes, milk and liver.* |
| *B Vitamins* | *Convert food to energy; promote normal digestion; aid in appetite and nerve function.* | *Meat, liver, poultry and fish; dried beans, lentils and peas; cheese; milk and yogurt; grains and enriched breads and cereals.* |
| *Vitamin C* | *Helps resist infection; heals wounds; maintains healthy gums.* | *Oranges, strawberries, grapefruits, papayas, tangerines; broccoli, bell peppers, tomatoes, dark green leafy vegetables; white and sweet potatoes.* |
| *Vitamin D* | *Maintains healthy bones.* | *Fortified milk, fortified margarine, eggs.* |
| *Vitamin E* | *Defends the body against potentially harmful oxidations.* | *Vegetable oils and margarines; wheat germ; nuts; dark green leafy vegetables.* |
| *Vitamin K* | *Aids in the formation of proteins that regulate blood clotting.* | *Dark green leafy vegetables.* |

## MINERALS

**Minerals** are inorganic substances derived from nonliving sources. There are many essential minerals. A few key minerals include the macrominerals calcium, potassium and sodium, which the body needs in relatively large amounts. Trace minerals include iron, zinc and iodine. Although your body needs only small amounts of trace minerals, they do perform important functions, and one of the reasons that **Weight Watchers recommends eating a wide variety of foods is to ensure getting certain vitamins and trace minerals.** The chart on page x indicates why all minerals are important and where to get them.

## An Important Word for Women

*If you're a woman of child-bearing age and you're thinking about becoming pregnant, folic acid, or folate, is an important nutrient that you should know about. A lack of folic acid has been linked to neural tube defects in infants. The Recommended Dietary Allowance (RDA) has recently been increased to 400 micrograms per day for all adults, an amount double previous recommendations. Food sources include dark leafy green vegetables, legumes, liver, yeast, sunflower seeds, whole grains, peanuts and oranges. If you're pregnant or thinking about having a baby and feel you may not be getting enough folic acid, talk to your physician about taking a supplement.*

| MINERAL | WHY YOU NEED IT | WHERE TO GET IT |
| --- | --- | --- |
| Calcium | The essential nutrient for building strong teeth and healthy bones, calcium also aids in normal blood clotting and muscle contraction (including the heart muscle). Adequate calcium intake is considered vital in the prevention of osteoporosis. | Milk, buttermilk, yogurt; canned salmon (with bones), broccoli, oysters. |
| Potassium | Contributes to the transmission of nerve impulses, muscle contraction and the maintenance of normal blood pressure. | Fruits, vegetables, fresh meat and milk. |
| Sodium | Regulates the amount of fluid in the body, helping to maintain blood pressure; necessary for muscle contraction, nerve impulses, transporting nutrients and maintaining cells. | Processed foods; salt is a primary source; consuming too much can cause bloating, limit intake. |

| TRACE MINERAL | WHY YOU NEED IT | WHERE TO GET IT |
| --- | --- | --- |
| Iron | Aids in formation of blood cells, absorption can be enhanced by including a food high in Vitamin C in the same meal. | Beef, poultry, fish; dried beans, lentils, peas; tofu, eggs, organ meats and liver; dark green leafy vegetables, asparagus, artichokes, broccoli; whole-grain and enriched bread, iron-fortified cereals; dried fruits (apricots, dates, figs, prunes, raisins). |
| Zinc | Aids in achievement of normal body height, the maturation of sex glands, normal hair and nail growth and wound healing. Also helps maintain a healthy immune system. | Seafood (especially oysters), meat, milk, cheese, eggs, wheat germ. |
| Iodine | Helps regulate metabolism, prevent goiter. | Seafoods and seaweed, yeast breads, dairy products, iodized salt. |

## Sneaky Sodium Sources

Medications—sedatives, antacids, headache remedies and laxatives

Convenience foods like soups, puddings, rice mixes and ready-to-eat cereals

Canned vegetables

Snack foods like chips, salted pretzels and nuts

## Should You Shun Salt?

Does sodium have you stumped? You may know that sodium is necessary for the body to perform certain functions (see the chart above), but you've also heard that too much sodium isn't good for you. If you have high blood pressure, or hypertension, as do one in five Americans over the age of twenty-five, you should know that a high sodium diet could be a contributing factor. And because high blood pressure is a major risk factor

## Say "See Ya" to Salt

*Instead of reaching for the salt shaker, give some of these herbs and spices a shake:*

*Allspice—great in gravies*

*Basil—livens up tomato sauce*

*Cumin—gives chili a kick*

*Curry Powder—adds life to rice*

*Mustard—bold in beef, ham, fish and vegetable dishes*

*Parsley—puts some freshness in rice, soups, salads, egg and poultry dishes*

*Saffron—a little goes a long way to sass up rice and potato dishes, breads and sauces*

for heart disease, stroke and kidney disease, you'll want to know how you can help to control it.

Although reducing sodium intake may not prevent high blood pressure, it *can* help lower it if you're "salt sensitive," a condition which may be linked to family history and aging. The National Research Council recommends that sodium be limited to 2,400 milligrams per day (the amount in 1 teaspoon of salt)—unfortunately, most people consume much more. It's a good idea to watch sodium intake as part of a healthy diet, so beware of hidden sources of sodium.

## *Dietary Fiber*

Found only in plant foods, fiber is the nondigestible part of carbohydrates. Although it has a whole host of benefits, fiber has no calories. Unfortunately, most people don't get enough of it (experts recommend twenty-five grams per day). So, you know that fiber is good for you and you probably need to get more, but the information out there can often be confusing—what are the two kinds of fiber, for example, what do they do and where do they come from?

### SOLUBLE FIBER

**Soluble fiber** slows down the absorption of food in the stomach, creating a feeling of fullness. It is also associated with reducing blood cholesterol and maintaining stable blood-sugar levels. The best sources? Get soluble fiber from oats, dried beans, lentils, peas, fresh fruits and vegetables—but be sure to introduce fiber-rich foods to your diet gradually over a period of several weeks to minimize gastrointestinal side effects, such as bloating.

### INSOLUBLE FIBER

**Insoluble fiber** speeds the movement of food through the digestive tract and is associated with reducing the risk of some forms of cancer. The best sources of insoluble fiber are whole-grain breads, dried beans, cereals, pasta and brown rice.

## *Water*

You may not think of water as an indispensable nutrient, but without drinking water, humans can survive only a few days. Water is the most abundant substance in the body and performs many functions, including regulating body temperature, assisting in the digestive process and transporting nutrients and waste products to and from the body cells.

Your body loses water every minute and needs daily replenishing. An added bonus of water: Drinking it can also help you to feel full and reduce hunger. If you exercise for a long period of time or in hot climates, drinking plenty of water will also reduce the risk of dehydration. **Weight Watchers recommends drinking six to eight 8-ounce glasses of water every day.**

Although tap water from a safe water supply is the easiest and least expensive way to fill up your glass, bottled water, mineral water, sugar-free seltzer and club soda are other options. Be sure to limit use of caffeinated beverages—they act as diuretics, causing you to lose more water than you would otherwise.

# What Is 1•2•3 Success™?

Now that you know the basic nutritional elements for losing weight and following a balanced diet, you'll want to know about Weight Watchers' revolutionary program that can help you get there. **1•2•3 Success** is the first major change to the Weight Watchers Program—and it's the breakthrough you've been waiting for.

What's so earth-shattering about **1•2•3 Success**? Anyone who has ever tried losing weight knows that it is one of the hardest things to do—that's why we created **1•2•3 Success**. This simple plan makes dieting *easier*. Using our **POINTS®** food system, if you can count, you can lose weight on **1•2•3 Success**. Every food has been assigned a **POINT** value based on fat, fiber and calories. Here's how it works: If you're a woman who weighs 160 pounds, for example, your Daily **POINTS** Range is 20–27. Each day, simply add up the **POINTS** for the foods you eat and stay within the specific range for your weight. Choose your **POINTS** from a wide variety of foods each day and be sure to include at least two servings of dairy products and at least five servings of fruits and vegetables. That way you'll be getting the good nutrition you need, along with the weight loss you want.

Here are the allotted **POINTS** ranges for all weights:

| CURRENT WEIGHT | DAILY POINTS RANGE |
|---|---|
| *Less than 150 pounds* | *18–25* |
| *150 to 174 pounds* | *20–27* |
| *175 to 199 pounds* | *22–29* |
| *200 to 224 pounds* | *24–31* |
| *225 to 250 pounds* | *26–33* |
| *Over 250 pounds* | *28–35* |

# Can You Survive Three Days on 1•2•3 Success?

On **1•2•3 Success**, it's easy to enjoy satisfying portions of your favorite foods because it's so flexible. If you don't like fish, don't include it in your daily menu; if you have to have chocolate, have a piece—at only 3 **POINTS** per ounce, you can! With **1•2•3 Success** there are no shakes to blend, no pills to take, no tasteless ingredients to search for—eat the foods you enjoy, alongside everyone else. **1•2•3 Success** even considers the special occasions in your life by allowing you to bank **POINTS** so you can enjoy life's little celebrations to their fullest. What makes **1•2•3 Success** so easy to follow is that it's customized to fit your lifestyle and tastes.

**For a 160-pound woman, here's what three days on 1•2•3 Success might look like:**

## DAY ONE

*Breakfast*

   1 whole small bagel (3)
   2 tablespoons light cream cheese (1)
   1 cup coffee with fat-free milk (0)
   1 cup honeydew and cantaloupe chunks (1)

*Lunch*

   ½ cup canned tomato soup with 7 fat-free
      saltine crackers (2)
   ½ cup chicken salad on a bed of mixed greens (6)
   1 cup baby carrots with 2 tablespoons fat-free
      ranch dressing (1)

*Snack*

   3 graham crackers (2½" squares) (2)

*Dinner*

   1 salmon fillet, grilled (7)
   ½ cup mashed potatoes (2)
   *Haricots verts*, steamed (0)
   1 cup reduced-calorie butterscotch pudding
      (prepared with fat-free milk) (2)

## DAY TWO

*Breakfast*

1 large blueberry muffin (6)
1 tablespoon apricot preserves (1)
1 cup coffee with fat-free milk (0)
½ cup orange juice (1)

*Lunch*

1 slice frozen vegetable pizza (6)
1 cup mixed greens with 2 tablespoons
  fat-free Italian dressing (0)
1 Granny Smith apple (1)

*Snack*

1 cup aspartame-sweetened coconut-cream
  pie yogurt (2)

*Dinner*

Tea (0)
1 cup egg drop soup (1)
1 cup Chinese vegetables with shrimp (5)
½ cup brown rice (2)
1 fortune cookie (1)
1 navel orange (1)

## DAY THREE

*Breakfast*

¼ cup fat-free egg substitute, scrambled (spray
  pan with nonstick cooking spray) with 1
  tablespoon grated cheddar cheese and ¼ cup
  chopped tomato (2)
1 piece high-fiber toast (1)
1 slice bacon (1)
½ cup pink grapefruit juice (1)

*Snack*

1 cup grapes (1)

*Lunch*

Pastrami sandwich with 2 slices lean turkey
  pastrami with lettuce, tomato and mustard
  on 2 slices reduced-calorie rye bread (3)
12 tortilla chips with ¼ cup salsa (3)
1 peach (1)

*Dinner*

1 glass red wine (2)
1 cup baked ziti (5)
2 long breadsticks (1)
1 cup Caesar salad (3)
1 slice angel food cake with ½ cup sliced
  strawberries, drizzled with chocolate syrup
  and 2 tablespoons whipped cream (3)

# Fitting in Fitness

By now, you know that losing weight *isn't* just
about food. That's why Weight Watchers considers activity and behavior modification in the
weight-loss equation.

To lose weight, you know that you'll need to
burn more calories than you take in; to maintain,
you'll need to strike a balance between input and
output. At Weight Watchers, we know the many
benefits of physical activity, which include
increasing your energy, relieving stress, reducing
the risk of chronic diseases and simply making
you look and feel great. The **1•2•3 Success** plan
provides you with all you need to know to get
started on an activity program, and it gives you
plenty of incentive by allowing you to earn extra
**POINTS** (just twenty minutes of *extra* activity
earns you one extra **POINT**!). Weight Watchers
answers all your fitness questions, everything
from when you'll see results and how to rate your
intensity level to what shoes to wear. Of course,
before beginning this or any exercise regime, consult with your physician.

# Weight Watchers 1•2•3 **Success** Food List

| FOOD LIST | SERVING | POINTS |
|---|---|---|
| **Beverages** | | |
| *Beer, light* | *1 can or bottle* | 2 |
| *Champagne* | *1 small glass* | 2 |
| *Coffee or tea, black, w/o sugar* | *1 cup* | 0 |
| *Seltzer, unsweetened* | *1 can or bottle* | 0 |
| *Soft drink, diet* | *1 can or bottle* | 0 |
| *Water or mineral water* | *1 cup* | 0 |
| **Breads and Bread Products** | | |
| *Bread, high fiber* | *(3 grams or more dietary fiber per slice), 1 slice* | 1 |
| *Bread, reduced-calorie, any type* | *2 slices* | 1 |
| *Bread crumbs, dried* | *3 tablespoons* | 1 |
| *English muffin, any type* | *1* | 2 |
| *Pita, any type* | *1 small or ½ large* | 1 |
| **Breakfast Cereals and Other Breakfast Items** | | |
| *Cereal, cold:* | | |
| *Bran flakes* | *1 cup* | 1 |
| *Cereals, high fiber* | *(10 grams or more dietary fiber per ½ cup), ½ cup* | 1 |
| *Shredded wheat* | *1 biscuit* | 1 |
| *Cereal, hot cooked:* | | |
| *Cream of wheat* | *1 cup* | 2 |
| *Grits* | *1 cup* | 2 |
| *Oatmeal* | *1 cup* | 2 |
| *Other Breakfast Items:* | | |
| *Pancake, any type, made from mix* | *1 (4″ diameter)* | 2 |
| *Waffle, any type, frozen* | *1 (4″ round or square)* | 3 |
| **Cheese** | | |
| *Cottage cheese, 1%, 2% or nonfat* | *⅓ cup* | 1 |
| *Cream cheese, nonfat* | *4 tablespoons* | 1 |
| *Hard or semisoft cheese, low-fat* | *1 slice, 1 (1″) cube, 3 tablespoons shredded, or 2 tablespoons grated* | 2 |
| *Hard or semisoft cheese, nonfat* | *1 slice, 1 (1″) cube, 3 tablespoons shredded, or 2 tablespoons grated* | 1 |
| *Ricotta, part-skim* | *⅓ cup* | 3 |

| FOOD LIST | SERVING | POINTS |
|---|---|---|
| **Chicken and Poultry (cooked w/o added fat)** | | |
| *Chicken breast (w/o skin)* | 1 | 3 |
| *Chicken leg (w/o skin)* | 1 | 1 |
| *Chicken thigh (w/o skin)* | 1 | 3 |
| *Chicken, light or dark meat* | 1 slice or ½ cup cubed or shredded | 2 |
| *Luncheon meat, lean* | 1 slice, less than 2 grams fat per ounce | 1 |
| *Turkey, light or dark meat* | 1 slice or ½ cup cubed or shredded | 2 |
| **Chicken and Poultry Dishes** | | |
| *Chicken salad* | ½ cup | 6 |
| **Chinese Food** | | |
| *Chinese vegetables w/shrimp or tofu* | 1 cup | 5 |
| *Chow mein noodles w/chicken or shrimp* | 1 cup | 6 |
| *Egg drop soup* | 1 cup | 1 |
| **Crackers** | | |
| *Crackers, fat-free* | 7 | 1 |
| *Melba toast* | 6 rounds or 4 slices | 1 |
| *Rice cakes* | 2 or 6 mini | 1 |
| **Cream and Creamers** | | |
| *Cream, light* | 2 tablespoons | 2 |
| *Creamer, nonfat, flavored, liquid* | 2 tablespoons | 1 |
| *Half and half* | 2 tablespoons | 1 |
| *Sour cream, light* | 3 tablespoons | 1 |
| *Sour cream, nonfat* | ¼ cup | 1 |
| **Desserts, Frozen** | | |
| *Ice cream, nonfat, no sugar added* | 1 scoop | 2 |
| *Yogurt, frozen, nonfat, no sugar added* | 1 scoop | 2 |
| **Desserts, Other** | | |
| *Angel food cake* | 1/16 of 10″ tube | 2 |
| *Cookies, any type* | 2 small | 3 |
| *Pudding, reduced-calorie (made w/fat-free or low-fat [1%] milk)* | 1 cup | 2 |

# Weight Watchers 1•2•3 Success Food List (cont.)

| FOOD LIST | SERVING | POINTS |
|---|---|---|
| **Eggs and Egg Dishes** | | |
| Egg | 1 | 2 |
| Egg substitute, fat-free | ¼ cup | 1 |
| Egg whites | 3 | 1 |
| **Fats** | | |
| Margarine, fat-free | 4 tablespoons | 1 |
| Margarine, reduced-calorie | 2 teaspoons | 1 |
| Mayonnaise, fat-free | 4 tablespoons | 1 |
| Mayonnaise, reduced-calorie | 2 teaspoons | 1 |
| Vegetable oil | 1 teaspoon | 1 |
| **Fish and Shellfish (cooked w/o added fat)** | | |
| Fish, (except those listed below) | 1 fillet | 4 |
| Fish, fresh, flaked (except those listed below) | ½ cup | 1 |
| Fish, anchovies | 6 | 1 |
| Fish, salmon | 1 fillet | 7 |
| Shellfish, fresh (clams, crab, crayfish, lobster, mussels, oysters, scallops, shrimp) | ½ cup | 1 |
| Tuna, canned in water, drained | ½ cup | 3 |
| **Fish and Shellfish Dishes** | | |
| Sushi, nori maki (raw fish and rice rolled in seaweed) | 4 pieces | 2 |
| **Fruits and Fruit Juices** | | |
| Apple | 1 | 1 |
| Applesauce, unsweetened | 1 cup | 1 |
| Apricots | 3 | 1 |
| Banana | 1 | 2 |
| Berries: blackberries, blueberries, cranberries, raspberries, strawberries | 1 cup each | 1 pt. each |
| Cantaloupe | ¼ melon or 1 cup | 1 |
| Cherries | 1 cup | 1 |
| Fruit salad | 1 cup | 2 |
| Grapefruit sections | 1 cup | 1 |

| FOOD LIST | SERVING | POINTS |
|---|---|---|
| **Fruits and Fruit Juices (continued)** | | |
| Grapes | 1 cup | 1 |
| Honeydew melon | $^1/_8$ melon or 1 cup | 1 |
| **Juices** | | |
| Cranberry juice cocktail, low-calorie | 1 cup | 1 |
| Grapefruit juice | $^1/_2$ cup | 1 |
| Orange juice | $^1/_2$ cup | 1 |
| Prune juice | $^1/_2$ cup | 1 |
| Kiwi fruit | 1 | 1 |
| Mandarin orange | 1 | 1 |
| Olives | 10 small or 6 large | 1 |
| Orange | 1 | 1 |
| Peach | 1 | 1 |
| Pear | 1 | 1 |
| Pineapple | $^1/_4$ or 1 cup | 2 |
| Watermelon | 2" slice or 1 cup | 1 |
| **Grains** | | |
| Barley, cooked | 1 cup | 2 |
| Couscous (semolina), cooked | 1 cup | 2 |
| Flour, any type | 3 tablespoons | 1 |
| Wheat germ | 3 tablespoons | |
| **Legumes and Legume Dishes (cooked)** | | |
| Dry beans (black, garbanzo, kidney, lima, navy, pinto) | $^1/_3$ cup | 1 |
| Dry peas (black-eyed, chick) | $^1/_3$ cup | 1 |
| Lentils | $^1/_3$ cup | 1 |
| **Meat and Meat Products (cooked w/o added fat)** | | |
| Beef, lean | 1 slice or $^1/_2$ cup cubed or shredded | 3 |
| Lamb, lean | 1 slice, 1 chop or $^1/_2$ cup cubed or shredded | 3 |
| Luncheon meat, lean | 1 slice, less than 2 grams fat per ounce | 1 |
| Steak, lean | 1 small | 5 |
| Veal, lean | 1 slice, 1 chop or $^1/_2$ cup cubed or shredded | 3 |

# Weight Watchers 1•2•3 **Success** Food List (cont.)

| FOOD LIST | SERVING | POINTS |
|---|---|---|
| **Meat Substitutes, Dishes and Products** | | |
| *Vegetarian breakfast patty (sausage-type)* | 1 | 1 |
| *Vegetarian burger* | 1 | 2 |
| **Mexican Food** | | |
| *Guacamole* | $\frac{1}{4}$ cup | 2 |
| *Taco, hard or soft, fast food* | 1 | 4 |
| *Taco shells, store-bought* | 2 | 2 |
| *Tortilla* | 1 (6″ diameter) | 2 |
| *Tostada shells, store-bought* | 2 | 2 |
| **Milk Products** | | |
| *Milk:* | | |
| *buttermilk, nonfat, 1%, 1.5% or 2%* | 1 cup | 2 |
| *evaporated, skimmed or low-fat* | $\frac{1}{2}$ cup | 2 |
| *instant nonfat dry milk powder* | $\frac{1}{3}$ cup | 2 |
| *skim, nonfat, or fat-free* | 1 cup | 2 |
| **Nuts and Peanut Butter** | | |
| *Peanut butter* | 1 tablespoon | 2 |
| **Pasta and Noodles (cooked)** | | |
| *Noodles, egg* | 1 cup | 3 |
| **Pizza** | | |
| *Cheese pizza, thin or thick crust* | 1 slice ($\frac{1}{8}$ of 12″ or $\frac{1}{12}$ of 14″–16″ pie) | 4 |
| *Cheese pizza w/vegetable, frozen* | 1 slice (5 ounces) | 6 |
| **Rice and Rice Dishes (cooked)** | | |
| *Brown rice* | 1 cup | 4 |
| *White rice* | 1 cup | 5 |
| **Salad Dressings** | | |
| *Fat-free, salad dressing (except Italian)* | 2 tablespoons | 1 |
| *Fat-free, salad dressing, Italian* | 2 tablespoons | 0 |
| **Salads** | | |
| *Salad, mixed greens* | 1 cup | 0 |

| FOOD LIST | SERVING | POINTS |
|---|---|---|
| **Sandwiches and Burgers** | | |
| *Fast Food:* | | |
| Cheeseburger on bun | 1 small | 7 |
| Hamburger on bun | 1 small | 5 |
| **Sauces and Gravies** | | |
| Chili sauce | 1 tablespoon | 0 |
| Cocktail sauce | ¼ cup | 1 |
| Ketchup | ¼ cup | 1 |
| Spaghetti sauce, bottled, any type | ½ cup | 2 |
| Taco sauce | 1 tablespoon | 0 |
| Tomato sauce | ½ cup | 0 |
| **Seeds** | | |
| Sesame | 1 teaspoon | 0 |
| Sunflower | 1 tablespoon | 1 |
| **Snacks** | | |
| Cereal bar, fat-free | 1 | 2 |
| Popcorn, hot-air or light microwave-popped | 3 cups | 1 |
| **Soups** | | |
| Broth, any type | 1 cup | 0 |
| Chicken noodle soup, canned | 1 cup | 1 |
| Lentil soup, canned | 1 cup | 2 |
| Vegetable soup, canned | 1 cup | 2 |
| **Spreads** | | |
| Jam, jelly, or preserves | 1 tablespoon | 1 |
| **Sweets and Candy** | | |
| Honey | 1 tablespoon | 1 |
| Syrup, low-calorie | 2 tablespoons | 1 |
| **Vegetable Dishes** | | |
| French fries, fast food | 1 small serving | 5 |
| **Yogurt** | | |
| Fruit-flavored, nonfat, sweetened w/sugar | 1 cup | 4 |

## Is It What You Eat or What's Eating *You*?

In order to lose weight successfully and keep it off, overweight individuals must develop strong motivation. By employing behavior modification and cognitive restructuring techniques, Weight Watchers helps you to adopt positive attitudes and strategies for dealing with weight-loss challenges. **1•2•3 Success** addresses the issues that affect *you*, like eating high-fat foods out of habit, dealing with social situations and stress, overeating—and provides *solutions* for handling them. The self-reinforcement of successfully managing such obstacles enhances motivation and confirms the wisdom of making long-term lifestyle changes. A few simple tips to try today:

- *Eat slowly.*
- *Choose a designated eating area.*
- *Plan ahead.*
- *Place healthful foods within easy reach.*

## Can We Talk?

### The Importance of Group Support

Many people are concerned about eating right and losing weight, but the stress of daily living, pressures of work and family obligations combined with a lack of time often cause other things to take precedence. That's why sometimes nothing works better than a Weight Watchers meeting to help you achieve successful weight loss. By sharing your successes and failures, hopes and concerns with caring leaders and a supportive group, it becomes easier to learn the necessary skills to lose weight and improve your overall well-being. More than thirty-five years of Weight Watchers meetings can't be wrong.

## A Final Word

If you're reading this book, you're probably interested in losing weight and feeling healthy and have taken the first step toward achieving that end. Now that you understand the importance of basic nutrition, fitting the following recipes into your daily life can help you to reach those goals.

# RECIPES

Basics

# Chapter 1

# Basics

You might be tempted to skip past this chapter to get to the real recipes, but don't: If you're serious about changing your eating habits and learning to cook more healthfully, these recipes—for flavor-enhancing sauces, condiments, marinades and other basic standbys—will prove invaluable.

## The Crucial Role of Fat

It all comes down to fat. Fat supplies food with flavor, as well as helps to distribute the flavors of foods throughout your mouth. For instance, if you've ever tried to cut calories by serving vegetables plain rather than drenched in butter, you've experienced fat's facilitator role. Once you start to reduce the amount of fat in your favorite recipes, you need to up the taste in other ways.

## Marvelous Marinades

Clever health-conscious cooks have a repertoire of easy tips and techniques for losing the fat, but not the flavor. Consider marinades: If you're a steak-lover, you know that lean cuts of meat like London broil are practically inedible if they aren't marinated. Marinades work their magic thanks to the enzymes in their acidic ingredients—vinegar, citrus juices, wine, even yogurt—that help tenderize lean cuts.

Chicken and fish reap the benefits of marinating as well. Because these foods are more tender than most meats, you'll want to use a less acidic marinade or marinate them just briefly. Heed this advice; otherwise, they'll be partially cooked before you get them near the heat. (Think of seviche, the Latin American seafood dish in which raw fish actually "cooks" in its lime juice marinade!)

## Super Stocks

In classic French cuisine, stocks are so important that they are known as the *fond du cuisine*—the foundation of cooking. If you've ever made a pot of soup with the bones from a roast and vegetables, you know how much more flavor a homemade stock provides. Although stocks from cans or cubes are certainly convenient, don't be intimidated by making stock from scratch—not only is it easy, but it's economical and environmental as well. Just stockpile vegetable peelings and trimmings, along with chicken or beef bones, in sealable plastic bags and freeze until you have the time to make your stock.

## Delicious Dressings

If you are drowning your greens in bottled salad dressing, it's time to change your ways. Homemade dressings have flavors that their store-bought counterparts just can't match. Many are simple to make; use these recipes as a starting point.

Once you've gotten the basics down, do a little experimentation: Try a fruit or herb vinegar, or use lemon or orange juice. Replace the oil with broth and a bit of honey (this helps to mimic the texture fat provides). Use different herbs or replace the mustard with horseradish.

# Lemon-Dill Sauce

*This creamy sauce gives a Greek touch to chicken, fish and veal.*

MAKES 8 SERVINGS

⅓ cup fresh lemon juice

2 teaspoons cornstarch

½ teaspoon sugar

¼ teaspoon dried thyme leaves

¼ teaspoon salt

4 teaspoons snipped dill

4 teaspoons unsalted margarine

1 tablespoon chopped parsley

¼ teaspoon grated lemon zest

In a medium nonreactive saucepan, whisk the lemon juice and cornstarch. Add ⅓ cup water, the sugar, thyme and salt; bring to a boil. Boil, stirring constantly, 2 minutes. Remove from the heat; stir in the dill, margarine, parsley and lemon zest.

**Per serving**: 23 Calories, 2 g Total Fat, 0 g Saturated Fat, 0 mg Cholesterol, 73 mg Sodium, 2 g Total Carbohydrate, 0 g Dietary Fiber, 0 g Protein, 3 mg Calcium. **POINTS** per serving: 1.

# Peanut Sauce

*A lighter variation on Indonesian satay sauce, this makes a wonderful dip for grilled foods. Thread strips of pork, or vegatable chunks, on skewers (marinate briefly in soy sauce, if you like) and grill.*

MAKES 8 SERVINGS

3 tablespoons creamy peanut butter

2 garlic cloves, crushed

2 tablespoons soy sauce

4 teaspoons sugar

1 tablespoon water

1¼ teaspoons rice-wine vinegar

1 tablespoon chopped fresh cilantro, or ½ teaspoon dried

In a mini food processor or blender, combine the peanut butter and garlic; puree. Add the remaining ingredients and process until combined.

**Per serving**: 44 Calories, 3 g Total Fat, 1 g Saturated Fat, 0 mg Cholesterol, 283 mg Sodium, 4 g Total Carbohydrate, 0 g Dietary Fiber, 2 g Protein, 5 mg Calcium. **POINTS** per serving: 1.

# Béchamel Sauce

*Béchamel sauce—better known as white sauce—finds its way into all kinds of rich dishes. Once you've mastered this simple, low-fat version, you can adapt it to many recipes.*

MAKES 4 SERVINGS

4 teaspoons reduced-calorie margarine

¼ cup all-purpose flour

3 cups low-fat (1%) milk

2 whole cloves

1 small bay leaf

3 black peppercorns

¼ teaspoon salt

Pinch nutmeg

In a medium nonstick saucepan over medium-low heat, melt the margarine. Whisk in the flour, then gradually add the milk, whisking constantly, until smooth. Add the cloves and bay leaf; stir in the peppercorns, salt and nutmeg. Reduce the heat and simmer, whisking frequently, until thickened, about 10 minutes. Strain, discarding the solids.

**Per serving:** 120 Calories, 4 g Total Fat, 1 g Saturated Fat, 7 mg Cholesterol, 283 mg Sodium, 14 g Total Carbohydrate, 0 g Dietary Fiber, 7 g Protein, 226 mg Calcium. **POINTS** per serving: 3.

# Mornay Sauce

*With its cheese flavor, Mornay sauce adds a rich touch to vegetables or fish.*

MAKES 8 SERVINGS

3 cups low-fat (1%) milk

¼ cup all-purpose flour

1 small onion, peeled

3 whole cloves

1 bay leaf

3 black peppercorns

¼ teaspoon salt

⅛ teaspoon ground nutmeg

2 slices reduced-fat processed Swiss cheese, diced

2 tablespoons grated Parmesan cheese

Pinch cayenne pepper

1. In a medium nonstick saucepan over low heat, whisk the milk and flour. Stud the onion with the cloves and bay leaf; add to the milk mixture. Stir in the peppercorns, salt and nutmeg. Simmer, whisking frequently, until thickened, about 10 minutes. Strain, discarding the solids.

2. Return to the heat; stir in the Swiss and Parmesan cheeses and the cayenne. Cook, stirring, just until the cheese melts.

**Per serving:** 85 Calories, 3 g Total Fat, 2 g Saturated Fat, 9 mg Cholesterol, 260 mg Sodium, 9 g Total Carbohydrate, 0 g Dietary Fiber, 6 g Protein, 203 mg Calcium. **POINTS** per serving: 2.

# Horseradish Sauce

*With a nip of horseradish, this sauce is a natural with roast beef; try it on hamburgers, too.*

<small>MAKES 8 SERVINGS</small>

½ cup drained prepared horseradish

½ cup plain nonfat yogurt

⅓ cup nonfat sour cream

2 teaspoons whole-grain mustard

1 teaspoon sugar

½ teaspoon Worcestershire sauce

⅛ teaspoon freshly ground pepper

2 tablespoons chopped parsley

In a medium bowl, whisk the horseradish, yogurt, sour cream, mustard, sugar, Worcestershire sauce and pepper. Refrigerate, covered, until ready to use. Stir in the parsley just before serving.

**Per serving**: 53 Calories, 3 g Total Fat, 2 g Saturated Fat, 7 mg Cholesterol, 89 mg Sodium, 4 g Total Carbohydrate, 0 g Dietary Fiber, 2 g Protein, 62 mg Calcium. *POINTS* per serving: 1.

# Salsa

*Sure, it's on every supermarket shelf, but once you've tasted it fresh, you won't go back to the jarred stuff.*

<small>MAKES 4 SERVINGS</small>

6 plum tomatoes, seeded and chopped

3 tablespoons chopped basil

3 tablespoons chopped cilantro

1 tablespoon minced green bell pepper

1 scallion, minced

2 garlic cloves, minced

½ teaspoon coarse (kosher) salt

1 tablespoon red-wine vinegar

1. In a medium nonreactive bowl, combine the tomatoes, basil, cilantro, bell pepper, scallion, garlic and salt. Let stand 30 minutes; drain off any liquid that accumulates.

2. Sprinkle the vinegar over the salsa; toss again.

**Per serving**: 34 Calories, 0 g Total Fat, 0 g Saturated Fat, 0 mg Cholesterol, 305 mg Sodium, 7 g Total Carbohydrate, 2 g Dietary Fiber, 1 g Protein, 18 mg Calcium. *POINTS* per serving: 0.

## How We Did It

Acidic ingredients like tomatoes can react with metals to produce off-colors and off-flavors. Be sure to mix the salsa in a glass, ceramic or plastic—nonreactive—bowl.

# Chocolate Sauce

*When you've got a chocolate craving, this nonfat sauce fills the bill. Try it drizzled over a graham cracker or a sliced apple.*

MAKES 4 SERVINGS

3 tablespoons unsweetened cocoa powder

½ cup evaporated skimmed milk

⅓ cup sugar

4 teaspoons light corn syrup

¾ teaspoon vanilla extract

Put the cocoa in a medium heavy-bottomed saucepan; slowly pour in ¼ cup water, whisking until dissolved. Whisk in the evaporated milk, sugar, corn syrup and vanilla. Set the saucepan over medium-high heat; bring just to a boil. Reduce the heat and simmer, stirring constantly, until thickened, 6–8 minutes. If you want a thicker sauce, refrigerate 1–2 hours. Serve warm or at room temperature.

**Per serving**: 118 Calories, 0 g Total Fat, 0 g Saturated Fat, 1 mg Cholesterol, 47 mg Sodium, 28 g Total Carbohydrate, 0 g Dietary Fiber, 3 g Protein, 99 mg Calcium. **POINTS** per serving: 2.

## How We Did It

You don't need a campfire to make these s'mores! Line a baking sheet with foil, then layer graham crackers with a drizzle or two of chocolate sauce and a few mini marshmallows. Bake at 400° F until the marshmallows start to melt, 4–5 minutes.

# Raspberry Sauce

*This is delightful on frozen yogurt or sorbet—especially peach and chocolate flavors. Or, drizzle it over your favorite fat-free chocolate brownie.*

MAKES 8 SERVINGS

1½ cups fresh or thawed frozen raspberries

¼ cup raspberry spreadable fruit

1 tablespoon honey

¾ teaspoon vanilla extract

⅛ teaspoon ground allspice

In a food processor or blender, puree the raspberries. Push the puree through a strainer, discarding the seeds; return the puree to the food processor. Add the spreadable fruit, honey, vanilla and allspice; puree.

**Per serving**: 38 Calories, 0 g Total Fat, 0 g Saturated Fat, 0 mg Cholesterol, 0 mg Sodium, 9 g Total Carbohydrate, 2 g Dietary Fiber, 0 g Protein, 5 mg Calcium. **POINTS** per serving: 0.

*Chocolate Sauce*

# Pesto

*We've cut the oil dramatically from this popular Italian specialty, without sacrificing the fresh basil flavor. For best results, use the highest quality Parmesan cheese, Parmigiano-Reggiano. Its nutty flavor will make all the difference.*

MAKES 6 SERVINGS

2½ cups packed basil leaves, washed and dried

3 tablespoons pine nuts

1 tablespoon olive oil

2 garlic cloves, crushed

¼ teaspoon salt

½ cup + 2 tablespoons grated Parmesan cheese

In a food processor or blender, combine the basil, pine nuts, oil, garlic and salt with ½ cup water; puree. Add the cheese and puree 30 seconds.

Per serving: 135 Calories, 10 g Total Fat, 4 g Saturated Fat, 14 mg Cholesterol, 428 mg Sodium, 2 g Total Carbohydrate, 0 g Dietary Fiber, 9 g Protein, 275 mg Calcium. **POINTS** per serving: 4.

# Pepper and Apple Chutney

*This versatile condiment turns plain broiled chicken or pork into something special.*

MAKES 8 SERVINGS

2 red bell peppers, seeded and diced

2 onions, diced

¼ cup sugar

2 tablespoons raisins

3 garlic cloves, slivered

1 teaspoon mustard seeds

¾ teaspoon ground ginger

½ teaspoon salt

⅔ cup cider vinegar

¼ cup thawed frozen apple juice concentrate

1 Granny Smith apple, peeled, cored and cut into ½" chunks

1. In a medium nonreactive saucepan, combine the bell peppers, onions, sugar, raisins, garlic, mustard seeds, ginger and salt. Stir in the vinegar and apple juice concentrate; bring to a boil. Reduce the heat and simmer, covered, until the vegetables are tender, 30–35 minutes.

2. Stir in the apple; cook, uncovered, until the apple is tender and the chutney has thickened, 7–10 minutes longer.

Per serving: 80 Calories, 0 g Total Fat, 0 g Saturated Fat, 0 mg Cholesterol, 151 mg Sodium, 20 g Total Carbohydrate, 2 g Dietary Fiber, 1 g Protein, 16 mg Calcium. **POINTS** per serving: 1.

# Herbed Cheese Sauce

*A great pick-me-up for simple, steamed vegetables. The intensely flavored Parmesan cheese allows you to use less of the cheddar, cutting fat without sacrificing cheesy goodness.*

MAKES 4 SERVINGS

1 cup low-fat (1%) milk

1 tablespoon all-purpose flour

3/4 cup shredded reduced-fat cheddar cheese

1 tablespoon grated Parmesan cheese

1 tablespoon chopped basil

1 teaspoon chopped tarragon

1 teaspoon minced thyme

3/4 teaspoon Dijon mustard

1/4 teaspoon freshly ground pepper

Pinch ground nutmeg

1. In a medium nonstick saucepan over medium heat, whisk 1/3 cup of the milk and the flour until smooth; bring to a boil, stirring constantly. Boil, stirring constantly, until very thick, about 5 minutes.

2. Meanwhile, in a small nonstick saucepan over medium heat, heat the remaining 2/3 cup of milk. Gradually whisk the warm milk into the flour mixture; whisk in the cheddar, Parmesan, basil, tarragon, thyme, mustard, pepper and nutmeg. Cook over low heat, stirring, until the cheese melts.

**Per serving**: 108 Calories, 5 g Total Fat, 3 g Saturated Fat, 18 mg Cholesterol, 216 mg Sodium, 6 g Carbohydrate, 0 g Dietary Fiber, 9 g Protein, 290 mg Calcium. *POINTS* per serving: 3.

# Mushroom Sauce

*Perfect for chicken and turkey, this sauce is also divine over fettuccine.*

MAKES 4 SERVINGS

2 teaspoons unsalted margarine

1 shallot, minced

1 garlic clove, minced

4 cups thinly sliced mushrooms

1/2 teaspoon rubbed sage

1/4 teaspoon salt

1/8 teaspoon freshly ground pepper

2 tablespoons brandy

1 tablespoon + 1 1/2 teaspoons all-purpose flour

1 cup evaporated skimmed milk

2 tablespoons nonfat sour cream

1. In a large nonstick skillet, melt the margarine. Sauté the shallot until soft, about 2 minutes. Add the garlic; cook 1 minute longer. Stir in the mushrooms, sage, salt and pepper; cook, stirring frequently, until the mushrooms are tender, about 6 minutes.

2. Increase the heat to high; cook until almost all the liquid evaporates, about 3 minutes. Add the brandy; cook 1 minute. Stir in the flour; cook, stirring constantly, until smooth. Stir in the evaporated milk; reduce the heat and simmer until thickened, about 7 minutes. Remove from the heat and stir in the sour cream.

**Per serving**: 121 Calories, 2 g Total Fat, 0 g Saturated Fat, 2 mg Cholesterol, 232 mg Sodium, 14 g Total Carbohydrate, 1 g Dietary Fiber, 7 g Protein, 202 mg Calcium. *POINTS* per serving: 2.

# Vegetable Stock

*Make this pantry staple when you have lots of odds and ends of vegetables on hand. You can substitute or make additions as you wish, but it's best to avoid stongly flavored vegetables like cabbage and broccoli.*

MAKES 8 SERVINGS

    4 onions, quartered

    3 leeks, cleaned and sliced

    1 carrot, scrubbed and chopped

    2 celery stalks with leaves, chopped

    2 parsnips, scrubbed and chopped

    6 large dried mushrooms

    12 sprigs flat-leaf parsley

    6 sprigs fresh dill

    12 black peppercorns

    1½ teaspoons salt, or to taste

1. Spray a large stockpot with nonstick cooking spray; heat. Add the onions, leeks, carrot, celery and parsnips; cook, stirring occasionally, until the vegetables are soft, about 10 minutes. Add 12 cups water, the mushrooms, parsley, dill, peppercorns and salt; bring to a boil. Reduce the heat and simmer, partially covered, about 2 hours.

2. Line a colander with a paper towel or a double layer of cheesecloth; place over a large bowl. Strain the stock through the colander, pressing the vegetables with a wooden spoon to extract the juices; discard the solids. Use the stock immediately, or, cool and transfer to 1-cup freezer containers to freeze for later use.

**Per serving**: 17 Calories, 0 g Total Fat, 0 g Saturated Fat, 0 mg Cholesterol, 423 mg Sodium, 4 g Total Carbohydrate, 1 g Dietary Fiber, 1 g Protein, 0 mg Calcium. **POINTS** per serving: 0.

## Tip

For flavorful stock, don't peel the vegetables—scrub the carrots and parsnips. Use the leek tops and celery leaves, too.

## Handy Equivalents

*Use this handy chart to figure out dry and liquid measure equivalents.*

*3 teaspoons = ½ fluid ounce = 1 tablespoon*

*⅛ cup = 1 fluid ounce = 2 tablespoons*

*¼ cup = 2 fluid ounces = 4 tablespoons*

*⅓ cup = 5 tablespoons + 1 teaspoon or 16 teaspoons*

*½ cup = 4 fluid ounces = 8 tablespoons*

*⅔ cup = 10 tablespoons + 2 teaspoons or 32 teaspoons*

*¾ cup = 6 fluid ounces = 12 tablespoons*

*1 cup = 8 fluid ounces = 16 tablespoons*

*1 pint = 16 fluid ounces = 2 cups*

*1 quart = 32 fluid ounces = 4 cups or 2 pints*

*½ gallon = 64 fluid ounces = 8 cups or 2 quarts*

*1 gallon = 128 fluid ounces = 16 cups or 4 quarts*

*16 ounces (dry-measure weight) = 1 pound*

# Beef Stock

*Make this rich-tasting stock and use it to flavor soups, stews and sauces without fat. It freezes well, so you can always have it handy.*

MAKES 8 SERVINGS

4 pounds meaty beef neck bones or beef soup bones

1 large onion, unpeeled, root end trimmed and cut into chunks

2 carrots, scrubbed and cut into 1" pieces

1 large celery stalk with leaves, cut into 1" pieces

1 large leek, cleaned and cut into 1" pieces

1 small purple turnip, cut into chunks

8 sprigs flat-leaf parsley

2 sprigs thyme

1 bay leaf

12 black peppercorns

1½ teaspoons salt, or to taste

1. Preheat the oven to 400° F. In a shallow roasting pan, roast the bones, turning occasionally with tongs, until they begin to brown, about 30 minutes.

2. With the tongs, transfer the bones to a large stockpot. Add 12 cups water and the remaining ingredients; bring just to a boil. Reduce the heat and simmer, partially covered, skimming off any foam and fat occasionally, about 2 hours.

3. Line a colander with a paper towel or a double layer of cheesecloth; place over a large bowl. Strain the stock through the colander, pressing the solids with a wooden spoon to extract the juices; discard the solids. Refrigerate the stock until the fat rises to the surface; scrape off and discard the fat. Or, cool and transfer to 1-cup freezer containers to freeze; remove the fat when ready to use.

**Per serving**: 19 Calories, 0 g Total Fat, 0 g Saturated Fat, 0 mg Cholesterol, 427 mg Sodium, 3 g Total Carbohydrate, 0 g Dietary Fiber, 1 g Protein, 0 mg Calcium. **POINTS** per serving: 0.

## Stuff About Nuts

- *Shelled nuts should be stored in the freezer or refrigerator to preserve freshness (because their fat content is high, nuts can turn rancid under less-than-ideal conditions).*

- *Store nuts in sealable plastic freezer bags; label with name and date before storing.*

- *Bring nuts to room temperature before adding to a recipe.*

- *Nuts are one ingredient best processed by hand; a blender or food processor tends to pulverize them and release their oils, causing them to clump. By hand-chopping or grinding, you have more control over the texture. A time-saving prep tip is to put nuts in a plastic bag; press out the air and seal tightly. Then pound with a mallet until the desired texture is achieved.*

# Chicken Stock

---

*Use this versatile stock whenever a recipe calls for chicken broth, and discover the delicious difference homemade stock can make. If you plan to freeze it to use later, conserve freezer space by boiling the stock down to reduce it by half. Thin it with an equal amount of water when you use it.*

MAKES 8 SERVINGS

4 pounds chicken wings, backs, or a mixture of wings, backs and giblets (no liver)

1 large onion, quartered

2 carrots, scrubbed and cut into 1" pieces

2 large celery stalks with leaves, cut into 1" pieces

1 large leek, cleaned and cut into 1" pieces

8 sprigs flat-leaf parsley

2 sprigs thyme

12 black peppercorns

1½ teaspoons salt, or to taste

1. In a large stockpot, combine the chicken and 12 cups water; bring to a boil. Skim off the foam that rises to the surface; add the onion, carrots, celery, leek, parsley, thyme, peppercorns and salt. Reduce the heat and simmer, partially covered, skimming off any foam and fat occasionally, about 2 hours.

2. Line a colander with a paper towel or a double layer of cheesecloth; place over a large bowl. Strain the stock through the colander, pressing the solids with a wooden spoon to extract the juices; discard the solids. Refrigerate the stock until the fat rises to the surface; scrape off and discard the fat. Or, cool and transfer to 1-cup freezer containers to freeze; remove the fat when ready to use.

**Per serving**: 23 Calories, 1 g Total Fat, 0 g Saturated Fat, 0 mg Cholesterol, 446 mg Sodium, 3 g Total Carbohydrate, 0 g Dietary Fiber, 1 g Protein, 0 mg Calcium. **POINTS** per serving: 1.

## Microwave Cooking Tips

*Using the microwave can slash prep time as well as cleanup time (note that times can vary depending on your microwave's wattage). You'll find these tips helpful and easy:*

- *For greater volume when whipping egg whites, place them in a glass measuring cup; microwave 8–10 seconds for 2 whites, 10–12 seconds for 3 whites.*

- *For maximum juice from a lemon or lime, prick with a fork and microwave 30–60 seconds before squeezing.*

- *Melt 2 tablespoons margarine in 20–30 seconds.*

- *One-half cup fat-free milk can be warmed in 30–45 seconds, scalded in 45–60 seconds.*

- *Plump dried fruits by sprinkling with a teaspoon of water; microwave for 15–45 seconds.*

- *Soften lumpy sugar in a microwavable dish or container with a slice of apple or bread; microwave 15 seconds.*

# Basic Marinade

*This is a good marinade for beef, lamb or pork. Cool the marinade and then add the meat; marinate in the refrigerator several hours or overnight.*

MAKES 4 SERVINGS

1 onion, thinly sliced

½ carrot, thinly sliced

2 garlic cloves, thinly sliced

1 cup dry red wine

2 sprigs fresh thyme, or ½ teaspoon dried

1 bay leaf

¼ teaspoon juniper berries, lightly crushed

6 black peppercorns

Spray a medium nonreactive saucepan with non-stick cooking spray; heat. Sauté the onion, carrot and garlic until softened, about 5 minutes. Add the wine, thyme, bay leaf, juniper berries and peppercorns; bring to a boil. Boil until slightly reduced, 7–8 minutes. Strain, discarding the solids.

**Per serving**: 61 Calories, 0 g Total Fat, 0 g Saturated Fat, 0 mg Cholesterol, 17 mg Sodium, 5 g Total Carbohydrate, 1 g Dietary Fiber, 1 g Protein, 18 mg Calcium. *POINTS* per serving: 1.

# Teriyaki Marinade

*This fat-free marinade turns pork, beef, chicken or fish into a Japanese delight; it also doubles as a tempting dipping sauce! (If you plan to use leftover marinade as a sauce, boil it several minutes to kill any bacteria from the raw meat.)*

MAKES 6 SERVINGS

¼ cup reduced-sodium soy sauce

3 tablespoons light corn syrup

3 tablespoons orange juice

1 tablespoon packed dark brown sugar

1 garlic clove, crushed

½ teaspoon ground ginger

In a small jar with a tight-fitting lid, combine all the ingredients; cover and shake well. To use, transfer to a sealable plastic bag or nonreactive dish.

**Per serving**: 48 Calories, 0 g Total Fat, 0 g Saturated Fat, 0 mg Cholesterol, 417 mg Sodium, 12 g Total Carbohydrate, 0 g Dietary Fiber, 1 g Protein, 11 mg Calcium. *POINTS* per serving: 1.

# Yogurt Marinade

*Inspired by the tandoori marinades of India, this fat-free mixture makes chicken, beef, lamb or fish uncommonly tender and flavorful. The recipe makes enough for four chicken breast halves or fish fillets.*

MAKES 4 SERVINGS

½ onion, coarsely chopped

4 garlic cloves, crushed

2 tablespoons chopped peeled gingerroot

1 tablespoon fresh lemon juice

1 cup plain low-fat yogurt

½ teaspoon salt

½ teaspoon ground coriander

½ teaspoon ground cumin

¼ teaspoon pepper

¼ teaspoon cinnamon

⅛ teaspoon ground cardamom

⅛ teaspoon ground cloves

In a food processor or blender, combine the onion, garlic, gingerroot and lemon juice; puree. Add the yogurt, salt, coriander, cumin, pepper, cinnamon, cardamom and cloves; process until combined.

**Per serving**: 54 Calories, 1 g Total Fat, 1 g Saturated Fat, 3 mg Cholesterol, 333 mg Sodium, 8 g Total Carbohydrate, 1 g Dietary Fiber, 4 g Protein, 121 mg Calcium. **POINTS** per serving: 1.

# Herb Marinade

*This versatile marinade recipe easily doubles. Rub on chicken or lamb, and marinate in the refrigerator for at least one hour or overnight.*

MAKES 6 SERVINGS

2 tablespoons Dijon mustard

4 teaspoons minced rosemary leaves

2 teaspoons chopped oregano

1 shallot, minced

1½ teaspoons red-wine vinegar

2 garlic cloves, minced

In a small jar with a tight-fitting lid, combine all the ingredients and 1 tablespoon water; cover and shake well.

**Per serving**: 9 Calories, 0 g Total Fat, 0 g Saturated Fat, 0 mg Cholesterol, 29 mg Sodium, 1 g Total Carbohydrate, 0 g Dietary Fiber, 0 g Protein, 10 mg Calcium. **POINTS** per serving: 0.

# Dry-Rub Marinade

*As their name implies, dry rubs contain no liquids; they are rubbed onto meats and poultry to permeate them with intense flavor.*

MAKES 12 SERVINGS

1½ teaspoons coarse (kosher) salt

1 bay leaf, crumbled

½ teaspoon rubbed sage

½ teaspoon sugar

⅛ teaspoon ground allspice

⅛ teaspoon ground ginger

⅛ teaspoon cinnamon

In a small bowl, combine all the ingredients. To use, rub onto meat (pork roast, thin chops or cutlets, flank steak, roast beef, steak or lamb) about 2 hours before cooking, using about 1 teaspoon per ¾ pound uncooked meat.

**Per serving:** 1 Calorie, 0 g Total Fat, 0 g Saturated Fat, 0 mg Cholesterol, 387 mg Sodium, 1 g Total Carbohydrate, 0 g Dietary Fiber, 0 g Protein, 2 mg Calcium. **POINTS** per serving: 0.

# Herbed Vinegar

*Fresh herbs give the vinegar a delightful, complex flavor. Make extra in pretty bottles for gifts.*

MAKES 1 QUART

1 quart distilled white vinegar

¼ cup packed basil leaves, washed and dried

8 sprigs rosemary, washed and dried

8 sprigs thyme, washed and dried

3 strips orange zest, cut into 3 × ½" pieces

8 black peppercorns

5 allspice berries

1 cinnamon stick, split lengthwise

In a medium nonreactive saucepan, bring the vinegar to a boil. Add the remaining ingredients; boil 1 minute. Transfer to a sterilized 1-quart jar or bottle. Store in a cool, dark place and allow the flavors to blend before using, about 2 weeks.

**Per quart:** 2 Calories, 0 g Total Fat, 0 g Saturated Fat, 0 mg Cholesterol, 0 mg Sodium, 1 g Total Carbohydrate, 0 g Dietary Fiber, 0 g Protein, 1 mg Calcium. **POINTS** per serving: 0.

# Basic Pie Crust

*The secret of good pastry? Keep it cold, work quickly and let it rest to relax the gluten before rolling it out. For best results, make the crust about 24 hours before you'd like to bake it.*

MAKES 8 SERVINGS

1 cup all-purpose flour

1 teaspoon sugar

⅛ teaspoon salt

3 tablespoons cold unsalted margarine, diced

⅓ cup low-fat (1%) cottage cheese

¼ cup plain low-fat yogurt

1. In a large bowl, combine the flour, sugar and salt. With two knives, cut in the margarine until the mixture resembles coarse crumbs. Stir in the cottage cheese and yogurt until the mixture forms a soft ball. Gather the dough into a ball; wrap in plastic wrap. Refrigerate several hours or overnight.

2. On a floured surface, roll out the dough to a 13" circle. Fit the dough into a 9" pie plate, pressing to fit and rolling the dough over to form a rim; flute the rim, if desired. Refrigerate until chilled. Prick the bottom with a fork.

*For Prebaked Crust*

Preheat the oven to 400° F. Line the crust with foil; fill with dried beans. Bake until the crust is set, about 10 minutes; remove the foil and beans. Bake until golden, 5–8 minutes longer. Cool on a rack.

**Per serving**: 106 Calories, 4 g Total Fat, 1 g Saturated Fat, 1 mg Cholesterol, 80 mg Sodium, 14 g Total Carbohydrate, 0 g Dietary Fiber, 3 g Protein, 22 mg Calcium. **POINTS** per serving: 2.

## Tip

If you're making something savory like a pot pie, omit the sugar.

# Crumb Crust

*Freezing the margarine ensures that it will coat the crumbs evenly without mashing them together—an essential step in keeping the crust tender.*

MAKES 8 SERVINGS

¾ cup honey graham cracker crumbs

¾ cup fine plain dried bread crumbs

1½ teaspoons sugar

¼ teaspoon cinnamon

⅛ teaspoon ground cloves

4 teaspoons unsalted stick margarine, cut into very small pieces and frozen

2 tablespoons apple juice

1. Preheat the oven to 375° F. Spray a 9" spring-form pan with nonstick cooking spray.

2. In a medium bowl, combine the graham cracker crumbs, bread crumbs, sugar, cinnamon and cloves. With two knives, cut in the margarine until the mixture resembles cornmeal. Stir in the apple juice until the mixture is thoroughly moistened. Press the mixture onto the bottom and up the sides of the pan. Bake until golden, about 15 minutes. Cool slightly on a rack before filling.

**Per serving**: 96 Calories, 3 g Total Fat, 0 g Saturated Fat, 0 mg Cholesterol, 138 mg Sodium, 15 g Total Carbohydrate, 1 g Dietary Fiber, 2 g Protein, 25 mg Calcium. **POINTS** per serving: 2.

# Tart Crust

*This is a versatile recipe for sweet pies or tarts. Stick margarine works better than tub.*

MAKES 8 SERVINGS

1 cup all-purpose flour, chilled

2 tablespoons sugar

½ teaspoon salt

3 tablespoons cold unsalted stick margarine, diced

¼ cup plain low-fat yogurt

1 egg yolk

1. In a large bowl, combine the flour, sugar and salt. With two knives, cut in the margarine until the mixture resembles coarse crumbs. Stir in the yogurt and egg yolk. Gather the dough into a ball; wrap in plastic wrap. Refrigerate several hours or overnight.

2. On a floured surface, roll out the dough to a 13" circle. Fit the dough into a 9" tart pan, pressing to fit and rolling the dough over to form a rim. Refrigerate. Prick the bottom with a fork.

### For Prebaked Crust

Preheat the oven to 400° F. Line the crust with foil; fill with dried beans. Bake until the crust is set, about 15 minutes; remove the foil and beans. Bake until golden, 5–8 minutes longer. Cool on a rack.

**Per serving**: 117 Calories, 5 g Total Fat, 1 g Saturated Fat, 27 mg Cholesterol, 152 mg Sodium, 16 g Total Carbohydrate, 0 g Dietary Fiber, 2 g Protein, 19 mg Calcium. **POINTS** per serving: 3.

## Tip

For an easy dessert, bake and cool the crust; fill with low-fat French vanilla pudding and top with sliced mango, peaches and strawberries.

*Tart Crust*

# Croutons

*You can either use your own day-old bread or buy it from a local bakery at a reduced price. You can also freeze leftover bread until you have enough to make croutons.*

MAKES 8 SERVINGS

    8 slices day-old bread, cubed
    1 tablespoon salt-free seasoning blend
    2 teaspoons garlic powder

1. Preheat the oven to 300° F.

2. On a baking sheet, arrange the bread cubes in a single layer, keeping the cubes close together; sprinkle with the seasoning blend and garlic powder. Bake until golden brown and thoroughly dried, 30–40 minutes. Store in a sealable plastic bag for up to one week, or freeze in an airtight container 2–3 months.

**Per serving**: 83 Calories, 1 g Total Fat, 0 g Saturated Fat, 15 g Total Carbohydrate, 154 mg Sodium, 0 mg Cholesterol, 1 g Dietary Fiber, 3 g Protein, 31 mg Calcium. **POINTS** per serving: 2.

## Tip

Whirl the croutons in a food processor for low-in-fat and low-in-sodium seasoned dried bread crumbs.

# Yogurt Cheese

*This cheese is extraordinarily versatile, substituting for cream cheese and for sour cream; you'll find it used in several of our recipes, too.*

MAKES 4 SERVINGS

    3 cups plain nonfat yogurt

Spoon the yogurt into a coffee filter or cheese-cloth-lined sieve; place over a bowl. Refrigerate, covered with plastic wrap, several hours. Discard the liquid.

**Per serving**: 73 Calories, 0 g Total Fat, 0 g Saturated Fat, 2.5 mg Cholesterol, 86 mg Sodium, 8 g Total Carbohydrate, 0 g Dietary Fiber, 9 g Protein, 249 mg Calcium. **POINTS** per serving: 1.

## Tip

The longer you drain the yogurt cheese, the thicker it will be—for sour cream consistency, drain 6–8 hours; for cream cheese consistency, drain about 24 hours.

# Creamy Garlic and Chive Dressing

*When choosing garlic, look for firm, plump bulbs that are heavy for their size; avoid those with soft or shriveled cloves.*

MAKES 4 SERVINGS

10 garlic cloves, peeled

½ cup part-skim ricotta cheese

¼ cup plain nonfat yogurt

2 tablespoons chopped chives

½ teaspoon salt

¼ teaspoon freshly ground pepper

In a small saucepan, combine the garlic and 1 cup water; bring to a boil. Reduce the heat and simmer 10 minutes. With a slotted spoon, transfer the garlic and 2 tablespoons of the cooking liquid to a blender or food processor. Add the ricotta and yogurt; puree. Transfer to a bowl; stir in the chives, salt and pepper. Refrigerate, covered, at least 2 hours. Stir again before serving.

**Per serving**: 62 Calories, 2 g Total Fat, 2 g Saturated Fat, 10 mg Cholesterol, 324 mg Sodium, 5 g Total Carbohydrate, 0 g Dietary Fiber, 5 g Protein, 129 mg Calcium. *POINTS* per serving: 1.

# Honey-Mustard Dressing

*For superior flavor, try Dijon or country-style mustard, rather than yellow "hot dog" mustard. This dressing is also an ideal spread for a grilled chicken sandwich— or mix some into fresh potato salad instead of some of the mayo.*

MAKES 4 SERVINGS

½ cup plain nonfat yogurt

4 teaspoons prepared mustard

4 teaspoons honey

1 tablespoon snipped dill

2 teaspoons white-wine vinegar

½ teaspoon sugar

⅛ teaspoon ground white pepper

In a small bowl, whisk all the ingredients. Refrigerate, covered, 2–3 hours. Whisk again before serving.

**Per serving**: 44 Calories, 0 g Total Fat, 0 g Saturated Fat, 1 mg Cholesterol, 87 mg Sodium, 9 g Total Carbohydrate, 0 g Dietary Fiber, 2 g Protein, 65 mg Calcium. *POINTS* per serving: 1.

## Tip

Dressings can be prepared in advance and stored in a covered container in the refrigerator for a few days; small glass jars are ideal containers. Just shake well or whisk to blend before serving.

# Italian Dressing

*Feel free to alter this dressing to suit your taste—garlic lovers will want to use at least a clove! But don't substitute for the olive oil—its flavor is matchless.*

MAKES 4 SERVINGS

¼ cup low-sodium chicken broth

1 tablespoon minced red bell pepper

1 tablespoon chopped basil

1 tablespoon white-wine vinegar

2 teaspoons extra virgin olive oil

½ teaspoon grated lemon zest

½ teaspoon salt

½ garlic clove, minced

¼ teaspoon dried oregano leaves, crumbled

⅛ teaspoon freshly ground pepper

In a jar with a tight-fitting lid, combine all the ingredients; cover and shake well. Refrigerate, covered, overnight. Shake again before serving.

**Per serving**: 24 Calories, 2 g Total Fat, 0 g Saturated Fat, 0 mg Cholesterol, 314 mg Sodium, 1 g Total Carbohydrate, 0 g Dietary Fiber, 0 g Protein, 11 mg Calcium. **POINTS** per serving: 1.

# Pesto Dressing

*This dressing is so easy to prepare. Of course, put it on your favorite greens, but also experiment with it as a creamy pasta sauce.*

MAKES 4 SERVINGS

2 cups packed basil leaves

½ cup packed flat-leaf parsley leaves

¼ cup part-skim ricotta cheese

3 tablespoons grated Parmesan cheese

3 garlic cloves

½ teaspoon freshly ground pepper

2 tablespoons plain nonfat yogurt

In blender or food processor, combine the basil, parsley, ricotta, Parmesan, garlic and pepper; puree. Transfer to a small bowl with a tight-fitting lid; stir in the yogurt. Refrigerate, covered, until the flavors are blended, at least 2 hours. Stir again before serving.

**Per serving**: 69 Calories, 3 g Total Fat, 1 g Saturated Fat, 8 mg Cholesterol, 99 mg Sodium, 8 g Total Carbohydrate, 0 g Dietary Fiber, 5 g Protein, 305 mg Calcium. **POINTS** per serving: 2.

# Russian Dressing

*Use fresh horseradish for an extra kick.*

MAKES 4 SERVINGS

3 tablespoons orange juice

3 tablespoons reduced-calorie mayonnaise

2 tablespoons minced green bell pepper

2 tablespoons minced red bell pepper

2 tablespoons tomato paste

2 tablespoons plain nonfat yogurt

1 tablespoon drained prepared horseradish

1 tablespoon grated onion

1 teaspoon Dijon mustard

½ teaspoon chili powder

¼ teaspoon freshly ground pepper

In a jar with a tight-fitting lid, combine all the ingredients; cover and shake well. Refrigerate, covered, 2–3 hours. Shake again before serving.

**Per serving**: 49 Calories, 3 g Total Fat, 1 g Saturated Fat, 3 mg Cholesterol, 148 mg Sodium, 5 g Total Carbohydrate, 1 g Dietary Fiber, 1 g Protein, 24 mg Calcium. *POINTS* per serving: 1.

## How We Did It

When prepared traditionally, this dressing is loaded with fat and calories. We've lightened it up by using nonfat yogurt and reduced-calorie mayo.

## All Dressed Up

*Salad dressing can be a fat trap, since a high percentage of calories comes from fat. An easy way to add great, fat-free flavor to your salad is to splash on different vinegars, such as red- or white-wine vinegar; rice, cider or malt varieties; herb-flavored vinegars such as tarragon or dill; or fruit-infused versions like cranberry or raspberry.*

## RECIPES

Appetizers and Snacks

# Chapter 2

# Appetizers and Snacks

Remember bacon-wrapped chicken livers? Creamed meatballs? Those old-fashioned hors d'oeuvres were purposely rich to counteract the effects of cocktails. Nowadays, the cocktail hour is practically obsolete and today's appetizer menu is designed to *stimulate* the appetite, not quench it.

## Appealing Appetizers

Using small portions and lean ingredients, appetizers are the perfect way to open a meal. Try to contrast with and complement the foods you'll serve later. Or, you can take a cue from experienced restaurant-goers and make a meal of appetizers alone. If you're not in the habit of serving your meals in courses, remember that some of the plated appetizers could double as side dishes, too.

## Snack Smarts

Snacks don't have to be your downfall; in fact, they can help you stick to your weight-loss goals.

Think of a snack as a planned event: a mini-meal that can help curb your cravings, rather than a surreptitious nibble you sneak when no one's looking. If you take a few minutes to make yourself a snack, you'll get a more satisfying (and nutritious) experience than simply reaching for a bag of chips.

Plan your snacks and appetizers around vegetables and grains, and include a small protein component for staying power—like a bean-based dip with baked chips or roasted vegetables dusted with a sprinkling of flavorsome cheese. Be sure to vary colors, textures, flavors, even temperatures, so all the senses can feast.

# Asparagus with Sherry Vinaigrette

*The ends of asparagus can be fibrous, so they should always be trimmed. To determine where to trim, hold a spear just below the tip and at the end and bend—it should snap about two inches from the end.*

MAKES 4 SERVINGS

1 pound asparagus, trimmed and cut into 2" lengths

2 tablespoons sherry-wine vinegar

4 teaspoons olive oil

1 teaspoon sugar

¼ teaspoon salt

2 tablespoons chopped chives

2 teaspoons sesame seeds, toasted

1. In a large pot of boiling water, cook the asparagus until just tender, about 2 minutes; drain. Rinse under cold running water; drain thoroughly and pat dry with paper towels.

2. In a large bowl, whisk the vinegar, oil, sugar and salt with 4 teaspoons water. Add the asparagus; toss to coat. Sprinkle with the chives and sesame seeds.

**Per serving:** 77 Calories, 6 g Total Fat, 1 g Saturated Fat, 0 mg Cholesterol, 139 mg Sodium, 6 g Total Carbohydrate, 1 g Dietary Fiber, 3 g Protein, 44 mg Calcium. *POINTS* per serving: 2.

# Broccoli with Caesar Dressing

*This is adapted from the classic Caesar dressing. It is also good as a salad dressing for greens.*

MAKES 4 SERVINGS

1 pound broccoli florets

3 ounces soft tofu

¼ cup chicken or vegetable broth

2 anchovy fillets, or 1 teaspoon anchovy paste

1 garlic clove

1 teaspoon Dijon mustard

1 teaspoon fresh lemon juice

1. In a large pot of boiling water, cook the broccoli until just tender, about 4 minutes; drain. Rinse under cold running water; drain thoroughly. Transfer to a large bowl.

2. In a food processor or blender, combine the tofu, broth, anchovies, garlic, mustard and lemon juice; puree. Pour the dressing over the broccoli; toss to coat.

**Per serving:** 68 Calories, 2 g Total Fat, 0 g Saturated Fat, 1 mg Cholesterol, 220 mg Sodium, 10 g Total Carbohydrate, 5 g Dietary Fiber, 7 g Protein, 94 mg Calcium. *POINTS* per serving: 1.

## How We Did It

Caesar dressing usually features a raw egg, along with plenty of oil. To avoid fat, not to mention potentially harmful bacteria, we based our version on tofu thinned with chicken broth. A bonus: The tofu provides a boost of protein, not pure fat.

# Green Beans in Tomato Vinaigrette

*Be sure to use a glass, ceramic or plastic bowl to marinate the beans. The acids in the tomato mixture will react with metals, giving the dish an unpleasant flavor.*

MAKES 4 SERVINGS

1 pound green beans, cut into 2" lengths

1 teaspoon olive oil

3 garlic cloves, minced

½ cup chicken or vegetable broth

½ cup canned crushed tomatoes

¼ cup mixed vegetable juice

1 tablespoon red-wine vinegar

1 teaspoon minced fresh oregano, or ½ teaspoon dried

1 teaspoon minced fresh marjoram, or ½ teaspoon dried

½ teaspoon salt

¼ teaspoon freshly ground pepper

¼ teaspoon sugar

1. In a large pot of boiling water, cook the green beans until just tender, about 4 minutes; drain. Rinse under cold running water; drain thoroughly.

2. In a large nonstick skillet, heat the oil. Sauté the garlic until lightly browned, about 1 minute. Stir in the broth, tomatoes, vegetable juice, vinegar, oregano, marjoram, salt, pepper and sugar; bring to a boil. Reduce the heat and simmer 5 minutes.

3. Transfer the tomato mixture to a large nonreactive bowl. Add the green beans; toss to coat. Marinate 1 hour at room temperature before serving.

**Per serving:** 56 Calories, 1 g Total Fat, 0 g Saturated Fat, 0 mg Cholesterol, 507 mg Sodium, 10 g Total Carbohydrate, 2 g Dietary Fiber, 3 g Protein, 54 mg Calcium. *POINTS* per serving: 1.

# Hearts of Palm in Lemon Dressing

*Hearts of palm have a delicate artichoke-like flavor; this recipe enhances it with a light lemon-infused dressing.*

MAKES 4 SERVINGS

2 tablespoons fresh lemon juice

1 tablespoon chopped dill

2 teaspoons olive oil

1 garlic clove, minced

⅛ teaspoon sugar

One 14-ounce can hearts of palm, rinsed, drained, dried and cut into 1" lengths

In a medium bowl, whisk the lemon juice, dill, oil, garlic and sugar; add the hearts of palm and toss to coat.

**Per serving:** 42 Calories, 2 g Total Fat, 0 g Saturated Fat, 0 mg Cholesterol, 1 mg Sodium, 5 g Total Carbohydrate, 0 g Dietary Fiber, 2 g Protein, 5 mg Calcium. *POINTS* per serving: 1.

# Leeks in Orange Vinaigrette

*The vinaigrette in this recipe is so delicious and easy to make, you'll want to try it on other veggies as well—we like it drizzled over watercress.*

MAKES 4 SERVINGS

4 leeks, cleaned

1 fennel bulb, trimmed and thinly sliced

3 garlic cloves

4 teaspoons olive oil

¼ teaspoon dried sage leaves

½ cup orange juice

2 tablespoons balsamic vinegar

½ teaspoon sugar

½ teaspoon salt

1. Preheat the oven to 400° F. Tear off a 24" sheet of foil and place on a baking sheet. Arrange the leeks, fennel and garlic on half of the sheet of foil; sprinkle with 2 teaspoons of the oil and the sage. Fold the remaining foil over the vegetables; seal the ends securely to make a tight packet. Bake about 15 minutes, turning the packet over after 7–8 minutes.

2. Meanwhile, in a small skillet over high heat, cook the orange juice until it is reduced to ¼ cup, about 5 minutes. Remove from the heat; stir in the remaining 2 teaspoons of oil, the vinegar, sugar and salt, stirring until the sugar dissolves.

3. Carefully transfer the vegetables from the foil to a shallow bowl, pouring any cooking juices over them. Drizzle with the orange juice mixture; toss to coat. Refrigerate, covered, until thoroughly chilled, about 3 hours.

**Per serving:** 101 Calories, 5 g Total Fat, 0 g Saturated Fat, 0 mg Cholesterol, 339 mg Sodium, 14 g Total Carbohydrate, 1 g Dietary Fiber, 2 g Protein, 67 mg Calcium. *POINTS* per serving: 2.

## Tip

**The bottoms of leeks grow underground, so they're usually filled with sand. To clean, cut off the tops, leaving 2" of pale green. Slice in half, lengthwise, to within ½" from the bottom; rinse under running water, spreading the leaves to get out all the dirt.**

# Snow Peas with Ginger Dressing

*Snow peas and radishes give this dish a lot of crunch, but this refreshing dressing works well on spinach, too. Serve it before—or alongside—rich roast pork.*

MAKES 4 SERVINGS

3 cups snow peas, stems and strings removed

2 tablespoons soy sauce

2 tablespoons honey

4 teaspoons grated peeled gingerroot

2 teaspoons peanut oil

1½ teaspoons Dijon mustard

1¼ teaspoons rice-wine vinegar

8 radishes, thinly sliced

1. In a large pot of boiling water, cook the snow peas until just tender, about 1 minute; drain. Rinse under cold running water; drain thoroughly and pat dry with paper towels.

2. In a medium bowl, whisk the soy sauce, honey, gingerroot, oil, mustard and vinegar with 1 tablespoon water. Add the snow peas and radishes; toss gently to coat. Refrigerate, covered, about 1 hour.

**Per serving**: 108 Calories, 3 g Total Fat, 0 g Saturated Fat, 0 mg Cholesterol, 496 mg Sodium, 18 g Total Carbohydrate, 4 g Dietary Fiber, 4 g Protein, 58 mg Calcium. **POINTS** per serving: 2.

# Potato-Vegetable Pancake

*A food processor makes short work of shredding the vegetables in this recipe. Although it's easier to make one big pancake and cut it into wedges, you can drop the potato mixture by tablespoons into the hot oil if you prefer.*

MAKES 4 SERVINGS

3 small Idaho potatoes, peeled and shredded

1 medium parsnip, peeled and shredded

½ carrot, peeled and shredded

1 egg

2 tablespoons all-purpose flour

¾ teaspoon salt

¼ teaspoon baking powder

2 teaspoons olive oil

1. In a large bowl, mix the potatoes, parsnip, carrot, egg, flour, salt and baking powder.

2. In a large nonstick skillet, heat the oil until very hot. Spread the potato mixture into the skillet, flattening with a spatula until even. Cook over medium-high heat until crisp, browned and set, about 8 minutes on each side. Cut into quarters before serving.

**Per serving**: 131 Calories, 4 g Total Fat, 1 g Saturated Fat, 53 mg Cholesterol, 469 m Sodium, 21 g Total Carbohydrate, 3 g Dietary Fiber, 4 g Protein, 42 mg Calcium. **POINTS** per serving: 2.

## Substitution

This recipe works nicely with sweet potatoes instead of the Idahos.

# Savory Pumpkin Pie

*Herbs and cheese add a rich flavor to the pumpkin filling in the crisp phyllo crust (add more pepper for more kick). This dish is ideal for a Thanksgiving buffet, or any Fall get together.*

MAKES 8 SERVINGS

4 teaspoons olive oil

1 garlic clove, peeled

½ teaspoon dried sage leaves

Six 12 × 17" sheets phyllo dough, at room temperature

One 15-ounce can pumpkin puree

3 tablespoons grated Parmesan cheese

1 egg

2 egg whites

½ teaspoon salt

⅛ teaspoon freshly ground pepper

⅛ teaspoon freshly grated nutmeg

1. Preheat the oven to 400° F. In a small nonstick skillet, heat the oil. Sauté the garlic and sage until the garlic is browned and fragrant, about 4 minutes. Discard the garlic and sage.

2. To prepare the crust, in a 9" pie plate, arrange the phyllo dough, 1 sheet at a time, rotating the sheets so they completely cover the bottom and sides of the pie plate. Brush the last sheet with 2 teaspoons of the garlic oil.

3. To prepare the filling, in a medium bowl, mix the pumpkin puree, cheese, egg, egg whites, salt, pepper and nutmeg. Spoon the filling into the crust; brush the top with the remaining 2 teaspoons of garlic oil. Bake 10 minutes; reduce the oven temperature to 350° F. Bake until the filling is just set, about 30 minutes longer.

**Per serving**: 108 Calories, 4 g Total Fat, 1 g Saturated Fat, 28 mg Cholesterol, 281 mg Sodium, 13 g Total Carbohydrate, 3 g Dietary Fiber, 5 g Protein, 60 mg Calcium. **POINTS** per serving: 4.

*Savory Pumpkin Pie*

# Baba Ghanouj

*Serve this Middle Eastern dip with a crudité platter or with other flat breads.*

MAKES 4 SERVINGS

1 medium (1-pound) eggplant

3 tablespoons chopped cilantro

3 tablespoons plain nonfat yogurt

4 teaspoons fresh lemon juice

1 garlic clove

1 teaspoon paprika

¾ teaspoon ground coriander

¾ teaspoon salt

4 small pitas

1. Preheat the oven to 425° F. Line a baking sheet with foil; spray with nonstick cooking spray.

2. With a knife, pierce the eggplant several times; place on the baking sheet. Bake, turning once or twice, until soft and the skin is charred, about 45 minutes; let stand until cool enough to handle. Peel off the skin, then coarsely chop the eggplant.

3. In a food processor or blender, puree the eggplant, cilantro, yogurt, lemon juice, garlic, paprika, coriander and salt. Serve with the pitas.

**Per serving**: 138 Calories, 1 g Total Fat, 0 g Saturated Fat, 0 mg Cholesterol, 595 mg Sodium, 29 g Total Carbohydrate, 4 g Dietary Fiber, 5 g Protein, 100 mg Calcium. **POINTS** per serving: 2.

# Caponata

*Commercial caponata is loaded with fat, so try this tasty version instead. Caponata can be served chilled or at room temperature; it's also a delicious pasta sauce.*

MAKES 4 SERVINGS

1 small (¾-pound) eggplant, peeled and cubed

1½ teaspoons coarse (kosher) salt

2 teaspoons olive oil

1 onion, chopped

3 garlic cloves, minced

1 celery stalk, diced

1 cup canned diced tomatoes

2 tablespoons golden raisins

1 tablespoon chopped mint

1 tablespoon capers, rinsed and drained

1 teaspoon chopped thyme leaves

2 heads Belgian endive, separated into leaves

1. In a colander, toss the eggplant with the kosher salt; let stand in the sink about 1 hour. Rinse well under cold running water; drain and dry thoroughly with paper towels.

2. In a large nonstick skillet, heat the oil. Sauté the onion and garlic until just fragrant, about 2 minutes. Add ¼ cup water and cook, stirring, until softened, about 5 minutes. Add the celery and 2 tablespoons water; cook, covered, 5 minutes. Add the eggplant and ⅓ cup water; cook, covered, 5 minutes. Stir in the tomatoes, raisins, mint, capers and thyme; cook, covered, 10 minutes. Uncover and cook 4 minutes longer.

3. To serve, arrange the endive on 4 plates; top with the caponata.

**Per serving**: 79 Calories, 3 g Total Fat, 0 g Saturated Fat, 0 mg Cholesterol, 356 mg Sodium, 14 g Total Carbohydrate, 3 g Dietary Fiber, 2 g Protein, 50 mg Calcium. **POINTS** per serving: 1.

# Guacamole

*A little avocado goes a long way, boosted by spinach, buttermilk and classic guacamole seasonings. If you like, serve with plenty of baked nonfat tortilla chips instead of the pita chips.*

MAKES 4 SERVINGS

4 small pitas, halved horizontally and cut into wedges

2 cups packed cleaned spinach leaves

¼ cup low-fat buttermilk

½ red onion, finely chopped

1 tablespoon drained canned chopped green chiles

1 teaspoon fresh lime juice

¼ medium avocado, peeled and sliced

2 plum tomatoes, chopped

¼ cup chopped cilantro

1. Preheat the oven to 400° F. Arrange the pita wedges on a large nonstick baking sheet. Bake until crisp, 4–5 minutes.

2. In a pot of large boiling water, cook the spinach about 1 minute; drain well and squeeze dry.

3. In a food processor, combine the spinach, buttermilk, half of the onion, the chiles and lime juice; puree until the spinach is finely chopped and the mixture is well-combined (do not overblend).

4. In a medium bowl, mash the avocado. Stir in the spinach mixture, the tomatoes, cilantro and the remaining onion. Serve with the pita chips.

**Per serving**: 124 Calories, 3 g Total Fat, 0 g Saturated Fat, 1 mg Cholesterol, 212 mg Sodium, 20 g Total Carbohydrate, 2 g Dietary Fiber, 5 g Protein, 67 mg Calcium. *POINTS* per serving: 2.

## How We Did It

Guacamole—usually loaded with fat—is lightened up by replacing much of the fatty avocado with spinach, buttermilk and tomato. Creative seasoning with chiles, cilantro and lime juice helps replace the lost fat with more flavor.

## Great Grilling

*Looking for a flexible summer appetizer? Get out your grill! Have fun finding the freshest, prettiest vegetables, then make small skewers of mixed vegetables. Here are some pointers to help you get started:*

- *If you're serving a large group, use several small grills, and let friends and family grill their own skewers of vegetables.*

- *Start your fire early enough so that cooking can begin as soon as people arrive.*

- *Prepare vegetables in advance and have them all ready on skewers.*

- *Leftover grilled vegetables? Add them to sandwiches or soups, or mix into pasta or grain salads.*

# Chicharos Guacamole

*Green peas—called chicharos in Mexico—are a delicious, low-fat substitute for the avocado commonly used in making guacamole. Serve with fat-free tortilla chips or raw vegetables, or use it as a spread for your next turkey sandwich.*

MAKES 6 SERVINGS

One 8-ounce can green peas, rinsed and drained (reserve 2 tablespoons liquid)

²⁄₃ cup canned pinto beans, rinsed and drained

2 tablespoons fat-free mayonnaise

1 tablespoon fresh lime or lemon juice

2 teaspoons Mexican (hot) chili powder

2 garlic cloves

½ teaspoon ground cumin

6 scallions, thinly sliced

1 tablespoon minced cilantro

½ jalapeño pepper, seeded, deveined and minced (wear gloves to prevent irritation)

1. In a food processor, combine the peas, beans, mayonnaise, lime juice, chili powder, garlic and cumin; puree.

2. Transfer to a medium bowl; stir in the scallions, cilantro and jalapeño. If the dip is too thick, add 1–2 tablespoons of the reserved green pea liquid until it reaches the desired consistency. Refrigerate, covered, until the flavors are blended, at least 1 hour.

**Per serving**: 75 Calories, 0 g Total Fat, 0 g Saturated Fat, 0 mg Cholesterol, 163 mg Sodium, 14 g Total Carbohydrate, 3 g Dietary Fiber, 4 g Protein, 32 mg Calcium. **POINTS** per serving: 1.

# Creamy Vegetable Salsa Dip

*Chopped raw cauliflower gives this creamy, rich-tasting dip a surprise crunch—try it with broccoli, too. Serve it with baked tortilla wedges or crudités. The recipe can easily be halved for a nutritious nosh for two.*

MAKES 4 SERVINGS

1½ cups plain nonfat yogurt

1 cup salsa

8 sun-dried tomato halves (not oil-packed), finely chopped

½ cup finely chopped cauliflower

1 celery stalk, finely chopped

6 scallions, thinly sliced

½ carrot, finely chopped

½ green bell pepper, seeded and finely chopped

2 teaspoons Dijon mustard

2 teaspoons sugar

¼ teaspoon freshly ground pepper

¼ cup chopped chives

In a medium bowl, combine the yogurt and salsa; stir in the tomatoes, cauliflower, celery, scallions, carrot, bell pepper, mustard, sugar and ground pepper. Let stand until the flavors are blended, about 10 minutes. Sprinkle with the chives before serving.

**Per serving**: 113 Calories, 1 g Total Fat, 0 g Saturated Fat, 2 mg Cholesterol, 769 mg Sodium, 20 g Total Carbohydrate, 3 g Dietary Fiber, 7 g Protein, 206 mg Calcium. **POINTS** per serving: 2.

# Herbed Yogurt Cheese

*Depending on how long you drain the yogurt, it will range in consistency from sour cream-like to cream cheese-like. Yogurt cheese works equally well in savory or sweet variations. Mix it with your favorite herb combination, spreadable fruit, or a combination of nuts and seeds. Spread it on whole-grain crisp breads, or dip veggies in it—we especially like it on cucumber spears.*

MAKES 4 SERVINGS

8 garlic cloves, unpeeled

½ teaspoon fresh lemon juice

1½ cups Yogurt Cheese (page 20)

1 scallion, thinly sliced

2 teaspoons chopped fresh oregano, or ¾ teaspoon dried

¼ teaspoon salt

1. Preheat the oven or toaster oven to 400° F. Wrap the garlic in foil and roast until soft, about 30 minutes. Unwrap the foil and let the garlic cool slightly. Squeeze the garlic from the skins into a mini food processor; add the lemon juice and puree.

2. In a medium bowl, mix the yogurt cheese, garlic, scallion, oregano and salt.

**Per serving:** 90 Calories, 1 g Total Fat, 0 g Saturated Fat, 0 mg Cholesterol, 212 mg Sodium, 12 g Total Carbohydrate 1 g Dietary Fiber, 8 g Protein, 267 mg Calcium. *POINTS* per serving: 2.

# Hummus
### (pictured on page 39)

*This basic chickpea spread is always delicious with warmed pita triangles, but also try it in a roasted veggie wrap.*

MAKES 8 SERVINGS

One 15-ounce can chickpeas, rinsed and drained

½ cup plain nonfat yogurt

2 tablespoons fresh lemon juice

3 garlic cloves

2 teaspoons olive oil

½ teaspoon salt

½ teaspoon ground cumin

⅛ teaspoon ground allspice

In food processor or blender, puree all the ingredients with 1 tablespoon water.

**Per serving:** 91 Calories, 2 g Total Fat, 0 g Saturated Fat, 0 mg Cholesterol, 151 mg Sodium, 13 g Total Carbohydrate, 1 g Dietary Fiber, 5 g Protein, 54 mg Calcium. *POINTS* per serving: 2.

## Tip

Hummus sometimes includes tahini, a paste made from ground sesame seeds. If you have some on hand, add a teaspoon or so. Believe it or not, peanut butter (creamy, not chunky) is a great "fake-out" for the tahini flavor.

# Moroccan Red Bean Dip

(*pictured on page 39*)

---

*The dried fruit and warm spices typical of Moroccan cuisine give this dip a marvelous, mysterious flavor. Serve it with crisp vegetable slices or toasted pita wedges.*

MAKES 4 SERVINGS

1 teaspoon olive oil

½ red onion, chopped

1 garlic clove, finely chopped

1 plum tomato, chopped

1 tablespoon golden raisins

3 dried apricot halves, chopped

1 tablespoon orange juice

¾ cup canned red kidney beans, rinsed and drained

¼ teaspoon ground cumin

⅛ teaspoon cinnamon

⅛ teaspoon ground cloves

⅛ teaspoon curry powder

⅛ teaspoon chili powder

⅛ teaspoon salt

In a medium nonstick skillet, heat the oil. Sauté the onion and garlic until just softened, 2–3 minutes. Reduce the heat and simmer, covered, 2–3 minutes. Stir in the tomato, raisins, apricots and orange juice. Cook, covered, 2–3 minutes. Stir in the beans, cumin, cinnamon, cloves, curry powder, chili powder and salt. Remove from the heat; let cool slightly. Transfer the mixture to a food processor or blender; puree. Refrigerate, covered, until ready to serve.

**Per serving**: 106 Calories, 2 g Total Fat, 0 g Saturated Fat, 0 mg Cholesterol, 74 mg Sodium, 19 g Total Carbohydrate, 3 g Dietary Fiber, 5 g Protein, 27 mg Calcium. *POINTS* per serving: 2.

# Roasted Red Pepper Dip

---

*Keep a container of this in your refrigerator for snacking; it complements any cutup vegetables and is a fabulous baked potato topper.*

MAKES 4 SERVINGS

2 large red bell peppers

2 teaspoons tomato paste

2 teaspoons balsamic vinegar

1 garlic clove

⅛ teaspoon cayenne pepper

1. Preheat the broiler; line a baking sheet with foil. Arrange the bell peppers on the baking sheet; broil 3" from the heat, turning frequently, until charred on all sides, about 10 minutes. Let stand until cool enough to handle, about 15 minutes.

2. Place a strainer over a small bowl. Peel the peppers over the strainer, discarding the cores and seeds and allowing the juices to drip into the bowl.

3. In a food processor, puree the peppers and juice, the tomato paste, vinegar, garlic and cayenne until almost smooth.

**Per serving**: 16 Calories, 0 g Total Fat, 0 g Saturated Fat, 0 mg Cholesterol, 23 mg Sodium, 4 g Total Carbohydrate, 1 g Dietary Fiber, 1 g Protein, 7 mg Calcium. *POINTS* per serving: 0.

## Tip

If you're short on time, use a 7-ounce jar of roasted red peppers. Drain the peppers, and slowly add the liquid to the food processor to reach the right consistency.

# White Bean–Garlic Dip with Vegetables

*Use more cayenne if you like it spicy! With the addition of some toasted baguette slices, this can be a light meal.*

MAKES 6 SERVINGS

½ garlic bulb (about 6 large cloves)

⅔ cup canned cannellini beans, rinsed and drained

2 tablespoons fresh lime juice

1 tablespoon extra virgin olive oil

3 scallions, minced

¼ orange or red bell pepper, seeded and finely chopped

1½ teaspoons minced cilantro

⅛–¼ teaspoon cayenne pepper

1 cup broccoli florets

1 cup cauliflower florets

1 carrot, cut into sticks

1. Preheat the oven or toaster oven to 400° F. Cut off a thin slice from the pointed end of the garlic bulb. Wrap the garlic in foil and roast until soft, about 30 minutes. Unwrap the foil and let the garlic cool slightly. Squeeze the garlic from the skins into a food processor or blender. Add ⅓ cup of the beans, the lime juice and oil; puree.

2. Transfer to a medium bowl; stir in the remaining ⅓ cup of beans, the scallions, bell pepper, cilantro and cayenne. Refrigerate, covered, until the flavors are blended, at least 1 hour. Serve with the broccoli, cauliflower and carrot.

**Per serving:** 84 Calories, 3 g Total Fat, 0 g Saturated Fat, 0 mg Cholesterol, 17 mg Sodium, 13 g Total Carbohydrate, 3 g Dietary Fiber, 4 g Protein, 38 mg Calcium. **POINTS** per serving: 1.

# Deviled Eggs

*The secret to perfect hard-cooked eggs: Put the eggs in a saucepan and add enough water to cover by one inch. Bring the water just to a boil; then remove the pan from the heat, cover and let stand 15 to 17 minutes. Run cold water over the eggs to stop the cooking process.*

MAKES 4 SERVINGS

4 hard-cooked eggs, peeled and halved lengthwise

1 tablespoon finely chopped chutney

2 teaspoons reduced-calorie mayonnaise

1 teaspoon Dijon mustard

¼ teaspoon cayenne pepper

⅛ teaspoon salt

1. Remove the yolks from the egg halves; set the whites aside. In a medium bowl, mash the egg yolks with a fork; mix in the chutney, mayonnaise, mustard, cayenne and salt.

2. Spoon the yolk mixture evenly into the egg whites.

**Per serving:** 98 Calories, 6 g Total Fat, 2 g Saturated Fat, 213 mg Cholesterol, 226 mg Sodium, 4 g Total Carbohydrate, 0 g Dietary Fiber, 6 g Protein, 26 mg Calcium. **POINTS** per serving: 2.

## Tip

For a pretty presentation, spoon the yolk mixture into a pastry bag fitted with a star tip; pipe into the whites. Sprinkle with paprika or minced parsley for a burst of color.

# Dolmades

*Dolmades, or stuffed grape leaves, make exquisite hors d'oeuvres that can be served chilled or at room temperature. All you'll need is some plain nonfat yogurt for dipping.*

MAKES 4 SERVINGS

1 teaspoon olive oil

¼ cup minced carrot

1 garlic clove, minced

4 scallions, thinly sliced

1¼ cups chicken broth

⅓ cup long-grain white rice

3 tablespoons chopped dill

¼ teaspoon grated lemon zest

2 tablespoons fresh lemon juice

12 bottled large grape leaves, drained, soaked and rinsed several times

8 large dill sprigs

¼ cup plain nonfat yogurt

1. In a medium nonstick saucepan, heat the oil. Sauté the carrot and garlic until softened, about 4 minutes. Stir in the scallions and ¼ cup of the broth; cook, stirring occasionally, until most of the liquid evaporates, about 5 minutes. Stir in the remaining cup of broth, the rice, dill, lemon zest and lemon juice. Reduce the heat and simmer, covered, until the rice is tender and the broth is absorbed, about 17 minutes.

2. On a clean work surface, arrange the grape leaves in a single layer. Spoon the rice mixture onto the stem end of each leaf; fold the stem end over. Fold the sides of the leaves over the filling to enclose. From the stem end, roll up the leaves, jelly-roll style. Place the dolmades seam-side down in a large skillet. Place 4 of the dill sprigs over the dolmades. Pour ½ cup water into the skillet; bring to a boil. Reduce the heat and simmer, covered, about 30 minutes. Let cool to room temperature.

3. To serve, arrange 3 dolmades and 1 tablespoon of the yogurt on each of 4 plates; garnish each with a remaining dill sprig.

**Per serving:** 94 Calories, 2 g Total Fat, 0 g Saturated Fat, 0 mg Total Cholesterol, 329 mg Sodium, 16 g Total Carbohydrate, 1 g Dietary Fiber, 4 g Protein, 92 mg Calcium. *POINTS* per serving: 2.

## Got Leftovers?

**Chances are you'll have some grape leaves left after making this recipe. Try using them to wrap a whole fish for grilling or baking, or stuff them with a traditional stuffed cabbage filling, and steam.**

*Clockwise from right: Moroccan Red Bean Dip (page 36), Hummus (page 35), Dolmades*

# Tomato Mini Pizzas

*Pizzas—the perfect kid-friendly cuisine! Let your children's creativity run wild by providing the toppings—try pepper strips, sliced olives, carrot coins—and let them do the decorating. If you prefer, use four small pitas instead of two large ones.*

MAKES 4 SERVINGS

2 large pocketless pitas

2 large plum tomatoes, thinly sliced

¼ teaspoon salt

2 tablespoons chopped basil

2 teaspoons olive oil

2 garlic cloves, minced

⅓ cup shredded part-skim mozzarella cheese

1. Preheat the oven to 400° F. Spray a large non-stick baking sheet with nonstick cooking spray. Place the pitas on the baking sheet.

2. In a small bowl, mix the tomatoes and salt; stir in the basil, oil and garlic. Top the pitas with the tomato mixture, drizzling any liquid in the bowl over the toppings. Bake until the tomatoes are hot and softened, about 8 minutes. Sprinkle with the cheese; bake until the cheese is melted, about 3 minutes longer. Cut the pitas in half before serving.

**Per serving:** 131 Calories, 4 g Total Fat, 1 g Saturated Fat, 4 mg Cholesterol, 346 mg Sodium, 18 g Total Carbohydrate, 1 g Dietary Fiber, 6 g Protein, 118 mg Calcium. **POINTS** per serving: 3.

*Tomato Mini Pizzas*

# Red Onion Pizzas

*An Italian favorite with a Greek accent, these little pizzas are built on pita crusts with a tangy topping. Cook the onions ahead of time; heat the onions briefly before spooning onto the pizzas, or bake the pizzas a bit longer before topping with the cheese.*

MAKES 4 SERVINGS

2 teaspoons olive oil

4 red onions, thinly sliced

2 teaspoons red-wine vinegar

1 teaspoon orange zest

1 medium zucchini, thinly sliced

4 small pitas

¾ cup crumbled feta cheese

4 teaspoons chopped oregano

1. In a large nonstick skillet over low heat, heat 1 teaspoon of the oil and ¼ cup water. Add the onions and cook until very tender, about 30 minutes. Stir in the vinegar and orange zest; cook until all the liquid is absorbed, about 10 minutes.

2. In a small bowl, combine the zucchini and the remaining teaspoon of oil with 1 tablespoon water; toss to coat.

3. Preheat the oven to 400° F; spray a baking sheet with nonstick cooking spray. Arrange the pitas on the baking sheet; top with the zucchini slices. Bake 8 minutes. Spoon the onions onto the pitas; bake 6 minutes. Sprinkle the pitas with the feta cheese and oregano; bake until the cheese melts, 3–5 minutes longer.

**Per serving**: 210 Calories, 8 g Total Fat, 4 g Saturated Fat, 19 mg Cholesterol, 403 mg Sodium, 29 g Total Carbohydrate, 3 g Dietary Fiber, 8 g Protein, 169 mg Calcium. *POINTS* per serving: 4.

# Mango and Black Bean Salsa

*Serve this alongside grilled chicken or fish for a tropical flair, or spoon it into a lettuce leaf.*

MAKES 4 SERVINGS

1 red onion, diced

1 cup ice water

1 mango, peeled, pitted and diced

½ red bell pepper, seeded and diced

½ cup fresh or thawed frozen corn kernels

½ cup canned black beans, rinsed and drained

2 tablespoons fresh lime juice

¼ teaspoon salt

1. In a small bowl, cover the onion with the ice water; soak about 30 minutes. Drain; dry well.

2. In a medium bowl, mix the onion, mango, bell pepper, corn, beans, lime juice and salt.

**Per serving**: 90 Calories, 1 g Total Fat, 0 g Saturated Fat, 0 mg Cholesterol, 140 mg Sodium, 21 g Total Carbohydrate, 2 g Dietary Fiber, 3 g Protein, 24 mg Calcium. *POINTS* per serving: 1.

## How We Did It

Stymied by mangoes? Try this technique to prep one: With the mango on a cutting board, cut it in half just off-center, running the knife along the pit; turn it over and repeat the motion. Discard the pit; cut a cross-hatch pattern into the mango flesh (don't cut through the skin). Push on the skin-side to "pop" the cubes, which can easily be removed.

# RECIPES

Breads and Baked Goods

# Chapter 3

# Breads and Baked Goods

What's the difference between someone who occasionally bakes and someone who calls herself a baker? Confidence, plus a few easily learned techniques. Here are some basics to boost your skills.

## Know Your Flours

The two types of wheat that make up most flours are classified by their content of gluten, a protein that gives dough its elastic texture. Hard wheat is high in gluten, so it's ideal for producing the expanding dough needed for yeast breads; *bread flour* is made from mostly hard wheat. By contrast, soft wheat is low in gluten, producing the tender crumbs needed for cakes; *cake flour* is mostly soft wheat.

*All-purpose flour*, a mixture of both hard and soft wheat, can be used for both breads and cakes. Although your results won't be the same, substituting all-purpose for bread flour in a bread recipe is fine. Similarly, you can use 1 cup minus 2 tablespoons of all-purpose flour for each cup of cake flour called for in a recipe, and $1\frac{1}{8}$ cups of cake flour for each cup of all-purpose.

*Self-rising flour* is all-purpose flour to which baking powder and salt have been added; omit both ingredients if you're substituting it for regular flour in a recipe.

## Yeast or Baking Powder?

Yeast and baking powder raise dough in different ways. Yeast, a living organism, feeds on sugar and produces the carbon dioxide gas that forms expanding bubbles in the dough. Water, heat and kneading allow the gluten to develop; more kneading and long rising in a warm place will produce a coarse-textured product, as they activate more gluten. Yeast is the best leavening for sturdy baking like breads, rolls and coffee cakes.

By contrast, baking powder uses the combination of acid (cream of tartar) and alkaline (baking soda) to produce carbon dioxide gas. It makes for a faster rise and a lighter crumb, so it's ideal for cakes, quick breads and muffins. However, with baking powder you'll need to work fast: If you overbeat a batter or let it stand too long before putting it in the oven, too much gas will escape to allow for proper rising.

## Dry versus Compressed Yeast

You can buy yeast in dry, granular form or in compressed cakes: Both forms work equally well in recipes. Dry yeast (usually called "active dry" yeast) has a long shelf life if it is stored in a cool, dry place; choose regular or rapid-rise varieties. The cake form will keep about two weeks in the refrigerator and two months in the freezer; check expiration dates on the package.

One $\frac{1}{2}$-ounce package of dry yeast (just under one tablespoon) is equivalent to one $\frac{3}{5}$-ounce cake of compressed yeast.

# Basic White Bread

*Baking your own bread is enormously satisfying— plus you can vary it to suit your mood! Try the cheese variation for a loaf with extra flavor, the raisin bread to make morning toast a treat.*

MAKES 16 SERVINGS

½ cup lukewarm (105–115° F) fat-free milk

¼ cup lukewarm (105–115° F) water

2 teaspoons sugar

1 envelope active dry yeast

2 cups all-purpose flour

1 teaspoon salt

1 teaspoon fat-free milk

1. In a small bowl, combine the lukewarm milk, water and sugar; sprinkle with the yeast. Let stand until foamy, about 10 minutes.

2. In a food processor, combine the flour and salt. With the machine running, scrape the yeast mixture through the food tube just until the dough forms a ball. Knead the dough by pulsing until it is smooth and no longer sticky, about 30 times.

3. Spray a large bowl with nonstick cooking spray; place the dough in the bowl. Cover loosely with plastic wrap or a damp towel and let the dough rise in a warm, draft-free place until it doubles in volume, 40–50 minutes.

4. Punch down the dough; lightly sprinkle a work surface with flour. Turn out the dough; pat into an 8 × 12" rectangle. Fold into thirds lengthwise, pinching the seams to seal, and form into an 8" loaf. Spray an 8 × 4" loaf pan with nonstick cooking spray. Place the dough in the pan, seam-side down; cover with plastic wrap or a damp towel and let it rise in a warm, draft-free place until doubled in volume, 35–40 minutes. Preheat the oven to 425° F.

5. Brush the bread with the teaspoon of milk. Bake on the center oven rack about 20 minutes; reduce the oven temperature to 375° F. Bake until the bread is golden brown, 25–30 minutes longer. Remove from the pan and cool completely on a rack.

**Per serving:** 58 Calories, 0 g Total Fat, 0 g Saturated Fat, 0 mg Cholesterol, 138 mg Sodium, 12 g Total Carbohydrate, 0 g Dietary Fiber, 2 g Protein, 13 mg Calcium. *POINTS* per serving: 1.

## Cheese Bread

Add 2 tablespoons grated Parmesan cheese, ¾ cup shredded extra-sharp cheddar cheese and a pinch each of cayenne pepper and ground nutmeg with the flour.

**Per serving:** 86 Calories, 2 g Total Fat, 1 g Saturated Fat, 7 mg Cholesterol, 195 mg Sodium, 12 g Total Carbohydrate, 1 g Dietary Fiber, 4 g Protein, 70 mg Calcium. *POINTS* per serving: 2.

## Raisin Bread

Add 1 teaspoon cinnamon with the flour and sprinkle with ½ cup raisins just before shaping the loaf in step 4.

**Per serving:** 72 Calories, 0 g Total Fat, 0 g Saturated Fat, 0 mg Cholesterol, 138 mg Sodium, 16 g Total Carbohydrate, 1 g Dietary Fiber, 2 g Protein, 17 mg Calcium. *POINTS* per serving: 1.

# Sourdough White Bread

*Sourdough bread is based on a "starter" instead of plain yeast. You'll want to begin this tangy bread at least two days before you plan to bake it. Apple butter is an ideal topping for sourdough toast.*

MAKES 12 SERVINGS

### Starter

¾ cup all-purpose flour

¾ cup lukewarm (105–115° F) water

1 envelope active dry yeast

### Bread

1½ cups all-purpose flour, plus more for dusting

2 teaspoons salt

1. To prepare the starter, in a glass bowl, combine the flour and water; sprinkle with the yeast. Cover and let stand at room temperature 2 days; the starter should be bubbling and have a grapefruit-like odor.

2. To prepare the bread, in a food processor, combine flour and salt. With the machine running, scrape the starter through the feed tube just until the dough forms a ball. Knead the dough by pulsing until it is smooth and no longer sticky, about 30 times.

3. Spray a large bowl with nonstick cooking spray; place the dough in the bowl. Cover loosely with plastic wrap or a damp towel and let the dough rise in a warm, draft-free place until it doubles in volume, about 1 hour.

4. Punch down the dough; lightly sprinkle a work surface with flour. Turn out the dough; form into a 6" round loaf. Spray a baking sheet with non-stick cooking spray. Place the loaf on the baking sheet; cover loosely with plastic wrap or a damp towel and let it rise in a warm, draft-free place until doubled in volume, about 1 hour.

5. Preheat the oven to 400° F; place a pan of boiling water on the lowest oven rack. Dust the loaf with about 1 teaspoon of flour; with a sharp knife or single-edge razor blade, slash the top of the loaf twice vertically and twice horizontally to make a crosshatch pattern. Bake about 20 minutes; reduce the oven temperature to 350° F. Bake until the bread is well-browned and sounds hollow when tapped on the bottom, 20–30 minutes longer. Remove from the pan and cool completely on a rack.

**Per serving:** 80 Calories, 0 g Total Fat, 0 g Saturated Fat, 0 mg Cholesterol, 356 mg Sodium, 17 g Total Carbohydrate, 1 g Dietary Fiber, 2 g Protein, 6 mg Calcium. **POINTS** per serving: 1.

## Measuring the Right Way

*Baking is a precise science, and accurate measurements are critical for best results. Use liquid measuring cups (clear glass or plastic, with pour spouts) for liquid ingredients; place them on a level surface, then pour in exactly what you need, viewing from the side to fill to the right level.*

*For dry or solid ingredients like flour or yogurt, use dry measuring cups; their flat tops allow you to fill the cup to the brim and level off with a knife or straight edge.*

# Bran Bread

*Slather slices of this fiber-rich bread with honey mustard, and then top with Black Forest ham and Swiss cheese for hearty open-faced sandwiches.*

MAKES 12 SERVINGS

1 envelope active dry yeast

1⅓ cups lukewarm (105–115° F) water

2 cups all-purpose flour

1 cup + 2 tablespoons wheat bran

½ cup + 2 tablespoons whole-wheat flour

2 teaspoons salt

1. In a small bowl, sprinkle the yeast over the water. Let stand until foamy, about 10 minutes.

2. In a food processor, combine the all-purpose flour, wheat bran, whole-wheat flour and salt. With the machine running, scrape the yeast mixture through the feed tube just until the dough forms a ball. Knead the dough by pulsing until it is smooth and no longer sticky, about 30 times.

3. Spray a large bowl with nonstick cooking spray; place the dough in the bowl. Cover loosely with plastic wrap or a damp towel and let the dough rise in a warm, draft-free place until it doubles in volume, about 1 hour.

4. Punch down the dough. Cover loosely with plastic wrap or a damp towel and let it rise in a warm, draft-free place about 30 minutes.

5. Punch down the dough; lightly sprinkle a work surface with flour. Turn out the dough; pat into an 8 × 12" rectangle. Fold into thirds, lengthwise, pinching the seams to seal, and form into an 8" loaf. Spray an 8 × 4" loaf pan with nonstick cooking spray. Place the loaf in the pan, seam-side down. Cover loosely with plastic wrap or a damp towel and let it rise until the dough is about 1" above the rim of the pan, about 1 hour. Preheat the oven to 375° F.

6. Lightly brush the loaf with water. Bake on the center oven rack until golden brown and the loaf sounds hollow when tapped on the bottom, 45–50 minutes. Remove from the pan and cool completely (preferably overnight) on a rack.

**Per serving**: 112 Calories, 1 g Total Fat, 0 g Saturated Fat, 0 mg Cholesterol, 356 mg Sodium, 25 g Total Carbohydrate, 5 g Dietary Fiber, 4 g Protein, 14 mg Calcium. **POINTS** per serving: 1.

# Microwave-Baked English Muffin Bread

*Your microwave can give you hearty bread in short order! And, just like regular English muffins, this bread is best toasted before serving.*

MAKES 11 SERVINGS

2 cups + 1 tablespoon all-purpose flour

1 envelope active dry yeast

2 teaspoons sugar

½ teaspoon salt

1 cup lukewarm (105–115° F) fat-free milk

¼ teaspoon baking soda

1. In a large bowl, mix the flour, yeast, sugar and salt. Pour in the milk; with a sturdy spoon, stir to form a very thick batter, then stir vigorously for 15–20 seconds (the batter will become very stretchy as you beat). Cover loosely with plastic wrap or a damp towel and let the batter rise in a warm, draft-free place until it doubles in volume, about 45 minutes.

2. In a small bowl, dissolve the baking soda in 1 tablespoon water; add to the batter and stir vigorously until it becomes stretchy again.

3. Spray an 8 × 4" glass loaf pan with nonstick cooking spray. Scrape the batter into the loaf pan; cover loosely with plastic wrap or a damp towel and let it rise in a warm, draft-free place until it fills the pan about two-thirds to three-quarters full, about 40 minutes.

4. Microwave on High, uncovered, until no wet spots remain on the top of the loaf, about 4 minutes. Cool in the pan 10 minutes, then gently but firmly pull on the sides of the loaf to release it from the pan. Remove from the pan and cool completely on a rack. Toast before serving.

**Per serving:** 91 Calories, 0 g Total Fat, 0 g Saturated Fat, 0 mg Cholesterol, 137 mg Sodium, 19 g Total Carbohydrate, 1 g Dietary Fiber, 3 g Protein, 32 mg Calcium. *POINTS* per serving: 2.

## Yeast Bread Tips

*Choose a warm, draft-free spot to let dough rise; a gas oven lit only by a pilot light is ideal. If you cover the dough with plastic wrap, spray the wrap with nonstick cooking spray. Cover the dough, sprayed-side down, to avoid sticking.*

*To test whether the dough has risen sufficiently, poke two fingers into the dough. If it pops back right away, the dough is ready.*

*When the dough has doubled in bulk, which should take from 45 minutes to an hour, make a fist and punch it down to release the air and return the dough to its original, unleavened size. Now it's ready for the second rise.*

# Whole-Wheat Bread

*This bread makes wonderful croutons—rub one or two day-old slices with garlic, then cut into cubes—or use it as the base for a poultry stuffing.*

MAKES 12 SERVINGS

1 cup lukewarm (105–115° F) water

4 teaspoons honey

1 envelope active dry yeast

2½ cups whole-wheat flour

1 teaspoon salt

1. In a small bowl, combine the lukewarm water and honey; sprinkle with the yeast. Let stand until foamy, about 10 minutes.

2. In a food processor, combine the flour and salt. With the machine running, scrape the yeast mixture through the feed tube just until the dough forms a ball. Knead the dough by pulsing until it is smooth and no longer sticky, about 30 times.

3. Spray a large bowl with nonstick cooking spray; place the dough in the bowl. Cover loosely with plastic wrap or a damp towel and let the dough rise until it doubles in volume, about 1 hour.

4. Punch down the dough; lightly sprinkle a work surface with flour. Turn out the dough; pat into an 8 × 12" rectangle. Fold into thirds, lengthwise, pinching the seams to seal, and form into an 8" loaf. Spray an 8 × 4" loaf pan with nonstick cooking spray. Place the dough in the pan, seam-side down; cover loosely with plastic wrap or a damp towel and let it rise in a warm, draft-free place until doubled in volume, about 1 hour.

5. Preheat the oven to 350° F. Bake on the center oven rack until the loaf sounds hollow when tapped on the bottom, about 1 hour. Remove from the pan and cool completely on a rack.

**Per serving**: 94 Calories, 0 g Total Fat, 0 g Saturated Fat, 0 mg Cholesterol, 179 mg Sodium, 20 g Total Carbohydrate, 3 g Dietary Fiber, 4 g Protein, 10 mg Calcium. **POINTS** per serving: 1.

## Bread Machine Baking

*If you'd like to convert a conventional recipe to use in your bread machine, first adjust the amount of flour to fit your machine's capacity, then decrease or increase the amount of the other ingredients proportionately. Use this chart for guidance on proportions for bread ingredients:*

| INGREDIENT | MACHINE'S CAPACITY | | |
|---|---|---|---|
| | 1-lb. loaf | 1½-lb. loaf | 2-lb. loaf |
| *Flour* | 2 cups | 3 cups | 4 cups |
| *Liquid** | ⅔ cup– ¾ cup | ¾ cup– 1¼ cups | 1⅓ cups– 1½ cups |
| *Yeast* | 1 tsp.– 1½ tsp. | 1½ tsp.– 2 tsp. | 1½ tsp.– 3 tsp. |
| *Salt* | ½ tsp.– ¾ tsp. | ¾ tsp.– 1¼ tsp. | 1 tsp.– 1½ tsp. |

*\*Egg, milk, honey and molasses are all liquid ingredients; count 1 egg as ¼ cup liquid.*

# Challah

*This traditional Jewish bread makes a lovely braided loaf. Leftover challah makes exceptional French toast.*

MAKES 10 SERVINGS

½ cup lukewarm (105–115° F) water

1½ cups + 2 tablespoons all-purpose flour

1 envelope active dry yeast

1 egg, beaten

2 teaspoons corn oil

2 teaspoons sugar

¾ teaspoon salt

1 egg white, beaten with 1 tablespoon water

½ teaspoon poppy seeds

1. In a small bowl, combine the water and 1 tablespoon of the flour; sprinkle with the yeast. Let stand until foamy, about 10 minutes. Stir in the egg and oil.

2. In a food processor, combine the remaining flour, the sugar and salt. With the machine running, scrape the yeast mixture through the feed tube just until the dough forms a ball. Knead the dough by pulsing until it is smooth and elastic, about 30 times.

3. Spray a large bowl with nonstick cooking spray; place the dough in the bowl. Cover loosely with plastic wrap or a damp towel and let the dough rise in a warm, draft-free place until it doubles in volume, about 1 hour.

4. Punch down the dough; lightly sprinkle a work surface with flour. Turn out the dough; divide into 3 equal pieces. Roll each piece between your palms into an 18" rope. Pinch the ropes together at one end and braid loosely. Spray a baking sheet with nonstick cooking spray; gently transfer the braided loaf to the baking sheet. Cover loosely with plastic wrap or a damp towel and let it rise in a warm, draft-free place until doubled in volume, about 1 hour.

5. Preheat the oven to 350° F. Brush the loaf with half of the egg white. Bake about 20 minutes; brush with the remaining egg white and sprinkle with the poppy seeds. Bake until the loaf sounds hollow when tapped on the bottom, 10–15 minutes longer. Remove from the baking sheet and cool completely on a rack.

**Per serving:** 102 Calories, 2 g Total Fat, 0 g Saturated Fat, 21 mg Cholesterol, 172 mg Sodium, 18 g Total Carbohydrate, 1 g Dietary Fiber, 4 g Protein, 9 mg Calcium. **POINTS** per serving: 2.

## Tip

**Be sure to braid the three ropes loosely to allow room for the dough to rise the second time.**

## Testing Yeast for Freshness

*If you're not sure that the yeast is fresh, test or "proof" it first; you'll save yourself a lot of disappointment. To proof cake yeast, cream a small amount with an equal quantity of sugar. It should become liquid immediately. To proof dry yeast, dissolve one package in ¼ cup of warm water with 2 tablespoons flour and a teaspoon of sugar. If in 10 minutes it hasn't become foamy, discard any remaining yeast.*

# Whole-Wheat Pizza Dough

*Let this delicious crust be the base for your favorite pizza. Try the tomato-basil topping, or add mushrooms and olives, feta cheese and scallions, sliced cooked turkey, cooked shrimp or any combination you prefer.*

MAKES 8 SERVINGS

### Sponge

2 teaspoons active dry yeast

¼ cup lukewarm (105–115° F) water

¼ cup all-purpose flour

### Pizza Dough

½ cup fat-free milk

1⅓ cups all-purpose flour

½ cup whole-wheat flour

¼ teaspoon salt

1. To prepare the sponge, in a large bowl, sprinkle the yeast over the water; when the yeast looks wet, add the flour and stir hard. Cover loosely with plastic wrap or a damp towel and let stand at room temperature about 40 minutes.

2. To make the dough, stir the milk into the sponge. In a medium bowl, combine the all-purpose flour, whole-wheat flour and salt. Add to the sponge and stir to blend.

3. Lightly sprinkle a work surface with flour. Turn out the dough; knead until it becomes elastic and resilient, 10–12 minutes.

4. Spray a large bowl with nonstick cooking spray; place the dough in the bowl; cover loosely with plastic wrap or a damp towel and let the dough rise in a warm, draft-free place until doubled in volume, 45–60 minutes.

5. Preheat the oven to 500° F. Punch down the dough; lightly sprinkle a work surface with flour. Roll out the dough to a 14" circle; transfer to a pizza pan or large baking sheet. Arrange the toppings of your choice on the crust. Bake until lightly browned, about 10 minutes.

**Per serving**: 117 Calories, 0 g Total Fat, 0 g Saturated Fat, 0 mg Cholesterol, 76 mg Sodium, 24 g Total Carbohydrate, 2 g Dietary Fiber, 4 g Protein, 26 mg Calcium. **POINTS** per serving: 2.

### Tomato-Basil Topping

MAKES 8 SERVINGS

2 tomatoes, sliced

24 cherry tomatoes (use a combination of red and yellow), sliced

2–3 tablespoons shredded basil leaves

2 tablespoons olive oil

¼ cup coarsely grated Parmesan cheese

Distribute the tomatoes and basil over the pizza dough; drizzle with the oil and sprinkle with the cheese. Bake as directed.

**Per serving**: 77 Calories, 5 g Total Fat, 2 g Saturated Fat, 4 mg Cholesterol, 109 mg Sodium, 5 g Total Carbohydrate, 1 g Dietary Fiber, 3 g Protein, 80 mg Calcium. **POINTS** per serving: 2.

# Calzones

*Calzones, originally from Naples, are stuffed pizzas. Although they are traditionally filled with heavy cheese, our lightened spinach-and-cheese version keeps all the great flavor of the original.*

MAKES 6 SERVINGS

1¼ teaspoons (about ½ envelope) active dry yeast

¾ cup lukewarm (105–115° F) water

2 cups all-purpose flour

1 teaspoon salt

2 teaspoons olive oil

3 shallots, minced

5 garlic cloves, minced

¾ cup thawed frozen chopped spinach, squeezed dry

½ cup part-skim ricotta cheese

½ cup crumbled feta cheese

1 egg, lightly beaten

3 tablespoons chopped mint

1 teaspoon dried oregano leaves

¼ teaspoon freshly ground pepper

1. In a small bowl, sprinkle the yeast over ¼ cup of the lukewarm water. Let stand until foamy, about 10 minutes.

2. In a food processor, combine 1¾ cups + 2 tablespoons of the flour and ¼ teaspoon of the salt. With the machine running, scrape the yeast mixture and the remaining ½ cup of lukewarm water through the feed tube just until the dough forms a ball. Knead the dough by pulsing until it is smooth and elastic, about 30 times.

3. Spray a large bowl with nonstick cooking spray; place the dough in the bowl. Cover loosely with plastic wrap or a damp towel and let the dough rise in a warm, draft-free place until it doubles in volume, about 1 hour.

4. Meanwhile, in small nonstick skillet, heat the oil. Sauté the shallots and garlic until softened, about 7 minutes. Add the spinach; cook about 2 minutes. Transfer to a medium bowl; stir in the ricotta, feta, egg, mint, oregano, the remaining ¾ teaspoon of salt and the pepper.

5. Preheat the oven to 400° F; spray a baking sheet with nonstick cooking spray. Sprinkle a work surface with the remaining 2 tablespoons of flour. Turn out the dough; divide into 6 pieces. Roll out each piece into a 6" circle. Place about 2 heaping tablespoons of filling on one side of each circle, then dampen all around the edge; fold over and press with a wet thumb to seal. Transfer the calzones to the baking sheet. Bake until golden brown and crisp, 20–25 minutes.

**Per serving**: 231 Calories, 7 g Total Fat, 3 g Saturated Fat, 51 mg Cholesterol, 529 mg Sodium, 33 g Total Carbohydrate, 1 g Dietary Fiber, 10 g Protein, 160 mg Calcium. *POINTS* per serving: 5.

# Mushroom Whole-Wheat Calzones

*With quick-rising yeast, this Italian favorite is ready to eat in half the usual time. To reheat in a hurry, microwave, covered with a paper towel, for about 30 seconds.*

MAKES 4 SERVINGS

2/3 cup lukewarm (105–115° F) water

1/4 teaspoon sugar

1 envelope rapid-rise active dry yeast

1 cup bread flour

1/2 cup whole-wheat flour

1 teaspoon salt

1 onion, chopped

1 teaspoon Italian seasoning

3 cups coarsely chopped mushrooms

Half 10-ounce box frozen chopped spinach, thawed and squeezed dry

3/4 cup shredded nonfat mozzarella cheese

1 cup tomato sauce, heated

1. In a small bowl, combine the lukewarm water and the sugar; sprinkle on the yeast. Let stand until foamy, about 5 minutes.

2. In a food processor, combine the bread flour, whole-wheat flour and salt. With the machine running, scrape the yeast mixture through the feed tube just until the dough forms a ball. Knead the dough by pulsing until it is smooth and elastic, 20–30 times.

3. Spray a large bowl with nonstick cooking spray; place the dough in the bowl. Cover loosely with plastic wrap or a damp towel and let the dough rise in a warm, draft-free place until it doubles in volume, 30–45 minutes.

4. Meanwhile, spray a large nonstick skillet with nonstick cooking spray; heat. Add the onion and Italian seasoning; sauté until softened, about 3 minutes. Transfer to a plate.

5. In the skillet, cook the mushrooms, stirring occasionally, until most of their liquid evaporates, about 25 minutes. Stir in the onion and the spinach; set aside.

6. Spray a baking sheet with nonstick cooking spray. Punch down the dough; lightly sprinkle a work surface with flour. Turn out the dough; divide into 4 pieces. Roll out each piece into a 7" circle. Mound the vegetables and the cheese in the center of each piece of dough, then fold the dough over the filling, pressing the edges to seal tightly. Place seam-side down on the baking sheet. Cover loosely with plastic wrap or a damp towel and let rise in a warm, draft-free place 30 minutes.

7. While the calzones rise, adjust the racks to divide the oven into thirds. Fill a shallow roasting pan with 2" hot water; place on the bottom oven rack. Preheat the oven to 400° F. Bake the calzones on the top rack until they just begin to brown, about 20 minutes. Serve immediately, with the tomato sauce on the side.

**Per serving**: 278 Calories, 2 g Total Fat, 0 g Saturated Fat, 2 mg Cholesterol, 1,179 mg Sodium, 50 g Total Carbohydrate, 6 g Dietary Fiber, 17 g Protein, 240 mg Calcium. **POINTS** per serving: 5.

# Focaccia

*Focaccia is an Italian bread of great versatility and, usually, a great amount of olive oil. You may want to experiment with your own toppings such as fresh rosemary or oregano, or thinly sliced onions or olives.*

MAKES 12 SERVINGS

1 envelope active dry yeast

1 cup minus 1 tablespoon lukewarm (105–115° F) water

2 cups + 2 tablespoons all-purpose flour

2 tablespoons whole-wheat flour

1 teaspoon salt

Topping (recipes follow)

1. In a small bowl, sprinkle the yeast over the water. Let stand until foamy, about 10 minutes.

2. In a food processor, combine the all-purpose flour, whole-wheat flour and salt. With the machine running, scrape the yeast mixture through the feed tube just until the dough forms a ball. Knead the dough by pulsing 30 times; the dough will still be sticky.

3. Spray a large bowl with nonstick cooking spray; place the dough in the bowl. Cover loosely with plastic wrap or a damp towel and let the dough rise until it doubles in volume, about 1 hour.

4. Spray a baking sheet with nonstick cooking spray. Punch down the dough. Flour your hands and form the dough into a ball. Place it on the baking sheet and press it into a 10" circle. Cover loosely with plastic wrap or a damp towel and let it rise in a warm, draft-free place until doubled in volume, about 30 minutes.

5. Meanwhile, prepare the topping. When the dough has risen, preheat the oven to 425° F. Without piercing the dough, make dimples all over it with your fingertips; cover with the topping. Bake on the center oven rack until browned, 15–20 minutes. Serve hot or at room temperature.

### Potato-Tomato Topping

¼ cup boiling water

4 sun-dried tomato halves (not oil-packed), minced

1 onion, thinly sliced

3 garlic cloves, minced

2 teaspoons olive oil

2–3 new potatoes, cooked and thinly sliced

1½ teaspoons chopped basil

1½ teaspoons chopped parsley

⅛ teaspoon freshly ground pepper

4½ teaspoons grated Parmesan cheese

1. In a medium bowl, pour the boiling water over the tomatoes. Let stand about 10 minutes; drain well. Add the onion, garlic and oil; toss to coat. Add the potatoes, basil, parsley and pepper; toss gently.

2. Distribute over the focaccia crust; sprinkle with the cheese. Bake as directed.

**Per serving:** 116 Calories, 2 g Total Fat, 0 g Saturated Fat, 1 mg Cholesterol, 208 mg Sodium, 22 g Total Carbohydrate, 1 g Dietary Fiber, 4 g Protein, 27 mg Calcium. **POINTS** per serving: 2.

*Continued on next page.*

*Focaccia*

### Feta Cheese Topping

3 shallots, thinly sliced

3 garlic cloves, minced

2 teaspoons olive oil

$\frac{1}{3}$ cup crumbled drained feta cheese

6 large black olives, pitted and chopped

1 tablespoon chopped parsley

$\frac{1}{2}$ teaspoon dried oregano

$\frac{1}{8}$ teaspoon freshly ground pepper

1. In a small bowl, toss the shallots, garlic and oil. Stir in the cheese, olives, parsley, oregano and pepper.

2. Distribute over the focaccia crust. Bake as directed.

**Per serving**: 110 Calories, 2 g Fat, 1 g Saturated Fat, 3 mg Cholesterol, 245 mg Sodium, 19 g Total Carbohydrate, 1 g Dietary Fiber, 3 g Protein, 29 mg Calcium. **POINTS** per serving: 2.

### Onion and Roasted Red Pepper Topping

2 teaspoons olive oil

1 onion, thinly sliced

$\frac{1}{2}$ teaspoon sugar

1 roasted red pepper (from a jar), thinly sliced

1. In a medium nonstick skillet, heat the oil. Sauté the onion and sugar until the onion is lightly browned, about 10 minutes. Stir in the pepper.

2. Distribute over the focaccia crust. Bake as directed.

**Per serving**: 100 Calories, 1 g Total Fat, 0 g Saturated Fat, 0 mg Cholesterol, 221 mg Sodium, 19 g Total Carbohydrate, 1 g Dietary Fiber, 3 g Protein, 7 mg Calcium. **POINTS** per serving: 2.

## In a Pinch

*Sometimes you can't avoid using a substitute when baking. If you're ever caught short-handed, try these easy baking substitutes:*

| INSTEAD OF | USE |
| --- | --- |
| 1 teaspoon baking powder | $\frac{1}{4}$ teaspoon baking soda and $\frac{5}{8}$ teaspoon cream of tartar, combined |
| 1 package active dry yeast | 1 cake compressed yeast |
| 1 teaspoon finely shredded lemon peel | $\frac{1}{2}$ teaspoon lemon extract |
| 1 cup fat-free milk | $\frac{1}{3}$ cup instant nonfat dry milk powder + water to make 1 cup |

# Italian Bread

*Top thin slices of this hearty loaf with Caponata (page 32) for an easy crostini or bruschetta.*

MAKES 12 SERVINGS

1 envelope active dry yeast

¾ cup lukewarm (105–115° F) water

2 cups all-purpose flour, plus more for dusting

¼ cup whole-wheat flour

1½ teaspoons salt

1 teaspoon cornmeal

1. In a small bowl, sprinkle the yeast over ¼ cup of the water. Let stand until foamy, about 5 minutes.

2. In a food processor, combine the all-purpose flour, whole-wheat flour and salt. With the machine running, scrape the yeast mixture and the remaining ½ cup of water through the feed tube just until the dough forms a ball. Knead the dough by pulsing until it is smooth and no longer sticky, about 30 times.

3. Spray a large bowl with nonstick cooking spray; place the dough in the bowl. Cover loosely with plastic wrap or a damp towel and let the dough rise in a warm, draft-free place until it doubles in volume, 40–50 minutes.

4. Punch down the dough; lightly sprinkle a work surface with flour. Turn out the dough; form into a 12 × 16" rectangle. Fold into thirds, lengthwise, and pinch the seams to seal, forming into a 12" tapered oval loaf. Spray a baking sheet with nonstick cooking spray; sprinkle the cornmeal in a 12" strip down the center. Place the loaf on the baking sheet; cover loosely with plastic wrap or a damp towel and let it rise in warm, draft-free place until doubled in volume, about 30 minutes.

5. Dust the loaf with about 1 teaspoon flour; with a sharp knife or single-edge razor blade, cut 2–3 slashes into the top. Place in the upper third of a cold oven; set the oven to 400° F. Bake about 20 minutes; reduce the oven temperature to 350° F. Bake until the loaf sounds hollow when tapped on the bottom, 25–30 minutes longer. Remove from the baking sheet and cool completely on a rack.

**Per serving**: 89 Calories, 1 g Fat, 0 g Saturated Fat, 0 mg Cholesterol, 275 mg Sodium, 18 g Total Carbohydrate, 1 g Dietary Fiber, 3 g Protein, 6 mg Calcium. *POINTS* per serving: 2.

# Irish Soda Bread

In Ireland, soda bread is served with plenty of butter. To save **POINTS**, top it with spreadable fruit.

MAKES 10 SERVINGS

1½ cups + 1 tablespoon all-purpose flour

½ cup whole-wheat flour

½ cup currants

2 teaspoons caraway seeds

2 teaspoons grated lemon zest

1 teaspoon baking soda

½ teaspoon salt

1 cup low-fat buttermilk

3 tablespoons honey

1 teaspoon sugar

1. Preheat the oven to 350° F; spray a baking sheet with nonstick cooking spray.

2. In a large bowl, combine the all-purpose flour, whole-wheat flour, currants, caraway seeds, lemon zest, baking soda and salt. In a small bowl, combine the buttermilk and honey. Pour over the flour mixture; stir just until the flour disappears (do not overmix).

3. Lightly sprinkle a work surface with flour; turn out the dough. Flour your hands and knead the dough lightly 7 times. Form into a 7" round loaf; place on the baking sheet. With a sharp knife or single-edge razor blade, slash a cross on the top; sprinkle with the sugar. Bake in the upper third of the oven until browned and a toothpick inserted in the center comes out clean, 40–45 minutes. Remove from the pan and cool completely on a rack.

**Per serving:** 137 Calories, 1 g Total Fat, 0 g Saturated Fat, 1 mg Cholesterol, 260 mg Sodium, 30 g Total Carbohydrate, 2 g Dietary Fiber, 4 g Protein, 44 mg Calcium. **POINTS** per serving: 2.

# Naan

An Indian flatbread, naan is excellent to serve when you'd like to tone down spicy dishes.

MAKES 8 SERVINGS

½ cup fat-free milk

1 egg

2 cups all-purpose flour

1½ teaspoons baking powder

1 teaspoon sugar

¼ teaspoon salt

⅛ teaspoon baking soda

1. In a small bowl, beat the milk and egg. In a food processor, combine the flour, baking powder, sugar, salt and baking soda. With the machine running, pour the milk mixture through the feed tube until the dough forms a ball. Knead the dough by pulsing until it is smooth, about 30 times.

2. Spray a large bowl with nonstick cooking spray; place the dough in the bowl. Cover loosely with plastic wrap or a damp towel and let the dough rise in a warm, draft-free place 3 hours.

3. Place a large baking sheet on the center oven rack; preheat the oven to 450° F. Lightly sprinkle a work surface with flour; turn out the dough. Divide the dough into 8 pieces; flatten each into a ⅜" thick teardrop shape. Transfer the teardrops to the baking sheet. Bake until firm, 10–12 minutes. If you like, run briefly under a broiler to brown the tops lightly. Serve hot or at room temperature.

**Per serving:** 122 Calories, 1 g Total Fat, 0 g Saturated Fat, 27 mg Cholesterol, 178 mg Sodium, 23 g Total Carbohydrate, 1 g Dietary Fiber, 4 g Protein, 57 mg Calcium. **POINTS** per serving: 2.

# Banana Bread

*Bananas, not fat, are what give this dense loaf its moist texture. Toast it and top with nonfat cream cheese for a speedy breakfast or snack.*

MAKES 12 SERVINGS

1¾ cups all-purpose flour

3 tablespooons packed light brown sugar

2¼ teaspoons baking powder

½ teaspoon salt

½ teaspoon cinnamon

8 dried dates, chopped

6 dried apricot halves, chopped

1 egg

1 very ripe banana, mashed

¼ cup fat-free milk

1. Preheat the oven to 350° F; spray an 8 × 4" loaf pan with nonstick cooking spray.

2. In a medium bowl, combine the flour, brown sugar, baking powder, salt and cinnamon; stir in the dates and apricots. In a small bowl, beat the egg; add the banana and milk. Pour over the flour mixture; stir just until blended (do not overmix).

3. Transfer to the pan. Bake until a toothpick inserted in the center comes out clean, about 1 hour. Cool completely on a rack.

**Per serving**: 111 Calories, 1 g Total Fat, 0 g Saturated Fat, 18 mg Cholesterol, 174 mg Sodium, 24 g Total Carbohydrate, 1 g Dietary Fiber, 3 g Protein, 49 mg Calcium. **POINTS** per serving: 2.

## Tip

If you don't have any baking powder on hand, see the chart on page 56 to make your own. Just remember: Homemade baking powder doesn't store well; make only what you will use right away.

# Carrot Tea Bread

*When you want something sweet in the morning, a warmed slice of this carrot-studded bread makes a satisfying breakfast.*

MAKES 8 SERVINGS

1 cup all-purpose flour

½ cup whole-wheat flour

½ cup packed dark brown sugar

1½ teaspoons cinnamon

½ teaspoon salt

½ teaspoon baking soda

¼ teaspoon baking powder

¼ teaspoon ground nutmeg

Pinch ground cloves

1 egg

2 egg whites

4 teaspoons vegetable oil

2¾ cups unsweetened applesauce

½ cup sliced cooked carrots

½ cup dried currants

1. Preheat the oven to 400° F; spray two 5 × 3" nonstick loaf pans with nonstick cooking spray.

2. In a large strainer, combine the all-purpose flour, whole-wheat flour, brown sugar, cinnamon, salt, baking soda, baking powder, nutmeg and cloves; sift by shaking into a medium bowl.

3. In food processor, combine the egg and egg whites until frothy, 30 seconds. With the machine running, gradually drizzle in the oil; process 10 seconds longer. Add ¾ cup of the applesauce and the carrots; process until smooth. Add the flour mixture; pulse 2 times to blend. Add the currants; pulse 4 times to chop.

4. Divide the batter between the loaf pans. Bake until a toothpick inserted in the center comes out clean, 35–40 minutes. Remove from the pan and cool completely on a wire rack. Serve with the remaining applesauce on the side.

**Per serving**: 237 Calories, 4 g Total Fat, 1 g Saturated Fat, 27 mg Cholesterol, 267 mg Sodium, 48 g Total Carbohydrate, 3 g Dietary Fiber, 5 g Protein, 48 mg Calcium. **POINTS** per serving: 4.

# Sweet Brown Bread

*This whole-wheat quick bread is simplicity itself. Whip up a loaf and serve with a hearty soup for an easy Sunday supper.*

MAKES 12 SERVINGS

1¼ cups whole-wheat flour

1 teaspoon baking powder

1 teaspoon grated orange or lemon zest

½ teaspoon baking soda

½ teaspoon cinnamon

⅛ teaspoon salt

½ cup low-fat buttermilk

1 egg

3 tablespoons molasses

2 tablespoons packed dark brown sugar

1. Preheat the oven to 375° F; spray an 8 × 4" loaf pan with nonstick cooking spray.

2. In a medium bowl, combine the flour, baking powder, orange zest, baking soda, cinnamon and salt. In another bowl, combine the buttermilk, egg, molasses and brown sugar. Pour over the flour mixture, mixing quickly to blend (do not overmix).

3. Transfer to the pan. Bake until a toothpick inserted in the center comes out clean, 35–40 minutes. Cool completely on a rack.

**Per serving**: 80 Calories, 1 g Total Fat, 0 g Saturated Fat, 18 mg Cholesterol, 127 mg Sodium, 16 g Total Carbohydrate, 2 g Dietary Fiber, 3 g Protein, 45 mg Calcium. *POINTS* per serving: 1.

# Corn Bread

*This is especially nice with Vegetarian Bean Chili (page 233).*

MAKES 12 SERVINGS

1¼ cups yellow cornmeal

¾ cup all-purpose flour

4 teaspoons sugar

2½ teaspoons baking powder

½ teaspoon salt

1 cup + 2 tablespoons low-fat buttermilk

1 egg

1. Preheat the oven to 400° F; spray an 8" square pan or a 12-cup muffin tin with nonstick cooking spray.

2. In a large bowl, combine the cornmeal, flour, sugar, baking powder and salt. In a small bowl, beat the buttermilk and egg. Pour over the flour mixture; stir just until blended (do not overmix).

3. Transfer to the pan. Bake until golden brown and a toothpick inserted in the center comes out clean, 20–25 minutes. Cool in the pan on a rack 10 minutes; serve warm.

**Per serving**: 100 Calories, 1 g Total Fat, 0 g Saturated Fat, 18 mg Cholesterol, 202 mg Sodium, 19 g Total Carbohydrate, 1 g Dietary Fiber, 3 g Protein, 64 mg Calcium. *POINTS* per serving: 2.

## Cheese Corn Bread

Omit the sugar; add ⅓ cup shredded extra-sharp cheddar cheese, ¼ cup grated Parmesan cheese, 1 cup cooked or frozen corn kernels and 1–2 teaspoons minced jalapeño peppers.

**Per serving**: 124 Calories, 3 g Total Fat, 1 g Saturated Fat, 23 mg Cholesterol, 298 mg Sodium, 20 g Total Carbohydrate, 1 g Dietary Fiber, 5 g Protein, 139 mg Calcium. *POINTS* per serving: 3.

# Pumpkin Apple Bread

*When you're short on time, bake this in a muffin tin instead of a loaf pan. Start testing for doneness after 15–20 minutes.*

MAKES 10 SERVINGS

2 cups all-purpose flour

¼ cup granulated sugar

1 teaspoon baking powder

½ teaspoon baking soda

½ teaspoon salt

½ teaspoon cinnamon

1 egg

1 cup low-fat buttermilk

1 apple, peeled, cored and grated

½ cup canned pumpkin puree

1 teaspoon confectioners' sugar

1. Preheat the oven to 350° F; spray a 9 × 5" loaf pan with nonstick cooking spray.

2. In a large bowl, combine the flour, granulated sugar, baking powder, baking soda, salt and cinnamon. In a small bowl, beat the egg; add the buttermilk, apple and pumpkin. Pour over the flour mixture; stir just until blended (do not overmix).

3. Spoon into the pan. Bake until a toothpick inserted in the center comes out clean, 1–1¼ hours. Cool in the pan on a rack 10 minutes; remove from the pan and cool completely on the rack. Dust with the confectioners' sugar and serve.

**Per serving:** 137 Calories, 1 g Total Fat, 0 g Saturated Fat, 22 mg Cholesterol, 243 mg Sodium, 28 g Total Carbohydrate, 1 g Dietary Fiber, 4 g Protein, 57 mg Calcium. **POINTS** per serving: 3.

# Zucchini Bread

*Don't peel the zucchini before you grate it—the dark green makes for pretty flecks of color when you slice the bread.*

MAKES 7 SERVINGS

1 egg

3 tablespoons sugar

1¼ cups + 1 tablespoon all-purpose flour

2 teaspoons baking powder

½ teaspoon salt

¼ teaspoon nutmeg

½ cup low-fat buttermilk

2 teaspoons unsalted butter, melted

1 teaspoon grated lemon zest

1 medium zucchini, grated and squeezed dry

1. Preheat the oven to 425° F; spray an 8 × 4" loaf pan with nonstick cooking spray.

2. In a large bowl, beat the egg until pale yellow, gradually adding the sugar.

3. Sift the flour, baking powder, salt and nutmeg onto a sheet of wax paper. In a small bowl, whisk the buttermilk, butter and lemon zest. Alternately beat half the flour mixture and half the buttermilk mixture into the egg mixture. Fold in the zucchini; the batter will be thick.

4. Transfer to the pan. Bake on the upper oven rack 10 minutes; reduce the oven temperature to 400° F. Bake until a toothpick inserted in the center comes out clean, 50–60 minutes longer. Cool in the pan on a rack 10 minutes; remove from the pan and cool completely on the rack.

**Per serving:** 127 Calories, 2 g Total Fat, 1 g Saturated Fat, 31 mg Cholesterol, 307 mg Sodium, 23 g Total Carbohydrate, 1 g Dietary Fiber, 4 g Protein, 77 mg Calcium. **POINTS** per serving: 3.

# Yogurt Biscuits

*(pictured on page 58)*

---

*These biscuits make a good base for fruit shortcake or a crust for chicken pot pie. They also freeze very well.*

MAKES 16 SERVINGS

2 cups all-purpose flour

1 cup plain nonfat yogurt

1 teaspoon sugar

2 teaspoons baking powder

½ teaspoon baking soda

½ teaspoon salt

1. In a large bowl, combine 1 cup of the flour with the yogurt; blend until very smooth. Sprinkle with the sugar; cover loosely with plastic wrap or a damp towel and let stand in a warm, draft-free place at least 4 hours or overnight.

2. Preheat the oven to 425° F. In a medium bowl, combine the remaining 1 cup of flour, the baking powder, baking soda and salt. Stir into the yogurt mixture.

3. Spray a baking sheet with nonstick cooking spray; lightly sprinkle a work surface with flour. Turn out the dough; pat into an 8 × 6" rectangle. Cut into 16 pieces; place the biscuits 1" apart on the baking sheet. Bake 10 minutes; reduce the oven temperature to 400° F. Bake until golden brown, about 10 minutes longer. Serve hot.

**Per serving:** 60 Calories, 0 g Total Fat, 0 g Saturated Fat, 0 mg Cholesterol, 167 mg Sodium, 12 g Total Carbohydrate, 0 g Dietary Fiber, 2 g Protein, 51 mg Calcium. **POINTS** per serving: 1.

# Currant Scones

---

*A British teatime treat, scones are perfect for breakfast, for parties or any time you'd like a sweet bread. They are also good when split, toasted and topped with spreadable fruit.*

MAKES 12 SERVINGS

1 cup + 2 tablespoons all-purpose flour

¼ cup + 2 tablespoons currants

1 teaspoon sugar

1 teaspoon baking powder

¼ teaspoon baking soda

¼ teaspoon salt

½ cup low-fat buttermilk

1 egg

1 teaspoon unsalted butter, melted

1. Preheat the oven to 425° F; spray a baking sheet with nonstick cooking spray.

2. In a large bowl, combine the flour, currants, sugar, baking powder, baking soda and salt. In a small bowl, combine the buttermilk, egg and butter. Pour over the flour mixture; stir just until the flour disappears (do not overmix).

3. Lightly sprinkle a work surface with flour; turn out the dough. Pat into a ¼" thick circle; cut into 12 rounds with a 2" cutter, or into 12 triangles with a sharp knife. Transfer to the baking sheet, placing the scones 1" apart. Reduce the oven temperature to 400° F and bake until golden brown, 12–15 minutes. Serve warm.

**Per serving:** 67 Calories, 1 g Total Fat, 0 g Saturated Fat, 18 mg Cholesterol, 124 mg Sodium, 12 g Total Carbohydrate, 1 g Dietary Fiber, 2 g Protein, 33 mg Calcium. **POINTS** per serving: 1.

# Fruit Mini Muffins

*Store dried dates in an airtight container in the refrigerator for up to one year.*

MAKES 12 SERVINGS

1⅓ cups wheat germ

1 cup quick-cooking rolled oats

¼ cup + 2 tablespoons whole-wheat flour

1 tablespoon grated lemon zest

1 teaspoon cinnamon

1 teaspoon baking soda

¼ teaspoon salt

Pinch ground cloves

½ cup low-fat buttermilk

½ cup fat-free egg substitute

2 tablespoons honey

1 teaspoon vanilla extract

8 dried dates, pitted and finely chopped

1 small apple, peeled, cored and grated

½ medium banana, finely mashed

1. Preheat the oven to 350° F; spray two 12-cup mini muffin tins with nonstick cooking spray.

2. In a large bowl, combine the wheat germ, oats, flour, lemon zest, cinnamon, baking soda, salt and cloves. In a medium bowl, combine the buttermilk, egg substitute, honey and vanilla; stir in the dates, apple and banana. Add to the wheat germ mixture; stir just until combined (do not overmix).

3. Spoon the batter into the cups, filling each about two-thirds full. Bake until golden, 15–20 minutes. Cool in the pan on a rack 5 minutes; remove from the pan and cool completely on the rack.

**Per serving**: 133 Calories, 2 g Total Fat, 0 g Saturated Fat, 0 mg Cholesterol, 179 mg Sodium, 24 g Total Carbohydrate, 3 g Dietary Fiber, 6 g Protein, 31 mg Calcium. *POINTS* per serving: 2.

# Jam Muffins

*There is no need to spread jam on these tasty muffins—it is already inside.*

MAKES 6 SERVINGS

⅔ cup all-bran cereal flakes, crumbled

¼ cup + 1 tablespoon whole-wheat flour

3 tablespoons all-purpose flour

¼ cup sugar

1 teaspoon baking powder

½ teaspoon baking soda

½ teaspoon cinnamon

¼ teaspoon salt

Pinch ground nutmeg

½ cup low-fat buttermilk

2 tablespoons vegetable oil

1 egg white

½ teaspoon vanilla extract

¼ cup black raspberry spreadable fruit

1. Preheat the oven to 350° F; spray a 6-cup muffin tin with nonstick cooking spray, then sprinkle lightly with flour.

2. In a medium bowl, combine the cereal, flours, sugar, baking powder, baking soda, cinnamon, salt and nutmeg. In a small bowl, beat the buttermilk, oil, egg white and vanilla. Add to the cereal mixture; stir just until combined (do not overmix).

3. Spoon the batter into the cups, filling each about two-thirds full. Spoon 2 teaspoons of the spreadable fruit on each muffin, pressing it gently into the batter. Bake until lightly golden and a toothpick inserted in a muffin (not the spreadable fruit) comes out clean, about 25 minutes. Cool in the pan on a rack 10 minutes; remove from the pan and cool completely on the rack.

**Per serving**: 168 Calories, 5 g Total Fat, 1 g Saturated Fat, 1 mg Cholesterol, 331 mg Sodium, 29 g Total Carbohydrate, 3 g Dietary Fiber, 3 g Protein, 79 mg Calcium. *POINTS* per serving: 3.

# Easy Pumpkin Muffins

*Serve these low-fat muffins hot from the oven if you can; baked goods with no added fat tend to toughen slightly as they cool.*

MAKES 6 SERVINGS

⅓ cup all-purpose flour

⅓ cup whole-wheat flour

⅓ cup sugar

¼ cup + 2 tablespoons raisins

3 tablespoons wheat germ

1½ teaspoons baking powder

½ teaspoon baking soda

½ teaspoon salt

1 cup pumpkin puree

1 egg

¼ cup orange juice

1 teaspoon pumpkin pie spice

½ teaspoon vanilla extract

2 tablespoons chopped walnuts

1. Preheat the oven to 350° F. Spray a 6-cup muffin tin with nonstick cooking spray, then sprinkle lightly with flour.

2. In a large bowl, combine the all-purpose flour, whole-wheat flour, sugar, raisins, wheat germ, baking powder, baking soda and salt. In a medium bowl, whisk the pumpkin puree, egg, orange juice, pumpkin pie spice and vanilla. Add to the flour mixture; stir just until combined (do not overmix).

3. Spoon the batter into the cups, filling each about two-thirds full; sprinkle with the walnuts. Bake until a toothpick inserted in a muffin comes out clean, 25–30 minutes. Cool in the pan on a rack 10 minutes; remove from the pan and serve warm.

**Per serving**: 202 Calories, 3 g Total Fat, 1 g Saturated Fat, 35 mg Cholesterol, 424 mg Sodium, 40 g Total Carbohydrate, 3 g Dietary Fiber, 5 g Protein, 99 mg Calcium. **POINTS** per serving: 4.

# Just Plain Muffins

*Use this very basic recipe and the variations to make your favorite muffins.*

MAKES 12 SERVINGS

1¾ cups all-purpose flour

4 teaspoons granulated sugar

2 teaspoons baking powder

½ teaspoon salt

1 cup fat-free milk

1 egg

4 teaspoons unsalted butter, melted

1. Preheat the oven to 400° F; spray a 12-cup muffin tin with nonstick cooking spray.

2. In a large bowl, combine the flour, sugar, baking powder and salt. In a small bowl, combine the milk, egg and butter. Pour over the flour mixture, stirring just until blended (do not overmix).

3. Spoon the batter into the cups, filling each about two-thirds full. Bake until a toothpick inserted in a muffin comes out clean and the muffins are golden brown, 20–25 minutes. Cool in the pan on a rack 5 minutes; remove from the pan and serve hot.

**Per serving**: 91 Calories, 2 g Total Fat, 0 g Saturated Fat, 18 mg Cholesterol, 186 mg Sodium, 15 g Total Carbohydrate, 0 g Dietary Fiber, 3 g Protein, 58 mg Calcium. *POINTS* per serving: 2.

## Berry Muffins

Add ¾ cup fresh blueberries or raspberries to the flour mixture.

**Per serving**: 96 Calories, 2 g Total Fat, 0 g Saturated Fat, 18 mg Cholesterol, 187 mg Sodium, 17 g Total Carbohydrate, 1 g Dietary Fiber, 3 g Protein, 58 mg Calcium. *POINTS* per serving: 2.

## Sweet Muffins

Substitute dark brown sugar or maple sugar for the granulated.

**Per serving**: 91 Calories, 2 g Total Fat, 0 g Saturated Fat, 18 mg Cholesterol, 186 mg Sodium, 15 g Total Carbohydrate, 0 g Dietary Fiber, 3 g Protein, 58 mg Calcium. *POINTS* per serving: 2.

## Orange Muffins

Mix ½ cup fat-free milk, ½ cup orange juice (the milk will curdle) and 2 teaspoons orange zest; use instead of the fat-free milk.

**Per serving**: 93 Calories, 2 g Total Fat, 0 g Saturated Fat, 18 mg Cholesterol, 181 mg Sodium, 16 g Total Carbohydrate, 0 g Dietary Fiber, 3 g Protein, 47 mg Calcium. *POINTS* per serving: 2.

## Lemon Muffins

Mix ¾ cup + 2 tablespoons fat-free milk, 2 tablespoons fresh lemon juice (the milk will curdle) and 2 teaspoons lemon zest; use instead of the fat-free milk.

**Per serving**: 91 Calories, 2 g Total Fat, 0 g Saturated Fat, 18 mg Cholesterol, 185 mg Sodium, 15 g Total Carbohydrate, 0 g Dietary Fiber, 3 g Protein, 55 mg Calcium. *POINTS* per serving: 2.

## Chocolate Muffins

Use 2 tablespoons unsweetened cocoa powder and 1½ cups flour; increase the sugar to 3 tablespoons. Add 1 teaspoon vanilla extract to the liquid. Dust with 1 teaspoon confectioners' sugar when slightly cooled.

**Per serving**: 92 Calories, 2 g Total Fat, 0 g Saturated Fat, 18 mg Cholesterol, 187 mg Sodium, 16 g Total Carbohydrate, 0 g Dietary Fiber, 3 g Protein, 58 mg Calcium. *POINTS* per serving: 2.

# Maple Bran Muffins

*If you normally use pancake syrup, try real maple syrup in this recipe.*

MAKES 8 SERVINGS

⅔ cup low-fat (1%) milk

½ cup wheat bran

⅓ cup maple syrup

¼ cup unsweetened applesauce

1 egg, lightly beaten

1 cup + 2 tablespoons all-purpose flour

½ teaspoon baking powder

½ teaspoon salt

½ teaspoon ground allspice

¼ teaspoon baking soda

½ cup raisins

1. In a large bowl, combine the milk and bran; let stand about 20 minutes. Stir in the syrup, apple-sauce and egg.

2. Preheat the oven to 400° F. Spray 8 muffin cups with nonstick cooking spray.

3. In a medium bowl, sift together the flour, baking powder, salt, allspice and baking soda. Add the bran mixture, stirring just until combined; stir in the raisins.

4. Spoon the batter into the cups, filling each about two-thirds full. Bake until a toothpick inserted in a muffin comes out clean, 18–20 minutes. Cool in the pan on a rack 5 minutes; remove from the pan and cool completely on the rack.

**Per serving**: 160 Calories, 2 g Total Fat, 0 g Saturated Fat, 27 mg Cholesterol, 227 mg Sodium, 35 g Total Carbohydrate, 3 g Dietary Fiber, 4 g Protein, 67 mg Calcium. *POINTS* per serving: 3.

## Bake a Better Muffin

- *Spray muffin cups with nonstick cooking spray; fill the cups two-thirds full with batter; add a few tablespoons water to any empty cups to keep them from burning and to help the muffin tin heat more evenly.*

- *For easier removal, let the muffins "rest" in tins a few moments after baking.*

- *To reheat muffins, wrap them loosely in foil, then heat in a 450° F oven about 5 minutes.*

# Sticky Buns

---

*These are a wonderful treat for a holiday morning or brunch.*

MAKES 8 SERVINGS

1 envelope active dry yeast

2 tablespoons lukewarm (105–115° F) water

½ cup lukewarm (105–115° F) fat-free milk

1 egg

2 teaspoons unsalted butter, melted

2¼ cups all-purpose flour

3 tablespoons granulated sugar

1½ teaspoons cinnamon

½ teaspoon salt

½ cup dark raisins

2 teaspoons fat-free milk

¼ cup confectioners' sugar

½ teaspoon vanilla extract

1. In a small bowl, sprinkle the yeast over the water. Let stand until foamy, about 10 minutes.

2. In a small bowl, combine the lukewarm milk, egg and butter. In a food processor, combine the flour, granulated sugar, cinnamon and salt. With the machine running, scrape the yeast mixture and milk mixture through the feed tube until the dough forms a ball. Knead the dough by pulsing until it is smooth and no longer sticky, about 30 times.

3. Spray a large bowl with nonstick cooking spray; place the dough in the bowl. Cover loosely with plastic wrap or a damp towel and let the dough rise in a warm, draft-free place until it doubles in volume, 30–45 minutes.

4. Spray an 8" cake pan with nonstick cooking spray. Punch down the dough; lightly sprinkle a work surface with flour. Turn out the dough; knead in the raisins and divide the dough into 8 pieces. Roll each piece of dough into an 8" rope, then coil the ropes into buns. Place the buns in the pan; cover loosely with plastic wrap or a damp towel and let them rise until doubled in volume, 35–40 minutes.

5. Preheat the oven to 375° F. Brush the tops of the buns with the milk. Bake on the center oven rack until lightly browned, 20–25 minutes.

6. Meanwhile, in a small bowl, combine the confectioners' sugar, vanilla and 1½ teaspoons warm water. Spread over the buns as soon as you remove them from the oven. Serve warm.

**Per serving:** 204 Calories, 2 g Total Fat, 0 g Saturated Fat, 27 mg Cholesterol, 163 mg Sodium, 42 g Total Carbohydrate, 2 g Dietary Fiber, 5 g Protein, 40 mg Calcium. **POINTS** per serving: 4.

# Pancakes

*Mixing the batter in a blender makes for easy cleanup: no bowls or spoons to wash (just add a bit of soapy water to the empty blender and whirl). Also, you can avoid drips by pouring the batter onto the griddle.*

MAKES 4 SERVINGS

1 egg

1 egg white

1½ cups plain nonfat yogurt

2 tablespoons vegetable oil

1 cup all-purpose flour

¼ cup sugar

1½ teaspoons baking powder

¼ teaspoon baking soda

¼ teaspoon salt

¼ teaspoon cinnamon

1 cup old-fashioned rolled oats

Maple syrup (optional)

1. In a blender, combine the egg, egg white, yogurt and oil; whirl until smooth. Add the flour, sugar, baking powder, baking soda, salt and cinnamon; whirl to blend. Add the oats; whirl briefly just to mix.

2. Spray a griddle or large skillet with nonstick cooking spray; heat. Pour about 3 tablespoons of batter for each pancake onto the griddle; cook until bubbles form around the edges on top, 2–3 minutes. Flip over; cook until browned, about 2 minutes longer. Serve at once, topped with maple syrup (if desired).

**Per serving**: 395 Calories, 10 g Total Fat, 2 g Saturated Fat, 55 mg Cholesterol, 458 mg Sodium, 62 g Total Carbohydrate, 4 g Dietary Fiber, 14 g Protein, 239 mg Calcium. *POINTS* per serving: 8.

# Baked French Toast with Apples

*If you're not a morning person, make the bread mixture and the topping the night before. Refrigerate them separately overnight, so all you'll have to do is combine and bake in the morning.*

MAKES 4 SERVINGS

2 eggs

½ cup fat-free milk

3 tablespoons packed dark brown sugar

1¼ teaspoons cinnamon

4 slices whole-wheat bread, cubed

2 small apples, peeled, cored and diced

3 tablespoons all-purpose flour

2 teaspoons reduced-calorie margarine

1. Preheat the oven to 350° F. Spray two 5 × 3" loaf pans with nonstick cooking spray. In a medium bowl, lightly beat the eggs; blend in the milk, 1 tablespoon of the brown sugar and 1 teaspoon of the cinnamon. Add the bread cubes and apples, stirring gently; let stand until the bread absorbs all the liquid, 2–3 minutes.

2. To make the topping, in a small bowl, combine with a fork the flour, the remaining 2 tablespoons of brown sugar, the margarine and the remaining ¼ teaspoon of cinnamon.

3. Divide the bread mixture between the loaf pans; sprinkle with the topping. Bake until golden brown, 35–40 minutes. Cool slightly and serve warm.

**Per serving**: 223 Calories, 5 g Total Fat, 1 g Saturated Fat, 107 mg Cholesterol, 220 mg Sodium, 38 g Total Carbohydrate, 3 g Dietary Fiber, 8 g Protein, 91 mg Calcium. *POINTS* per serving: 4.

# RECIPES

Soups

# Chapter 4

# Soups

Soups are perennially popular, and with good reason: They're simple, satisfying, and, for the chef, they're a nearly foolproof way to use up leftovers. Almost any soup recipe can take some improvising and substituting; consider the following recipes a framework for your creativity.

## Making Them Healthy

You can trim the fat from soups by starting with a fat-free broth or homemade stock and sautéing the ingredients in a nonstick skillet with nonstick cooking spray. Take advantage of the fact that fat rises to the surface of soups: Let the finished soup stand unstirred for a few hours, then skim off the fat with a shallow spoon or gravy skimmer. If the soup is thick, float a paper towel on the surface to absorb the fat. Or, chill the soup until the fat on the surface hardens and can be scraped away.

If you're cooking a thick or creamy soup, try thickening it with pureed rice or potatoes instead of a cream sauce. A little cornstarch-and-water mixture can also add body to a soup with virtually no fat or calories.

Then, bump up the vegetables: Add an extra handful of leftover cooked or frozen veggies. Try throwing in chopped steamed broccoli, carrots or string beans, or frozen chopped spinach or kale.

## Making Them Last

Most soups are big-batch food; plan for leftovers. Luckily, most soups taste even better if they've sat in the fridge a few days (just thin with a little water as needed). If you're doubling or halving a soup recipe, taste often while you add the seasonings; you might need more or less than called for in the original recipe.

If you're planning to freeze a soup, just prepare the recipe as usual, but undercook the vegetables a little (especially potatoes). Keep in mind that the flavors may change after thawing: Onions, pepper, cloves and garlic tend to become stronger; salt and some herb flavors may weaken. If you can, wait to season until after the soup has been frozen and thawed.

While most thawed soups can be simply brought back to a boil to reheat, creamy soups should be gently heated and stirred constantly to prevent separation. A frozen cold soup should be served as soon as it has thawed.

# Beef Barley Soup

*This soup thickens after standing, so when reheating, add a bit of water to thin it.*

MAKES 4 SERVINGS

10 ounces boneless round steak, cut into
1" cubes

½ cup pearl barley

¼ cup dried lima beans, picked over, rinsed
and drained

1 carrot, chopped

1 onion, chopped

1 celery stalk, sliced

1 teaspoon salt

¼ teaspoon fennel seeds (optional)

⅛ teaspoon freshly ground pepper

1 cup sliced mushrooms

1. In a large saucepan, combine the meat, barley,
lima beans and 5 cups water; bring to a boil. Skim
off any foam, then add the carrot, onion, celery,
salt, fennel seeds (if using) and pepper; bring back
to a boil. Reduce the heat and simmer, covered,
1½ hours.

2. Stir in the mushrooms; cook, covered, until the
meat is tender, 15 minutes longer.

**Per serving:** 237 Calories, 4 g Total Fat, 1 g Saturated
Fat, 35 mg Cholesterol, 645 mg Sodium, 30 g Total
Carbohydrate, 5 g Dietary Fiber, 22 g Protein, 50 mg
Calcium. **POINTS** per serving: 4.

## Tip

If you like, brown the beef before you add the
barley, lima beans and water.

# Black Bean Soup

*Top this hearty soup with crushed baked tortilla chips
and chopped jalapeño instead of the onion and
cilantro, if you like.*

MAKES 4 SERVINGS

2 teaspoons olive oil

2 onions, chopped

2 jalapeño peppers, seeded, deveined and
chopped (wear gloves to prevent irritation)

1 garlic clove, minced

One 15-ounce can black beans, rinsed and
drained

2 cups low-sodium chicken broth

1 teaspoon ground cumin

1 teaspoon ground coriander

2 tablespoons dry sherry

1 teaspoon lime juice

½ teaspoon salt

2 tablespoons chopped cilantro

1 small onion or 2 scallions, minced

1. In a medium nonstick saucepan, heat the oil.
Sauté the chopped onions, jalapeños and garlic
until softened, about 5 minutes. Stir in the beans,
broth, cumin, coriander and 1 cup water; bring to
a boil. Reduce the heat and simmer, covered,
until the flavors are blended, about 45 minutes.
Remove from the heat; stir in the sherry, lime
juice and salt. Cool slightly.

2. Transfer the soup to a food processor or blender;
puree. Pour back into the saucepan and heat to
serving temperature. Serve, topped with the
minced onion and cilantro.

**Per serving:** 207 Calories, 4 g Total Fat, 1 g Saturated
Fat, 0 mg Cholesterol, 292 mg Sodium, 31 g Total
Carbohydrate, 7 g Dietary Fiber, 11 g Protein, 78 mg
Calcium. **POINTS** per serving: 3.

# Minestrone

Minestra *is Italian for soup. This version of the classic pasta and bean soup calls for spaghetti, but a cup of cooked ditalini or tubetti works well, too.*

MAKES 8 SERVINGS

3 cups low-sodium chicken broth

2 cups shredded green cabbage

2 onions, chopped

1 carrot, diagonally sliced

2 celery stalks, diagonally sliced

1 purple turnip, peeled and chopped

1 cup canned whole tomatoes

1 medium all-purpose potato, peeled and chopped

2 teaspoons Italian herb seasoning

1 teaspoon salt

¼ teaspoon freshly ground pepper

1 cup chopped trimmed green beans (1" lengths)

1 medium zucchini, halved lengthwise and sliced

1 cup cooked thin spaghetti, broken into halves

½ cup canned red kidney beans, rinsed and drained

¼ cup grated Romano or Parmesan cheese

1. In a large saucepan, combine the broth, cabbage, onions, carrot, celery, turnip, tomatoes, potato, Italian seasoning, salt and pepper with 3 cups water; bring to a boil. Reduce the heat and simmer, covered, 20 minutes.

2. Stir in the green beans and zucchini; cook, covered, 15 minutes longer. Stir in the spaghetti and kidney beans; heat to serving temperature. Serve, sprinkled with the cheese.

**Per serving:** 181 Calories, 3 g Total Fat, 1 g Saturated Fat, 6 mg Cholesterol, 494 mg Sodium, 31 g Total Carbohydrate, 5 g Dietary Fiber, 8 g Protein, 145 mg Calcium. **POINTS** per servings: 3.

## Tip

When freezing leftover soup, leave ½ inch of air on top in pint containers and 1 inch in quart containers to allow the soup to expand when it freezes.

## Power Lunches

*Soup makes a wonderful lunch, whether it's a warm soup on a chilly day, or a cold soup when it's hot and sultry. It's easy to take to work or school, even if you don't have access to a refrigerator or a microwave oven. Just pour it into a vacuum bottle, and you can enjoy a hot or cold soup whenever you please. Before filling the bottle with hot soup, rinse it with hot water to warm the inside. You may also want to buy a lunch box, which helps to keep food insulated.*

# Navy Bean Soup

*Fresh lemon juice, rosemary and lots of parsley add plenty of spirit and flavor to this nourishing, simple-to-make soup. Use any small white bean in this soup.*

MAKES 4 SERVINGS

2 teaspoons extra virgin olive oil

2 garlic cloves, minced

One 15-ounce can navy beans, rinsed and drained

½ cup chopped parsley

2 tablespoons fresh lemon juice

4 teaspoons chopped rosemary leaves

½ teaspoon freshly ground pepper

2 cups low-sodium chicken broth

½ teaspoon salt

1. In a large nonstick saucepan, heat the oil. Sauté the garlic until fragrant, about 1 minute. Stir in the beans, parsley, lemon juice, rosemary and pepper, then add the broth; bring to a boil. Reduce the heat and simmer 10 minutes; then cool slightly.

2. With a slotted spoon, transfer about 3 cups of the soup to a blender or food processor; puree, then return to the saucepan. Add the salt and heat to serving temperature.

**Per serving**: 202 Calories, 4 g Total Fat, 1 g Saturated Fat, 0 mg Cholesterol, 335 mg Sodium, 33 g Total Carbohydrate, 5 g Dietary Fiber, 12 g Protein, 108 mg Calcium. **POINTS** per serving: 3.

# Pistou

*Pistou is a classic, hearty French vegetable soup that uses a variation of pesto (minus the pine nuts) to create a rich flavor.*

MAKES 4 SERVINGS

2 leeks, cleaned and sliced

1 carrot, scrubbed and diagonally sliced

1 medium all-purpose potato, peeled and cubed

¾ teaspoon salt

¾ teaspoon freshly ground pepper

1 medium zucchini, sliced

1 cup chopped trimmed green beans

1 cup fusilli

⅓ cup canned lima beans or red kidney beans, rinsed and drained

2 tablespoons grated Parmesan cheese

2 tablespoons minced basil

1 tablespoon tomato paste

1 garlic clove, minced

4 teaspoons olive oil

1. In a large saucepan, combine the leeks, carrot, potato, salt, pepper and 6 cups water; bring to a boil. Reduce the heat and simmer, covered, stirring occasionally, about 30 minutes.

2. Stir in the zucchini, green beans and fusilli; simmer, stirring occasionally, about 10 minutes. Stir in the lima beans.

3. In a small bowl, whisk the cheese, basil, tomato paste and garlic. Whisk in the oil in a slow, steady stream. Stir ½ cup of the hot broth into the basil mixture; gradually stir the basil mixture into the soup.

**Per serving**: 257 Calories, 7 g Total Fat, 2 g Saturated Fat, 4 mg Cholesterol, 617 mg Sodium, 41 g Total Carbohydrate, 6 g Dietary Fiber, 9 g Protein, 145 mg Calcium. **POINTS** per serving: 5.

# Chicken Soup with Matzo Balls

*A hot bowl of this savory broth will lift your spirits even if it does not cure your cold.*

MAKES 4 SERVINGS

1 egg, separated

1 egg white

Pinch cream of tartar

1 tablespoon seltzer water

⅛ teaspoon salt

¼ cup + 2 tablespoons matzo meal

1 scallion, minced

1 tablespoon snipped dill

4 cups low-sodium chicken broth

4 baby carrots, quartered lengthwise

¼ cup julienned parsnip

Dill sprigs, to garnish

1. In a medium bowl, with an electric mixer at high speed, beat both of the egg whites with the cream of tartar until stiff but not dry peaks form; set aside.

2. In a large bowl, beat the egg yolk with the seltzer and salt until thick and doubled in volume. With a rubber spatula, fold in the egg whites. On a sheet of wax paper, combine the matzo meal, scallions and dill; fold into the egg mixture. Refrigerate at least 30 minutes.

3. In a large saucepan, bring 2 quarts water to a boil (add a pinch of salt, if desired). Shape the matzo mixture into 8 balls; drop into the boiling water. Reduce the heat and simmer, covered, 25–30 minutes.

4. Meanwhile, in a medium saucepan, combine the broth, carrots and parsnip; bring to a boil. Reduce the heat and simmer, covered, until the vegetables are tender, about 5 minutes. With a slotted spoon, transfer the matzo balls to the soup. Serve, garnished with a dill sprig.

**Per serving**: 162 Calories, 6 g Total Fat, 2 g Saturated Fat, 60 mg Cholesterol, 101 mg Sodium, 3 g Total Carbohydrate, 1 g Dietary Fiber, 24 g Protein, 27 mg Calcium. **POINTS** per serving: 4.

# Chicken-Tomato Chowder

*Thick with vegetables, potatoes and beans, this chowder is a great midweek supper for the whole family. If you have leftovers, take some along in a wide-mouth vacuum bottle for a hearty lunch.*

MAKES 4 SERVINGS

4 teaspoons olive oil

2 carrots, thinly sliced

6 scallions, chopped

2 celery stalks, chopped

2 garlic cloves, minced

One 14½-ounce can crushed tomatoes

2 cups low-sodium chicken broth

2 medium all-purpose potatoes, peeled and cubed

½ teaspoon dried marjoram

¼ teaspoon dried oregano

¼ teaspoon freshly ground pepper

½ pound skinless boneless chicken breast, cubed

½ cup canned cannellini beans, rinsed and drained

2 tablespoons chopped parsley

1. In a medium saucepan, heat 2 teaspoons of the oil. Sauté the carrots, scallions, celery and garlic until softened, 5–7 minutes. Stir in the tomatoes and broth; bring to a boil, then stir in the potatoes, marjoram, oregano and pepper. Reduce the heat and simmer, covered, until the potatoes are tender, 15–20 minutes.

2. Meanwhile, in a medium nonstick skillet, heat the remaining 2 teaspoons of the oil. Sauté the chicken until cooked through, 6–8 minutes. Stir into the chowder; stir in the beans and parsley. Simmer until heated through, about 5 minutes.

**Per serving:** 277 Calories, 7 g Total Fat, 1 g Saturated Fat, 41 mg Cholesterol, 314 mg Sodium, 32 g Total Carbohydrate, 5 g Dietary Fiber, 24 g Protein, 98 mg Calcium. *POINTS* per serving: 5.

*Chicken-Tomato Chowder*

# Corn Chowder

*For superior flavor, use corn kernels cut fresh off the cob. For more visual appeal, use yellow and red bell peppers.*

MAKES 4 SERVINGS

2 slices turkey bacon, cut into ½" pieces

1 onion, chopped

½ yellow bell pepper, seeded and chopped

2½ cups low-sodium chicken broth

2 medium all-purpose potatoes, peeled and cubed

2 cups whole corn kernels

¼ cup light cream

1. In a medium nonstick saucepan, cook the bacon in 2 tablespoons water until crisp. With a slotted spoon, transfer to a paper towel; discard the liquid.

2. Add the onion, bell pepper and 2 teaspoons water to the saucepan; sauté until soft, about 5 minutes. Add the broth and potatoes; bring to a boil. Reduce the heat and simmer, partially covered, until the potatoes are almost tender, about 15 minutes. Stir in the corn; simmer 5 minutes longer. Remover from the heat; cool slightly.

3. Transfer 2 cups of the soup to a food processor or blender; puree. Pour back into the saucepan; stir in the cream and heat to serving temperature. Serve, topped with the bacon pieces.

**Per serving:** 209 Calories, 8 g Total Fat, 4 g Saturated Fat, 22 mg Cholesterol, 175 mg Sodium, 30 g Total Carbohydrate, 4 g Dietary Fiber, 6 g Protein, 28 mg Calcium. *POINTS* per serving: 4.

## Got Leftovers?

**If you have light cream left over, don't leave it in the fridge to tempt you when you make coffee. Instead, pour it into ice cube trays and freeze. Remove the cubes and store in a sealable plastic bag; they will keep up to 3 months. Each cube holds 1–2 tablespoons—you need only a small amount to give richness to soup recipes.**

# Mulligatawny

*This east Indian curry soup is now a common offering on countless menus. Try it with a warmed piece of Naan, the Indian flatbread (page 60).*

MAKES 4 SERVINGS

4 teaspoons reduced-calorie margarine

1 onion, chopped

½ carrot, chopped

1 celery stalk, chopped

½ green bell pepper, seeded and chopped

1 tart apple, peeled, cored and diced

¼ cup all-purpose flour

2 teaspoons curry powder

⅛ teaspoon ground mace or nutmeg

1 whole clove

2 cups low-sodium chicken broth

1 tomato, peeled, seeded and chopped

1 teaspoon fresh lemon juice

1½ cups diced cooked chicken breast

¼ teaspoon salt

In a medium nonstick saucepan, melt the margarine. Sauté the onion, carrot, celery, bell pepper and apple until softened, about 5 minutes. Stir in the flour, curry, mace and clove; cook, stirring, 1 minute; gradually stir in the broth. Add the tomato and lemon juice; bring to a boil, stirring occasionally. Reduce the heat and simmer, covered, stirring occasionally, 30 minutes. Add the chicken and salt; heat to serving temperature.

**Per serving**: 187 Calories, 7 g Total Fat, 2 g Saturated Fat, 38 mg Cholesterol, 278 mg Sodium, 17 g Total Carbohydrate, 3 g Dietary Fiber, 15 g Protein, 39 mg Calcium. *POINTS* per serving: 4.

# Tortellini in Chicken Broth

*In Italy, this soup is called tortellini en* brodo. *If you keep your freezer stocked, this soup is a snap to whip up after a long day at the office.*

MAKES 4 SERVINGS

2 cups low-sodium chicken broth

Half 16-ounce package frozen cheese tortellini (about 2 cups)

1 cup slivered watercress leaves

2 scallions, sliced

3 drops hot red pepper sauce (optional)

2 tablespoons grated Romano or Parmesan cheese

Freshly ground pepper

In a medium saucepan, combine the broth and ⅔ cup water. Add the tortellini and cook according to package directions. Stir in the watercress and scallions; cook until the watercress wilts, about 2 minutes. Add the pepper sauce (if using). Serve, sprinkled with the cheese and pepper to taste.

**Per serving:** 211 Calories, 7 g Total Fat, 3 g Saturated Fat, 36 mg Cholesterol, 308 mg Sodium, 26 g Total Carbohydrate, 2 g Dietary Fiber, 12 g Protein, 174 mg Calcium. *POINTS* per serving: 4.

# Faux Gumbo

*Authentic gumbo begins with a roux, which is made by cooking flour in butter until it's a deep rich brown. It ends with filé powder, which is stirred in after the gumbo is removed from the heat. Our easy version of this Creole favorite showcases shrimp, chicken and kielbasa in a savory broth. Use frozen sliced okra if your market doesn't have fresh.*

MAKES 4 SERVINGS

4 teaspoons reduced-calorie margarine

1 green bell pepper, seeded and chopped

1 celery stalk, chopped

6 scallions, sliced

1 garlic clove, minced

One 14½-ounce can no-salt-added crushed tomatoes

2 cups low-sodium chicken broth

1 cup trimmed sliced fresh or thawed frozen okra

½ teaspoon dried thyme leaves, crumbled

1 bay leaf

⅛–¼ teaspoon cayenne pepper

½ cup regular long-grain rice

½ pound shrimp, peeled and deveined

¼ pound boneless chicken breast, cut into ½" pieces

One 2" piece kielbasa, cut into 8 slices

1. In a large nonstick saucepan, melt the margarine. Sauté the bell pepper, celery, scallions and garlic until softened, about 5 minutes. Stir in the tomatoes, broth, okra, thyme, bay leaf and cayenne; bring to a boil. Reduce the heat and simmer, covered, 15 minutes.

2. Stir in the rice and simmer, covered, 15 minutes. Add the shrimp, chicken and kielbasa; simmer, covered, until the shrimp is pink, the chicken is cooked through and the rice is tender, about 5 minutes longer. Discard the bay leaf.

**Per serving:** 255 Calories, 9 g Total Fat, 3 g Saturated Fat, 58 mg Cholesterol, 297 mg Sodium, 28 g Total Carbohydrate, 4 g Dietary Fiber, 17 g Protein, 101 mg Calcium. *POINTS* per serving: 5.

# Bouillabaisse

*A French favorite, this classic seafood stew is served over crusty bread so you can savor every last bit of broth.*

MAKES 4 SERVINGS

2 teaspoons olive oil

4 shallots, chopped

1 garlic clove, minced

One 14½-ounce can no-salt-added tomatoes

½ cup bottled clam juice

½ cup dry white wine

1 tablespoon chopped parsley

1 tablespoon tomato paste

½ teaspoon dried thyme leaves, crumbled

1 bay leaf

⅛ teaspoon crushed saffron threads, dissolved in 1 tablespoon hot water

⅛ teaspoon fennel seeds, crushed

10 ounces boneless firm white fish (tilefish, red snapper or monkfish), cut in ½" chunks

Four 3-ounce fresh or thawed frozen lobster tails, halved

12 medium littleneck clams, scrubbed

Four 1" slices French bread

1. In a large nonstick saucepan, heat the oil. Sauté the shallots and garlic until softened, about 3 minutes. Stir in the tomatoes, clam juice, wine, parsley, tomato paste, thyme, bay leaf, dissolved saffron, fennel seeds and 1½ cups water; bring to a boil. Reduce the heat and simmer, covered, 30 minutes.

2. Add the fish, lobster and clams; bring back to a boil. Reduce the heat and simmer, covered, until the clams open and the fish and lobster are cooked through, 6–8 minutes. Discard any unopened clams and the bay leaf.

3. To serve, place the bread into 4 shallow soup bowls; ladle the bouillabaisse over the bread.

**Per serving**: 320 Calories, 6 g Total Fat, 1 g Saturated Fat, 42 mg Cholesterol, 347 mg Sodium, 31 g Total Carbohydrate, 3 g Dietary Fiber, 30 g Protein, 104 mg Calcium. **POINTS** per serving: 6.

# Cioppino

*Don't be tempted to double this recipe so you'll have leftovers—it's best eaten right after it's made.*

MAKES 4 SERVINGS

2 teaspoons olive oil

1 onion, finely chopped

½ green bell pepper, seeded and diced

4 garlic cloves, finely chopped

One 14½-ounce can crushed tomatoes

1 cup dry white wine

¼ cup tomato paste

¼ cup chopped fresh flat-leaf parsley

¼ teaspoon freshly ground pepper

¼ teaspoon dried basil

¼ teaspoon dried oregano

1 bay leaf

10 ounces boneless firm white fish (hake, tilefish or monkfish), cut in 1½" chunks

12 medium littleneck clams, scrubbed

12 medium mussels, scrubbed and debearded

8 medium shrimp, peeled and deveined

1. In a large nonstick saucepan, heat the oil. Sauté the onion, bell pepper and garlic until softened, about 5 minutes. Stir in the tomatoes, wine, tomato paste, parsley, pepper, basil, oregano, bay leaf and ½ cup water; bring to a boil. Reduce the heat and simmer, covered, 30 minutes.

2. Add the fish; simmer, uncovered, 3–5 minutes. Add the clams and mussels; simmer, covered, 3–5 minutes. Add the shrimp; simmer, covered, 3–5 minutes, until the clams and mussels are open and the shrimp is pink. Discard any unopened clams and mussels and the bay leaf.

**Per serving:** 261 Calories, 7 g Total Fat, 1 g Saturated Fat, 39 mg Cholesterol, 516 mg Sodium, 14 g Total Carbohydrate, 2 g Dietary Fiber, 26 g Protein, 104 mg Calcium. **POINTS** per serving: 5.

# Creamy Clam Chowder

*This lightened version of New England clam chowder has all of the richness of the traditional with much less fat.*

## Makes 4 servings

2 medium all-purpose potatoes, peeled and diced

1 celery stalk, chopped

1 onion, chopped

4 teaspoons reduced-calorie margarine

1 cup fat-free milk

1 cup evaporated skimmed milk

1 tablespoon all-purpose flour

One 10-ounce can clams, drained (reserve ½ cup juice)

½ teaspoon dried thyme leaves, crumbled

⅛ teaspoon ground white pepper

2 slices bacon, crisp-cooked and crumbled (optional)

1. In a medium saucepan, combine the potatoes, celery, onion, margarine and 1 cup water; bring to a boil. Reduce the heat and simmer, covered, until the potatoes are tender, about 15 minutes.

2. In a medium bowl, mix the milk, evaporated milk and flour until smooth; add to the saucepan. Stir in the clams, the reserved clam juice, thyme and pepper; cook, stirring, until the chowder thickens slightly, about 10 minutes (do not let the soup boil). Serve, sprinkled with the bacon (if desired).

**Per serving:** 250 Calories, 3 g Total Fat, 1 g Saturated Fat, 41 mg Cholesterol, 300 mg Sodium, 31 g Total Carbohydrate, 2 g Dietary Fiber, 23 g Protein, 332 mg Calcium. **POINTS** per serving: 5.

## Tip

Recipes for pale foods often call for ground white pepper to avoid the dark specks of black pepper or a pepper blend. If the flecks don't bother you, feel free to use whatever type of pepper you have on hand.

# Fish Chowder

*This versatile chowder lets you take advantage of the freshest fish available at the market. For added nutrition, toss in ½ cup chopped spinach with the parsley.*

MAKES 4 SERVINGS

4 teaspoons reduced-calorie margarine

1 onion, chopped

½ carrot, chopped

1 garlic clove, minced

4 cups low-sodium chicken broth

1 medium all-purpose potato, peeled and cubed

1 pound boneless firm white fish (orange roughy, red snapper, tilefish or sea bass), cut in ½" chunks

3 tablespoons chopped parsley

1 tablespoon snipped dill

⅛ teaspoon ground white pepper

1 cup fat-free milk

1. In a medium nonstick saucepan, melt the margarine. Sauté the onion, carrot and garlic until softened, about 5 minutes. Add the broth and potato; bring to a boil. Reduce the heat and simmer, covered, until the potato is tender, about 15 minutes.

2. Stir in the fish, parsley, dill and pepper; simmer, covered, until the fish is just opaque, about 5 minutes. Stir in the milk; heat to serving temperature.

**Per serving**: 179 Calories, 5 g Total Fat, 1 g Saturated Fat, 19 mg Cholesterol, 190 mg Sodium, 14 g Total Carbohydrate, 2 g Dietary Fiber, 18 g Protein, 104 mg Calcium. **POINTS** per serving: 4.

# Borscht

*Fresh beets give borscht its unmatched ruby color, making it an eye-catching first course.*

MAKES 4 SERVINGS

2 cups low-sodium chicken broth

2–3 fresh beets, peeled and shredded

6 scallions, sliced

½ teaspoon packed light brown sugar

½ cup shredded red cabbage

2 tablespoons snipped dill

1 teaspoon grated lemon zest

2 tablespoons fresh lemon juice

¼ teaspoon salt

⅛ teaspoon ground white pepper

¼ cup light sour cream

Fresh dill sprigs, to garnish

1. In a medium nonreactive saucepan, combine the broth, beets, scallions, brown sugar and 1½ cups water; bring to a boil. Reduce the heat and simmer, covered, 15 minutes. Add the cabbage and dill; cook, covered, until the beets and cabbage are soft, about 5 minutes longer. Remove from the heat.

2. Stir in the lemon zest, lemon juice, salt and pepper; pour into a medium nonreactive bowl. Refrigerate, covered, until chilled. Serve, topped with the sour cream and a dill sprig.

**Per serving**: 72 Calories, 2 g Total Fat, 1 g Saturated Fat, 5 mg Cholesterol, 219 mg Sodium, 10 g Total Carbohydrate, 2 g Dietary Fiber, 3 g Protein, 51 mg Calcium. **POINTS** per serving: 1.

## Got Leftovers?

**Red cabbage will keep in the refrigerator for up to 3 weeks; just wrap it in a perforated plastic bag. Try sautéing it with some onions in a little oil until soft, then sprinkle with dill.**

# Cabbage and Apple Soup

*Serve this unusual soup hot or cold, with pumpernickel bread, if desired. If you decide to serve it cold, puree all of the soup; then refrigerate, covered, until chilled. The recipe can be doubled.*

MAKES 4 SERVINGS

1 teaspoon canola oil

1½ cups shredded green cabbage

2 onions, chopped

1 small Granny Smith apple, cored, peeled and chopped

3 cups reduced-sodium vegetable broth

1 garlic clove, minced

1 teaspoon grated peeled gingerroot

½ teaspoon sugar

¼ teaspoon cinnamon (optional)

Freshly ground pepper, to taste

1 small red apple, cored and finely diced

1. In a medium nonstick saucepan, heat the oil over low heat. Add the cabbage, onions and Granny Smith apple; simmer, covered, stirring occasionally, 10 minutes.

2. Add the broth and garlic; bring to a boil. Reduce the heat and simmer, covered, until the cabbage is tender, about 10 minutes. With a slotted spoon, transfer half of the solids to a blender or food processor; puree, then return to the saucepan. Add the gingerroot, sugar, cinnamon (if using) and pepper; bring just to a boil. Serve, garnished with the red apple.

**Per serving:** 83 Calories, 1 g Total Fat, 0 g Saturated Fat, 0 mg Cholesterol, 197 mg Sodium, 16 g Total Carbohydrate, 3 g Dietary Fiber, 3 g Protein, 32 mg Calcium. *POINTS* per serving: 1.

# Indian Carrot Soup

*There are a large variety of flavored pitas available, and they make a nice accompaniment to hot or cold soups. Try this soup with sesame or onion-flavor.*

MAKES 4 SERVINGS

2 teaspoons olive oil

1 onion, chopped

2 teaspoons curry powder

¼ teaspoon ground coriander

¼ teaspoon ground cardamom

4 carrots, peeled and cut into 1" chunks

3 cups low-sodium chicken broth

¼ cup plain low-fat yogurt

Carrot curls and mint sprigs, to garnish

1. In a medium nonstick saucepan, heat the oil. Sauté the onion until softened, about 5 minutes. Add the curry powder, coriander and cardamom; cook, stirring, 1 minute. Add the carrots and broth; bring to a boil. Reduce the heat and simmer, covered, until the carrots are tender, about 20 minutes. Strain the broth into a large bowl.

2. In a food processor or blender, puree the carrots with 1 cup of the broth. Stir the puree into the remaining broth; refrigerate, covered, until chilled. Serve, topped with the yogurt and garnished with a carrot curl and mint sprig.

**Per serving:** 133 Calories, 5 g Total Fat, 1 g Saturated Fat, 1 mg Cholesterol, 144 mg Sodium, 20 g Total Carbohydrate, 6 g Dietary Fiber, 4 g Protein, 92 mg Calcium. *POINTS* per serving: 2.

## Tip

**Stirring in the yogurt, as we did in the photograph, tames some of the spiciness—good to know if your curry powder has lots of kick.**

*Indian Carrot Soup*

# Cream of Asparagus Soup

*This is a lusciously rich soup that's perfect to serve at your most elegant dinner party. For a pretty garnish, float a thin lemon slice in the center of the soup.*

MAKES 4 SERVINGS

2 slices whole-wheat bread, cut into ½" cubes

1 pound asparagus, trimmed

1 teaspoon canola oil

1 onion, chopped

1 garlic clove, minced

1 cup low-sodium chicken broth

¼ cup finely chopped parsley

1 cup evaporated skimmed milk

2 tablespoons whole-wheat flour

1 teaspoon fresh lemon juice

Freshly ground pepper, to taste

1. To prepare the croutons, preheat the oven to 300° F. Place the bread cubes on a baking sheet; bake until crisp and golden, 20–25 minutes.

2. To prepare the soup, chop the top 4" of the asparagus spears into 1" lengths; chop the rest of the asparagus into ½" lengths; keep in separate piles.

3. In a medium nonstick saucepan, heat the oil. Sauté the onion and garlic until the garlic is lightly browned, about 3 minutes. Add the ½" pieces of asparagus, the broth, parsley and 1½ cups water; bring to a boil. Reduce the heat and simmer, covered, until the asparagus is very tender, about 20 minutes. With a slotted spoon, transfer the solids to a blender or food processor; puree, then return to the saucepan.

4. In a small bowl, whisk the milk and flour until smooth; whisk into the asparagus mixture. Add the reserved asparagus; bring to simmer, stirring constantly (do not let the soup boil). Reduce the heat and simmer, stirring often, about 15 minutes. Stir in the lemon juice and pepper. Serve, sprinkled with the croutons.

**Per serving:** 137 Calories, 3 g Total Fat, 1 g Saturated Fat, 3 mg Cholesterol, 181 mg Sodium, 21 g Total Carbohydrate, 3 g Dietary Fiber, 10 g Protein, 223 mg Calcium. *POINTS* per serving: 2.

# Cream of Broccoflower Soup

*Broccoflower is a vegetable that is a combination of broccoli and cauliflower. If it is unavailable, simply substitute broccoli or a mixture of broccoli and cauliflower.*

MAKES 4 SERVINGS

1½ cups low-sodium chicken broth or Vegetable Stock (page 11)

1 pound broccoflower, coarsely chopped (about 2 cups)

6 scallions, sliced

2 tablespoons reduced-calorie margarine

2 tablespoons all-purpose flour

½ teaspoon dried marjoram leaves

¼ teaspoon salt

⅛ teaspoon ground white pepper

1 cup evaporated skimmed milk

Broccoflower florets, to garnish

1. In a medium saucepan, combine the broth, broccoflower and scallions; bring to a boil. Reduce the heat and simmer, covered, until the broccoflower is tender, about 10 minutes. Remove from the heat; cool slightly. Transfer the soup to a food processor or blender; puree, scraping down the sides of the work bowl, until the broccoflower is completely smooth.

2. Wipe the saucepan with a paper towel. In the saucepan, melt the margarine. Blend in the flour, marjoram, salt and pepper; gradually stir in the milk until the mixture is smooth. Cook over medium heat, stirring, until thick and bubbling. Stir in the pureed soup; heat to serving temperature. Serve, garnished with broccoflower florets.

**Per serving**: 116 Calories, 4 g Total Fat, 1 g Saturated Fat, 2 mg Cholesterol, 302 mg Sodium, 13 g Total Carbohydrate, 1 g Dietary Fiber, 7 g Protein, 216 mg Calcium. *POINTS* per serving: 2.

# Cream of Mushroom Soup

*This creamy soup is especially satisfying in cold weather. You can also use it as a sauce over veggies or pasta, or as a base for casseroles.*

MAKES 4 SERVINGS

1 pound mushrooms, coarsely chopped (about 4 cups)

3 cups low-sodium chicken broth

1 teaspoon vegetable oil

2 onions, chopped

1 carrot, peeled and thinly sliced

1 celery stalk, finely chopped

1 cup evaporated skimmed milk

3 tablespoons whole-wheat flour

¼ cup finely chopped parsley

¼ teaspoon dried thyme leaves, crumbled

¼ teaspoon dried marjoram leaves, crumbled

Freshly ground pepper, to taste

1. In a medium saucepan, combine 3 cups of the mushrooms with 1½ cups of the broth; bring to a boil. Reduce the heat and simmer, covered, about 20 minutes. Transfer to a blender or food processor; puree, then return to the saucepan.

2. Meanwhile, in a large nonstick skillet, heat the oil. Sauté the onions, carrot and celery until softened, about 5 minutes. Add the remaining mushrooms; cook, stirring occasionally, until the vegetables are wilted, about 10 minutes. Add to the mushroom puree in the saucepan, along with the remaining broth.

3. In a small bowl, whisk the milk and flour until smooth; whisk into the mushroom mixture. Bring to a simmer, stirring constantly (do not let the soup boil). Reduce the heat and simmer, stirring occasionally, about 15 minutes. Add the parsley, thyme, marjoram and pepper; simmer 5 minutes.

**Per serving:** 157 Calories, 4 g Total Fat, 1 g Saturated Fat, 3 mg Cholesterol, 190 mg Sodium, 25 g Total Carbohydrate, 4 g Dietary Fiber, 11 g Protein, 234 mg Calcium. **POINTS** per serving: 3.

## Tip

**Combine wild and cultivated mushrooms, or soak ½ ounce dried mushrooms in warm water and add them.**

# Herbed Split Pea Soup

*Turkey ham (or Canadian bacon) imparts the smoky flavor of ham without a lot of fat in this slimmed-down version of classic split pea soup. This soup thickens upon standing; when reheating, add water to thin.*

MAKES 4 SERVINGS

2 teaspoons olive oil

1 onion, chopped

½ carrot, chopped

1 garlic clove, minced

1 cup dried green or yellow split peas, picked over, rinsed and drained

½ cup slivered no-sugar-added turkey ham

1 teaspoon dried marjoram

¾ teaspoon salt

⅛ teaspoon freshly ground pepper

1. In a medium nonstick saucepan, heat the oil. Sauté the onion, carrot and garlic until softened, about 5 minutes. Add the split peas and 4 cups water; bring to a boil. Reduce the heat and simmer, covered, until the peas are tender, stirring once, about 1 hour.

2. Add the turkey ham, marjoram, salt and pepper; heat to serving temperature.

**Per serving:** 199 Calories, 3 g Total Fat, 1 g Saturated Fat, 10 mg Cholesterol, 579 mg Sodium, 30 g Total Carbohydrate, 12 g Dietary Fiber, 14 g Protein, 38 mg Calcium. **POINTS** per serving: 2.

# Lentil and Swiss Chard Soup

*Lentils are so satisfying, they can be used as a substitute for meat. Top this hearty soup with grated or slivered lemon zest for a refreshing hint of flavor and color. Don't discard the Swiss chard stalks; use them as you would use celery in another recipe.*

MAKES 4 SERVINGS

2 teaspoons olive oil

1 onion, chopped

1 garlic clove, minced

2 cups low-sodium beef broth

1 cup dried lentils, picked over, rinsed and drained

1 cup packed shredded Swiss chard leaves

1 tablespoon chopped cilantro

¼ teaspoon ground cumin

¼ teaspoon salt

⅛ teaspoon freshly ground pepper

2 teaspoons fresh lemon juice

Cilantro sprigs, to garnish

1. In a medium nonstick saucepan, heat the oil. Sauté the onion and garlic until soft, about 5 minutes. Add the broth, lentils and 2 cups water; bring to a boil. Reduce the heat and simmer, covered, until the lentils are tender, about 45 minutes.

2. Add the Swiss chard, cilantro, cumin, salt and pepper; cook, stirring once, until the chard wilts, about 5 minutes. Stir in the lemon juice and serve, garnished with the cilantro.

**Per serving:** 196 Calories, 4 g Total Fat, 1 g Saturated Fat, 0 mg Cholesterol, 228 mg Sodium, 28 g Total Carbohydrate, 14 g Dietary Fiber, 14 g Protein, 54 mg Calcium. **POINTS** per serving: 1.

# Herbed Cucumber and Yogurt Soup

*The flavors of this refreshing cold soup are similar to the Greek salad called tzatiki. Serve with toasted pocketless pita triangles for a cool summertime meal.*

MAKES 4 SERVINGS

3 cups plain low-fat yogurt

2 cucumbers, peeled, seeded and chopped

1 tablespoon snipped dill

1 tablespoon finely chopped mint

1 tablespoon snipped chives

1 garlic clove, minced

1 teaspoon fresh lemon juice (optional)

¼ teaspoon salt

⅛ teaspoon ground white pepper

Mint, dill or chives, to garnish

In a large nonreactive bowl, combine the yogurt, cucumbers, dill, mint, chives, garlic, lemon juice (if using), salt, pepper and 1 cup water; blend thoroughly. Refrigerate, covered, until chilled. Serve, garnished with the mint, dill or chives.

**Per serving:** 121 Calories, 3 g Total Fat, 2 g Saturated Fat, 10 mg Cholesterol, 255 mg Sodium, 15 g Total Carbohydrate, 1 g Dietary Fiber, 10 g Protein, 328 mg Calcium. **POINTS** per serving: 2.

# Gazpacho with Garlicky Croutons

*This is virtually a liquid salad! The croutons add crunch and texture to this refreshing soup. If you like, whip up a batch of the soup (without croutons) and keep in your fridge as an appetite-cutting drink.*

MAKES 4 SERVINGS

4 plum tomatoes, peeled and sliced

½ cucumber, seeded and chopped (do not peel)

6 scallions, sliced

2 tablespoons tarragon-wine vinegar

1 large garlic clove

2 cups spicy mixed vegetable juice

1 teaspoon dried tarragon

1 tablespoon reduced-calorie margarine

2 teaspoons olive oil

1 garlic clove, minced

2 slices nine-grain or whole-wheat bread, cut in 1" cubes

1. In food processor or blender, combine the tomatoes, cucumber, scallions, vinegar and garlic clove; pulse until fairly smooth. Pour into a nonreactive large bowl. Stir in the vegetable juice and tarragon, then salt to taste. Refrigerate, covered, until chilled.

2. Just before serving, in a medium skillet, melt the margarine with the oil. Sauté the minced garlic until fragrant, about 30 seconds. Add the bread cubes; toss to coat. Cook, stirring, just until bread begins to brown, 2–3 minutes. Serve the soup, topped with the croutons.

**Per serving:** 113 Calories, 4 g Total Fat, 1 g Saturated Fat, 0 mg Cholesterol, 803 mg Sodium, 17 g Total Carbohydrate, 3 g Dietary Fiber, 3 g Protein, 49 mg Calcium. **POINTS** per serving: 2.

# Turnip Bisque with Crispy Shallots

*Turnips make a thick, creamy, satisfying soup. You can substitute rutabaga—or any root vegetable—for the turnips, if you prefer.*

MAKES 4 SERVINGS

1 pound purple turnips, peeled and cut into 1" cubes

2 medium potatoes, peeled and cut into 1" cubes

3 cups low-sodium chicken broth

2 teaspoons olive oil

8 shallots, thinly sliced

$\frac{1}{8}$ teaspoon ground white pepper

$\frac{1}{8}$ teaspoon ground nutmeg

1. In a medium saucepan, combine the turnips, potatoes and 2 cups of the broth; bring to a boil. Reduce the heat and simmer until vegetables are tender, about 15 minutes; cool slightly.

2. While the vegetables cook, in a medium non-stick skillet, heat the oil. Stir in the shallots; reduce the heat and cook, covered, stirring occasionally, until golden brown, 13–15 minutes. Remove from the heat.

3. Transfer the turnip mixture to a food processor; puree, then return to the saucepan. Stir in the remaining cup of broth, the pepper and nutmeg; heat to serving temperature. Serve, sprinkled with the shallots.

**Per serving**: 154 Calories, 4 g Total Fat, 1 g Saturated Fat, 0 mg Cholesterol, 171 mg Sodium, 28 g Total Carbohydrate, 3 g Dietary Fiber, 6 g Protein, 66 mg Calcium. *POINTS* per serving: 3.

# Vichyssoise

*This French soup is wonderful as a warm-weather luncheon or as an elegant first course.*

MAKES 4 SERVINGS

4 teaspoons reduced-calorie margarine

1 small leek, cleaned and sliced

2 medium all-purpose potatoes, peeled and diced

2 cups low-sodium chicken broth

1 cup evaporated skimmed milk

$\frac{1}{4}$ teaspoon salt

$\frac{1}{4}$ teaspoon ground white pepper

$\frac{1}{4}$ teaspoon ground nutmeg

$\frac{1}{4}$ cup light cream

Snipped chives, to garnish

1. In a medium nonstick saucepan, melt the margarine. Sauté the leek until soft, about 5 minutes. Add the potatoes, broth, milk, salt, pepper and nutmeg; bring to a boil. Reduce the heat and simmer, uncovered, until the potatoes are fork-tender, about 10 minutes. Remove from the heat; cool slightly.

2. Transfer to a food processor or blender, puree, then pour into a large bowl. Stir in the cream. Refrigerate, covered, until chilled. Serve, garnished with the chives.

**Per serving**: 190 Calories, 6 g Total Fat, 3 g Saturated Fat, 12 mg Cholesterol, 285 mg Sodium, 26 g Total Carbohydrate, 2 g Dietary Fiber, 8 g Protein, 228 mg Calcium. *POINTS* per serving: 4.

## How We Did It

Vichyssoise is traditionally thickened with cream and butter, but our version uses rich-flavored evaporated skimmed milk and light cream instead. The fat savings are substantial, but you won't notice a difference in the flavor.

# Spanish Pepper Soup

*Poblano chiles, dark green peppers shaped like long bell peppers, are available in some supermarkets and Latino grocery stores. They range from mild to fairly hot and are commonly used for chiles rellenos. If unavailable, substitute drained canned whole green chiles. Just add cornbread and this beautiful soup makes a satisfying meal.*

MAKES 4 SERVINGS

2 red bell peppers

2 poblano chile peppers

2 large garlic cloves

3½ cups reduced-sodium vegetable broth

2 cups green beans, trimmed and cut into ½" lengths

1 cup canned tomato puree

¼ cup brown rice

1 tablespoon red-wine vinegar

1 teaspoon packed brown sugar

1 teaspoon paprika

⅛ teaspoon cayenne pepper

Tiny pinch saffron

¼ cup parsley

1. Preheat the broiler, setting the rack 6" below the heat. Line a baking sheet with foil; place both kinds of peppers and garlic on the foil. Roast, turning as needed, until the peppers are evenly blistered and lightly charred on all sides and the garlic is deep brown, 7–10 minutes. Set aside 10 minutes to cool.

2. Wearing gloves, peel and seed the peppers over a bowl, saving the juices. Chop the peppers and place in a medium saucepan. Peel and smash the garlic; add to the peppers.

3. Strain the pepper juices into the saucepan. Add the broth, green beans, tomato puree, rice, vinegar, brown sugar, paprika, cayenne and saffron; bring to a boil. Reduce the heat and simmer, covered, until the rice and beans are tender, about 45 minutes. Serve, sprinkled with the parsley.

**Per serving**: 113 Calories, 1 g Total Fat, 0 g Saturated Fat, 0 mg Cholesterol, 327 mg Sodium, 24 g Total Carbohydrate, 3 g Dietary Fiber, 5 g Protein, 58 mg Calcium. *POINTS* per serving: 2.

## Soup Economics

*Soup is an economical dish, as it comfortably incorporates leftovers. Try making soups such as Minestrone (page 75) when you have leftover vegetables or Mulligatawny (page 81) with leftover chicken. You can also get the maximum use from chicken or beef bones by making your own stocks—see pages 12 and 13. Homemade broth freezes well and can be easily stored for soup or to use in other recipes. And fans of croutons can make their own from leftover bread—see page 20.*

**Spanish Pepper Soup**

# Sweet and Sour Cabbage Soup

*Use regular green or red cabbage rather than Savoy in this recipe—they hold up better during long simmering. Serve with thick slices of black bread.*

MAKES 4 SERVINGS

2 teaspoons canola or vegetable oil

2 onions, chopped

6 cups shredded green cabbage

4 cups low-sodium beef broth

1 cup canned crushed tomatoes

¼ cup raisins

2 tablespoons packed light brown sugar

2 tablespoons fresh lemon juice

1 teaspoon salt

¼ teaspoon caraway seeds

Pinch freshly ground pepper

In a large nonstick saucepan, heat the oil. Sauté the onions until golden, about 5 minutes. Add the cabbage, broth, tomatoes, raisins, brown sugar, lemon juice, salt, caraway seeds, pepper and 2 cups water; bring to a boil. Reduce the heat and simmer, covered, stirring occasionally, until the flavors are blended, about 1 hour.

**Per serving:** 167 Calories, 5 g Total Fat, 1 g Saturated Fat, 0 mg Cholesterol, 747 mg Sodium, 28 g Total Carbohydrate, 5 g Dietary Fiber, 5 g Protein, 103 mg Calcium. **POINTS** per serving: 3.

# Summer Squash Soup

*This is the perfect recipe for making use of a gardenful of zucchini. For a pretty color contrast, chop up a few fresh tomatoes or use quartered cherry tomatoes instead of the julienned zucchini and basil.*

MAKES 4 SERVINGS

2 teaspoons olive oil

6 scallions, sliced

1 celery stalk, chopped

1 garlic clove, minced

2 medium zucchini, shredded

2 medium yellow squash, shredded

1½ cups low-sodium chicken broth

¼ teaspoon salt

¼ teaspoon ground white pepper

¼ cup chopped basil

¼ cup nonfat sour cream

Julienned zucchini or yellow squash and basil sprigs, to garnish

1. In a medium nonstick saucepan, heat the oil. Sauté the scallions, celery and garlic until soft, about 5 minutes. Add the zucchini, yellow squash, broth, salt and pepper; bring to a boil. Reduce the heat and simmer, uncovered, 15 minutes. Remove from the heat; cool slightly.

2. In a food processor or blender, puree the soup with the basil. Pour into a large bowl; refrigerate, covered, until chilled. When ready to serve, swirl in the sour cream. Garnish with the julienned zucchini and basil sprigs.

**Per serving:** 63 Calories, 3 g Total Fat, 1 g Saturated Fat, 0 mg Cholesterol, 174 mg Sodium, 6 g Total Carbohydrate, 2 g Dietary Fiber, 4 g Protein, 52 mg Calcium. **POINTS** per serving: 1.

# Pumpkin Soup with Cinnamon Toast

*If you like, you can substitute frozen butternut squash for the pumpkin.*

### MAKES 4 SERVINGS

2 cups frozen chopped yellow turnips, cooked

1 cup low-sodium chicken broth

1 cup canned pumpkin puree

$\frac{1}{4}$ teaspoon salt

$\frac{1}{4}$ teaspoon ground ginger

$\frac{1}{4}$ teaspoon cinnamon

$\frac{1}{8}$ teaspoon ground nutmeg

Dash ground white pepper

1 cup evaporated skimmed milk

4 teaspoons reduced-calorie margarine

$\frac{3}{4}$ teaspoon sugar

2 slices multigrain or whole-wheat bread

Parsley sprigs, to garnish

1. In a medium saucepan over low heat, combine the turnips, broth, pumpkin, salt, ginger, $\frac{1}{8}$ teaspoon of the cinnamon, the nutmeg, white pepper and $\frac{1}{4}$ cup water; blend in the milk. Heat slowly to serving temperature, stirring occasionally.

2. Meanwhile, in a small bowl, combine the margarine, sugar and the remaining $\frac{1}{8}$ teaspoon of cinnamon; spread over the bread. Toast in a toaster oven or under the broiler until golden; cut each slice into 4 triangles. Serve the soup, garnished with a parsley sprig, with toast on the side.

**Per serving**: 144 Calories, 3 g Total Fat, 1 g Saturated Fat, 2 mg Cholesterol, 382 mg Sodium, 23 g Total Carbohydrate, 4 g Dietary Fiber, 8 g Protein, 231 mg Calcium. **POINTS** per serving: 2.

# Mushroom-Tofu Soup

*Asian or dark sesame oil, made from toasted sesame seeds, Chinese black mushrooms and brown rice udon can be found in health food or Asian food stores.*

MAKES 4 SERVINGS

1 cup (1 ounce) dried Chinese black mushrooms

2 cups boiling water

1½ cups low-sodium chicken broth

1 cup snow peas, strings removed

6 scallions, sliced

2 teaspoons Asian sesame oil

½ pound firm tofu, cut into ¼" slices, then into 1" cubes

3 ounces brown rice udon, broken into halves and cooked

⅛ teaspoon salt

⅛ teaspoon ground white pepper

1½ teaspoons white-wine vinegar

1. In a small bowl, soak the mushrooms in the boiling water 10 minutes. Strain the liquid into a medium saucepan; add the broth and bring to a boil.

2. Meanwhile, trim the tough stems from the mushrooms; cut the caps into strips.

3. Add the mushrooms, snow peas, scallions and oil to the broth; heat 1 minute. Stir in the tofu, udon, salt and pepper; heat to serving temperature. Remove from the heat and stir in the vinegar.

**Per serving**: 227 Calories, 9 g Total Fat, 1 g Saturated Fat, 0 mg Cholesterol, 297 mg Sodium, 26 g Total Carbohydrate, 4 g Dietary Fiber, 15 g Protein, 145 mg Calcium. **POINTS** per serving: 4.

# Onion Soup Gratinée

*This recipe can easily be doubled when you'd like to serve four. To make short work of slivering the onion, first cut it into quarters, then cut each quarter into very thin slices.*

MAKES 2 SERVINGS

1 tablespoon reduced-calorie margarine

2 Spanish onions, slivered

1 small leek, cleaned and sliced

1 cup low-sodium beef broth

⅛ teaspoon freshly ground pepper

2 slices semolina bread, toasted

4 teaspoons grated Parmesan cheese

⅓ cup shredded reduced-fat Swiss cheese

1. In a small nonstick saucepan, melt the margarine. Sauté the onions and leek until the onions are golden, about 15 minutes. Add the broth, pepper and 1 cup water; bring to a boil. Reduce the heat and simmer, covered, 15 minutes.

2. Preheat the broiler. Set 2 flameproof bowls on a baking sheet. Ladle the soup into the bowls; top with the bread. Sprinkle with the Parmesan, then with the Swiss cheese. Broil until the cheese melts, about 2 minutes.

**Per serving**: 277 Calories, 10 g Total Fat, 2 g Saturated Fat, 14 mg Cholesterol, 427 mg Sodium, 34 g Total Carbohydrate, 4 g Dietary Fiber, 13 g Protein, 132 mg Calcium. **POINTS** per serving: 6.

# RECIPES

# Chapter 5

# Poultry

Not long ago, chicken nudged out beef as America's favorite meat, and turkey isn't far behind. That's a healthy trend, since poultry (without the skin) is one of the leanest meats you can buy.

The leanest part of any bird is the breast, followed by the drumsticks. The fattiest parts are the wings, which have a lot of skin, and the thighs. But regardless of which part you choose, you'll get dramatic fat savings when you remove the skin—before cooking, if possible.

When buying poultry, check the freshness date on the package. Avoid any parts with dark or dried-out areas; they indicate freezer burn and improper storage. Rinse the poultry well when you get home and pat it dry with a paper towel; refrigerate in loose plastic wrap for up to two days.

**Note: All raw poultry should be handled with care, because it can contain infectious organisms. See pages 104 and 146 for safety tips.**

## Choosing Chicken

Chickens are sold by age and weight: The youngest, fryers or broilers, weigh between 2½ to 4 pounds. Roasters, slightly older and thus bigger, weigh 5 to 6 pounds. Stewing hens (sometimes called soup fowl), are the most mature, averaging about 6 pounds. They're best suited for long-cooking dishes and for making soups. Cornish hens—chickens with a strain of Cornish game in their pedigree—usually average 1 to 1½ pounds apiece.

## Choosing Turkey

Turkeys come in a range of sizes: Young fryer-roasters, at around 4 to 8 pounds; hens, at 7 to 15 pounds; and the more mature (Tom) turkeys, 15 to 30 pounds. White-meat lovers can also buy just the bone-in breast, halved or whole, from around 3½ to 7 pounds.

## Roasting Times for Whole Poultry

Chickens and turkeys vary, but the following will give you an idea of how long you'll need to cook them at 325° F. Use the internal cooking temperature, measured by an instant-read thermometer, as your guide: Cook until the thigh meat has reached an internal temperature of 180° F, measured in the thickest part of the thigh.

| WEIGHT | APPROXIMATE ROASTING TIME* |
|---|---|
| *Up to 6 pounds* | *20–25 minutes/pound* |
| *6–16 pounds* | *15–20 minutes/pound* |
| *More than 16 pounds* | *12–15 minutes/pound* |

*\*Add 5 minutes per pound if the bird is stuffed.*

# Garlic Roasted Chicken with Gravy

*The chicken cavity can be stuffed with just about anything and doing so will infuse the meat with wonderful flavor. Try onion quarters and lots of rosemary or lemon wedges and parsley.*

MAKES 4 SERVINGS

One 3½-pound chicken

1 lemon, halved

1 onion, halved

4 rosemary sprigs

4 thyme sprigs

6 garlic cloves, peeled

1 cup low-sodium chicken broth

2 tablespoons fresh lemon juice

1 tablespoon cornstarch

2 tablespoons dry white wine

1 scallion, minced

1 tablespoon reduced-sodium soy sauce

¼ teaspoon crumbled dried sage leaves

1. Preheat the oven to 400° F; spray the rack of a roasting pan with nonstick cooking spray. Remove the chicken giblets and neck from body cavity; refrigerate or freeze for another use. Rinse the chicken under cold running water inside and out; pat dry with paper towels.

2. Place the lemon, onion, rosemary, thyme and garlic in the body cavity. Place the chicken, breast-side up, on the rack in the roasting pan. Roast 30 minutes; pour the broth and lemon juice over the chicken. Reduce the oven temperature to 325° F. Roast, basting frequently, until cooked through and the juices run clear when the thigh is pierced in the thickest part with a fork, about 1 hour longer. Transfer the chicken to a cutting board; let stand 15 minutes.

3. Meanwhile, pour the pan juices into a medium saucepan, skimming off any fat and reserving 1 tablespoon of the juices in a small bowl. Dissolve the cornstarch in the reserved juices. Add the wine, scallion, soy sauce, sage and ¼ cup water to the saucepan; bring to a boil and boil 5 minutes. Reduce the heat to low and whisk in the dissolved cornstarch; cook, stirring constantly, until the gravy thickens, about 1 minute. Carve the chicken and serve with gravy. Remove the skin before eating.

**Per serving:** 293 Calories, 10 g Total Fat, 3 g Saturated Fat, 114 mg Cholesterol, 277 mg Sodium, 9 g Total Carbohydrate, 0 g Dietary Fiber, 39 g Protein, 71 mg Calcium. *POINTS* per serving: 7.

*Garlic Roasted Chicken with Gravy with Cornbread-Cranberry Dressing (page 339)*

# Southern Oven "Fried" Chicken

*Though buttermilk may sound sinful, it is actually nonfat or low-fat milk with added bacteria, which produces a slightly sour taste. If you don't have buttermilk, add 1 teaspoon of vinegar to $^{1}/_{2}$ cup skim milk for this recipe.*

MAKES 4 SERVINGS

$^{1}/_{2}$ cup fat-free buttermilk

2–3 drops hot red pepper sauce

$^{1}/_{2}$ cup cornflakes, crushed

3 tablespoons all-purpose flour

$^{1}/_{4}$ teaspoon salt

$^{1}/_{4}$ teaspoon freshly ground pepper

2 pounds chicken parts, skinned

4 teaspoons canola oil

1. Preheat the oven to 400° F; spray a large baking sheet with nonstick cooking spray.

2. In a large shallow bowl, combine the buttermilk and pepper sauce. On a sheet of wax paper, combine the cornflake crumbs, flour, salt and pepper. Dip the chicken in the buttermilk, then dredge in the cornflake mixture, coating completely. Place the chicken on the baking sheet; drizzle with the oil. Bake 30 minutes; turn the chicken over. Bake until cooked through, 15–20 minutes longer.

**Per serving:** 229 Calories, 10 g Total Fat, 2 g Saturated Fat, 64 mg Cholesterol, 295 mg Sodium, 11 g Total Carbohydrate, 0 g Dietary Fiber, 23 g Protein, 49 mg Calcium. *POINTS* per serving: 5.

## How We Did It

Cornflake crumbs add plenty of crunch and toastiness without fat; nobody will miss the traditional fried-chicken coating.

## Chicken Checklist

- *Check "sell by" date on package labels before buying.*

- *Refrigerate raw chicken immediately—don't leave it in the car while you run errands or on the countertop while you unpack groceries.*

- *It will take about 24 hours to thaw a 4-pound chicken. To thaw more quickly, place the chicken in a watertight plastic bag and place in cold water; change the water frequently as it warms up. A 4-pound chicken will thaw in about 2 hours.*

- *Don't refreeze raw or cooked chicken that has thawed.*

- *Always marinate chicken in the refrigerator.*

- *Never stuff an uncooked bird in advance—stuff it just before you put it in to roast.*

- *When refrigerating a cooked chicken with stuffing, remove the stuffing and refrigerate the chicken and the stuffing in separate containers.*

# Chicken Stuffed with Orange Rice

*Try this dish with basmati rice, the long-grain rice grown in the foothills of the Himalayas. It imparts a nutty, perfumed flavor.*

MAKES 6 SERVINGS

3 cups hot cooked white rice

½ cup raisins

Three 5-ounce skinless boneless chicken breasts, pounded ¼" thick

3 sprigs fresh tarragon, or ½ teaspoon dried leaves

2 tablespoons margarine

2 garlic cloves, minced

1 cup dry white wine

1 cup orange juice

2 teaspoons chopped tarragon

2 tablespoons cornstarch, dissolved in ¼ cup water

1. In a small bowl, combine ¼ cup + 2 tablespoons of the rice and the raisins. Place the chicken on a work surface; top with the rice-raisin mixture, then the tarragon sprigs. Starting from the narrow end, roll each chicken breast jelly-roll style, enclosing the stuffing. Secure the ends with toothpicks.

2. In a large nonstick skillet, melt the margarine. Sauté the garlic 2 minutes; add the chicken and brown on all sides. Transfer to a plate.

3. In the skillet, combine the wine, orange juice and chopped tarragon; return the chicken to the skillet. Reduce the heat and simmer until the chicken is cooked through, about 30 minutes. With a slotted spoon, transfer the chicken to a cutting board; discard the toothpicks. Slice each breast into thirds.

4. Add the dissolved cornstarch to the pan juices; cook, stirring frequently, until the sauce thickens. Arrange the remaining rice on a platter; top with the chicken. Spoon the sauce over the chicken.

**Per serving**: 341 Calories, 5 g Total Fat, 1 g Saturated Fat, 41 mg Cholesterol, 98 mg Sodium, 46 g Total Carbohydrate, 1 g Dietary Fiber , 20 g Protein, 47 mg Calcium. **POINTS** per serving: 7.

# Chicken and Asparagus Stir-Fry

*This is the ultimate do-ahead dish. Make the marinade, prepare all the remaining ingredients and refrigerate overnight. Just whip it up the next night after work!*

## MAKES 4 SERVINGS

2 tablespoons low-sodium chicken broth

1 tablespoon grated peeled gingerroot

1 tablespoon reduced-sodium soy sauce

1 tablespoon Worcestershire sauce

2 teaspoons packed brown sugar

1 teaspoon cornstarch

1 teaspoon Asian sesame oil

¼ teaspoon baking soda

¾ pound skinless boneless chicken breasts, cut into strips

2 tablespoons sesame seeds

1 tablespoon peanut oil

6 scallions, cut into 1" lengths

2 garlic cloves, minced

¼ teaspoon crushed red pepper flakes

12 asparagus spears, cut into 2" lengths

1 cup trimmed watercress

1. To prepare the marinade, in a gallon-size sealable plastic bag, combine the broth, gingerroot, soy sauce, Worcestershire sauce, brown sugar, cornstarch, sesame oil and baking soda; add the chicken. Seal the bag, squeezing out the air; turn to coat the chicken. Refrigerate, turning the bag occasionally, at least 2 hours or overnight. Drain and discard the marinade.

2. Heat a large nonstick skillet until very hot; add the sesame seeds and stir-fry until golden, 2–3 minutes. Transfer to a small bowl.

3. In the skillet, heat the peanut oil. Stir-fry the scallions, garlic and pepper flakes 2 minutes; add the asparagus and stir-fry until tender, 4–5 minutes. Add the chicken and watercress; stir-fry until the chicken is cooked through, 6–8 minutes. Serve, sprinkled with the sesame seeds.

**Per serving:** 184 Calories, 8 g Total Fat, 1 g Saturated Fat, 41 mg Cholesterol, 327 mg Sodium, 9 g Total Carbohydrate, 1 g Dietary Fiber, 20 g Protein, 95 mg Calcium. *POINTS* per serving: 4.

# Creole Poached Chicken Breasts

*This dish uses many of the ingredients that define Creole cooking, including onion, green pepper, celery and tomatoes.*

MAKES 4 SERVINGS

2 teaspoons olive oil

2 onions, chopped

1 green bell pepper, seeded and chopped

1 celery stalk, chopped

½ carrot, chopped

One 14½-ounce can stewed tomatoes

½ cup low-sodium chicken broth

2 tablespoons chopped parsley

1 teaspoon ground thyme

¼ teaspoon salt

⅛ teaspoon cayenne pepper

Four 4-ounce skinless boneless chicken breasts

1. In a large nonstick skillet, heat the oil. Sauté the onions, bell pepper, celery and carrot until tender, 4–5 minutes. Stir in the tomatoes, broth, parsley, thyme, salt and cayenne; add the chicken and bring to a boil. Reduce the heat and poach, partially covered, until the chicken is cooked through, 8–10 minutes.

2. With a slotted spoon, transfer the chicken to a platter. Simmer the sauce, uncovered, until reduced by half, 4–5 minutes. Spoon the sauce over the chicken.

**Per serving:** 182 Calories, 4 g Total Fat, 1 g Saturated Fat, 49 mg Cholesterol, 541 mg Sodium, 16 g Total Carbohydrate, 5 g Dietary Fiber, 22 g Protein, 82 mg Calcium. **POINTS** per serving: 3.

# Chicken with Feta Sauce

*A lesson from the Greeks is learned in this fortuitous pairing of olive oil, oregano and feta cheese.*

MAKES 4 SERVINGS

Four 4-ounce skinless boneless chicken breasts

2 tablespoons balsamic vinegar

½ teaspoon ground thyme

2 teaspoons olive oil

1 tablespoon + 1½ teaspoons all-purpose flour

½ teaspoon ground oregano

1 cup fat-free milk

1 cup thawed frozen broccoli, carrot and cauliflower medley

⅓ cup crumbled peppercorn-flavored or plain feta cheese

1 teaspoon fresh lemon juice

2 cups hot cooked orzo or white rice

1. On a sheet of wax paper, sprinkle the chicken with the vinegar and thyme. In a large nonstick skillet, heat the oil. Cook the chicken until browned and cooked through, 4–5 minutes on each side. Transfer to a plate.

2. Sprinkle the flour and oregano over the pan juices; cook, stirring constantly, 1 minute. Gradually whisk in the milk; cook, whisking constantly, until thick and bubbling, 2–3 minutes. Stir in the vegetables, cheese and lemon juice. Reduce the heat and simmer until the cheese melts, about 2 minutes. Place the rice on a large platter; top with the chicken. Spoon the sauce over the chicken.

**Per serving:** 319 Calories, 6 g Total Fat, 2 g Saturated Fat, 60 mg Cholesterol, 219 mg Sodium, 37 g Total Carbohydrate, 1 g Dietary Fiber, 27 g Protein, 169 mg Calcium. **POINTS** per serving: 7.

# Chicken with Sausage and Capers

*Capers, the tiny flower buds of a shrub native to the Mediterranean, may be small but they add lots of zest to recipes. Keep a jar in your refrigerator to add a pungent kick to chicken and pasta dishes as well as sauces.*

MAKES 4 SERVINGS

2 teaspoons olive oil

¾ pound skinless boneless chicken breasts, cut into 1" pieces

¼ pound hot Italian turkey sausage, cut into ½" slices

2 tablespoons red-wine vinegar

2 green bell peppers, seeded and cut into strips

1 red onion, chopped

2 garlic cloves, minced

½ teaspoon dried basil leaves

½ teaspoon dried Italian seasoning

2½ cups canned crushed tomatoes

½ cup low-sodium chicken broth

2 tablespoons grated Parmesan cheese

2 tablespoons capers, rinsed and drained

1. In a large nonstick skillet, heat the oil. Sauté the chicken until golden and cooked through, 6–8 minutes. With a slotted spoon, transfer to a bowl.

2. In the skillet, cook the sausage, stirring frequently, until cooked through and browned, 8–10 minutes. Pour in the vinegar; cook until the liquid evaporates, 1–2 minutes. Add the peppers, onion, garlic, basil and seasoning; cook, stirring, until the peppers are tender, 4–5 minutes.

3. Stir in the tomatoes, broth, cheese and capers; bring to a boil. Return the chicken to the skillet. Reduce the heat and simmer until the sauce thickens slightly.

**Per serving:** 220 Calories, 8 g Total Fat, 1 g Saturated Fat, 73 mg Cholesterol, 633 mg Sodium, 13 g Total Carbohydrate, 2 g Dietary Fiber, 24 g Protein, 98 mg Calcium. **POINTS** per serving: 5.

# Chicken with Apples and Cider

*This is a perfect cool-weather dish for making use of fall apples. If you like, toss in a few tablespoons of golden raisins for sweetness.*

MAKES 4 SERVINGS

3 tablespoons reduced-calorie margarine

1 Granny Smith apple, cored and sliced

1 tablespoon packed dark brown sugar

Four 4-ounce skinless boneless chicken breasts

¼ teaspoon cinnamon

¼ teaspoon salt

¼ teaspoon freshly ground pepper

1 medium onion, thinly sliced and separated into rings

½ cup apple cider

¼ cup cider vinegar

2 cups hot cooked wide noodles

1. In a large nonstick skillet, melt half of the margarine. Sauté the apple until lightly browned, about 5 minutes. Sprinkle with the brown sugar; cook, stirring frequently, until tender, 3–5 minutes longer. Transfer to a plate.

2. On a sheet of wax paper, sprinkle the chicken with the cinnamon, salt and pepper. In the skillet, melt the remaining margarine. Sauté the chicken until browned, 4–5 minutes on each side. Transfer to another plate.

3. In the skillet, cook the onion, covered, until tender, 6–8 minutes; stir in the cider and vinegar. Reduce the heat and simmer 2 minutes. Return the chicken to the skillet; simmer, spooning the sauce over the chicken, until the chicken is cooked through and the liquid is reduced by half, 4–5 minutes.

4. Return the apples to the skillet; cook until heated through, about 2 minutes. Arrange the noodles on a platter; top with the chicken mixture, pouring any remaining juices over chicken.

**Per serving**: 287 Calories, 6 g Total Fat, 1 g Saturated Fat, 76 mg Cholesterol, 273 mg Sodium, 34 g Total Carbohydrate, 3 g Dietary Fiber, 24 g Protein, 34 mg Calcium. *POINTS* per serving: 6.

# Chicken Sauté with Escarole

*The slightly bitter edge of escarole adds piquant flavor to this quick but elegant sauté. Sauvignon blanc and Chablis are both suitable dry white wines to use in this recipe.*

MAKES 4 SERVINGS

3 tablespoons all-purpose flour

1 tablespoon grated Parmesan cheese

¼ teaspoon ground white pepper

Four 4-ounce skinless boneless chicken breasts

4 teaspoons olive oil

2 cups sliced mushrooms

6 scallions, sliced

¼ cup dry white wine

1 bunch escarole, cleaned and coarsely chopped

1. On a sheet of wax paper, combine the flour, cheese and pepper. Dredge the chicken in the flour mixture, coating both sides.

2. In a large nonstick skillet, heat 2 teaspoons of the oil. Cook the chicken until golden and cooked through, 4–5 minutes on each side. Transfer to a platter.

3. In the skillet, heat the remaining 2 teaspoons of oil. Sauté the mushrooms and scallions, stirring constantly, 2–3 minutes. Pour in the wine; cook until the liquid evaporates, 1–2 minutes. Add the escarole; cook until the escarole is tender, about 2 minutes. Spoon over the chicken.

**Per serving:** 196 Calories, 6 g Total Fat, 1 g Saturated Fat, 50 mg Cholesterol, 96 mg Sodium, 10 g Total Carbohydrate, 2 g Dietary Fiber, 23 g Protein, 75 mg Calcium. *POINTS* per serving: 4.

## Got Leftovers?

**Spoon the chicken mixture in a tortilla for a wrap for lunch.**

# Rosemary Chicken with Wild Rice

*Although wild rice is expensive—traditionally, it is harvested by hand—its rich hazelnut flavor makes it worth the price.*

MAKES 6 SERVINGS

1 cup wild rice

1 tablespoon olive oil

1¼ pounds skinless boneless chicken breasts, cubed

2 carrots, diced

1 tablespoon dried rosemary leaves, crumbled

¼ cup + 2 tablespoons reduced-calorie orange marmalade

¼ cup Dijon mustard

¼ teaspoon garlic powder

⅛ teaspoon freshly ground pepper

1. Cook the rice according to package directions.

2. In a large nonstick skillet, heat the oil. Sauté the chicken and carrots, stirring frequently, 3–4 minutes. Stir in the rosemary; cook until chicken is cooked through, 3–4 minutes longer.

3. Stir in the marmalade, mustard, garlic powder and pepper; cook, stirring frequently, until heated through, about 3 minutes. Add the rice; toss to combine.

**Per serving:** 270 Calories, 4 g Total Fat, 1 g Saturated Fat, 52 mg Cholesterol, 370 mg Sodium, 32 g Total Carbohydrate, 2 g Dietary Fiber, 25 g Protein, 31 mg Calcium. **POINTS** per serving: 5.

# Chicken-Chili Casserole

*A marvelous way to use leftover chicken, this hearty casserole is ideal on a chilly night. Just add a salad and some fruit for an easy dinner.*

MAKES 4 SERVINGS

6 ounces wide noodles

1 tablespoon reduced-calorie margarine

4 teaspoons all-purpose flour

2 cups fat-free milk

1 tablespoon grated Parmesan cheese

2 cups cubed cooked skinless chicken breast

1 red onion, chopped

2 tablespoons chopped canned green chiles

1 tablespoon Dijon mustard

4 teaspoons seasoned dried bread crumbs

1. Cook the noodles according to package directions; drain. Preheat the oven to 375° F; spray a 2-quart casserole with nonstick cooking spray.

2. In a medium nonstick saucepan, melt the margarine. Sprinkle with the flour; cook, whisking constantly, 2 minutes. Whisk in the milk and cheese; cook, whisking constantly, until thickened, 2–3 minutes. Remove from the heat. Stir in the noodles, chicken, onion, chiles and mustard. Transfer to the casserole; sprinkle with the bread crumbs. Bake until browned and bubbling, 20–25 minutes.

**Per serving:** 371 Calories, 9 g Total Fat, 2 g Saturated Fat, 94 mg Cholesterol, 396 mg Sodium, 43 g Total Carbohydrate, 2 g Dietary Fiber, 28 g Protein, 199 mg Calcium. **POINTS** per serving: 8.

# Chicken Chili

*Cocoa powder is the surprise ingredient in our chili recipe, giving it a rich taste and color.*

MAKES 4 SERVINGS

4 teaspoons olive oil

1 red bell pepper, seeded and chopped

1 green bell pepper, seeded and chopped

1 yellow bell pepper, seeded and chopped

1 red onion, chopped

¾ pound ground chicken

1 tablespoon all-purpose flour

1 tablespoon chili powder

1 tablespoon ground cumin

1 teaspoon unsweetened cocoa powder

⅛ teaspoon cayenne pepper

Three 14½-ounce cans crushed tomatoes

2 tablespoons balsamic vinegar

¾ cup canned chickpeas, rinsed and drained

1. In a large nonstick Dutch oven or saucepan, heat the oil. Sauté the bell peppers and onion until softened, about 5 minutes. Add the chicken; cook, breaking apart with a wooden spoon, until no longer pink, 5–7 minutes.

2. Sprinkle with the flour, chili powder, cumin, cocoa powder and cayenne; cook, stirring briskly and constantly, 1 minute. Stir in the tomatoes and vinegar; bring to a boil. Reduce the heat and simmer, stirring frequently, until thick, 30–40 minutes. Stir in the chickpeas; simmer until heated through, about 5 minutes.

**Per serving**: 377 Calories, 16 g Total Fat, 3 g Saturated Fat, 76 mg Cholesterol, 545 mg Sodium, 37 g Total Carbohydrate, 6 g Dietary Fiber, 25 g Protein, 155 mg Calcium. *POINTS* per serving: 8.

*Chicken Chili*

# Barley-Chicken Casserole

*This recipe uses pearl barley, which is processed to create grains of the same size and shape, giving it a wonderful feeling in the mouth—and no need to soak before cooking!*

MAKES 6 SERVINGS

2 teaspoons vegetable oil

2 onions, chopped

¾ cup pearl barley

2 teaspoons chicken bouillon granules

2 teaspoons low-sodium chicken bouillon granules

3 cups cubed cooked chicken breast

2 cups sliced mushrooms

¼ cup slivered almonds

1. Preheat the oven to 350° F. In a large nonstick Dutch oven, heat the oil. Sauté the onions and barley until the onions are wilted, 1–2 minutes.

2. Add both kinds of bouillon granules and 3 cups water, stirring until the bouillon dissolves. Bake 45 minutes, then add the chicken, mushrooms and half of the almonds; stir to combine. Bake until the liquid is absorbed and the barley is tender, about 30 minutes longer. Serve, sprinkled with the remaining almonds.

**Per serving**: 272 Calories, 9 g Total Fat, 1 g Saturated Fat, 52 mg Cholesterol, 424 mg Sodium, 23 g Total Carbohydrate, 4 g Dietary Fiber, 25 g Protein, 51 mg Calcium. *POINTS* per serving: 5.

## Tip

Use lentils instead of barley, and reduce the cooking time to 30 minutes.

# Chicken Hash

*Although hash usually includes potatoes, this version, inspired by New York City's famed 21 Club restaurant, is simply chicken in a rich, creamy sauce. If you like, toss in sautéed mushrooms or cooked diced potatoes.*

MAKES 4 SERVINGS

2 slices white bread

1 tablespoon + 1½ teaspoons grated Parmesan cheese

⅛ teaspoon ground white pepper

1 tablespoon reduced-calorie margarine

1 red onion, chopped

1 celery stalk, chopped

¾ pound skinless boneless chicken breasts, cut into ½" pieces

1 tablespoon all-purpose flour

1 teaspoon dried thyme leaves, crumbled

½ teaspoon minced chives

¼ teaspoon salt

1 cup fat-free milk

1 green bell pepper, seeded and chopped

¼ teaspoon paprika

1. In a mini food processor or blender, combine the bread, cheese and pepper; pulse until the mixture is the consistency of coarse crumbs. Preheat the oven to 350° F; spray a 2-quart casserole with nonstick cooking spray.

2. In a large nonstick skillet, melt the margarine. Sauté the onion and celery until softened, about 5 minutes. Add the chicken; sprinkle with the flour, thyme, chives and salt; cook, stirring frequently, 5 minutes. Stir in the milk; cook, stirring frequently, until the sauce thickens, 2–3 minutes. Remove from the heat; stir in the bell pepper. Transfer to the casserole; sprinkle with the crumbs and paprika. Bake until golden brown, 30–35 minutes.

**Per serving**: 185 Calories, 4 g Total Fat, 1 g Saturated Fat, 44 mg Cholesterol, 368 mg Sodium, 15 g Total Carbohydrate, 1 g Dietary Fiber, 21 g Protein, 145 mg Calcium. *POINTS* per serving: 4.

# Orange Couscous with Chicken

*Couscous gets a double dose of orange, complementing the grain and adding flavor to the cooked chicken. This recipe is a great way to make use of leftover chicken.*

MAKES 6 SERVINGS

¾ cup orange juice

2 teaspoons low-sodium chicken bouillon granules

1 teaspoon chicken bouillon granules

¾ cup couscous

3 cups shredded cooked skinless chicken breasts

One 11-ounce can mandarin orange sections, drained

½ cup chopped parsley

In a large Dutch oven, combine the orange juice, both kinds of bouillon granules and ½ cup water; bring to a boil. Remove from the heat; stir in the couscous. Let stand, covered, until the liquid is absorbed, about 5 minutes. Fluff with a fork, then stir in the chicken, all but ¼ cup of the orange sections, and the parsley. Cook over low heat, stirring frequently, until heated through, about 5 minutes. Serve, garnished with the remaining orange sections.

**Per serving**: 251 Calories, 2 g Total Fat, 1 g Saturated Fat, 48 mg Cholesterol, 239 mg Sodium, 34 g Total Carbohydrate, 0 g Dietary Fiber, 23 g Protein, 34 mg Calcium. *POINTS* per serving: 5.

# Shepherd's Pie

*Blanching is a technique often used to retain the color and nutrients in vegetables. To blanch veggies, simply plunge into rapidly boiling water in small quantities, remove and rinse under cold running water, which stops the cooking process.*

MAKES 4 SERVINGS

1 tablespoon reduced-calorie margarine

2 tablespoons all-purpose flour

1 cup low-sodium chicken broth

1 teaspoon reduced-sodium soy sauce

2 cups cubed cooked chicken breast

2 carrots, sliced and blanched

1 cup chopped cleaned spinach leaves

6 scallions, chopped

½ cup thawed frozen corn kernels

½ cup evaporated skimmed milk

1 teaspoon dried thyme leaves, crumbled

½ teaspoon ground marjoram

3 medium russet potatoes, cooked, peeled and mashed

1 tablespoon grated Parmesan cheese

¼ teaspoon paprika

1. In a medium nonstick saucepan, melt the margarine. Sprinkle with 1 tablespoon of the flour; cook, stirring constantly, 2 minutes. Whisk in the broth, soy sauce and ¼ cup water; bring to a boil. Reduce the heat and simmer, stirring constantly, until thickened, 3–4 minutes. Preheat the oven to 400° F; spray a 2-quart casserole with nonstick cooking spray.

2. In a large bowl, combine the chicken and the remaining tablespoon of flour. Stir in the carrots, spinach, scallions, corn, milk, thyme, marjoram and the sauce. Transfer to the casserole. Top with the potatoes, spreading to cover the filling completely; sprinkle with the cheese and paprika. Bake until bubbling and the potatoes are golden, 30–35 minutes.

**Per serving**: 268 Calories, 3 g Total Fat, 1 g Saturated Fat, 51 mg Cholesterol, 209 mg Sodium, 37 g Total Carbohydrate, 4 g Dietary Fiber, 25 g Protein, 160 mg Calcium. **POINTS** per serving: 5.

# Arroz con Pollo

*For many, saffron is most notable for its high price. Fortunately, a little goes a long way, adding a warm, spicy flavor and rich, golden color.*

MAKES 4 SERVINGS

4 teaspoons olive oil

1½ pounds chicken parts, skinned

1 teaspoon paprika

¼ teaspoon salt

¼ teaspoon freshly ground pepper

1 green bell pepper, seeded and chopped

1 celery stalk, chopped

1 red onion, chopped

2 garlic cloves, minced

One 14½-ounce can stewed tomatoes

½ cup low-sodium chicken broth

⅔ cup white rice

1 tablespoon capers, rinsed and drained

½ teaspoon dried oregano leaves

¼ teaspoon saffron

1 bay leaf

1 cup thawed frozen green peas

1 cup chopped roasted red peppers

1. Preheat the oven to 350° F. In a large nonstick skillet, heat the oil. Add the chicken and sprinkle with the paprika, salt and pepper; cook, turning frequently, until browned, 8–10 minutes. Transfer the chicken to a shallow 2-quart casserole.

2. In the skillet, combine the bell pepper, celery, onion and garlic; cook, stirring frequently, until softened, about 4–5 minutes. Stir in the tomatoes, broth and 2 tablespoons water; bring to a boil. Remove from the heat; stir in the rice, capers, oregano, saffron and bay leaf. Transfer to the casserole. Cover and bake 25 minutes; stir in the peas and roasted peppers. Cover and bake until the liquid is absorbed, about 15 minutes longer; discard the bay leaf before serving.

**Per serving**: 333 Calories, 6 g Total Fat, 1 g Saturated Fat, 49 mg Cholesterol, 635 mg Sodium, 43 g Total Carbohydrate, 6 g Dietary Fiber, 26 g Protein, 94 mg Calcium. **POINTS** per serving: 6.

# Chicken with Rice and Tomatoes

*The easiest way to cut up sun-dried tomatoes? Use your kitchen scissors.*

MAKES 4 SERVINGS

2 teaspoons olive oil

1½ pounds chicken parts, skinned

½ teaspoon dried oregano

¼ teaspoon salt

¼ teaspoon freshly ground pepper

⅔ cup brown rice

1 celery stalk, chopped

6 scallions, sliced

4 garlic cloves, minced

1 cup mixed vegetable juice

10 sun-dried tomato halves (not oil-packed)

½ cup canned chickpeas, rinsed and drained

1. In a large nonstick skillet, heat the oil. Add the chicken and sprinkle with the oregano, salt and pepper; cook, turning frequently, until browned, 8–10 minutes. Transfer to a plate.

2. In the skillet, combine the rice, celery, scallions and garlic; cook, stirring frequently, 2 minutes. Stir in the vegetable juice, tomatoes and 2 tablespoons water; bring to a boil. Reduce the heat; return the chicken to the skillet and simmer, covered, until the liquid is absorbed, 40–45 minutes. Stir in the chickpeas; cook until heated through, about 2 minutes.

**Per serving:** 309 Calories, 5 g Total Fat, 1 g Saturated Fat, 49 mg Cholesterol, 439 mg Sodium, 40 g Total Carbohydrate, 4 g Dietary Fiber, 26 g Protein, 69 mg Calcium. **POINTS** per serving: 6.

# Tandoori-Dijon Chicken

*Tandoori refers to a cooking method used throughout India in which food is cooked quickly in a special oven (a tandoor) at more than 500° F.*

MAKES 4 SERVINGS

¼ cup + 2 tablespoons plain nonfat yogurt

1 tablespoon grated peeled gingerroot

1 tablespoon red-wine vinegar

1 tablespoon Dijon mustard

½ teaspoon ground cumin

¼ teaspoon cinnamon

⅛ teaspoon cayenne pepper

1½ pounds chicken parts, skinned

1. To prepare the marinade, in a gallon-size sealable plastic bag, combine the yogurt, gingerroot, vinegar, mustard, cumin, cinnamon and cayenne; add the chicken. Seal the bag, squeezing out the air; turn to coat the chicken. Refrigerate, turning the bag occasionally, at least 2 hours or overnight. Drain and discard the marinade.

2. Spray the broiler rack with nonstick cooking spray; preheat the broiler. Broil the chicken 6–8" from the heat, turning occasionally, until cooked through, 15–20 minutes.

**Per serving:** 115 Calories, 3 g Total Fat, 1 g Saturated Fat, 49 mg Cholesterol, 171 mg Sodium, 3 g Total Carbohydrate, 0 g Dietary Fiber, 19 g Protein, 55 mg Calcium. **POINTS** per serving: 3.

## Got Leftovers?

**This dish is so tasty cold that you may just want to make a double batch and save the rest to slice into sandwiches or toss with cooked vegetables into a sweet-and-sour pasta salad.**

# Chicken with Olives and Dates

*This Middle Eastern–inspired dish combines warm spices and fruit with poultry; the olives add another rich note.*

MAKES 4 SERVINGS

1 tablespoon olive oil

2 garlic cloves, crushed

1 teaspoon ground ginger

1 teaspoon ground cumin

½ teaspoon paprika

¼ teaspoon turmeric

¼ teaspoon cinnamon

¼ teaspoon salt

1 pound skinless boneless chicken drumsticks

¼ cup low-sodium chicken broth

¼ cup dried apricot halves, chopped

2 pitted dates, coarsely chopped

10 small kalamata olives, pitted and chopped

1 tablespoon grated lemon zest

1. To prepare the marinade, in a gallon-size sealable plastic bag, combine the oil, garlic, ginger, cumin, paprika, turmeric, cinnamon and salt; add the chicken. Seal the bag, squeezing out the air; turn to coat the chicken. Refrigerate, turning once, 1 hour. Drain and discard the marinade.

2. Spray a large nonstick skillet sprayed with nonstick cooking spray; heat. Add the chicken and broth; cook, covered, 15 minutes. Turn the chicken over; sprinkle with the apricots, dates, olives, lemon zest and 1 tablespoon water. Cook, covered, checking occasionally, until the chicken is cooked through, about 15 minutes longer. If the chicken begins to stick to the skillet, add 1–2 tablespoons more water.

**Per serving:** 202 Calories, 8 g Total Fat, 2 g Saturated Fat, 82 mg Cholesterol, 296 mg Sodium, 9 g Total Carbohydrate, 1 g Dietary Fiber, 23 g Protein, 35 mg Calcium. **POINTS** per serving: 5.

# Chicken and Artichoke Packets

*Present these savory packets in their foil wrappers and let each diner slit his or hers open. For a more elegant presentation, use parchment paper instead of foil.*

MAKES 4 SERVINGS

Four 3-ounce skinless boneless chicken thighs

One 10½-ounce box frozen artichoke hearts, thawed

¾ cup canned chickpeas, rinsed and drained

½ cup chopped fennel

1 carrot, shredded

1 tablespoon grated Parmesan cheese

1 tablespoon minced thyme

¼ teaspoon salt

¼ cup Italian dressing

1. Preheat the oven to 350° F; cut four 12" squares of heavy-duty foil.

2. Place the chicken in the center of the foil; top with the artichoke hearts, chickpeas, fennel, carrot, cheese, thyme and salt; drizzle with the dressing. Make a packet by bringing 2 sides of the foil up to meet in the center and folding over the edges; then folding the edges of each end together. Allowing room for the packets to expand, crimp the edges to seal. Place the packets on a large baking sheet. Bake until cooked through, 20–30 minutes. To serve, carefully cut a cross in center of each packet to release steam.

**Per serving:** 310 Calories, 13 g Total Fat, 2 g Saturated Fat, 72 mg Cholesterol, 410 mg Sodium, 26 g Total Carbohydrate, 6 g Dietary Fiber, 25 g Protein, 87 mg Calcium. *POINTS* per serving: 6.

## Tip

Always take care when opening any dish cooked *en papillote*—in parchment—since steam escapes when you cut it open.

# Warm Chicken Salad with Roasted Pepper Dressing

*For another option, substitute turkey for the chicken and mesclun for the greens.*

MAKES 4 SERVINGS

¾ pound skinless boneless chicken breasts, pounded ¼" thick

3 garlic cloves, crushed

2 red bell peppers, seeded and sliced

1 onion, sliced

2 teaspoons olive oil

¼ cup chicken broth

1 teaspoon chopped rosemary

1 tablespoon red-wine vinegar

¼ teaspoon freshly ground pepper

⅛ teaspoon salt

3 cups torn red leaf lettuce

3 cups torn arugula leaves

1. Place the chicken on a plate; rub with one-third of the garlic. Refrigerate, covered, at least 1 hour.

2. Preheat the oven to 400° F. In a 2-quart casserole, combine the bell peppers, onion, the remaining garlic and the oil. Roast 25 minutes; stir in the broth, rosemary and ¼ cup water. Cover with foil and roast until tender, about 20 minutes longer. Cool slightly, then transfer to a food processor or blender. Add the vinegar and ⅛ teaspoon of the pepper; puree.

3. Spray a medium nonstick skillet with nonstick cooking spray; heat. Sauté the chicken until golden, 4–5 minutes; sprinkle with the salt and the remaining ⅛ teaspoon of pepper. Turn the chicken; sauté until cooked through, about 4 minutes longer. Transfer to cutting board; let stand 5 minutes. Slice the chicken on the diagonal.

4. On a platter, combine the lettuce and arugula; top with the chicken, then drizzle with the dressing.

**Per serving:** 137 Calories, 4 g Total Fat, 1 g Saturated Fat, 41 mg Cholesterol, 193 mg Sodium, 8 g Total Carbohydrate, 2 g Dietary Fiber, 18 g Protein, 81 mg Calcium. *POINTS* per serving: 3.

## Got Leftovers?

**Refrigerate any extra dressing in a small glass jar. Drizzle it over leftover rice and veggies for a savory lunch.**

# Provençal Chicken Strips

*If you keep your pantry well-stocked, this elegant yet easy dish can become a quick weeknight dinner. If you pick up chicken tenders on your way home from work, you won't even have to cut up the chicken breasts.*

MAKES 4 SERVINGS

2 teaspoons olive oil

¾ pound skinless boneless chicken breasts, cut into 2" strips

6 scallions, sliced

2 garlic cloves, minced

6–8 plum tomatoes, chopped

2 tablespoons chopped parsley

1 tablespoon capers, rinsed and drained

1 teaspoon red-wine vinegar

¼ teaspoon dried rosemary leaves, crumbled

3 cups hot cooked wide noodles

1. In a large nonstick skillet, heat the oil. Sauté the chicken, stirring constantly, 4 minutes. Add the scallions and garlic; cook, stirring frequently, until the chicken is cooked through, 2–4 minutes.

2. Stir in the tomatoes, parsley, capers, vinegar and rosemary. Reduce the heat and simmer until the liquid evaporates, about 10 minutes. Serve the chicken mixture over the noodles.

**Per serving**: 288 Calories, 5 g Total Fat, 1 g Saturated Fat, 81 mg Cholesterol, 123 mg Sodium, 36 g Total Carbohydrate, 5 g Dietary Fiber, 23 g Protein, 51 mg Calcium. **POINTS** per serving: 5.

# Orange-Flavored Fajitas

*Look for the tortillas at your supermarket with flavors like spinach, red pepper and tomato.*

MAKES 4 SERVINGS

¾ cup plain nonfat yogurt

2 tablespoons orange juice

1 tablespoon grated orange zest

2 teaspoons canola oil

1 teaspoon ground cumin

¼ teaspoon cayenne pepper

¾ pound skinless boneless chicken breasts, cut into strips

1 red bell pepper, seeded and cut into strips

6 scallions, sliced

2 garlic cloves, minced

Four 6" flour tortillas

¼ cup salsa

1. In a medium bowl, combine the yogurt, orange juice and orange zest. In a large nonstick skillet, heat the oil. Sauté the cumin and cayenne, stirring constantly, 1 minute. Add the chicken, bell pepper, scallions and garlic; sauté until the chicken is cooked through, 6–8 minutes. Add to the yogurt mixture; toss to coat.

2. Heat the tortillas according to package directions. Spoon 1 tablespoon of salsa across each tortilla; top with the chicken mixture, then roll up to enclose filling.

**Per serving**: 215 Calories, 5 g Total Fat, 1 g Saturated Fat, 42 mg Cholesterol, 270 mg Sodium, 21 g Total Carbohydrate, 2 g Dietary Fiber, 21 g Protein, 148 mg Calcium. **POINTS** per serving: 4.

# Chicken with Broccoli and Oranges

*This Chinese restaurant favorite begs to be served on plain white rice with chopsticks.*

MAKES 4 SERVINGS

4 teaspoons vegetable oil

One 2" piece gingerroot, peeled and julienned

1 pound skinless boneless chicken breasts, cut crosswise into ½" strips

2 cups broccoli florets

½ cup low-sodium chicken broth

¼ cup orange juice

3 tablespoons reduced-sodium soy sauce

1 teaspoon cornstarch, dissolved in 1 tablespoon water

1 orange, peeled and sectioned

1. In a medium nonstick skillet, heat the oil. Sauté the gingerroot until golden brown, 2–3 minutes. With a slotted spoon, transfer the gingerroot to a small plate.

2. In the skillet, sauté the chicken until cooked through, about 5 minutes. Transfer to another plate. In the skillet, combine the broccoli and ¼ cup water, stirring to scrape up the browned bits from the bottom of the pan; cook, covered, until tender-crisp, 3–4 minutes. Return the chicken to the skillet; stir in the broth, orange juice and soy sauce. Add the dissolved cornstarch; cook, stirring frequently, until the mixture boils and thickens slightly. Add the orange; heat through. Serve, garnished with the gingerroot.

**Per serving:** 221 Calories, 6 g Total Fat, 1 g Saturated Fat, 66 mg Cholesterol, 389 mg Sodium, 12 g Total Carbohydrate, 3 g Dietary Fiber, 29 g Protein, 49 mg Calcium. *POINTS* per serving: 4.

## Tip

To section an orange, slice a small piece off the top and bottom ends of the fruit. Using a sharp paring knife, slice off the rind and pith by sliding the edge from top to bottom. Slip the blade between the membrane and section and slice to the center, separating one side of the section. Slide the blade from the center out along the membrane to free each section.

# Polenta with Broccoli Rabe and Chicken

*If you have never tasted broccoli rabe (pronounced rah-BAY), you are in for a treat. It is an intensely flavored green, delicious in soups, with pasta, sautéed with garlic or as served here, with golden polenta that sets off its deep green color. To clean broccoli rabe, simply rinse in cold water, shake and cut off the ends of the stalks.*

MAKES 4 SERVINGS

1 bunch broccoli rabe, cleaned and chopped

1 teaspoon olive oil

½ pound skinless boneless chicken breast, cut into 4 equal pieces

1 onion, thinly sliced

1 large garlic clove, sliced

½ cup low-sodium chicken broth

¼ teaspoon crushed red pepper flakes

¾ cup instant polenta or cornmeal

3 tablespoons grated Parmesan cheese

1. In a large pot, bring 3 quarts of water to a boil. Add the broccoli rabe; reduce the heat and simmer 5 minutes. Drain and rinse with cold water; set aside.

2. In a medium nonstick skillet, heat the oil. Sauté the chicken until browned, about 2 minutes on each side. Transfer to a plate.

3. In the skillet, sauté the onion until golden, about 8 minutes. Add the garlic; cook, stirring, 1 minute longer. Add the broth, pepper flakes, the broccoli rabe and the chicken. Reduce the heat and simmer, covered, until chicken is cooked through, about 5 minutes.

4. Meanwhile, in a medium nonstick saucepan, bring 2¼ cups water to a boil. Stir in the polenta in a thin, steady stream; reduce the heat and cook, stirring constantly, 5 minutes. Remove from the heat and stir in the cheese; transfer into a serving dish. With a large spoon, smooth into an oval with a depression in middle. Spoon the chicken mixture over the polenta.

**Per serving**: 320 Calories, 4 g Total Fat, 1 g Saturated Fat, 36 mg Cholesterol, 188 mg Sodium, 48 g Total Carbohydrate, 8 g Dietary Fiber, 23 g Protein, 158 mg Calcium. *POINTS* per serving: 5.

## Tip

Polenta, a mush made from cornmeal, is available in regular or instant (quick-cooking) versions in gourmet grocery stores and some supermarkets.

# Chicken Pita Pizzas

*Try pocketless pitas instead of the regular pitas for a thicker crust. Don't forget to add the extra* **POINTS**, *though.*

MAKES 4 SERVINGS

8 sun-dried tomato halves (not oil-packed)

1 cup boiling water

4 small whole-wheat pitas

¼ cup low-sodium canned tomato sauce

1½ cups shredded cooked chicken breast

½ cup coarsely chopped arugula or watercress

20 small pitted black olives, thinly sliced

⅓ cup shredded part-skim mozzarella cheese

1. Preheat the oven to 425° F; spray a large baking sheet with nonstick cooking spray.

2. In a small bowl, combine the tomatoes and boiling water; let stand about 2 minutes. Drain and cut into thin strips.

3. Place the pitas on the baking sheet; spread with the tomato sauce, then divide the chicken, arugula, olives, tomato strips and cheese evenly over each. Bake until golden and the cheese melts, 10–12 minutes.

**Per serving**: 223 Calories, 8 g Total Fat, 2 g Saturated Fat, 44 mg Cholesterol, 372 mg Sodium, 22 g Total Carbohydrate, 4 g Dietary Fiber, 19 g Protein, 103 mg Calcium. **POINTS** per serving: 4.

## Storing Chicken

*It's always a good idea to have chicken on hand, and chicken is so versatile that it's tempting to stock up. Use the chart below as a guide to refrigerating and storing chicken. Before freezing raw chicken, remove the store's plastic wrapper, and rinse and dry. To freeze, wrap in foil, heavy-duty plastic wrap or sealable plastic freezer bags. Press the air out of the wrapper before sealing, and label with date.*

| FRESH RAW CHICKEN | REFRIGERATOR | FREEZER |
| --- | --- | --- |
| *Whole Chicken* | *1–2 days* | *1 year* |
| *Chicken Parts* | *1–2 days* | *9 months* |
| *Giblets* | *1–2 days* | *3–4 months* |
| *Ground Chicken* | *1–2 days* | *3–4 months* |
| *Cooked Chicken Leftovers* | *Refrigerator* | *Freezer* |
| *Whole Roasted Chicken* | *3–4 days* | *4 months* |
| *Cooked Chicken Dishes* | *3–4 days* | *4 months* |
| *Chicken Parts (plain)* | *3–4 days* | *4 months* |
| *Chicken Nuggets or Patties* | *1–2 days* | *1–3 months* |

# Dijon Chicken with Corn Salsa

*Serve this colorful salsa with a favorite chicken or fish recipe. It goes especially well with basic broiled or grilled dishes.*

MAKES 4 SERVINGS

1 cup thawed frozen corn kernels

1 green bell pepper, seeded and chopped

2 plum tomatoes, chopped

½ cucumber, seeded and chopped

2 tablespoons chopped cilantro

1 tablespoon chopped parsley

1 tablespoon orange juice

1 tablespoon red-wine vinegar

1 tablespoon canned chopped green chiles

½ teaspoon ground cumin

¼ teaspoon salt

¼ teaspoon chili powder

¾ pound skinless boneless chicken breasts, cut into 2" strips

2 tablespoons Dijon mustard

8 romaine lettuce leaves

1. To prepare the salsa, in a medium bowl, combine the corn, bell pepper, tomatoes, cucumber, cilantro, parsley, orange juice, vinegar, chiles, cumin, salt and chili powder.

2. Heat an indoor ridged grill sprayed with nonstick cooking spray until very hot, or spray the broiler rack with nonstick cooking spray and preheat the broiler.

3. Brush the chicken with the mustard; place on the grill or broiler rack. Grill or broil 4" from the heat until cooked through, 3–4 minutes on each side. Line 4 plates with the lettuce; top with the salsa, then the chicken.

**Per serving:** 164 Calories, 2 g Total Fat, 0 g Saturated Fat, 49 mg Cholesterol, 577 mg Sodium, 15 g Total Carbohydrate, 2 g Dietary Fiber, 22 g Protein, 28 mg Calcium. *POINTS* per serving: 3.

# Easy Chicken with Artichoke Salad

*Be sure to use frozen artichoke hearts, not jarred. The jarred variety is usually packed in a vinaigrette laden with fat.*

MAKES 4 SERVINGS

One 10½-ounce box frozen artichoke hearts, thawed and coarsely chopped

1 cup chopped roasted red pepper

¼ cup chopped basil

1 tablespoon grated lemon zest

2 tablespoons fresh lemon juice

¼ teaspoon salt

¼ teaspoon freshly ground pepper

3 tablespoons all-purpose flour

2 tablespoons yellow cornmeal

⅛ teaspoon ground white pepper

¾ pound skinless boneless chicken breasts, thinly sliced

2 teaspoons olive oil

1. In a medium bowl, combine the artichokes, roasted pepper, basil, lemon zest, lemon juice, salt and pepper.

2. On a sheet of wax paper, combine the flour, cornmeal and white pepper. Dredge the chicken in the flour mixture, coating all sides.

3. In a large nonstick skillet, heat the oil. Sauté the chicken until cooked through, 3–4 minutes on each side. Serve, with the salad on the side.

**Per serving**: 199 Calories, 4 g Total Fat, 1 g Saturated Fat, 49 mg Cholesterol, 232 mg Sodium, 18 g Total Carbohydrate, 4 g Dietary Fiber, 23 g Protein, 58 mg Calcium. **POINTS** per serving: 4.

# Classic Chicken Salad

*Serve this recipe in a classic way: on whole wheat toast or on top of a bed of greens.*

MAKES 4 SERVINGS

¾ cup plain nonfat yogurt

3 tablespoons reduced-calorie mayonnaise

1 tablespoon cider vinegar

2 teaspoons Dijon mustard

¼ teaspoon celery seeds

¼ teaspoon freshly ground pepper

2½ cups cubed cooked chicken breast

2 cups green beans, lightly steamed

2 celery stalks, chopped

2 tablespoons grated onion

1. In a small bowl, combine the yogurt, mayonnaise, vinegar, mustard, celery seeds and pepper.

2. In a medium bowl, combine the chicken, beans, celery and onion. Add the yogurt mixture; toss to coat. Refrigerate, covered, at least 1 hour before serving.

**Per serving**: 214 Calories, 8 g Total Fat, 2 g Saturated Fat, 67 mg Cholesterol, 252 mg Sodium, 10 g Total Carbohydrate, 2 g Dietary Fiber, 24 g Protein, 132 mg Calcium. **POINTS** per serving: 5.

# Oriental Chicken Salad

Although reduced-fat peanut butter is lower in fat, it can have at least as many calories as regular peanut butter and taste too sweet. Use regular peanut butter in this recipe—you only need a little for lots of peanut taste!

MAKES 4 SERVINGS

¾ cup plain nonfat yogurt

1 tablespoon smooth peanut butter

1 tablespoon rice-wine vinegar

1 teaspoon Asian sesame oil

1 garlic clove, crushed

¼ teaspoon ground coriander

2 cups cubed cooked chicken breast

1½ cups cooked cellophane noodles

6 scallions, cut into 1" lengths

1 red bell pepper, thinly sliced

One 8-ounce can water chestnuts, drained

2 cups trimmed watercress or mixed salad greens

4 teaspoons sesame seeds, toasted

In a medium bowl, combine the yogurt, peanut butter, vinegar, oil, garlic and coriander. Add the chicken, cellophane noodles, scallions, bell pepper and water chestnuts; toss to coat. Refrigerate, covered, at least 1 hour. Serve over the watercress, sprinkled with the sesame seeds.

**Per serving**: 279 Calories, 9 g Total Fat, 2 g Saturated Fat, 51 mg Cholesterol, 118 mg Sodium, 28 g Total Carbohydrate, 2 g Dietary Fiber, 22 g Protein, 147 mg Calcium. **POINTS** per serving: 6.

## Easy Poaching

*Poaching is a delicious way to cook chicken. The liquid in which you poach the chicken can add wonderful flavor, and a poached chicken breast is lovely with a sauce, as in Creole Poached Chicken Breasts (page 107).*

*Poaching is also an easy and fast way to cook chicken for recipes that require it, such as Oriental Chicken Salad (left).*

- *Place a boneless chicken breast in a deep skillet and add water or broth just to cover. Add a dash of salt, pepper and onion powder.*

- *Place wax paper on top of the chicken to hold in steam. Bring to a simmer and cook until the thickest part of the meat becomes white and opaque, 4–8 minutes. (You can reserve the liquid for soup stock.)*

- *Drain the meat; cool slightly before refrigerating.*

# Moo Shu Chicken

*Everyone's take-out favorite! Make the pancakes ahead of time; well wrapped in plastic wrap, they freeze beautifully. In a pinch, use flour tortillas in place of the pancakes.*

MAKES 4 SERVINGS

4 tablespoons reduced-sodium soy sauce

4 garlic cloves, minced

¾ pound skinless boneless chicken breasts, cut into 2" strips

1 teaspoon ground ginger

2 cups shredded napa cabbage

2 cups shredded bok choy (Chinese cabbage)

1 carrot, shredded

½ cup canned straw mushrooms, rinsed, drained and thinly sliced

½ cup canned bamboo shoots, rinsed, drained and thinly sliced

¼ teaspoon hot chili oil

8 Whole-Wheat Moo Shu Pancakes (recipe follows)

4 teaspoons hoisin sauce

1. To prepare the marinade, in a gallon-size sealable plastic bag, combine 2 tablespoons of the soy sauce and half of the garlic; add the chicken. Seal the bag, squeezing out the air; turn to coat the chicken. Refrigerate, turning the bag occasionally, 1 hour. Drain and discard the marinade.

2. In a small bowl, combine the remaining 2 tablespoons of soy sauce and the remaining garlic with the ginger; set aside.

3. Spray a large nonstick skillet with nonstick cooking spray; heat. Sauté the chicken until cooked through, 2–3 minutes. Transfer to a plate. In the skillet, combine the cabbage, bok choy,

carrot, mushrooms and bamboo shoots; cook, stirring frequently, until the cabbage and bok choy begin to wilt, 4–5 minutes. Add the chicken, the soy sauce mixture and the hot chili oil; toss to combine.

4. To serve, spread the pancakes with the hoisin sauce; top with the chicken mixture and roll up.

**Per serving**: 503 Calories, 3 g Total Fat, 1 g Saturated Fat, 41 mg Cholesterol, 726 mg Sodium, 88 g Total Carbohydrate, 9 g Dietary Fiber, 31 g Protein, 116 mg Calcium. **POINTS** per serving: 9.

### *Whole-Wheat Moo Shu Pancakes*

MAKES 4 SERVINGS

½ cup whole-wheat flour

½ cup all-purpose flour

1. In a medium bowl, combine both kinds of flours. Add 5 tablespoons water; with a wooden spoon, stir until a smooth dough forms, 3–4 minutes. If the dough is dry, add a few more drops of water. Knead the dough in the bowl until it is soft and elastic, about 3 minutes. Divide the dough into 8 pieces.

2. On a lightly floured work surface, roll each piece of dough into a 6" circle, about ⅛" thick. Layer between sheets of wax paper; cover with plastic wrap and refrigerate until ready to use, up to 2 hours. (If the pancakes shrink slightly, roll them out again just prior to cooking.)

3. Heat a medium nonstick skillet. One at a time, cook the pancakes, turning every 10 seconds, until light brown spots appear on both sides, 30–40 seconds. Wrap in foil and keep warm until ready to use.

**Per serving**: 121 Calories, 0 g Total Fat, 0 g Saturated Fat, 0 mg Cholesterol, 1 mg Sodium, 26 g Total Carbohydrate, 3 g Dietary Fiber, 4 g Protein, 8 mg Calcium. **POINTS** per serving: 2.

# Chicken "Fried" Rice

*When purchasing ground chicken, be sure it is skinless (since the skin is where most of the fat is). If it doesn't indicate that it is skinless on the package, ask the butcher to grind some fresh while you wait.*

MAKES 4 SERVINGS

½ pound ground skinless chicken

¼ cup low-sodium chicken broth

1 tablespoon reduced-sodium teriyaki sauce

½ teaspoon ground coriander

¼ teaspoon ground ginger

2 teaspoons peanut oil

2 eggs, lightly beaten

2 carrots, shredded

1 green bell pepper, seeded and chopped

6 scallions, sliced

1½ cups cold cooked brown rice

½ cup thawed frozen green peas

1. Spray a large nonstick skillet or wok with nonstick cooking spray; heat. Sauté the chicken until browned, 4–5 minutes. Transfer to a medium bowl; stir in the broth, teriyaki sauce, coriander and ginger.

2. In the skillet, heat 1 teaspoon of the oil. Stir-fry the eggs until set but still moist. Transfer to the bowl.

3. Heat the remaining teaspoon of oil; sauté the carrots, bell pepper and scallions until tender, about 5 minutes. Stir in the rice and peas; stir-fry until the rice begins to brown. Add the chicken mixture; cook until heated through, about 5 minutes.

**Per serving**: 272 Calories, 11 g Total Fat, 3 g Saturated Fat, 153 mg Cholesterol, 194 mg Sodium, 27 g Total Carbohydrate, 4 g Dietary Fiber, 17 g Protein, 68 mg Calcium. *POINTS* per serving: 6.

## How We Did It

**Recipes for fried rice vary in the amount of oil they call for; some specify as much as ¼ cup! Using chicken instead of high-fat ham or sausage also helps steer this classic out of the fat-trap territory.**

# Chicken Pot Stickers

*Wonton skins are available fresh or frozen in Asian specialty stores and some supermarkets. Fresh wonton skins will keep for about five days wrapped in plastic wrap and stored in the refrigerator.*

MAKES 4 SERVINGS

2 tablespoons chili sauce

1 tablespoon minced cilantro

1 tablespoon reduced-sodium teriyaki sauce

1 teaspoon rice-wine vinegar

½ teaspoon grated peeled gingerroot

Pinch cayenne pepper

½ pound ground skinless chicken breast

½ cup finely shredded napa cabbage

1 scallion, minced

2 teaspoons reduced-sodium soy sauce

1 teaspoon cornstarch, dissolved in 2 teaspoons water

¼ teaspoon mustard powder

⅛ teaspoon freshly ground pepper

20 wonton skins (3" squares)

4 teaspoons peanut oil

1 cup low-sodium chicken broth

1 teaspoon all-purpose flour

1 tablespoon sesame seeds, toasted

1. To prepare the sauce, in a small bowl, combine the chili sauce, cilantro, teriyaki sauce, vinegar, gingerroot and cayenne.

2. To prepare the filling, in a medium bowl, combine the chicken, cabbage, scallion, soy sauce, dissolved cornstarch, mustard and pepper.

3. Cover the wontons with plastic wrap; have a small bowl of water near your work area. Working with one wonton at a time, spoon 2 teaspoons of the filling into the center of each wonton. Moisten the edges of the wonton with water; fold diagonally to form a triangle. Seal the edges, pressing out any air. Repeat with the remaining wontons and filling.

4. In a large nonstick skillet, heat the oil until it's almost smoking. Place the dumplings in a circle in the skillet; reduce the heat slightly and cook until the bottoms are golden, 5–7 minutes.

5. Meanwhile, in a small saucepan, bring the broth to a boil. Remove from the heat; sprinkle in the flour and stir until the flour is dissolved. Pour the broth over the dumplings; cook, partially covered, until the liquid evaporates. Uncover and cook until the bottoms are crisp. Carefully loosen the dumplings with a spatula. Serve, sprinkled with the sesame seeds, with the sauce on the side.

**Per serving**: 262 Calories, 7 g Total Fat, 1 g Saturated Fat, 36 mg Cholesterol, 570 mg Sodium, 29 g Total Carbohydrate, 0 g Dietary Fiber, 19 g Protein, 60 mg Calcium. *POINTS* per serving: 6.

# Easy Enchiladas

*Although we like the combination of black beans and chickpeas, pinto beans and black beans would be tasty, too.*

MAKES 4 SERVINGS

2 teaspoons canola oil

½ pound hot Italian turkey sausage, casings removed

1 red bell pepper, seeded and chopped

6 scallions, sliced

1 teaspoon chili powder

½ teaspoon ground cumin

1 cup canned stewed tomatoes

¾ cup canned black beans, rinsed and drained

¾ cup canned chickpeas, rinsed and drained

⅛ teaspoon freshly ground white pepper

Four 6" flour tortillas

½ cup shredded reduced-fat Monterey Jack cheese

1. Preheat the oven to 350° F; spray a 2-quart casserole with nonstick cooking spray. In a large nonstick skillet, heat the oil. Sauté the sausage, bell pepper and scallions, stirring frequently to break up the sausage, until browned, 6–8 minutes. Add the chili powder and cumin; cook, stirring, 1 minute. Stir in the tomatoes, beans, chickpeas and pepper. Reduce the heat and simmer 5 minutes.

2. Place the tortillas on a work surface; spoon the turkey mixture down the center of the tortillas, then roll them into cylinders. Place, seam-side down, in the baking dish; sprinkle with the cheese. Bake until heated through and the cheese is melted, 30–35 minutes. Let stand 10 minutes before serving.

**Per serving**: 404 Calories, 14 g Total Fat, 3 Saturated Fat, 49 mg Cholesterol, 1,265 mg Sodium, 48 g Total Carbohydrate, 7 g Dietary Fiber, 23 g Protein, 140 mg Calcium. *POINTS* per serving: 8.

## Got Leftovers?

Spoon any leftover sausage mixture into a pita for lunch or a casual supper; a green salad rounds out the meal.

# Sancocho

*This thick, hearty stew (pronounced sahn-KOH-choh), is served throughout Central and South America. It makes a great one-dish supper.*

MAKES 4 SERVINGS

1 teaspoon corn oil

¼ pound skinless boneless chicken breast, diced

¼ pound skinless boneless chicken thigh, diced

2 onions, chopped

1 celery stalk, chopped

½ red bell pepper, seeded and diced

1 jalapeño pepper, seeded, deveined and minced (wear gloves to prevent irritation)

2 teaspoons ground cumin

3 cups low-sodium chicken broth

4 plum tomatoes, chopped

1 cup canned pumpkin puree

1 small sweet potato, peeled and diced

½ cup thawed frozen corn kernels

2 tablespoons minced cilantro or parsley

2 cups cooked long-grain rice

1. In a medium nonstick saucepan, heat the oil. Sauté the chicken until lightly browned, 4–5 minutes. Transfer to a plate.

2. In the skillet, sauté the onions until golden, 5–7 minutes. Add the celery, bell pepper, jalapeño and cumin; cook, stirring, 3 minutes. Stir in the broth, tomatoes, pumpkin and sweet potato; bring to a boil. Reduce the heat and simmer, covered, until the potato is tender, about 10 minutes. Add the chicken and the corn; simmer 10 minutes longer. Sprinkle with the cilantro and serve with the rice.

**Per serving:** 305 Calories, 4 g Total Fat, 1 g Saturated Fat, 30 mg Cholesterol, 102 mg Sodium, 50 g Total Carbohydrate, 3 g Dietary Fiber, 16 g Protein, 58 mg Calcium. **POINTS** per serving: 6.

# Turkey with Feta-Tomato Sauce

*Low-fat and fat-free feta are now available in many supermarket dairy cases. Because feta is "pickled" in brine, it should be rinsed to cut down on some of the saltiness.*

MAKES 4 SERVINGS

4 sun-dried tomato halves (not oil-packed)

½ cup boiling water

⅓ cup crumbled plain or peppercorn-flavored feta cheese

1 scallion, minced

2 garlic cloves, minced

½ teaspoon dried basil leaves

¼ teaspoon dried oregano leaves

Four 3-ounce turkey cutlets

1. Spray the broiler rack with nonstick cooking spray; preheat the broiler. In a small bowl, combine the tomatoes and boiling water; let stand 2 minutes. Drain and finely chop; return the tomatoes to the bowl. Stir in the cheese, scallion, garlic, basil and oregano.

2. Broil the turkey 4" from the heat 4 minutes; turn over and top with the cheese mixture. Broil until cooked through and cheese begins to melt, 4–5 minutes longer.

**Per serving:** 136 Calories, 3 g Total Fat, 2 g Saturated Fat, 62 mg Cholesterol, 164 mg Sodium, 3 g Total Carbohydrate, 1 g Dietary Fiber, 23 g Protein, 73 mg Calcium. **POINTS** per serving: 3.

# Tamale Casserole

*Tamales are a traditional Mexican dish that consists of various fillings, like chopped meat and veggies. They are coated with masa dough and wrapped in a corn husk. The package is tied and steamed until the dough is cooked through; it's eaten out of hand by pulling back the corn husk. We've turned it into an easy casserole.*

MAKES 4 SERVINGS

4 teaspoons canola oil

1 green bell pepper, seeded and chopped

2 red onions, chopped

1 jalapeño pepper, seeded, deveined and minced (wear gloves to prevent irritation)

1 garlic clove, minced

½ pound ground skinless turkey breast

1 cup no-salt-added tomato sauce

1 cup frozen corn kernels

¾ teaspoon salt

½–1 teaspoon hot Mexican chili powder

⅔ cup stone ground yellow cornmeal

⅓ cup shredded reduced-fat Monterey Jack cheese

1. In a large nonstick skillet, heat the oil. Sauté the bell pepper, onions, jalapeño and garlic until softened, about 5 minutes. Add the turkey and cook, breaking apart with a wooden spoon, until browned, 5–8 minutes. Stir in the tomato sauce, corn, ½ teaspoon of the salt and the chili powder; bring to a boil. Reduce the heat and simmer, covered, stirring once or twice, until the sauce thickens slightly, about 15 minutes. Transfer to an 8" square baking dish.

2. Preheat the oven to 350° F. In a medium saucepan, bring 1 cup water and remaining ¼ teaspoon salt to a boil. In a medium bowl, whisk the cornmeal into 1 cup water. Slowly pour the cornmeal into the boiling water in a thin steady stream, stirring constantly with a wooden spoon until the mixture comes back to a boil. Reduce the heat and cook, stirring constantly, until mixture thickens and begins to form large bubbles, about 5 minutes. Spread over the turkey so that it is completely covered. Bake 25 minutes, then sprinkle with the cheese and bake until the cheese melts, about 5 minutes longer. Let stand 10 minutes before serving.

**Per serving:** 293 Calories, 8 g Total Fat, 2 g Saturated Fat, 43 mg Cholesterol, 531 mg Sodium, 35 g Total Carbohydrate, 4 g Dietary Fiber, 22 g Protein, 122 mg Calcium. **POINTS** per serving: 6.

# Mushroom-Stuffed Turkey Breast

*Suitable for your best company, this beautiful roulade is filled with sautéed vegetables and carves into attractive pinwheel slices. Serve it surrounded with a mélange of roasted chestnuts, pearl onions and steamed Brussels sprouts.*

MAKES 12 SERVINGS

2 tablespoons stick margarine

2 red onions, chopped

2 cups sliced mushrooms

2 carrots, shredded

One 10-ounce box frozen chopped spinach, thawed and squeezed dry

2 tablespoons chopped parsley

1 tablespoon grated Parmesan cheese

½ teaspoon dried basil leaves

1 slice reduced-calorie white bread, finely chopped

1 cup low-sodium chicken broth

1 tablespoon grated lemon zest

One 3-pound skinless boneless turkey breast

1. In a large nonstick skillet, melt the margarine. Sauté the onions 4 minutes. Add the mushrooms and carrots; sauté until the vegetables are tender, 4–5 minutes. Stir in the spinach, parsley, cheese and basil; cook 2 minutes. Remove from the heat; stir in the bread, 2 tablespoons of the broth and the lemon zest.

2. Preheat the oven to 325° F; spray a 9 × 13" baking dish with nonstick cooking spray. Place the turkey between two sheets of plastic wrap; with a meat mallet or rolling pin, pound to an even thickness. Remove the top sheet of plastic wrap from the turkey; spread the mushroom mixture over the turkey breast, leaving a 2½" border on all sides. Starting with the short side, roll up the turkey breast jelly-roll style; tie at 2" intervals with kitchen string. Place the roll, seam-side down, in the baking dish, pour the remaining broth over the turkey and cover loosely with foil. Bake, basting frequently with the pan juices, until an instant-read thermometer inserted in the center of the roll reaches 180° F, 1–1½ hours. Transfer the turkey to cutting board; let stand 10 minutes before removing the string and slicing.

**Per serving:** 162 Calories, 3 g Total Fat, 1 g Saturated Fat, 71 mg Cholesterol, 119 mg Sodium, 5 g Total Carbohydrate, 2 g Dietary Fiber, 28 g Protein, 68 mg Calcium. **POINTS** per serving: 3.

# Toasted Almond Turkey Cutlets

*Almonds are especially nice in this dish, but you may also use walnuts or pecans. One caution: Both walnuts and pecans are higher in fat than almonds.*

MAKES 4 SERVINGS

Four 3-ounce turkey cutlets

1 tablespoon grated Parmesan cheese

¼ teaspoon freshly ground pepper

2 teaspoons olive oil

2 tablespoons sliced almonds

½ cup low-sodium chicken broth

2 tablespoons dry white wine

2 garlic cloves, crushed

2 tablespoons chopped basil

1 teaspoon stick margarine

1 teaspoon fresh lemon juice

1. On a sheet of wax paper, sprinkle the turkey on both sides with the cheese and pepper. In a large nonstick skillet, heat 1 teaspoon of the oil. Sauté the turkey until cooked through, about 4 minutes on each side. Transfer to a platter.

2. In the skillet, heat the remaining teaspoon of oil. Toast the almonds, stirring constantly, until golden, about 1 minute. Transfer to a small bowl.

3. In the skillet, combine the broth, wine, garlic and 2 tablespoons of water; bring to a boil. Boil until reduced by half, about 5 minutes. Remove from the heat; stir in the almonds, basil, margarine and lemon juice. Serve the turkey, topped with the sauce.

**Per serving:** 183 Calories, 8 g Total Fat, 1 g Saturated Fat, 54 mg Cholesterol, 85 mg Sodium, 3 g Total Carbohydrate, 0 g Dietary Fiber, 23 g Protein, 61 mg Calcium. *POINTS* per serving: 4.

# Turkey-Fruit Pilaf

*If you like, substitute mixed dried fruit for the raisins and apricots—dried cranberries, cherries and blueberries make a delicious blend.*

MAKES 4 SERVINGS

2 teaspoons olive oil

¾ pound turkey cutlets, cut into thin strips

2 celery stalks, chopped

6 scallions, sliced

2 garlic cloves, minced

1 teaspoon cinnamon

1 teaspoon packed dark brown sugar

¼ teaspoon ground nutmeg

⅔ cup white rice

1 cup low-sodium chicken broth

½ cup dried apricot halves, coarsely chopped

¼ cup raisins

1 tablespoon sesame seeds, toasted

1. Preheat the oven to 350° F. In a Dutch oven or large ovenproof skillet with a lid, heat the oil. Sauté the turkey until browned, 2–3 minutes on each side. Transfer to a plate.

2. In the skillet, sauté the celery, scallions and garlic until softened, 4–5 minutes. Reduce the heat and stir in the cinnamon, brown sugar and nutmeg; cook, stirring until fragrant, about 1 minute. Add the rice; cook, stirring, until coated, about 1 minute. Add the broth; bring to a boil. Remove from the heat; stir in the turkey. Bake, covered, 40 minutes; stir in the apricots, raisins and sesame seeds. Bake, covered, until the liquid is absorbed and the rice is tender, 10–15 minutes longer.

**Per serving:** 297 Calories, 5 g Total Fat, 1 g Saturated Fat, 44 mg Cholesterol, 83 mg Sodium, 42 g Total Carbohydrate, 3 g Dietary Fiber, 22 g Protein, 87 mg Calcium. *POINTS* per serving: 6.

# Turkey with Sweet Potato–Pear Puree

*A sweet potato puree makes a sensational accompaniment for sage-dusted turkey breasts. When purchasing pear nectar, choose bottled rather than canned to avoid any metallic taste.*

MAKES 4 SERVINGS

2 small sweet potatoes, peeled and cut into chunks

1 pear, peeled, cored and cut into chunks

⅓ cup pear nectar

1 onion, minced

1 teaspoon dried sage leaves, crumbled

¼ teaspoon salt

⅛ teaspoon freshly ground pepper

¾ pound skinless boneless turkey breast, cut into 4 pieces

1 tablespoon reduced-calorie margarine

1. In a medium saucepan, combine the sweet potatoes, pear, nectar and onion with ⅔ cup water; bring to a boil. Reduce the heat and cook, covered, until the potatoes are tender, about 15 minutes. Transfer to a food processor or blender; puree. Return to the saucepan; keep warm.

2. Meanwhile, in a small bowl, combine the sage, salt and pepper; rub over the turkey breast on both sides.

3. Spray a large nonstick skillet with nonstick cooking spray; heat. Add 1½ teaspoons of the margarine; let it melt, turning the skillet to coat evenly. Sauté the turkey breast, two pieces at a time, until browned, 2–3 minutes on each side. Transfer to a plate; keep warm. Repeat with the remaining 1½ teaspoons of margarine and the remaining turkey breast. Serve the puree, topped with a turkey breast.

**Per serving**: 208 Calories, 3 g Total Fat, 0 g Saturated Fat, 53 mg Cholesterol, 219 mg Sodium, 24 g Total Carbohydrate, 3 g Dietary Fiber, 22 g Protein, 33 mg Calcium. **POINTS** per serving: 4.

# Turkey Cutlets with Cranberry Sauce

*Green peppercorns are unripened black peppercorns; they have a softer texture and milder flavor.*

MAKES 4 SERVINGS

Four 3-ounce turkey cutlets

¼ teaspoon salt

¼ teaspoon freshly ground pepper

2 teaspoons canola oil

1 red onion, chopped

1 cup low-calorie cranberry juice cocktail

1 tablespoon packed dark brown sugar

1 tablespoon red-wine vinegar

1 teaspoon green peppercorns

½ teaspoon dried thyme leaves

¼ cup + 2 tablespoons dried cranberries

1 tablespoon cornstarch, dissolved in 2 tablespoons water

1. On a sheet of wax paper, sprinkle the cutlets on both sides with the salt and pepper. In a large nonstick skillet, heat the oil. Sauté the turkey and onion, stirring occasionally and turning the turkey once, until cooked through, 5–7 minutes on each side. Transfer the turkey to a platter.

2. In the same skillet, combine the cranberry juice, brown sugar, vinegar, peppercorns and thyme; bring to a boil. Stir in the cranberries. Reduce the heat and simmer 5 minutes. Stir in the dissolved cornstarch; bring to a boil. Cook, stirring constantly, until thickened, about 1 minute. Spoon over the turkey.

**Per serving:** 189 Calories, 3 g Total Fat, 0 g Saturated Fat, 53 mg Cholesterol, 183 mg Sodium, 19 g Total Carbohydrate, 0 g Dietary Fiber, 21 g Protein, 30 mg Calcium. **POINTS** per serving: 4.

## Got Leftovers?

Leftover cranberries freeze beautifully; just spread them on a baking sheet and freeze until hard, then pack into a sealable plastic bag. Use them to flavor pancakes and bread recipes. Or, toss them in the food processor with some granulated sugar, orange zest and chopped walnuts to make a quick cranberry relish; it will keep in the refrigerator for up to a month.

# Dilled Meatballs with Vegetable Sauce

*Our version of meatballs and sauce combines ground turkey with just the white of an egg and some bread crumbs; the sauce is rich with vegetables. Serve over your favorite rice or grain, such as bulgur.*

MAKES 4 SERVINGS

¾ pound ground skinless turkey

3 tablespoons seasoned dried bread crumbs

2 tablespoons minced dill

1 egg white, lightly beaten

1 tablespoon Dijon mustard

1 teaspoon salt-free lemon-herb seasoning

2 teaspoons olive oil

1 green bell pepper, seeded and chopped

1 red bell pepper, seeded and chopped

1 medium zucchini, sliced

1 cup chopped fennel

2 garlic cloves, minced

One 28-ounce can stewed tomatoes

2 teaspoons grated lemon zest

½ teaspoon dried oregano leaves

1. In a large bowl, combine the turkey, bread crumbs, dill, egg white, mustard and seasoning; blend well. Form into 12 meatballs.

2. In a large nonstick skillet, heat the oil. Cook the meatballs, turning frequently, until browned on all sides, 6–8 minutes. With a slotted spoon, transfer to a plate.

3. In the skillet, sauté the bell peppers, zucchini, fennel and garlic until softened, 4–5 minutes. Stir in the tomatoes, lemon zest and oregano. Reduce the heat and simmer 5 minutes. Add the meatballs to the sauce; simmer, partially covered, frequently spooning the sauce over the meatballs, until cooked through, about 10 minutes.

**Per serving**: 229 Calories, 8 g Total Fat, 2 g Saturated Fat, 52 mg Cholesterol, 859 mg Sodium, 23 g Total Carbohydrate, 6 g Dietary Fiber, 17 g Protein, 115 mg Calcium. **POINTS** per serving: 4.

## Tip

**If you like, prepare the meatballs ahead of time. They can be baked in a 350° F oven for about 15 minutes as well.**

# Parmesan-Turkey Meatloaf

*An American classic, meatloaf gets a nutritional update when made with turkey, fat-free milk and egg white. Leftovers are delicious served with a cold vegetable salad.*

MAKES 8 SERVINGS

1 tablespoon olive oil

1 onion, chopped

1¼ pounds ground skinless turkey

4 slices whole-wheat bread, made into fine crumbs

½ cup fat-free milk

1 egg white, lightly beaten

3 tablespoons ketchup

2 tablespoons grated Parmesan cheese

½ teaspoon garlic powder

½ teaspoon dried basil

¼ teaspoon dried thyme leaves, crumbled

¼ teaspoon freshly ground pepper

1. Preheat the oven to 350° F; spray an 8 × 5" loaf pan with nonstick cooking spray. In a small nonstick skillet, heat the oil. Sauté the onion until tender, 4–5 minutes.

2. In a medium bowl, combine the onion, turkey, bread crumbs, milk, egg white, ketchup, cheese, garlic powder, basil, thyme and pepper; blend well. Shape into a loaf and transfer to the pan. Bake until browned and cooked through, 50–60 minutes. Let stand 10 minutes before slicing.

**Per serving:** 181 Calories, 9 g Total Fat, 2 g Saturated Fat, 53 mg Cholesterol, 247 mg Sodium, 10 g Total Carbohydrate, 1 g Dietary Fiber, 15 g Protein, 64 mg Calcium. **POINTS** per serving: 4.

## Tip

When recipes call for ground turkey or chicken, why not make your own? If you have a food processor, it will take only a minute—and you can control the fat content. Use skinless, boneless breasts, and you'll have the leanest grind possible. Cut into 1-inch cubes and pulse several times until evenly ground.

*Parmesan-Turkey Meatloaf with Succotash*
*(page 313)*

# Monterey Jack Turkey Burgers

*Mixing the cheese into the meat adds moisture as well as lots of flavor. Serve this delicious combo on sourdough or whole-grain bread if you prefer a heartier roll for your burger. Don't forget to include a side of slaw (page 305 or 307) and a dill pickle spear.*

MAKES 4 SERVINGS

¾ pound ground skinless turkey breast

2 scallions, minced

1 tablespoon reduced-sodium soy sauce

1 tablespoon ketchup

¼ teaspoon garlic powder

¼ teaspoon freshly ground pepper

⅓ cup shredded Monterey Jack cheese

4 strips turkey bacon

4 hamburger buns, split and toasted

1 tomato, cut into 4 slices

1. In a large bowl, combine the turkey, scallions, soy sauce, ketchup, garlic powder and pepper. Blend in the cheese, then form into 4 burgers.

2. Heat an indoor ridged grill sprayed with nonstick cooking spray. Cook the burgers until cooked through, 6–8 minutes on each side. When you turn the burgers, add the bacon to the grill; cook until crisp, 3–4 minutes on each side. Serve the burgers in the buns, with the bacon and tomato slices.

**Per serving:** 306 Calories, 9 g Total Fat, 4 g Saturated Fat, 77 mg Cholesterol, 707 mg Sodium, 26 g Total Carbohydrate, 2 g Dietary Fiber, 31 g Protein, 130 mg Calcium. **POINTS** per serving: 6.

## Food Safety Tips

*Raw poultry (and raw meats and seafood as well) can harbor salmonella, E. coli and other harmful bacteria, so it's important to store and handle it properly. Follow these tips to help safeguard your family's health:*

- *Wash your hands, countertops and utensils in hot, soapy water after handling raw chicken. Never transfer cooked chicken to a plate or bowl that has held raw chicken, unless it has been cleaned. If you're grilling chicken, for example, cover a platter with foil before you place the raw chicken on it to carry outside; discard the foil before placing the cooked chicken on the platter.*

- *Defrost frozen chicken in the refrigerator or in a microwave, never on the counter.*

- *Cook chicken thoroughly. For chicken with bones, a meat thermometer should register 180° F; boneless parts should be cooked to an internal temperature of 170° F. When done, the juices of the chicken will be clear, not pink.*

- *Never leave raw chicken at room temperature for longer than 30 minutes; cooked, for no longer than 2 hours.*

*These guidelines apply to meat and seafood as well as poultry.*

# Sausage and Peppers

*This 20-minute skillet supper combines everyone's favorite Italian flavors. Serve with an escarole salad and garlic bread for an authentic trattoria meal.*

MAKES 4 SERVINGS

¼ pound hot Italian turkey sausage, cut into ¼" slices

1 red bell pepper, seeded and sliced

1 green bell pepper, seeded and sliced

1 yellow bell pepper, seeded and sliced

1 onion, sliced

¼ cup chicken broth

3 garlic cloves, minced

¼ teaspoon crushed red pepper flakes

¼ teaspoon dried oregano leaves

Spray a large nonstick skillet with nonstick cooking spray; heat. Cook the sausage, stirring frequently, until no longer pink, 4–6 minutes. Add the bell peppers, onion, broth, garlic, pepper flakes and oregano; cook, stirring frequently, until most of the liquid evaporates, about 5 minutes. Reduce the heat and simmer, covered, until the peppers are tender, 3–4 minutes.

**Per serving:** 92 Calories, 4 g Total Fat, 0 g Saturated Fat, 29 mg Cholesterol, 256 mg Sodium, 7 g Total Carbohydrate, 1 g Dietary Fiber, 7 g Protein, 15 mg Calcium. *POINTS* per serving: 2.

## Tip

If you find the slender, pale green Italian frying peppers, use them instead of the bell peppers.

# Smoked Turkey Panini

*Panini are simply sandwiches, Italian style. Here, we liven them up with piquant marinated peppers.*

MAKES 4 SERVINGS

1 red bell pepper

1 tablespoon balsamic vinegar

1 sprig fresh rosemary, or ½ teaspoon dried leaves

½ pound thinly sliced smoked turkey

8 large basil leaves

4 whole-wheat hard rolls, split

1. Spray the broiler rack with nonstick cooking spray; preheat the broiler. Broil the pepper, turning occasionally, until charred on all sides, about 10 minutes; place in a paper bag and fold closed; set aside 15 minutes to steam. Peel, seed and slice the pepper into thin strips.

2. In a quart-size sealable plastic bag, combine the vinegar, rosemary and 1 tablespoon water; add the pepper. Seal the bag, squeezing out the air; turn to coat the pepper. Refrigerate 8 hours or overnight, turning the bag occasionally. Drain and discard the marinade.

3. To assemble the sandwiches, layer the turkey, pepper and basil leaves on the rolls.

**Per serving:** 212 Calories, 4 g Total Fat, 1 g Saturated Fat, 29 mg Cholesterol, 873 mg Sodium, 29 g Total Carbohydrate, 4 g Dietary Fiber, 17 g Protein, 63 mg Calcium. *POINTS* per serving: 4.

# RECIPES

Meat

# Chapter 6

# Meat

From a juicy burger to sizzling lamb chops, red meat has an almost elemental appeal. But most of us need to cut down on our meat consumption, as it is a primary source of saturated fat and cholesterol. More than ever, meat producers are giving us leaner beef, pork and lamb, thanks to changes in livestock-farming techniques. By choosing wisely and cooking creatively, you'll find plenty of healthy ways to satisfy a red-meat craving.

Start with lean cuts and keep portions small—treating meat as a condiment in a meal rather than the centerpiece. Think of 2–3 ounces as a maximum serving size: about the size of a deck of playing cards. Trim off all visible fat before cooking.

**Note: All raw meat should be handled with care because it can contain infectious organisms. See page 146 for safety tips (they apply to meat as well as poultry).**

## Beef

Beef is sold at retail in three grades: prime, choice and select. Prime beef, usually available only at butcher shops and restaurants, is the fattiest and most tender. Supermarkets carry choice grade, with a mid-range fat content and tenderness, and select, which is leanest, and toughest, of all. Most select cuts require long, slow cooking to keep them tender.

*Leanest cuts: round, sirloin, top loin*

## Pork

Today's pork is about a third lower in fat than it used to be—good news for our arteries but more taxing on our cooking skills. Most pork cuts need gentle cooking to keep them tender. At the same time, they must be cooked thoroughly to protect against illness caused by the trichina parasite.

The line between "cooked through" and "over-cooked" can be a thin one, so be sure to use an instant-read thermometer to judge doneness: Cook pork to an internal temperature of 160° F.

"Ham" refers to meat from the hind leg of pork, which has been cured and smoked (though, confusingly, you can sometimes find "fresh ham," or uncured, unsmoked hind leg). Be sure to read the label; some hams are only partially cooked. Those labeled "cooked" or "fully cooked" need only be heated through before serving.

*Leanest cuts: tenderloin, loin, center-cut ham*

## Lamb

The term "lamb" refers to a sheep less than one year old; very young lamb, between 3–5 months old, is called "baby" or "milk-finished" lamb. "Spring lamb," another term for young, tender lamb, used to be only available between March and September. But now that lamb is imported from places like New Zealand and Australia, spring lamb is available virtually year-round.

*Leanest cuts: leg and top loin*

# London Broil

*Many steak lovers swear London broil is even better the day after it is cooked. Serve cold leftover strips over Romaine lettuce and drizzled with your favorite low-fat dressing for a satisfying lunch.*

MAKES 4 SERVINGS

One 1-pound top round or sirloin tip steak

½ cup dry red wine

1 garlic clove, minced

Freshly ground pepper, to taste

1 sprig fresh rosemary, chopped, or 1 teaspoon dried leaves, crumbled

Salt, to taste

1. Place the steak in a gallon-size sealable plastic bag; add the wine, garlic and pepper, then lightly rub the marinade into the meat. Add the rosemary (if using dried, add with other ingredients). Seal the bag, squeezing out any air; turn to coat the steak. Refrigerate, turning the bag occasionally, overnight or up to 24 hours. Remove the steak from the refrigerator about 30 minutes before broiling.

2. Preheat the broiler at least 20 minutes. Transfer the steak to the broiler rack; discard the marinade. Broil 3" from the heat, turning only once then salting the cooked side, about 4 minutes on each side. Transfer the steak to a cutting board; let stand 2–3 minutes before slicing thinly across the grain.

**Per serving:** 149 Calories, 4 g Total Fat, 1 g Saturated Fat, 67 mg Cholesterol, 316 mg Sodium, 0 g Total Carbohydrate, 0 g Dietary Fiber, 25 g Protein, 8 mg Calcium. **POINTS** per serving: 3.

# Grilled T-Bone Steak

*This steak is made for the grill. The perfect accompaniment? Grilled vegetables, such as eggplant, squash and onion, or try grilled skewers of cherry tomatoes with basil and spring onions.*

MAKES 4 SERVINGS

4 teaspoons extra virgin olive oil

2 teaspoons chopped rosemary

2 teaspoons chopped sage

One 1¼-pound T-bone or rib steak (at least 1–1½" thick), trimmed of all visible fat

Salt and freshly ground pepper, to taste

1. Spray the grill rack with nonstick cooking spray; preheat the grill.

2. In a small bowl, mix the oil, rosemary and sage. Rub the steak with the herb mixture; place on the grill rack. Grill 3" from the heat, turning once, until done to taste, 6 minutes on each side for rare. Season with salt and pepper as soon as the steak is done. Transfer the steak to a cutting board; let stand about 5 minutes before slicing.

**Per serving:** 228 Calories,  14 g Total Fat, 4 g Saturated Fat, 68 mg Cholesterol, 350 mg Sodium, 0 g Total Carbohydrate, 0 g Dietary Fiber, 24 g Protein, 13 mg Calcium. **POINTS** per serving: 6.

*Grilled T-Bone Steak*

# Marinated Flank Steak

*This is an ideal way to prepare flank steak, which has very little fat. The marinade provides lots of flavor and juiciness.*

MAKES 4 SERVINGS

¼ cup reduced-sodium soy sauce

2 teaspoons honey

2 teaspoons grated peeled gingerroot, or 1 teaspoon ground

2 teaspoons finely chopped fresh lemongrass or grated lemon zest

2 garlic cloves, minced

1 tablespoon dry sherry

Pinch crushed red pepper flakes

One 1-pound flank steak

2 teaspoons olive oil

Salt and freshly ground pepper, to taste

1. To prepare the marinade, in a gallon-size sealable plastic bag, combine the soy sauce, honey, gingerroot, lemongrass, garlic, sherry and pepper flakes; add the steak. Seal the bag, squeezing out the air; turn to coat the steak. Refrigerate, turning the bag occasionally, overnight or up to 24 hours. Remove the meat from the refrigerator at least 30 minutes before broiling.

2. Preheat the broiler. Discard the marinade; pat the steak dry with a paper towel, then rub very lightly with the oil. Broil 3" from the heat, turning only once and salting the cooked side, about 4 minutes on each side. Season with the pepper. Transfer the steak to a cutting board; let stand 2–3 minutes before slicing thinly on the diagonal.

**Per serving:** 207 Calories, 10 g Total Fat, 4 g Saturated Fat, 44 mg Cholesterol, 390 mg Sodium, 1 g Total Carbohydrate, 0 g Dietary Fiber, 26 g Protein, 7 mg Calcium. **POINTS** per serving: 5.

## What's the Beef?

*Recently, meat has taken on a bad reputation in the protein game, yet it's a rep that's really undeserved. It's easy to incorporate beef into a healthy eating plan when you follow a few sensible guidelines:*

- *Select the leanest cuts of beef—top round, top loin strip steak, top sirloin, eye round, tip and lean (10 percent or less fat) ground beef.*

- *Choose pork tenderloin, leg (fresh ham) and loin chops.*

- *Look for reduced-fat luncheon and processed meats.*

- *Trim all visible fat from the meat, then roast, broil or bake on a rack to keep any untrimmed fat from being reabsorbed.*

# Steak with Two Peppers

*Any dry red wine, such as Cabernet Sauvignon, works in this recipe.*

MAKES 4 SERVINGS

1 tablespoon drained green peppercorns packed in brine

1 teaspoon cracked black peppercorns

One 1-pound boneless top loin steak, trimmed of all visible fat and pounded slightly

2 teaspoons olive oil

Salt, to taste

2 teaspoons unsalted stick margarine

1 tablespoon grated shallots or red onion

¼ cup dry red wine

1 teaspoon tomato paste

⅓ cup low-sodium beef broth

1. Using your fingers, press 2 teaspoons of the green peppercorns and the black peppercorns into the steak. Heat a medium nonstick skillet over medium-high heat. Add the olive oil; let it heat. Sauté the steak, turning only once and salting the cooked side, 1–2 minutes on each side. Transfer the steak to a plate.

3. In the skillet, melt 1 teaspoon of the margarine. Sauté the shallots until wilted, about 1 minute. Add the wine; cook, stirring, until it evaporates, about 2 minutes. Dissolve the tomato paste in the beef broth and stir in with the remaining teaspoon of green peppercorns. Cook until the liquid is slightly reduced, about 2–3 minutes longer; swirl in the remaining teaspoon of margarine. Quickly return the steak and any accumulated juices to the sauce; reheat about 30–60 seconds. Remove and slice the steak. Serve with the sauce.

**Per serving**: 210 Calories, 11 g Total Fat, 3 g Saturated Fat, 61 mg Cholesterol, 408 mg Sodium, 1 g Total Carbohydrate, 0 g Dietary Fiber, 23 g Protein, 13 mg Calcium. *POINTS* per serving: 5.

## Tip

**When a recipe calls for wine, it's best to steer clear of cooking wines, which often contain salt and are generally inferior.**

# Peppered Roast Tenderloin

*Crack peppercorns in a mortar or between two spoons.*

MAKES 10 SERVINGS

One 2½-pound beef tenderloin

2 garlic cloves, slivered lengthwise

2 tablespoons olive oil

1 tablespoon cracked black peppercorns

1 teaspoon minced fresh rosemary, or ½ teaspoon dried leaves

1 teaspoon minced fresh thyme, or ½ teaspoon dried leaves

1 teaspoon minced fresh sage, or ½ teaspoon dried leaves

Salt, to taste

1. Preheat the oven to 425° F. With a small sharp knife, make several small incisions in the tenderloin; insert a sliver of garlic in each incision. Rub the tenderloin with the oil. In a small bowl, combine the peppercorns, rosemary, thyme, sage and salt; pat the mixture on all sides of the tenderloin.

2. Place the tenderloin in a shallow roasting pan. Roast 10 minutes; reduce the oven temperature to 350° F. Roast about 15 minutes longer for rare, about 20 minutes for medium. Transfer the roast to a cutting board; let stand 15 minutes before slicing.

**Per serving:** 202 Calories, 12 g Total Fat, 4 g Saturated Fat, 67 mg Cholesterol, 156 mg Sodium, 1 g Total Carbohydrate, 0 g Dietary Fiber, 23 g Protein, 13 mg Calcium. *POINTS* per serving: 5.

## Got Leftovers?

Leftovers can be used for cold beef salads, stir-fries or sandwiches.

## Using a Meat Thermometer

*There are so many variables when you cook meat—the temperature of your oven, grill or skillet; the thickness of the meat, for example—that it's impossible to have precise cooking times. Instead, rely on an instant-read meat thermometer to judge doneness. (It's more accurate than an old-fashioned meat thermometer, which is stuck in the meat throughout the entire cooking time.)*

*Stick the thermometer in the center of the thickest part of the meat, without touching the bone or fat, to get the most accurate reading. Wait until the indicator stops climbing before you read it; you'll have the result in seconds.*

# Beef Stew

*This beef stew is ideal cold weather fare. An easy green salad and freshly baked bread or biscuits to soak up every drop of the savory stew round out the meal.*

MAKES 4 SERVINGS

4 teaspoons olive oil

1 tablespoon minced onion

1 tablespoon minced carrot

1 tablespoon minced celery

1 pound beef round, cut into 1½" cubes

1 cup chopped canned plum tomatoes, with juice

½ cup dry red wine

1 teaspoon minced fresh thyme, or ½ teaspoon dried leaves

1 bay leaf

Salt and freshly ground pepper, to taste

8 frozen pearl onions

2 carrots, peeled and cut into 1" chunks

4 medium potatoes, peeled and cut into 1" cubes

1 cup thawed frozen peas

1 tablespoon minced flat-leaf parsley

1 tablespoon minced mint

1. In a medium nonstick Dutch oven or heavy saucepan, heat the oil. Sauté the minced onion, carrot and celery until translucent, 5–6 minutes. Add the beef and sauté until browned, about 5 minutes. Add the tomatoes, wine, thyme, bay leaf, salt and pepper; bring to a boil. Reduce the heat and simmer gently, partially covered, stirring occasionally, about 45 minutes.

2. Add the pearl onions, carrots, potatoes and 1 cup hot water. Cook, covered, 40 minutes.

3. Stir in the peas; cook 4 minutes, then add the parsley and mint and cook 1 minute longer. Discard the bay leaf.

**Per serving**: 356 Calories, 8 g Total Fat, 2 g Saturated Fat, 51 mg Cholesterol, 511 mg Sodium, 41 g Total Carbohydrate, 7 g Dietary Fiber, 25 g Protein, 75 mg Calcium. **POINTS** per serving: 6.

## Tip

If you can't find frozen pearl onions, use fresh— but you'll have to peel them.

# Classic Pot Roast

*Pot roast is one of those dishes where the flavor improves when made ahead, which also makes it easy to lower the fat of the final dish. Just remove the meat from the gravy and cool both to room temperature. Wrap the meat in plastic and refrigerate the meat and gravy separately. When cold, lift the fat from the gravy with a large spoon or spatula.*

MAKES 8 SERVINGS

2 tablespoons + 2 teaspoons olive oil

2 pounds bottom or top round boneless roast

2 onions, finely chopped

½ carrot, finely chopped

1 celery stalk, finely chopped

2 garlic cloves, minced

1½ teaspoons minced rosemary, or ½ teaspoon dried leaves, crumbled

1½ teaspoons minced sage

6 juniper berries, crushed (optional)

½ cup dry red wine

1 cup chopped canned plum tomatoes, with juice

1 cup low-sodium beef broth

Salt and freshly ground pepper, to taste

1. In a large nonstick saucepan or Dutch oven, heat the oil. Add the roast and brown on all sides. Transfer the roast to a plate. Add the onions, carrot, celery, garlic, rosemary, sage and juniper (if using). Sauté, stirring constantly, until the vegetables are golden and fragrant, about 10 minutes.

2. Add the wine, turning up the heat slightly and scraping up the browned bits from the bottom of the pan. Return the roast to the pan; cook 2 minutes. Stir in the tomatoes, broth, salt and pepper (the liquid should cover only about one-third of the meat); partially cover and bring to a boil. Reduce the heat and simmer gently, turning the meat occasionally, until tender when tested with a fork, about 2 hours. Skim all the fat from the gravy before serving. Slice the meat thinly across the grain and reheat it in the gravy over low heat. If you desire a thicker gravy, boil the gravy over high heat, keeping the sliced meat warm.

**Per serving:** 202 Calories, 10 g Total Fat,  2 g Saturated Fat, 60 mg Cholesterol, 245 mg Sodium, 5 g Total Carbohydrate, 1 g Dietary Fiber, 7 g Protein, 26 mg Calcium. **POINTS** per serving: 5.

## Tip

**If you don't have time to cook the meat ahead, use a gravy skimmer to remove the fat, or blot the top of the gravy with a few sturdy paper towels.**

# Spicy Meatloaf with Herbs

*Be sure to cook meatloaf thoroughly. If you don't have 1¼ hours to bake it, form into balls and bake in a muffin tin, or use a ring mold; bake for 30–45 minutes.*

MAKES 4 SERVINGS

2 teaspoons vegetable oil

1 cup finely chopped mushrooms

1 onion, finely chopped

¼ carrot, finely chopped

2 tablespoons minced celery

2 tablespoons minced seeded green bell pepper

1 pound lean ground beef (10% or less fat)

½ cup quick-cooking oats

1 egg

2 tablespoons tomato paste

1 tablespoon Worcestershire sauce

3–4 garlic cloves, minced

1 teaspoon minced fresh rosemary, or ½ teaspoon dried leaves, crumbled

1 teaspoon minced fresh sage, or pinch dried leaves

1 teaspoon minced fresh thyme, or ½ teaspoon dried leaves

¼ teaspoons hot red pepper sauce

¼ cup tomato puree or tomato sauce, diluted with ¼ cup water

1. Preheat the oven to 350° F; spray a 9" square baking pan with nonstick cooking spray. In a large nonstick skillet, heat the oil. Sauté the mushrooms, onion, carrot, celery, and bell pepper until softened, about 5 minutes.

2. In a large bowl, combine the sautéed vegetables, beef, oats, egg, tomato paste, Worcestershire sauce, garlic, rosemary, sage, thyme and pepper sauce. Shape into a loaf about 7 × 5 × 2" and place in the pan. Bake, basting with tomato puree after 30 minutes, until cooked through, about 1–1¼ hours. Let stand about 10 minutes before slicing.

**Per serving:** 268 Calories, 12 g Total Fat, 5 g Saturated Fat, 114 mg Cholesterol, 266 mg Sodium, 16 g Total Carbohydrate, 3 g Dietary Fiber, 24 g Protein, 42 mg Calcium. *POINTS* per serving: 6.

## Got Leftovers?

**As always, leftover meatloaf makes a very satisfying sandwich. Try it in a pita topped with Dijon mustard, ketchup or both.**

# Beef and Bean Chili

*Don't be put off by the lengthy ingredients list—this chili is a breeze to make. Double the batch and freeze half of it.*

MAKES 4 SERVINGS

4 teaspoons olive oil

2 onions, chopped

½ carrot, chopped

½ celery stalk, chopped

¼ cup green bell pepper, seeded and chopped

3–4 garlic cloves, minced

1 teaspoon minced deveined seeded jalapeño pepper, or to taste (wear gloves to prevent irritation)

¾ pound lean ground beef (10% or less fat)

1 tablespoon chili powder

2 teaspoons ground cumin

1 teaspoon dried oregano leaves

½ teaspoon ground coriander

One 14½-ounce can diced tomatoes

One 16-ounce can pinto or red kidney beans, rinsed and drained

½ teaspoon salt

Pinch freshly ground pepper

¼ cup chopped fresh cilantro

¼ cup nonfat sour cream

¼ cup chopped red onion

1. In a large nonstick Dutch oven or saucepan, heat the oil. Sauté the onions, carrot, celery, bell pepper, garlic and jalapeño until the onions are translucent, about 15 minutes. Add the beef and cook, breaking it apart with a wooden spoon, until no longer pink, 5–7 minutes. Stir in the chili powder, cumin, oregano and coriander; cook, stirring, 1 minute.

2. Add the tomatoes, beans, salt and pepper; bring to a boil. Reduce the heat and simmer gently, partially covered, stirring occasionally, until the flavors are blended, about 20 minutes. Stir in the cilantro. Serve, topped with the sour cream, red onion and some additional chopped cilantro, if you like.

**Per serving:** 402 Calories, 12 g Total Fat, 4 g Saturated Fat, 44 mg Cholesterol, 700 mg Sodium, 49 g Total Carbohydrate, 15 g Dietary Fiber, 27 g Protein, 171 mg Calcium. *POINTS* per serving: 6.

# Sloppy Joes

*Serve these wonderfully messy joes on hard rolls with plenty of napkins on hand. If you like, you can also serve the meat over plain white rice.*

MAKES 4 SERVINGS

4 teaspoons olive oil

2 onions, finely chopped

1 celery stalk, finely chopped

½ carrot, finely chopped

½ green bell pepper, seeded and finely chopped

½ teaspoon dried oregano leaves

½ teaspoon dried thyme leaves

1 pound lean ground beef (10% or less fat)

1 cup canned diced tomatoes

2 tablespoons tomato paste

1 tablespoon Worcestershire sauce

2 teaspoons red-wine vinegar

¼ teaspoon hot red pepper sauce

Salt and freshly ground pepper, to taste

4 rolls or hamburger buns

4 unsweetened pickles (optional)

1. In a medium nonstick saucepan, heat the oil. Sauté the onions, celery, carrot and bell pepper until the onions are translucent, 10–12 minutes. Stir in the oregano and thyme, then add the beef and cook, breaking it apart with a wooden spoon, until no longer pink, 5–7 minutes.

2. In a small bowl, combine the tomatoes, tomato paste and 2 tablespoons water; add to the beef mixture and cook 1 minute. Stir in the Worcestershire sauce, vinegar, pepper sauce, salt and pepper; bring to a boil. Reduce the heat and simmer, stirring occasionally, until the mixture thickens, about 10 minutes. Serve on the rolls with the pickles on the side, if desired.

**Per serving**: 419 Calories, 16 g Total Fat, 6 g Saturated Fat, 66 mg Cholesterol, 957 mg Sodium, 41 g Total Carbohydrate, 3 g Dietary Fiber, 28 g Protein, 132 mg Calcium. *POINTS* per serving: 9.

## Storing Meat

*How long is it safe to store meat in your refrigerator or freezer? Use the chart below to ensure that your meat is stored properly.*

| MEAT | REFRIGERATOR | FREEZER |
|---|---|---|
| *Beef Cuts* | *3–4 days* | *6–12 months* |
| *Veal Cuts* | *1–2 days* | *6–9 months* |
| *Pork Cuts* | *2–3 days* | *6 months* |
| *Lamb Cuts* | *3–5 days* | *6–9 months* |
| *Ground Beef, Veal and Lamb* | *1–2 days* | *3–4 months* |
| *Ground Pork* | *1–2 days* | *1–3 months* |

# Mushroom Hamburgers

*These hamburgers are great with sautéed onions. Slice the onions, then sauté in a nonstick pan with a little beef bouillon until tender.*

MAKES 4 SERVINGS

2 teaspoons olive oil

½ red or yellow bell pepper, seeded and finely chopped

½ onion, finely chopped

2 tablespoons minced carrot

2 tablespoons minced celery

2 garlic cloves, minced

2 cups finely chopped mushrooms

¾ pound lean ground beef (10% or less fat)

1 tablespoon steak sauce

Salt and freshly ground pepper, to taste

1. In a medium nonstick skillet, heat the oil. Sauté the bell pepper, onion, carrot, celery and garlic until the onion is translucent, 8–10 minutes. Add the mushrooms; sauté until the mushrooms brown and the liquid evaporates, about 8 minutes. Cool to room temperature.

2. Spray the broiler rack with nonstick cooking spray; preheat the broiler. In a medium bowl, combine the mushroom mixture, beef, steak sauce, salt and pepper. Form into 4 hamburgers. Broil the burgers 3–4" from heat, 5–7 minutes on each side.

**Per serving:** 153 Calories, 8 g Total Fat, 3 g Saturated Fat, 44 mg Cholesterol, 396 mg Sodium, 6 g Total Carbohydrate, 1 g Dietary Fiber, 15 g Protein, 15 mg Calcium. *POINTS* per serving: 4.

## How We Did It

Sautéed vegetables are a great way to "thin" out a burger, meatball or meatloaf recipe, adding bulk and nutrients without much fat. Other good candidates are chopped eggplant, shredded zucchini, drained chopped spinach or other greens, bean sprouts or scallions.

# Beef and Pasta

*This retro casserole is perfect for an informal family dinner. Consider using a fun-shaped pasta, like stars or ABC's, for the kids.*

MAKES 4 SERVINGS

4 teaspoons olive oil

2 onions, finely chopped

½ carrot, finely chopped

1 celery stalk, finely chopped

3–4 garlic cloves, minced

2 teaspoons minced fresh thyme, or 1 teaspoon dried leaves

½ pound lean ground beef (10% or less fat)

½ cup dry red wine

One 14½-ounce can diced tomatoes

1 cup thawed frozen green peas

2½ cups cooked tubetti, ditalini or elbow macaroni

¼ cup grated pecorino or Parmesan cheese

2 tablespoons chopped basil

Preheat the oven to 350° F; spray a 2-quart casserole with nonstick cooking spray. In a medium nonstick skillet, heat the oil. Sauté the onions, carrot, celery, garlic and thyme until the onions are translucent, 8–10 minutes. Add the beef and cook, breaking it apart with a wooden spoon, until no longer pink, 5–7 minutes. Stir in the wine; cook 2 minutes, then stir in the tomatoes and peas. Reduce the heat and cook, stirring occasionally, 20 minutes. Stir in the macaroni, cheese and basil; transfer to the casserole. Bake until the cheese is melted, about 20 minutes.

**Per serving:** 401 Calories, 12 g Total Fat, 5 g Saturated Fat, 46 mg Cholesterol, 575 mg Sodium, 44 g Total Carbohydrate, 6 g Dietary Fiber, 23 g Protein, 204 mg Calcium. **POINTS** per serving: 8.

# Stuffed Peppers

*To cut down on the fat in this recipe, use skinless ground turkey breast in place of the beef.*

MAKES 4 SERVINGS

½ pound lean ground beef (10% or less fat)

1 cup cooked white rice

1 onion, finely chopped

¼ cup thawed frozen green peas

¼ cup grated Parmesan cheese

2 tablespoons tomato paste

3 garlic cloves, minced

1 teaspoon minced thyme

1 teaspoon minced basil

½ teaspoon minced sage

½ teaspoon minced rosemary

4 green, red or yellow bell peppers, tops cut off and seeded

½ cup tomato puree or tomato sauce

Preheat the oven to 350° F. In a large bowl, combine the beef, rice, onion, peas, cheese, tomato paste, garlic, thyme, basil, sage and rosemary. Loosely stuff the peppers with the mixture; stand them in a baking dish or casserole. Pour the tomato puree over the peppers; add enough water so that the liquid comes about one-fourth up the sides of the peppers. Cover with foil and bake, basting occasionally with the juices, 30 minutes. Uncover and bake until the peppers and rice are tender and the filling is completely cooked, about 20 minutes longer. Let stand 5 minutes before serving.

**Per serving:** 284 Calories, 10 g Total Fat, 5 g Saturated Fat, 52 mg Cholesterol, 471 mg Sodium, 28 g Total Carbohydrate, 6 g Dietary Fiber, 23 g Protein, 188 mg Calcium. **POINTS** per serving: 5.

# Tacos with Salsa

*Store-bought taco shells, though convenient, are often deep-fried and loaded with fat. Our solution: Make low-in-fat taco shells by draping 6" corn tortillas directly over the bars of your oven rack; bake for 10 minutes at 400° F.*

MAKES 4 SERVINGS

2 tomatoes, diced

4 teaspoons olive oil

1 onion, finely chopped

2 garlic cloves, minced

1 teaspoon minced deveined seeded jalapeño pepper, or to taste (wear gloves to prevent irritation)

2 teaspoons ground cumin

1 teaspoon dried oregano leaves

1 teaspoon paprika

1 pound lean ground beef (10% or less fat)

1 cup canned diced tomatoes

Salt and freshly ground pepper, to taste

½ cup minced cilantro

1 red onion, finely chopped

2 tablespoons fresh lime juice

8 taco shells

2 cups shredded iceberg or romaine lettuce

¼ cup nonfat sour cream

1. Place the fresh tomatoes in a strainer or colander in the sink; drain 20–30 minutes.

2. In a medium nonstick saucepan, heat the oil. Sauté the onion, garlic and jalapeño until the onion is translucent, 6–8 minutes. Stir in the cumin, oregano and paprika; sauté until fragrant, about 1 minute. Add the beef and cook, breaking it apart with a wooden spoon, until no longer pink, 8–10 minutes. Add the canned tomatoes, salt and pepper. Reduce the heat and simmer until thickened, about 10 minutes.

3. To prepare the salsa, in a medium bowl, combine the fresh tomatoes, cilantro, red onion and lime juice; season with salt and pepper.

4. To assemble the tacos, divide the beef mixture among the taco shells; top with the lettuce, then the salsa and sour cream.

**Per serving:** 401 Calories, 20 g Total Fat, 6 g Saturated Fat, 66 mg Cholesterol, 634 mg Sodium, 32 g Total Carbohydrate, 6 g Dietary Fiber, 26 g Protein, 134 mg Calcium. *POINTS* per serving: 8.

## Tip

**If you'd rather make taco-shell bowls to serve this as a salad, crumple foil into balls and place them on a baking sheet; drape 6" corn tortillas over the balls, then bake at 400° F for about 10 minutes.**

# Taco Salad

*Have a bowl of hot salsa on hand so that those who like their Mexican food spicy can add just the right amount of heat.*

MAKES 4 SERVINGS

½ cup plain nonfat yogurt

¼ cup chopped cilantro

¼ cup nonfat sour cream

1 garlic clove, crushed

⅛ teaspoon salt

2 teaspoons olive oil

1½ onions, chopped

2 garlic cloves, minced

½ carrot, chopped

1 celery stalk, diced

¼ red bell pepper, seeded and chopped

¼ green bell pepper, seeded and chopped

4 teaspoons chili powder

1 teaspoon ground cumin

1 teaspoon dried oregano leaves, crumbled

¼ teaspoon cayenne pepper

¼ teaspoon freshly ground pepper

1 bay leaf

½ pound lean ground beef (10% or less fat)

One 14½-ounce can diced tomatoes

½ cup tomato paste

4 cups shredded iceberg lettuce

1 carrot, shredded

Four 6" corn tortillas, lightly toasted and cut into 4 triangles

¾ cup shredded reduced-fat cheddar cheese

1. To prepare the dressing, in a small bowl, combine the yogurt, cilantro, sour cream, crushed garlic and salt; let stand 30 minutes.

2. In a large nonstick skillet, heat the oil. Sauté about two-thirds of the onions and the minced garlic until the onion is translucent, 6–8 minutes. Add the chopped carrot, celery, bell peppers, chili powder, cumin, oregano, cayenne, pepper and bay leaf; cook, stirring constantly, 2 minutes. Add the beef, breaking it apart with a wooden spoon. Stir in the tomatoes, tomato paste and 1 cup water; bring to a boil. Reduce the heat and simmer, covered, until the beef is cooked through, about 20 minutes. Uncover and cook, stirring occasionally, until the liquid evaporates, about 15 minutes longer. Discard the bay leaf.

3. Meanwhile, in a large bowl, combine the lettuce, shredded carrot and one-fourth of the cilantro dressing; toss to coat.

4. To serve, divide the lettuce mixture among 4 plates; top with the meat, then surround with the tortilla triangles. Serve, sprinkled with the cheese and remaining onion and drizzled with the dressing.

**Per serving**: 429 Calories, 19 g Total Fat, 7 g Saturated Fat, 845 mg Sodium, 65 mg Cholesterol, 38 g Total Carbohydrate, 7 g Dietary Fiber, 29 g Protein, 440 mg Calcium. *POINTS* per serving: 9.

# Beef Kebabs with Moroccan Spices

*For these kebabs, 10" wooden or bamboo skewers work well. Soak the skewers in water for about half an hour before cooking to keep them from catching fire.*

MAKES 4 SERVINGS

1 onion, cubed

Grated zest of 1 lemon

2 tablespoons fresh lemon juice

4 teaspoons olive oil

2 garlic cloves, crushed

1 teaspoon ground cumin

1 teaspoon minced fresh thyme, or ½ teaspoon dried leaves

1 teaspoon chopped mint

½ teaspoon paprika

Dash cayenne pepper

1 pound boneless beef tenderloin, cut into 1" cubes

1 bay leaf

1 onion, cut into 8 wedges and blanched

1 red bell pepper, seeded, cut into 8 squares and blanched

8 medium mushroom caps

Chopped flat-leaf parsley, to garnish

1. To prepare the marinade, in a food processor or blender, combine the cubed onion, lemon zest, lemon juice, oil, garlic, cumin, thyme, mint, paprika and cayenne; puree. In a gallon-size sealable plastic bag, combine the beef, bay leaf and marinade. Seal the bag, squeezing out the air; turn to coat the beef. Refrigerate, turning the bag occasionally, 1 hour or overnight. Remove the meat from the refrigerator about 30 minutes before cooking. Drain the marinade into a small saucepan and bring to a rolling boil. Boil, stirring constantly, 3 minutes.

2. Preheat the broiler or grill. Thread the onion wedges, bell pepper, mushrooms and beef onto 4 skewers, beginning and ending with onion wedges. Set the skewers on the broiler or grill rack, keeping the rack 2–3" from the heat. Broil about 5 minutes on each side, basting with the marinade when turning. Serve the kebabs with any remaining marinade on the side.

**Per serving**: 256 Calories, 12 g Total Fat, 3 g Saturated Fat, 67 mg Cholesterol, 57 mg Sodium, 11 g Total Carbohydrate, 3 g Dietary Fiber, 25 g Protein, 39 mg Calcium. **POINTS** per serving: 6.

# Roast Beef Salad with Arugula

*A perfect recipe for making use of leftovers from a Sunday roast.*

MAKES 4 SERVINGS

1 red onion, halved lengthwise and sliced

1 cup ice water

10 sun-dried tomato halves (not oil-packed)

1 cup boiling water

1 tablespoon balsamic vinegar

2 teaspoons Dijon mustard

Salt and freshly ground pepper, to taste

4 teaspoons extra virgin olive oil

8 cups arugula, thick stems removed

1 cup thinly sliced mushrooms

½ pound thinly sliced roast beef, cut into strips

Cracked black pepper, to taste

1 lemon, cut into 4 wedges

1. Soak the onion in the ice water 1 hour; drain and pat dry. Soak the tomatoes in the boiling water 2 minutes; drain and pat dry, then finely dice.

2. To prepare the dressing, in a small bowl, whisk the vinegar, mustard, salt and pepper; whisk in the oil, a little at a time, then add the tomatoes and beat in 1 tablespoon water.

3. In a medium bowl, toss the arugula with 1 tablespoon of the dressing; divide among 4 plates. In the bowl, toss the onion and mushrooms with another tablespoon of the dressing; divide among the plates. Toss the roast beef with the remaining dressing and place on top of the salads. Sprinkle with the cracked pepper and serve with the lemon wedges.

**Per serving**: 202 Calories, 9 g Total Fat, 2 g Saturated Fat, 44 mg Cholesterol, 532 mg Sodium, 11 g Total Carbohydrate, 2 g Dietary Fiber, 19 g Protein, 88 mg Calcium. *POINTS* per serving: 4.

## The All-Fours Test

*Meat is muscle, and some muscles get more exercise than others. Therefore, meats cut from the parts of the animal that do the most amount of work are likely to be the toughest. One good rule of thumb is that the farther away the cut is from hoof or horn, the more tender the meat.*

*To understand the process, get down on all fours and do some "grazing" movements for a few minutes. You'll find that your neck, shoulders, chest and thighs work the hardest, while your back has it relatively easy. Accordingly, the shank (thigh), brisket (upper chest), flank and round (rump) cuts, which come from the hard-working areas, tend to yield the tougher meat that's best for long, slow cooking and grinding into burgers. By contrast, the rib, loin (back) and sirloin (upper back) parts do less work and have the tender meat that can cook quickly or make a juicy steak.*

# Spicy Beef and Broccoli Stir-Fry

*Soy sauce is the most frequently used condiment in Chinese cooking. It's made from fermented soybeans, wheat, salt, sugar and yeast. The dark variety is thick and slightly sweet while the light version is thinner and saltier.*

MAKES 4 SERVINGS

2 tablespoons dry sherry

2 tablespoons dark soy sauce

1 tablespoon grated peeled gingerroot

5–6 garlic cloves, minced

1 teaspoon Asian sesame oil

¼ teaspoon crushed red pepper flakes, or to taste

½ pound beef tenderloin, cut into strips

1 teaspoon cornstarch

1 tablespoon vegetable oil

4 cups chopped broccoli

3 scallions, thinly sliced

1. To prepare the marinade, in a gallon-size sealable plastic bag, combine the sherry, soy sauce, gingerroot, garlic, sesame oil and pepper flakes; add the beef. Seal the bag, squeezing out the air, turn to coat the beef. Refrigerate, turning the bag occasionally, about 1 hour.

2. Drain the marinade into a measuring cup; add enough water to make ⅓ cup liquid. Add the cornstarch and stir until it dissolves.

3. Heat a large nonstick skillet or wok with a lid over high heat. Add the vegetable oil and beef; stir-fry until the beef loses its red color, about 1 minute. With a slotted spoon, transfer to a plate. Reduce the heat slightly and add the broccoli; stir-fry 3 minutes, then cover and steam 1 minute. Return the beef to the skillet and add the marinade; increase the heat to high and stir-fry until the sauce thickens, 2–3 minutes. Serve, sprinkled with the scallions.

**Per serving**: 207 Calories, 11 g Total Fat, 3 g Saturated Fat, 44 mg Cholesterol, 573 mg Sodium, 8 g Total Carbohydrate, 3 g Dietary Fiber, 18 g Protein, 57 mg Calcium. *POINTS* per serving: 4.

## Tip

**If you usually discard broccoli stems because they're tough, peel them—you'll find they're actually quite tender.**

*Spicy Beef and Broccoli Stir-Fry*

# Moroccan-Style Roast Leg of Lamb

*Leftover lamb freezes well. After defrosting, serve it in sandwiches or use it in Lamb and Pepper Stir-Fry (page 170).*

MAKES 8 SERVINGS

4 teaspoons olive oil

1 tablespoon finely chopped mint

2 teaspoons paprika

2 teaspoons fresh lemon juice

3 garlic cloves, minced

½ teaspoon ground cumin

Pinch cayenne pepper

Salt and freshly ground pepper, to taste

One 2–2¼-pound half bone-in leg of lamb (preferably sirloin half)

1. Preheat the oven to 375° F. In a small bowl, thoroughly combine the oil, mint, paprika, lemon juice, garlic, cumin, cayenne, salt and pepper. Rub all over the lamb.

2. Place the lamb on a rack in a shallow roasting pan. Roast until tender and an instant-read thermometer inserted in the lamb (not touching the bone) registers 155° F. for medium, about 2½ hours. Let stand 10 minutes before slicing.

**Per serving**: 137 Calories, 7 g Total Fat, 2 g Saturated Fat, 53 mg Cholesterol, 187 mg Sodium, 1 g Total Carbohydrate, 0 g Dietary Fiber, 17 g Protein, 9 mg Calcium. **POINTS** per serving: 3.

## Got Leftovers?

**Turn leftover mint into a refreshing drink:**
**Crush a handful of leaves and steep in a pitcher of cold water with the juice of a fresh lemon or add to iced tea. Or, hang the leaves upside down to dry; they'll be fully dried in about one month.**

# Lamb Chops with Yogurt-Mint Sauce

*Fresh mint and cucumber give this sauce a cooling tang. If fresh mint is unavailable, don't substitute dried mint; look for fresh dill instead.*

MAKES 4 SERVINGS

Four 5-ounce bone-in loin lamb chops, about 1" thick

¾ cup plain nonfat yogurt

½ cucumber, peeled, seeded and chopped

¼ cup mint leaves

3 scallions, sliced

1 garlic clove, chopped

¼ teaspoon crushed red pepper flakes, or to taste

Salt and freshly ground pepper, to taste

½ teaspoon paprika

1. Remove the lamb chops from the refrigerator about 1 hour before cooking. Preheat the broiler.

2. In a blender or food processor, combine the yogurt, cucumber, mint, scallions and garlic; puree. Season with the pepper flakes and salt. Let stand at room temperature.

3. Meanwhile, season the lamb with the salt and pepper. Place on the broiler rack and broil 3–4" from heat until done to taste, 4–5 minutes per side for medium-rare; add 1–2 minutes per side for medium or well-done chops. Serve, topped with the sauce and sprinkled lightly with the paprika.

**Per serving**: 232 Calories, 11 g Total Fat, 4 g Saturated Fat, 78 mg Cholesterol, 399 mg Sodium, 5 g Total Carbohydrate, 1 g Dietary Fiber, 26 g Protein, 113 mg Calcium. **POINTS** per serving: 5.

# Savory Lamb Stew

*This stew is an ideal lunch on a winter's day. Make a double batch on Sunday afternoon and enjoy throughout the week.*

MAKES 4 SERVINGS

4 teaspoons olive oil

1 onion, finely chopped

½ carrot, finely chopped

½ celery stalk, finely chopped

2 garlic cloves, minced

1 pound boneless lamb (from the leg), cut into 1½" cubes

½ cup dry white wine

1 cup drained canned chopped plum tomatoes

2 teaspoons minced fresh rosemary, or 1 teaspoon dried leaves

2 teaspoons minced fresh sage, or 1 teaspoon dried leaves

2 teaspoons minced fresh thyme, or 1 teaspoon dried leaves

½ teaspoon grated lemon zest

Salt and freshly ground pepper, to taste

2 medium all-purpose potatoes, peeled and cubed

2 cups cut green beans

1 tablespoon minced parsley

1. Preheat the oven to 350° F. In a medium flameproof casserole, heat the oil. Sauté the onion, carrot, celery and garlic until the onion is translucent, 8–10 minutes. Add the lamb; sauté until no longer pink, about 3 minutes. Add the wine; cook 2 minutes. Stir in the tomatoes, rosemary, sage, thyme, lemon zest, salt, pepper and ½ cup hot water; bring to a boil. Bake, covered partially and stirring occasionally, 40 minutes.

2. Stir in the potatoes, green beans and another ½ cup hot water; cover tightly and bake until tender, about 20 minutes longer. If the sauce seems thin, remove the lamb, then boil the sauce over medium-high heat until thickened; return the lamb to the sauce. Serve, sprinkled with the parsley.

**Per serving**: 342 Calories, 12 g Total Fat, 3 g Saturated Fat, 73 mg Cholesterol, 518 mg Sodium, 27 g Total Carbohydrate, 5 g Dietary Fiber, 27 g Protein, 92 mg Calcium. *POINTS* per serving: 7.

# Lamb and Pepper Stir-Fry

*If you like, you can substitute pork loin for the lamb.*

MAKES 4 SERVINGS

1 tablespoon + 1½ teaspoons soy sauce

2 teaspoons honey

4 teaspoons vegetable oil

1 pound boneless lamb (from the loin), cut into thin strips

1 red bell pepper, seeded and cut into ½" strips

1 yellow bell pepper, seeded and cut into ½" strips

6 scallions, cut into 2" lengths

4 garlic cloves, minced

2 teaspoons grated peeled gingerroot

Grated zest of 1 orange

¼ teaspoon crushed red pepper flakes, or to taste

2 tablespoons low-sodium chicken broth

Coarsely ground pepper, to taste

1 tablespoon chopped mint

1. In a small bowl, combine the soy sauce and honey.

2. Heat a large nonstick wok or skillet over high heat. Add the oil and lamb; stir-fry until the lamb loses its red color, 1–2 minutes. With slotted spoon, transfer to a plate. Reduce the heat slightly. Add the bell peppers; stir-fry until slightly softened, about 4 minutes. Add the scallions, garlic, gingerroot, orange zest, pepper flakes and soy sauce mixture; stir-fry 30 seconds longer. Return the lamb to the wok. Add the broth and pepper; stir-fry 30 seconds longer. Serve, sprinkled with the mint.

**Per serving:** 251 Calories, 12 g Total Fat, 3 g Saturated Fat, 73 mg Cholesterol, 449 mg Sodium, 11 g Total Carbohydrate, 3 g Dietary Fiber, 25 g Protein, 31 mg Calcium. *POINTS* per serving: 5.

## Super Stir-Fries

*Stir-fries are a terrific way to showcase meat as part of a delicious meal that includes fresh vegetables and just a bit of oil. Serve over pasta or rice, and you have a complete meal. Try our Spicy Pork Stir-Fry (page 175) or Spicy Beef and Broccoli Stir-Fry (page 167) and you'll be hooked. It's simple to create your own stir-fries, combining meat and vegetables in a wok or heavy skillet. Have all your ingredients ready before you start, as stir-fries cook in a flash. Below you'll find suggested cuts of meat (pick one) and vegetables (pick a few!) to combine.*

| MEAT | VEGETABLES |
| --- | --- |
| *Sirloin Tip* | *Mushrooms* |
| *Strip Steak* | *Broccoli* |
| *Bottom Round* | *Bok Choy* |
| *Tenderloin* | *Cabbage* |
| *Top Round Steak* | *Spinach* |
| *Round Tip Steak* | *Pea Pods* |

# Shish Kebabs

*Experiment with different vegetables. Try chunks of zucchini and eggplant as well as cherry tomatoes in this classic recipe.*

MAKES 4 SERVINGS

1 onion, chopped

2 tablespoons fresh lemon juice

5–6 garlic cloves, minced

1 tablespoon minced dill

1 tablespoon dried oregano leaves

1 tablespoon paprika

½ teaspoon freshly ground pepper

1 pound boneless lamb (from the leg), cut into 1½" cubes

1 onion, cut into 8 wedges

1 red bell pepper, seeded and cut into 1" pieces

1. To prepare the marinade, in a blender or food processor, combine the onion, lemon juice, garlic, dill, oregano, paprika and pepper; puree. Put the lamb in a gallon-size sealable plastic bag; add the marinade. Seal the bag, squeezing out the air; turn to coat the lamb. Refrigerate, turning the bag occasionally, at least 3 hours or overnight. Remove the lamb from the refrigerator 1 hour before cooking. Soak four 10" bamboo skewers in water about 30 minutes to avoid burning under the broiler.

3. Preheat the broiler. Alternately thread the lamb, onion and pepper onto the skewers. Place on the broiler rack and broil 3–4" from heat until the lamb is done to taste, 3–4 minutes on each side for medium-rare; add 1–2 minutes per side for medium or well-done.

**Per serving:** 183 Calories, 8 g Total Fat, 3 g Saturated Fat, 73 mg Cholesterol, 59 mg Sodium, 5 g Total Carbohydrate, 2 g Dietary Fiber, 24 g Protein, 20 mg Calcium. *POINTS* per serving: 4.

## Grilling Guide

*Steaks on the grill are a universal favorite, whether cooked in the great outdoors or on a handy indoor grill. All steaks take well to marinades, and you can use ours (see pages 14–16) or a favorite of your own. Just follow these guidelines for irresistible sizzle.*

- *Trim excess fat before cooking to prevent flare-ups. Score edges of steaks before grilling to prevent curling. Use long-handled tongs to turn; piercing with a fork allows juices to escape.*

- *For cooking tender cuts such as club, rib-eye, T-bone, porterhouse and sirloin steaks, about 1¼" thick, sear over direct high heat on one side. Turn with tongs and continue to grill, reducing heat by raising the cooking rack.*

TIME TABLE

| | |
|---|---|
| *Medium-rare* | *3–5 minutes first side, 8 minutes second side* |
| *Medium* | *3–5 minutes first side, 10 minutes second side* |
| *Well Done* | *3–5 minutes first side, 12 minutes second side* |

# Honey-Mustard Pork Chops

*If you like, liquefy the honey in the microwave: Place in a small microwavable bowl and microwave at 20–30% power for 30 seconds.*

MAKES 4 SERVINGS

4 teaspoons honey

¼ cup Dijon mustard

1 teaspoon cider or wine vinegar

Salt and freshly ground pepper, to taste

Four 5-ounce bone-in loin pork chops, 1" thick

1. To prepare the marinade, in a small saucepan over low heat, heat the honey until it liquefies. Stir in the mustard, vinegar, salt and pepper; cool to room temperature.

2. Place the pork chops in a gallon-size sealable plastic bag; add the marinade. Seal the bag, squeezing out the air; turn to coat the chops. Refrigerate, turning the bag occasionally, at least 8 hours or overnight. Remove the chops from the refrigerator 30 minutes before broiling.

3. Preheat the broiler. Discard the marinade. Place the chops on the broiler rack and broil 3–4" from the heat until cooked through, 6–7 minutes on each side.

**Per serving:** 178 Calories, 7 g Total Fat, 3 g Saturated Fat, 10 mg Cholesterol, 124 mg Sodium, 2 g Total Carbohydrate, 0 g Dietary Fiber, 26 g Protein, 27 mg Calcium. **POINTS** per serving: 4.

# Tuscan-Style Pork Roast

*Ask the butcher to clean the fat and cartilage off the bones so they'll brown nicely, instead of getting burned and gristly. For a pretty accompaniment, poach peeled and cored miniature pears, dried cranberries and slivered dried apricots in wine; serve with the dried fruit in the pear cavities.*

MAKES 8 SERVINGS

One 2¼-pound bone-in pork loin roast

3 garlic cloves, slivered lengthwise

4 teaspoons olive oil

1 tablespoon minced rosemary

½ teaspoon salt

½ teaspoon freshly ground pepper

½ cup dry white wine

1. Preheat the oven to 350° F. With a small sharp knife, make several small incisions in the roast; insert a sliver of garlic in each incision. Rub the roast with the oil, rosemary, salt and pepper.

2. Place the roast, bone-side down, in a shallow roasting pan; pour the wine into the pan. Roast, basting occasionally with the pan juices, until cooked through and an instant-read thermometer inserted in the pork (not touching bone) registers 160° F, about 1½ hours. Let stand 10 minutes before slicing.

**Per serving:** 197 Calories, 11 g Total Fat, 3 g Saturated Fat, 45 mg Cholesterol, 195 mg Sodium, 1 g Total Carbohydrate, 0 g Dietary Fiber, 21 g Protein, 24 mg Calcium. **POINTS** per serving: 5.

## Got Leftovers?

Try to slice only the amount to be served; save the remainder unsliced. Refrigerate the leftovers, well wrapped, for two to three days. Use the leftovers in sandwiches.

*Tuscan-Style Pork Roast*

# Pork Chops with Pineapple Chutney

*When you're looking for a quick fix for the same old chicken cutlets, simply grill and serve with this versatile chutney.*

MAKES 4 SERVINGS

1 pound diced peeled cored fresh pineapple

1 Granny Smith apple, peeled, cored and finely chopped

½ cup golden raisins, chopped

½ red bell pepper, seeded and finely chopped

½ red onion, finely chopped

¼ cup cider vinegar

2 tablespoons grated peeled gingerroot

4 teaspoons orange marmalade

1 small jalapeño pepper, seeded, deveined and minced (wear gloves to prevent irritation)

2 garlic cloves, minced

1 teaspoon yellow mustard seeds (optional)

¼ teaspoon cinnamon

Pinch ground cloves

Salt and freshly ground pepper, to taste

4 teaspoons olive or vegetable oil

Four 5-ounce bone-in loin pork chops

1. To prepare the chutney, in a heavy medium saucepan over medium-low heat, combine all the ingredients except the oil and pork chops; bring to a simmer. Cook until thickened and the flavors are blended, 40–45 minutes. If the mixture is dry, add water, 1–2 tablespoons at a time.

2. Preheat the oven to 300° F. In a heavy medium ovenproof skillet, heat the oil. Sauté the chops until browned, 1–1½ minutes on each side. Place the skillet in the oven and bake, turning the chops occasionally, until cooked through, 10–15 minutes. Serve with the chutney.

**Per serving:** 384 Calories, 12 g Total Fat, 3 g Saturated Fat, 70 mg Cholesterol, 349 mg Sodium, 45 g Total Carbohydrate, 4 g Dietary Fiber, 28 g Protein, 59 mg Calcium. **POINTS** per serving: 8.

## Tip

**Look for fresh pineapple that's vacuum-packed and already peeled and cored in your supermarket's produce department. If you can't find it by the whole pineapples, check near the packaged foods like broccoli florets, baby carrots and salad blends.**

# Spicy Pork Stir-Fry

*Use care when cleaning and preparing jalapeño peppers—they contain an ingredient called capsaicin that can actually burn the skin. It is safest to wear gloves when handling them; of course, wash all utensils with soap and hot water after use.*

### MAKES 4 SERVINGS

1 tablespoon vegetable oil

1 pound pork tenderloin, cut into thin slices

1 red bell pepper, seeded and cut into ½" strips

8 scallions, cut into 2" lengths

One 20-ounce can pineapple chunks, drained

1 tomato, cut into 8 wedges

1 jalapeño pepper, seeded, deveined and finely chopped (wear gloves to prevent irritation)

2 teaspoons grated peeled gingerroot

2 garlic cloves, minced

4 teaspoons soy sauce

1 teaspoon Asian sesame oil

¼ cup chopped cilantro

1. Heat a large nonstick wok or skillet over high heat. Add the vegetable oil and pork; stir-fry until the pork is no longer pink, 1–2 minutes. With a slotted spoon, transfer to a plate.

2. Add the bell pepper; stir-fry 2–3 minutes. Add the scallions; stir-fry 30 seconds, then add the pineapple and stir-fry 30 seconds longer. Add the tomato, jalapeño, gingerroot, garlic, soy sauce and sesame oil. Return the pork to the wok and stir-fry 1–2 minutes longer. Serve, sprinkled with the cilantro.

**Per serving:** 278 Calories, 9 g Total Fat, 2 g Saturated Fat, 61 mg Cholesterol, 394 mg Sodium, 27 g Total Carbohydrate, 3 g Dietary Fiber, 24 g Protein, 49 mg Calcium. **POINTS** per serving: 6.

# Pork and Black Beans

*If you like, use turkey breast instead of the pork.*

### MAKES 4 SERVINGS

2 garlic cloves, minced

½ teaspoon hot paprika

¼ teaspoon ground cumin

¼ teaspoon salt

5 ounces lean pork tenderloin

1 teaspoon extra virgin olive oil

2 tablespoons white vinegar

One 15-ounce can black beans, rinsed and drained

½ carrot, finely diced

2 tablespoons fresh lime juice

½ tomato, diced

1 red onion, chopped

2 tablespoons chopped cilantro

1. In a small bowl, combine the garlic, paprika, cumin and salt; rub into the pork.

2. In a medium nonstick skillet, heat the oil. Sauté the pork until browned, 2–3 minutes on each side. Reduce the heat and cook, covered, turning occasionally, until cooked through, about 10 minutes. Transfer to a plate. Halve the pork lengthwise, then cut crosswise into thin slices.

3. Add the vinegar to the pan drippings and simmer, stirring, until the acidity cooks off, about 2 minutes. Add the beans, carrot and lime juice; cook, tossing, about 1 minute. Transfer to a medium bowl. Add the pork, tomato, onion and cilantro; toss to combine.

**Per serving:** 190 Calories, 3 g Total Fat, 1 g Saturated Fat, 23 mg Cholesterol, 163 mg Sodium, 26 g Total Carbohydrate, 3 g Dietary Fiber, 16 g Protein, 30 mg Calcium. **POINTS** per serving: 3.

# Italian Sausage with Peppers

*You can control the heat of this hearty dish by using hot or sweet sausages, or a combination of the two.*

MAKES 4 SERVINGS

2 teaspoons olive oil

1 Bermuda onion, halved lengthwise and thinly sliced

1 red bell pepper, seeded and thinly sliced

1 yellow bell pepper, seeded and thinly sliced

1 green bell pepper, seeded and thinly sliced

1 fennel bulb, trimmed and thinly sliced

2 garlic cloves, thinly sliced

1 cup canned diced tomatoes

Salt and freshly ground pepper, to taste

½ pound cooked Italian pork sausage (hot, sweet or a combination)

2 cups penne

¼ cup chopped basil

2 tablespoons chopped flat-leaf parsley

1. In a large nonstick skillet, heat the oil. Sauté the onion, bell peppers and fennel until the vegetables turn golden, 8–10 minutes. Add the garlic and sauté 1–2 minutes longer. Stir in the tomatoes, salt and pepper. Reduce the heat and simmer, stirring occasionally, 15 minutes. Add the sausage; simmer, covered, stirring occasionally, until the flavors are blended, about 20 minutes. If the sauce becomes too dry, add 1–2 tablespoons of water.

2. Meanwhile, cook the penne according to package directions; drain.

3. Add the basil, parsley and penne to the sausage mixture; toss to combine.

**Per serving**: 438 Calories, 20 g Total Fat, 6 g Saturated Fat, 44 mg Cholesterol, 972 mg Sodium, 50 g Total Carbohydrate, 6 g Dietary Fiber, 16 g Protein, 89 mg Calcium. **POINTS** per serving: 9.

# Orange-Glazed Ham

*Any leftovers? Toss some diced ham and tomato into scrambled eggs for a skillet lunch in minutes.*

MAKES 4 SERVINGS

One ¾-pound ready-to-eat boneless ham steak

4 whole cloves

4 slices canned pineapple, drained and quartered, with ½ cup juice

½ cup orange juice

3 tablespoons orange marmalade

¼ teaspoon cinnamon

1. Preheat the oven to 400° F. Make several cuts along the edge of the ham; stud with the cloves, then place in a shallow ovenproof pan. Place the pineapple around the ham.

2. To make the glaze, in a small saucepan, combine the pineapple juice, orange juice, marmalade and cinnamon; bring to a boil. Boil until slightly thickened, 5–6 minutes. Pour the glaze over the ham. Bake, basting occasionally with the glaze, about 15 minutes; the glaze should be thickened. If there is too much liquid, remove the ham from the pan; keep warm. Return the pineapple and glaze to the upper oven rack until the glaze thickens, 5–10 minutes. Serve the ham with the pineapple and glaze.

**Per serving:** 196 Calories, 4 g Total Fat, 1 g Saturated Fat, 40 mg Cholesterol, 1,224 mg Sodium, 23 g Total Carbohydrate, 17 g Protein, 1 g Dietary Fiber, 25 mg Calcium. *POINTS* per serving: 4.

# Red Beans and Rice

*Kidney beans are a great source of iron—more so than most types of beans. Serving them with something acidic, like the tomatoes in this recipe, helps make the iron more available to the body.*

MAKES 4 SERVINGS

4 teaspoons olive oil

2 onions, finely chopped

4 garlic cloves, finely chopped

One 16-ounce can kidney beans, rinsed and drained

1 cup low-sodium chicken broth

1 cup chopped canned plum tomatoes, with juice

½ cup diced lean smoked ham or turkey

6 scallions, thinly sliced

1 teaspoon minced thyme, or ½ teaspoon dried

2 bay leaves

¼ teaspoon hot red pepper sauce

Salt and freshly ground pepper, to taste

4 cups cooked white rice

1. In a medium nonstick saucepan, heat the oil. Sauté the onions and garlic until the onions are translucent, 6–7 minutes.

2. Stir in the beans, broth, tomatoes, ham, scallions, thyme, bay leaves and pepper sauce; bring to a boil. Reduce the heat and simmer, stirring occasionally, until the beans are creamy, 30–40 minutes. Season with the salt and pepper; discard the bay leaves. Serve over the rice.

**Per serving:** 442 Calories, 6 g Total Fat, 1 g Saturated Fat, 0 mg Cholesterol, 563 mg Sodium, 78 g Total Carbohydrate, 2 g Dietary Fiber, 19 g Protein, 126 mg Calcium. *POINTS* per serving: 9.

# RECIPES

Fish and Seafood

# Cod Stew with Potatoes

*Cod and potatoes are a classic Spanish combination. Although a Spanish cook would likely start with the dried salted cod known as* bacalao, *you can approximate the flavor—with a lot less time—by using fresh cod.*

MAKES 4 SERVINGS

4 medium all-purpose potatoes, peeled and chunked

3 onions, diced

2 celery stalks, diced

1 red bell pepper, seeded and diced

8 garlic cloves, chopped

1 teaspoon dried thyme leaves

½ teaspoon salt

1 bay leaf

1¼ pounds cod fillets, cut into 2" chunks

¼ cup chopped parsley

2 tablespoons fresh lemon juice

½ teaspoon freshly ground pepper

1. In a medium saucepan, combine the potatoes, onions, celery, bell pepper, garlic, thyme, salt and bay leaf with 4 cups water; bring to a boil. Reduce the heat and simmer, covered, until the potatoes are just tender, 15–20 minutes. Transfer 2 cups of the vegetables and about 1 cup of the cooking liquid to a food processor or blender; puree.

2. Return the puree to the saucepan and bring to simmer. Add the cod; cook until just opaque in the center, 3–4 minutes. Gently stir in the parsley, lemon juice and pepper; discard the bay leaf.

**Per serving**: 281 Calories, 1 g Total Fat, 0 g Saturated Fat, 61 mg Cholesterol, 399 mg Sodium, 38 g Total Carbohydrate, 5 g Dietary Fiber, 30 g Protein, 90 mg Calcium. **POINTS** per serving: 5.

# Flounder with Broiled Tomatoes

*Inspired by the flavors of southern France, this easy preparation is ideal for almost any white-fleshed fish, like sole, cod or halibut.*

MAKES 4 SERVINGS

4 teaspoons fat-free milk

¼ cup whole-wheat flour

1 egg white, lightly beaten

¾ cup dried whole-wheat bread crumbs

1¼ pounds flounder fillets, cut into 4 pieces

6 plum tomatoes, halved lengthwise

½ teaspoon dried thyme leaves

1. Spray the broiler rack with nonstick cooking spray; preheat the broiler.

2. Place the milk, flour, egg white and ½ cup of the bread crumbs separately into 4 shallow bowls. Dip each piece of flounder first into the milk, then the flour, egg white and finally the bread crumbs; transfer to the broiler rack. Broil 5" from the heat until the fish is just opaque in the center, 4–5 minutes on each side. Transfer to a platter; keep warm.

3. Place the tomatoes cut-side up in a small baking pan. Broil until lightly browned, 3–5 minutes. Let cool slightly. In a small bowl, combine the remaining ¼ cup bread crumbs with the thyme; sprinkle the bread crumbs onto the tomatoes; continue broiling until the crumbs are toasted, 3–4 minutes. Serve with the flounder.

**Per serving:** 200 Calories, 2 g Total Fat, 1 g Saturated Fat, 68 mg Cholesterol, 188 mg Sodium, 14 g Total Carbohydrate, 3 g Dietary Fiber, 30 g Protein, 49 mg Calcium. **POINTS** per serving: 4.

# "Fried" Flounder with Tartar Sauce

*Enjoy guilt-free tartar sauce with our lightened version of the classic. Here, its creamy texture adds extra flavor to the lemon-spiced flounder.*

MAKES 4 SERVINGS

¾ cup plain nonfat yogurt

2 tablespoons minced dill pickle

2 scallions, minced

2 tablespoons minced parsley

1 tablespoon fresh lemon juice

1 tablespoon reduced-calorie mayonnaise

2 teaspoons pickle relish

2 teaspoons capers, rinsed, drained and minced

1 teaspoon low-sodium Worcestershire sauce

¼ teaspoon freshly ground pepper

⅛ teaspoon cayenne pepper

¾ cup seasoned dried bread crumbs

½ cup mixed nuts, toasted and finely chopped

1 tablespoon dried thyme leaves

1½ teaspoons finely grated lemon zest

½ cup fat-free buttermilk

1¼ pound flounder fillets, cut into 4 pieces

4 lemon wedges

1. To prepare the tartar sauce, in a small bowl, combine the yogurt, pickle, scallions, parsley, lemon juice, mayonnaise, pickle relish, capers, Worcestershire sauce, pepper and cayenne. Refrigerate, covered, until the flavors are blended, at least 1 hour.

2. Preheat the oven to 400° F; spray a baking sheet with nonstick cooking spray.

3. On a sheet of wax paper, combine the bread crumbs, nuts, thyme and lemon zest. Pour the buttermilk into a shallow bowl. Dip each piece of flounder into the buttermilk, then the bread crumb mixture, pressing gently to coat. Place on the baking sheet and spray with nonstick cooking spray. Bake until just opaque in the center, about 10 minutes. Serve with the tartar sauce and lemon wedges.

**Per serving:** 355 Calories, 12 g Total Fat, 2 g Saturated Fat, 75 mg Cholesterol, 998 mg Sodium, 27 g Total Carbohydrate, 2 g Dietary Fiber, 35 g Protein, 200 mg Calcium. *POINTS* per serving: 8.

## How We Did It

**A small amount of nuts goes a long way in the crumb coating, adding a "fried" toasty taste and crunch without a lot of fat. Thinning the mayonnaise in the tartar sauce with yogurt yields big fat savings, too.**

# Paella

*Paella is a traditional Spanish dish that combines meats, sausage and fish in a rice base. Our version uses chicken, shrimp and mussels to create lots of flavor without lots of fat.*

MAKES 4 SERVINGS

4 teaspoons olive oil

1 red bell pepper, seeded and coarsely chopped

1 red onion, thinly sliced

5–6 garlic cloves, minced

1 cup regular long-grain rice

¼ pound thin-sliced chicken cutlets

3 cups low-sodium chicken broth

¾ pound medium shrimp, peeled (tails left on) and deveined

2–3 saffron strands (optional)

½ pound medium mussels, cleaned and cooked

½ cup canned chickpeas, rinsed and drained

2 tablespoons minced parsley

½ teaspoon salt

¼ teaspoon freshly ground pepper

1. In a large nonstick skillet, heat the oil. Sauté the bell pepper, onion and garlic until softened, about 5 minutes. Stir in the rice and chicken; cook, stirring, until the chicken is lightly browned, about 2 minutes.

2. Stir in the broth, shrimp and saffron (if using); bring to a low boil. Reduce the heat and simmer, covered, until most of the liquid is absorbed, 10–15 minutes. Stir in the mussels, chickpeas, parsley, salt and pepper. Cook, covered, until all the liquid is absorbed, about 5 minutes longer.

**Per serving:** 413 Calories, 10 g Total Fat, 2 g Saturated Fat, 143 mg Cholesterol, 626 mg Sodium, 47 g Total Carbohydrate, 4 g Dietary Fiber, 32 g Protein, 87 mg Calcium. *POINTS* per serving: 8.

# Tandoori Haddock

*Fascinating aromas will fill your kitchen as this Indian-seasoned dish bakes. Serve it with toasted wedges of pocketless pita bread.*

MAKES 4 SERVINGS

1½ cups plain nonfat yogurt

1 onion, chopped

2 tablespoons curry powder or garam masala

2 tablespoons fresh lemon juice

1 tablespoon minced seeded green chile pepper

1 tablespoon grated peeled gingerroot

1 large garlic clove, minced

1 teaspoon salt

1 teaspoon turmeric

1 pound haddock fillets, cut into 4 pieces

2 cups shredded green leaf lettuce

1 onion, sliced and separated into rings

4 lime wedges

1. To prepare the marinade, in a blender or food processor, combine the yogurt, onion, curry powder, lemon juice, chile, gingerroot, garlic, salt and turmeric; puree. Transfer to a gallon-size sealable plastic bag; add the haddock. Seal the bag, squeezing out the air; turn to coat the fish. Refrigerate, turning the bag occasionally, 6–8 hours.

2. Preheat the broiler. Place the fish in a shallow metal pan; top with the marinade. Broil until the fish is just opaque in the center, 4–6 minutes.

3. Line a platter with the lettuce and onion rings; top with the fish and lime wedges.

**Per serving:** 182 Calories, 2 g Total Fat, 0 g Saturated Fat, 66 mg Cholesterol, 730 mg Sodium, 14 g Total Carbohydrate, 2 g Dietary Fiber, 28 g Protein, 239 mg Calcium. *POINTS* per serving: 3.

*Tandoori Haddock*

# Caribbean Mahi Mahi

*If mahi mahi is unavailable, try substituting orange roughy or flounder in this island-inspired dish.*

MAKES 4 SERVINGS

1 banana, cut into ½" slices

1¼ pounds mahi mahi fillets, cut into 2" pieces

1 cup low-sodium chicken broth

⅔ cup pineapple juice

½ cup mango slices

¼ cup coconut milk

1 teaspoon salt

½ teaspoon freshly ground pepper

4 cups cooked white rice

1 cup watercress leaves

1. Spray a large nonstick skillet with nonstick cooking spray; heat. Cook the banana until golden brown, 1–2 minutes on each side. Add the mahi mahi; cook until just opaque in the center, 3–4 minutes. Stir in the broth, pineapple juice, mango, coconut milk, salt and pepper; heat through.

2. Line a platter with the rice. Top with the fish mixture and garnish with the watercress.

**Per serving**: 437 Calories, 6 g Total Fat, 4 g Saturated Fat, 104 mg Cholesterol, 721 mg Sodium, 63 g Total Carbohydrate, 2 g Dietary Fiber, 32 g Protein, 34 mg Calcium. **POINTS** per serving: 9.

# Fruity Monkfish Salad

*Star fruit has a thin, waxy skin that's completely edible.*

MAKES 4 SERVINGS

2 tablespoons olive oil

½ red onion, finely chopped

1 tablespoon poppy seeds

2 teaspoons ground coriander

1 teaspoon ground cumin

½ cup chopped mint

¼ cup red-wine vinegar

2 tablespoons fresh lemon juice

½ pound cooked monkfish fillet, cut into 1" pieces

1½ cups cooked couscous

2 tablespoons currants

1 medium star fruit, sliced

4 dates, pitted and chopped

1 teaspoon salt

½ teaspoon freshly ground pepper

2 cups shredded green leaf lettuce

1. To prepare the dressing, in a small saucepan, heat the oil. Cook the onion, poppy seeds, coriander and cumin until the onions begin to soften, 1–2 minutes. Cool slightly; stir in the mint, vinegar and lemon juice.

2. In a large bowl, combine the monkfish, couscous, currants, star fruit, dates, salt and pepper. Drizzle with the dressing; toss to coat. Line a serving platter with the lettuce; mound the salad in the center.

**Per serving**: 357 Calories, 10 g Total Fat, 1 g Saturated Fat, 18 mg Cholesterol, 611 mg Sodium, 50 g Total Carbohydrate, 6 g Dietary Fiber, 18 g Protein, 96 mg Calcium. **POINTS** per serving: 7.

# Thai Monkfish

*Basmati or jasmine rice, with their wonderful perfume, are the perfect match for Thai food.*

MAKES 4 SERVINGS

¼ cup low-fat (1%) milk

½ teaspoon coconut extract

1 pound monkfish fillets, cut into 12 slices

4 teaspoons chunky peanut butter

1 tablespoon grated peeled gingerroot

1 jalapeño pepper, seeded, deveined and minced (wear gloves to prevent irritation)

2 tablespoons chopped cilantro

2 tablespoons fresh lime juice

2 garlic cloves, minced

¾ teaspoon salt

¼ teaspoon freshly ground pepper

4 lime slices

2 cups cooked white or basmati rice

1. Spray the grill rack with nonstick cooking spray; place the grill rack 5" from the coals. Preheat the grill. In a small bowl, combine the milk and coconut extract.

2. Cut four 12 × 24" pieces of double-thickness heavy-duty foil. Arrange 3 slices of monkfish in the center of each piece of foil; dot with the peanut butter. Sprinkle with the milk mixture, the gingerroot, jalapeño, cilantro, lime juice, garlic, salt and pepper; top with the lime slices. Make a packet by bringing the sides of the foil up to meet in the center and folding over the edges, then folding the edges of each end together. Allowing room for the packets to expand, crimp the edges.

3. Grill the packets until cooked through 25–30 minutes; open the packets carefully when testing for doneness, as steam will escape. Serve with the rice, drizzled with the juices.

**Per serving**: 226 Calories, 5 g Total Fat, 1 g Saturated Fat, 26 mg Cholesterol, 491 mg Sodium, 26 g Total Carbohydrate, 1 g Dietary Fiber, 19 g Protein, 44 mg Calcium. **POINTS** per serving: 5.

## Tip

**If you prefer, bake the packets in a 400° F oven for 25–30 minutes.**

# Herb-Crusted Red Snapper

*Black peppercorns, which are picked when the berry is not quite ripe, are dried until their skin turns dark brown or black. They have a stronger flavor than white peppercorns, which have been allowed to ripen and have had their skins removed. White peppercorns are smaller, smoother and milder because of this, and are used primarily for their appearance.*

MAKES 4 SERVINGS

½ cup chopped flat-leaf parsley

¼ cup dry white wine

3 tablespoons plain dried bread crumbs

2 teaspoons grated lemon zest

2 tablespoons fresh lemon juice

1 tablespoon minced fresh oregano, or ½ teaspoon dried

1 tablespoon minced fresh thyme, or ½ teaspoon dried

2 teaspoons olive oil

1 garlic clove, minced

¼ teaspoon salt

¼ teaspoon ground white pepper

1¼ pounds red snapper fillets, cut into 4 pieces

4 carrots, thinly sliced

4 medium zucchini, thinly sliced

2 teaspoons reduced-calorie margarine, melted

1. Preheat the oven to 375° F; spray a 9 × 13" glass or ceramic baking dish with nonstick cooking spray.

2. In a small bowl, combine the parsley, wine, bread crumbs, lemon zest, lemon juice, oregano, thyme, oil, garlic, salt and pepper; let stand, covered, until it forms a paste-like consistency, about 10 minutes.

3. Place the fish, skin-side down, in the baking dish. With a spatula, spread the herb paste over the fillets. Bake until the fish is just opaque in the center and the herb paste has formed a crust, about 12 minutes.

4. Meanwhile, place the carrots in a steamer basket; set in a medium saucepan over 1" boiling water. Cover and steam 5 minutes; add the zucchinis and steam until the vegetables are firm but tender, about 3 minutes longer. Toss gently with the margarine. Serve the snapper, with the vegetables on the side.

**Per serving**: 275 Calories, 6 g Total Fat, 1 g Saturated Fat, 52 mg Cholesterol, 334 mg Sodium, 21 g Total Carbohydrate, 5 g Dietary Fiber, 33 g Protein, 128 mg Calcium. **POINTS** per serving: 5.

# Cajun Red Snapper

*Cajun cooking combines French flair with native Southern ingredients and lots of bold spices.*

## MAKES 4 SERVINGS

1¼ pounds red snapper fillets

1 tablespoon paprika

1 teaspoon garlic powder

1 teaspoon onion powder

1 teaspoon freshly ground pepper

1 teaspoon cayenne pepper

1 teaspoon ground white pepper

1 teaspoon dried oregano leaves, crumbled

½ teaspoon salt

½ teaspoon dried thyme leaves, crumbled

4 teaspoons reduced-calorie margarine

2 tablespoons fresh lemon juice

1 tablespoon chopped chives

1 lemon, cut into wedges

1. Preheat the grill; place the grill rack 5" from the coals.

2. Spray a double-thickness sheet of heavy-duty foil with nonstick cooking spray; place the snapper, skin-side down, in the center. Fold up the edges to make a pan. In a small bowl, mix the paprika, garlic powder, onion powder, ground pepper, cayenne, white pepper, oregano, salt and thyme. Spread the margarine on the fish; sprinkle with the spice mixture, lemon juice and chives.

3. Transfer the foil to the grill rack. Cover the grill, opening the top and bottom flues slightly. Cook the snapper until just opaque in the center, 10–15 minutes. Serve with the lemon wedges.

**Per serving:** 175 Calories, 4 g Total Fat, 1 g Saturated Fat, 52 mg Cholesterol, 400 mg Sodium, 4 g Total Carbohydrate, 1 g Dietary Fiber, 30 g Protein, 65 mg Calcium. **POINTS** per serving: 4.

## Fish on the Grill

*Fast, easy and delicious, fish and shellfish are ideal choices for grilling. Here are a few pointers for perfect results.*

- *Seafood cooks best over a moderately hot fire; if you're grilling a whole fish, bank the coals on either side of the grill and place the fish in the center.*

- *Fish steaks, fillets, kebabs and shellfish should be cooked over direct heat. For fragile fish, use a hinged basket or a mesh rack, or place the fish on a sheet of perforated aluminum foil. Grill racks, baskets and foil should be sprayed with nonstick cooking spray.*

- *Fish steaks should be turned halfway through cooking time; fillets under 1" do not need to be turned.*

- *Thin fillets are tricky on the grill. For best results, fold the ends under for an even thickness and use a basket or perforated foil for cooking.*

- *To estimate cooking time, measure the fish at its thickest part and allow 10 minutes per inch. A whole fish may take as long as 12 minutes per inch. Never overcook! Fish is done when it turns opaque; if it flakes easily with a fork, it's overdone. Shrimp, crab, lobster and scallops also turn opaque; shellfish such as oysters, clams, and mussels open when done.*

- *Add extra flavor by tossing a handful of soaked fruitwood or mesquite chips or whole sprigs of thyme, rosemary, dill, basil or oregano on the fire just before serving the fish.*

# Louisiana Stuffed Red Snapper

*Serve this Creole style, with rice, and follow with a crisp salad.*

MAKES 4 SERVINGS

3 tablespoons reduced-calorie margarine

2 onions, finely chopped

6 garlic cloves, minced

2 cups sliced mushrooms

1 tomato, chopped

¾ cup plain dried bread crumbs

1 teaspoon salt

¼ teaspoon cayenne pepper

One 1½-pound whole red snapper, pan-dressed

1 cup dry white wine

2 sprigs fresh parsley

2 sprigs fresh thyme

4 allspice berries

2 whole cloves

2 bay leaves

1. Preheat the oven to 375° F. In a medium non-stick skillet, melt the margarine. Sauté the onions and garlic until softened, about 5 minutes. Add the mushrooms and tomato; sauté until the mushrooms are tender, 3–4 minutes longer. Remove from the heat. Stir in the bread crumbs, salt and cayenne.

2. Stuff the cavity of the red snapper with the vegetables; fasten together in several places with toothpicks. Place in a shallow ovenproof dish; pour in the wine and ⅓ cup water, then surround the fish with the parsley, thyme, allspice, cloves and bay leaves. Bake until the fish is just opaque in the center, 25–30 minutes. Discard the allspice, cloves and bay leaves.

**Per serving**: 175 Calories, 4 g Total Fat, 1 g Saturated Fat, 52 mg Cholesterol, 400 mg Sodium, 4 g Total Carbohydrate, 1 g Dietary Fiber, 30 g Protein, 65 mg Calcium. **POINTS** per serving: 4.

## Substituting Fish in Recipes

*Don't be wedded to the fish specified in a recipe—instead, go with what looks freshest and best in the market. Try to match shape (round fish or flatfish, steaks or fillets) as well as flavor (lean or oily).*

*The following can be used interchangeably:*

- *Salmon, tuna, mako shark, bluefish, swordfish, mahi mahi, steelhead trout (sometimes called salmon trout)*

- *Snapper, halibut, rockfish, bass*

- *Cod, scrod, haddock, whiting, pollock, monkfish, tilefish*

- *Flounder, sole, turbot*

# Grilled Salmon with Herbs

*If you want to broil the salmon, mince the rosemary and thyme; add it to the herb mixture. Mackerel or bluefish also work beautifully in this simple recipe.*

MAKES 4 SERVINGS

One 10-ounce salmon fillet, skinned

2 teaspoons reduced-calorie margarine

1 tablespoon fresh lemon juice

2 tablespoons minced parsley

½ teaspoon garlic powder

½ teaspoon salt

½ teaspoon paprika

½ teaspoon freshly ground pepper

3–4 sprigs rosemary

3–4 sprigs thyme

1. Preheat the grill; place the grill rack 5" from the coals.

2. Spray a double-thickness sheet of heavy-duty foil with nonstick cooking spray; place the salmon in the center. Fold up the edges to make a pan. Spread both sides of the salmon with the margarine; sprinkle with the lemon juice. In a small bowl, mix the parsley, garlic powder, salt, paprika and pepper; sprinkle on both sides of the fish.

3. Drop the rosemary and thyme sprigs directly onto the coals. Transfer the foil pan to the grill rack. Cover the grill, opening the top and bottom flues slightly. Grill the salmon until just opaque in the center, 10–15 minutes. Cut into 4 pieces.

**Per serving**: 110 Calories, 5 g Total Fat, 1 g Saturated Fat, 38 mg Cholesterol, 310 mg Sodium, 1 g Total Carbohydrate, 0 g Dietary Fiber, 14 g Protein, 13 mg Calcium. **POINTS** per serving: 3.

# Salmon Salad with Horseradish

*Salmon is a terrific source of Omega-3 fatty acids, which some studies show can help reduce the risk of heart disease. With these Scandinavian-inspired flavorings, it's heartily delicious too.*

MAKES 4 SERVINGS

¾ pound salmon fillet, skinned

1¼ pounds small white potatoes, cooked and chopped

1 yellow bell pepper, seeded and diced

1 dill pickle, halved lengthwise and sliced

¼ cup chopped chives

¾ cup plain nonfat yogurt

3 tablespoons drained horseradish

3 tablespoons reduced-calorie mayonnaise

½ teaspoon salt

¼ teaspoon freshly ground pepper

2 cups arugula, cleaned

1. Place the salmon in a large skillet and add ½ cup cold water; bring to boil. Reduce the heat and poach, covered, until just opaque in the center, about 8 minutes. With a slotted spoon, transfer to a plate. Cool completely, then flake.

2. In a large bowl, combine the salmon, potatoes, bell pepper, pickle and chives.

3. In a small bowl, mix the yogurt, horseradish, mayonnaise, salt and pepper. Pour over the salmon mixture; toss to coat. Serve over the arugula.

**Per serving**: 325 Calories, 9 g Total Fat, 2 g Saturated Fat, 46 mg Cholesterol, 654 mg Sodium, 38 g Total Carbohydrate, 4 g Dietary Fiber, 23 g Protein, 147 mg Calcium. **POINTS** per serving: 6.

# Poached Salmon with Dill

*If you've never had cooked cucumbers before, this dish is a great place to start. Simmered just enough to bring out their grassy flavor and preserve their crunch, they're a perfect foil for the rich, silky textured salmon.*

MAKES 4 SERVINGS

2 cups low-sodium chicken broth

½ cup dry white wine

½ cucumber, peeled, seeded and thinly sliced

1 teaspoon grated lemon zest

1 cup cooked wild or long-grain rice

½ medium avocado, peeled and diced

2 tablespoons chopped dill

¼ teaspoon freshly ground pepper

¾ pound salmon fillet, skinned and cut into 4 pieces

In a large skillet, bring the broth and wine to a boil. Add the cucumber and lemon zest; reduce the heat and simmer until the cucumber is tender, about 2 minutes. Stir in the rice, avocado, dill and pepper, then add the salmon. Poach, covered, until the fish is just opaque in the center, 4–6 minutes.

**Per serving**: 246 Calories, 11 g Total Fat, 2 g Saturated Fat, 46 mg Cholesterol, 63 mg Sodium, 12 g Total Carbohydrate, 3 g Dietary Fiber, 20 g Protein, 29 mg Calcium. **POINTS** per serving: 5.

## Storing Seafood

*Here's a handy guide for storing fresh or frozen seafood.*

| FISH | REFRIGERATOR | FREEZER |
|---|---|---|
| **Fillets or Steaks:** | | |
| *Cod, Flounder, Haddock, Halibut* | *3 days* | *6–8 months* |
| *Pollock, Ocean Perch, Sea Trout, Rockfish* | *3 days* | *4 months* |
| *Mullet, Salmon* | *3 days* | *3 months* |
| **Shellfish:** | | |
| *Crab* | *5 days* | *6 months* |
| *Surimi Seafoods* | *2 weeks* | *9 months* |
| *Shrimp* | *4 days* | *5 months* |
| *Oysters, shucked* | *4–7 days* | *Don't freeze* |
| *Clams, shucked* | *5 days* | *Don't freeze* |

# Salmon Salad with Cucumber and Rice

*For a delicious and pretty twist, make the salad without the arugula, and serve it in hollowed-out tomatoes.*

MAKES 4 SERVINGS

4 cups cooked rice

1 cup drained canned pink or red salmon

1 cucumber, diced

1 cup radishes, thinly sliced

¼ cup white-wine vinegar

3 tablespoons fresh lemon juice

2 tablespoons chopped dill

1 tablespoon vegetable oil

1 tablespoon honey

1 teaspoon salt

1 teaspoon freshly ground pepper

2 cups arugula or other lettuce leaves, cleaned

1. In a large bowl, combine the rice, salmon, cucumber and radishes.

2. In a small bowl, whisk the vinegar, lemon juice, dill, oil, honey, salt and pepper.

3. Line a platter with the arugula. Mound the salad in the center and drizzle with the dressing.

**Per serving**: 365 Calories, 9 g Total Fat, 2 g Saturated Fat, 31 mg Cholesterol, 915 mg Sodium, 55 g Total Carbohydrate, 2 g Dietary Fiber, 16 g Protein, 178 mg Calcium. **POINTS** per serving: 8.

*Salmon Salad with Cucumber and Rice*

# Salmon with Fennel

*Chances are you'll find more than one type of salmon in your market. Atlantic salmon is delicately flavored, while Pacific salmon has a more assertive flavor and darker hue.*

MAKES 4 SERVINGS

4 teaspoons margarine

1 fennel bulb, trimmed and thinly sliced

2 leeks, cleaned and thinly sliced

6 shallots, finely chopped

¾ pound salmon fillet, skinned and cut into 4 pieces

1¼ cups low-sodium chicken broth

2 tablespoons dry white wine

½ teaspoon Dijon mustard

¼ teaspoon salt

Pinch freshly ground pepper

2 tablespoons half-and-half

1. In a large nonstick skillet, melt the margarine. Sauté the fennel, leeks and shallots until golden brown, about 10 minutes. With a slotted spoon, transfer to a platter. Add the salmon to the skillet; cook until just opaque in the center, 4–5 minutes on each side. Arrange the salmon over the vegetables; keep warm.

2. In the skillet, combine the broth, wine, mustard, salt and pepper; bring to a boil. Stir in the half-and-half; simmer, stirring, 1 minute. Pour the sauce over the salmon and vegetables.

**Per serving**: 221 Calories, 9 g Total Fat, 2 g Saturated Fat, 48 mg Cholesterol, 256 mg Sodium, 16 g Total Carbohydrate, 2 g Dietary Fiber, 19 g Protein, 95 mg Calcium. **POINTS** per serving: 5.

## Tip

When buying fennel, look for firm, unbrowned bottoms and deep-green feathery tops.

# Baked Scrod with Ratatouille

*Make this dish at summer's end, when the vegetables are glorious and bursting with flavor.*

MAKES 4 SERVINGS

2 onions, chopped

4 garlic cloves, minced

1 small (¾-pound) eggplant, diced

1 red bell pepper, seeded and diced

½ green bell pepper, seeded and diced

1 medium zucchini, diced

2 tomatoes, seeded and chopped

3 tablespoons shredded basil

2 tablespoons minced oregano

1 teaspoon salt

½ teaspoon freshly ground pepper

1 pound scrod fillets, cut into 4 pieces

2 tablespoons tomato paste

4 teaspoons olive oil

8 taco or tostado shells, crushed

⅓ cup shredded cheddar cheese

1. Preheat the oven to 350° F. Spray a large skillet with nonstick cooking spray; heat. Sauté the onions and garlic until softened, about 5 minutes. Add the eggplant and bell peppers; cook, stirring frequently, until the peppers are softened, about 5 minutes. Stir in the zucchini, tomatoes, basil, oregano, salt and pepper; cook, stirring, until the vegetables are tender, about 5 minutes longer. Transfer half the vegetables to a shallow 2-quart baking dish.

2. Arrange the scrod over the vegetables. In a small bowl, mix the tomato paste and oil; spread over the fish. Top with the remaining vegetables, then sprinkle with the taco shells and cheese. Bake until the top is golden brown and the fish is just opaque in the center, 20–30 minutes.

**Per serving**: 375 Calories, 16 g Total Fat, 4 g Saturated Fat, 60 mg Cholesterol, 900 mg Sodium, 34 g Total Carbohydrate, 7 g Dietary Fiber, 28 g Protein, 172 mg Calcium. **POINTS** per serving: 7.

## Nothing Fishy!

*When buying fresh fish and shellfish, use your nose—there should be no sour odor or smell of ammonia. Whole fish should have bright, bulging (not sunken) eyes and shiny, resilient skin. Look for compact and moist, fresh fillets with no dryness around the edges. Shrimp should be clear and pinkish. Both shrimp and scallops should have a firm texture and a sweet smell.*

*When you get your fish home, remove it from the supermarket wrapping and rewrap it in an airtight package and keep it in the coldest part of the refrigerator; use within three days. Clams, mussels and oysters should be tightly closed; when shucked, their meat should be plump and juicy. If any shells don't open after cooking, discard them.*

# Asian Sea Bass

*Based on the Chinese-restaurant classic, which uses whole fish, this quick version is every bit as flavorful. If you can't find sea bass, grouper, snapper or cod are good substitutes.*

MAKES 4 SERVINGS

1 pound sea bass fillets, cut into 4 pieces

3 scallions, cut into thin strips

1 tablespoon finely chopped peeled gingerroot

2 tablespoons reduced-sodium soy sauce

2 teaspoons Asian sesame oil

4 scallion tops, cut into fans

2 cups cooked white rice

1. Place the sea bass in a single layer in the center of an 18 × 12" piece of heavy-duty foil. Sprinkle with the scallions, gingerroot, 1 tablespoon of the soy sauce, and the oil. Make a packet by bringing the sides of the foil up to meet in the center and folding over the edges, then folding the ends together. Allowing room for the packet to expand, crimp the edges.

2. In a large skillet, bring 1" water to a boil. Place the packet in the skillet; reduce heat and steam, tightly covered, until the fish is just opaque in the center, about 10 minutes. Open the packet carefully when testing for doneness, as steam will escape.

3. With a slotted spatula, transfer the fillets and scallions to a platter. Pour any cooking juices and the remaining tablespoon of soy sauce over the fillets. Garnish with the scallion fans; serve with the rice.

**Per serving:** 144 Calories, 5 g Total Fat, 1 g Saturated Fat, 47 mg Cholesterol, 384 mg Sodium, 2 g Total Carbohydrate, 1 g Dietary Fiber, 22 g Protein, 34 mg Calcium. **POINTS** per serving: 3.

## How We Did It

To make scallion fans, slit the green tops of the scallions lengthwise into thin strips; place in cold water to curl.

# Sea Bass with Potatoes

*If you like, try a mixture of mushrooms to add differ-
ent textures and flavors, such as meaty shiitakes or
portobellos, or earthy-brown creminis.*

MAKES 4 SERVINGS

½ cup low-sodium chicken broth

1¼ pounds sea bass fillets, cut into 4 pieces

2 cups sliced mushrooms

3 tablespoons cornstarch

1¼ cups low-fat (1%) milk

½ cup dry white wine

4 teaspoons reduced-calorie margarine

1 teaspoon salt

½ teaspoon freshly ground pepper

2⅓ cups dry instant mashed potatoes

4 teaspoons grated Parmesan cheese

1 tablespoon chopped chives

1. Preheat the broiler. In a large skillet, bring the
broth to a boil; add the sea bass and mushrooms.
Reduce the heat and poach, covered, until the
fish is just opaque in the center, 3–4 minutes.
With a slotted spoon, transfer the fillets and
mushrooms to a shallow 2-quart flameproof baking dish.

2. Dissolve the cornstarch in the milk; whisk into
the broth in the skillet, then add the wine, margarine, salt and pepper; bring to a boil, stirring
constantly. Reduce the heat and simmer, stirring,
until thickened, 2–3 minutes. Pour the sauce over
the fish.

3. Mix the instant mashed potatoes with enough
boiling water to reach the desired consistency.
Spoon or pipe the potatoes around the edges of
the baking dish. Sprinkle with the cheese. Broil
until the top is golden brown and bubbling, 6–10
minutes. Sprinkle with the chives.

**Per serving**: 400 Calories, 7 g Total Fat, 2 g Saturated
Fat, 63 mg Cholesterol, 846 mg Sodium, 45 g Total
Carbohydrate, 0 g Dietary Fiber, 34 g Protein, 170 mg
Calcium. **POINTS** per serving: 9.

# Swordfish Mexicana

*This zesty Mexican dish is also very nice with turbot or bluefish.*

MAKES 4 SERVINGS

1 carrot, julienned

½ cup fresh or thawed frozen corn kernels

1 onion, thinly sliced

½ green bell pepper, seeded and julienned

½ red bell pepper, seeded and julienned

1¼ pounds swordfish steaks, cut into 4 pieces

1 cup chopped drained canned peeled tomatoes

¼ cup fresh cilantro, minced

1 jalapeño pepper, seeded, deveined and minced (wear gloves to prevent irritation)

4 teaspoons vegetable oil

1 teaspoon salt

4 lime slices

1. Preheat the oven to 425° F. In a medium saucepan, bring 1" water to a boil; add the carrot, corn, onion and bell peppers. Reduce the heat and steam, covered, until slightly wilted but still crunchy, 1–2 minutes; drain.

2. Cut out four 12" squares of baking parchment or foil; fold in half on the diagonal. Unfold and lay flat. Layer the steamed vegetables, swordfish, tomatoes, cilantro, jalapeño, oil and salt on one-half of each piece of parchment. Fold in half again on the diagonal, forming 4 triangular packets. Starting at one corner, make a series of small overlapping folds to seal each packet tightly.

3. Transfer to 2 baking sheets and bake until the fish is just opaque in the center, 10–12 minutes. Transfer to plates and cut each packet open slightly in the center. Serve with the lime.

**Per serving**: 276 Calories, 10 g Total Fat, 2 g Saturated Fat, 56 mg Cholesterol, 887 mg Sodium, 14 g Total Carbohydrate, 4 g Dietary Fiber, 31 g Protein, 46 mg Calcium. **POINTS** per serving: 6.

# Jamaican Jerked Grilled Swordfish

*The spicy hot seasoning typical of the islands are what makes a dish "jerked." Catfish can be substituted for the swordfish.*

MAKES 4 SERVINGS

1 onion, chopped

3 scallions, thinly sliced

1 jalapeño pepper, seeded, deveined and minced (wear gloves to prevent irritation)

1 teaspoon hot red pepper sauce

1 teaspoon salt

1 teaspoon minced thyme

½ teaspoon ground allspice

½ teaspoon freshly ground pepper

¼ teaspoon cinnamon

⅛ teaspoon ground nutmeg

1¼ pounds swordfish steaks, cut into 4 pieces

1. To prepare the marinade, in a blender or food processor, combine the onion, scallions, jalapeño, pepper sauce, salt, thyme, allspice, pepper, cinnamon and nutmeg; puree. Transfer to a gallon-size sealable plastic bag; add the swordfish steaks. Seal the bag, squeezing out the air; turn to coat the fish. Refrigerate, turning the bag occasionally, 6–8 hours. Drain and discard the remaining marinade.

2. Spray the grill rack with nonstick cooking spray; preheat the grill. Grill the swordfish 5" from the heat until just opaque in the center, 5–6 minutes on each side.

**Per serving**: 184 Calories, 6 g Total Fat, 2 g Saturated Fat, 56 mg Cholesterol, 716 mg Sodium, 3 g Total Carbohydrate, 1 g Dietary Fiber, 28 g Protein, 21 mg Calcium. **POINTS** per serving: 4.

## Tip

If you'd rather broil, prepare the fish as in Step 1. Spray the broiler rack with nonstick cooking spray; preheat the broiler. Broil the fish 5" from heat, 2 minutes on each side.

# Baked Trout with Tomato

*Once known as rich man's parsley, chervil has a uniquely delicate flavor that works well with mild fish like trout. Use it in egg dishes and creamy sauces, too.*

MAKES 4 SERVINGS

2 cups arugula or other lettuce, cleaned and shredded

Four 5-ounce trout fillets

2 tomatoes, peeled, seeded and chopped

¼ cup tomato juice

4 teaspoons Worcestershire sauce

1 tablespoon chopped chervil or thyme

½ teaspoon salt

½ teaspoon freshly ground pepper

4 teaspoons reduced-calorie margarine

4 lemon wedges

1. Preheat the oven to 425° F. Cut out four 12" squares of baking parchment or foil; fold in half on the diagonal. Unfold and lay flat. Layer the arugula, trout, tomatoes, tomato juice, Worcestershire sauce, chervil, salt, pepper and margarine on one-half of each piece of parchment. Fold in half again on the diagonal, forming 4 triangular packets. Starting at one corner, make a series of small overlapping folds to seal each packet tightly.

2. Transfer to 2 baking sheets and bake until the fish is just opaque in the center, about 5 minutes. Transfer to plates and cut each packet open slightly in the center. Serve with the lemon.

**Per serving:** 213 Calories, 7 g Total Fat, 1 g Saturated Fat, 81 mg Cholesterol, 477 mg Sodium, 8 g Total Carbohydrate, 1 g Dietary Fiber, 31 g Protein, 135 mg Calcium. **POINTS** per serving: 5.

## Got Leftovers?

If you've got some chervil left over, get your omelet pan out; this delicately flavored herb is a natural with eggs. Snip a few leaves into a salad, or sprinkle over cooked spinach.

# Trout Florentine

*When a dish is called Florentine, it means that it is made with spinach.*

MAKES 4 SERVINGS

2 cups cooked spinach, well drained and chopped

¼ cup part-skim ricotta cheese

2 tablespoons chopped chives

½ teaspoon grated lemon zest

1 teaspoon salt

½ teaspoon freshly ground pepper

¼ teaspoon ground nutmeg

Four 5-ounce trout fillets

2 cups skim milk

¼ cup all-purpose flour

1 slice reduced-calorie bread, made into crumbs

4 teaspoons grated Parmesan cheese

1. Preheat the oven to 375° F; spray an 8" square baking dish with nonstick cooking spray. In a medium bowl, combine the spinach, ricotta, chives, lemon zest, ½ teaspoon of the salt, ¼ teaspoon of the pepper and the nutmeg. Spread the spinach mixture over the trout fillets and roll up; transfer to the baking dish, seam-side down.

2. In a medium nonstick saucepan over low heat, combine the milk, flour, the remaining ½ teaspoon of salt and ¼ teaspoon of pepper; cook, whisking constantly, until thickened, about 5 minutes. Pour over the fillets.

3. In a small bowl, combine the bread crumbs and Parmesan; sprinkle over the fillets. Bake until the fish is just opaque in the center and golden brown on top, about 30 minutes.

**Per serving:** 311 Calories, 7 g Total Fat, 2 g Saturated Fat, 89 mg Cholesterol, 844 mg Sodium, 21 g Total Carbohydrate, 4 g Dietary Fiber, 40 g Protein, 470 mg Calcium. **POINTS** per serving: 6.

# Tuna Provençal Sandwiches

*These delicious tuna sandwiches "marinate" in the refrigerator, so use day-old bread if you can.*

MAKES 4 SERVINGS

Two 6-ounce cans light water-packed tuna, drained

1 cup cooked broccoli florets

1 red onion, minced

10 small black olives, pitted and sliced

¼ cup + 2 tablespoons plain nonfat yogurt

1 tablespoon balsamic vinegar

1 tablespoon reduced-calorie mayonnaise

1 tablespoon Dijon mustard

¼ teaspoon freshly ground pepper

One 8-ounce loaf whole-wheat Italian bread, split horizontally

4 large romaine lettuce leaves

4 plum tomatoes, sliced

1. In a medium bowl, combine the tuna, broccoli, onion and olives. In a small bowl, combine the yogurt, vinegar, mayonnaise, mustard and pepper. Pour over the tuna mixture; toss to coat.

2. Line the bottom half of the bread with the lettuce and tomatoes; top with the tuna salad. Cover with the top half of the bread, wrap in plastic wrap and refrigerate at least 1 hour. With a serrated knife, cut into 4 sandwiches.

**Per serving:** 273 Calories, 5 g Total Fat, 1 g Saturated Fat, 25 mg Cholesterol, 702 mg Sodium, 34 g Total Carbohydrate, 6 g Dietary Fiber, 25 g Protein, 120 mg Calcium. **POINTS** per serving: 5.

# Salad Niçoise

*If time allows, use fresh tuna: The flavor is superb. Broil an 8-ounce tuna steak and flake it into the salad.*

MAKES 4 SERVINGS

1¼ pounds small red potatoes, scrubbed

2 cups trimmed green beans

Two 6-ounce cans chunk light water-packed tuna, drained and flaked

24 cherry tomatoes, halved

4 cups thinly sliced romaine lettuce leaves

2 eggs, hard-cooked, peeled and quartered

6 large black olives, pitted and sliced crosswise

8 anchovy fillets, rinsed

¼ cup red-wine vinegar

2 tablespoons fresh lemon juice

1 tablespoon olive oil

¼ teaspoon salt

¼ teaspoon freshly ground pepper

1. Place the potatoes in a large pot and add cold water to cover; bring to a boil. Reduce the heat and simmer until tender, 15–20 minutes. With a slotted spoon, transfer to a colander; rinse with cold water. Coarsely chop and place in a large bowl. Add the green beans to the boiling water; cook until bright green and tender-crisp, about 3 minutes. Rinse with cold water, drain. Toss the green beans, tuna and tomatoes with the potatoes.

2. Line a large platter with the lettuce; mound the tuna mixture in the center. Arrange the eggs, olives and anchovy fillets over the tuna mixture.

3. In a small bowl, whisk the vinegar, lemon juice, oil, salt and pepper. Drizzle over the salad.

**Per serving**: 351 Calories, 9 g Total Fat, 2 g Saturated Fat, 130 mg Cholesterol, 749 mg Sodium, 44 g Total Carbohydrate, 8 g Dietary Fiber, 26 g Protein, 115 mg Calcium. *POINTS* per serving: 6.

# Tuna with White Beans and Onions

*Canned tuna is available in three grades: solid, chunk and flaked. Solid, somethimes called fancy, is considered the best.*

MAKES 4 SERVINGS

One 16-ounce can cannellini beans, rinsed and drained

Two 6-ounce cans light tuna packed in olive oil, drained

1 red onion, chopped

½ cup dry red wine

2 tablespoons chopped fresh sage, or 2 teaspoons dried

2 tablespoons fresh lemon juice

1 tablespoon red-wine vinegar

2 teaspoons balsamic vinegar

2 garlic cloves, minced

1 teaspoon olive oil

¼ teaspoon freshly ground pepper

¼ teaspoon salt

In a large bowl, combine all the ingredients. Refrigerate, covered, until the flavors are blended, at least 2 hours.

**Per serving**: 406 Calories, 7 g Total Fat, 2 g Saturated Fat, 40 mg Cholesterol, 499 mg Sodium, 44 g Total Carbohydrate, 7 g Dietary Fiber, 38 g Protein, 93 mg Calcium. *POINTS* per serving: 7.

## Got Leftovers?

**This tuna mix makes a satisfying lunch on a crusty baguette.**

# Tuna-Noodle Casserole

*The ultimate comfort food, this all-time favorite is perfect on a cold, dreary night or after a stressful day.*

MAKES 4 SERVINGS

1½ cups medium egg noodles

2 onions, chopped

2 celery stalks, chopped

1 green, red or yellow bell pepper, seeded and chopped

1 cup sliced mushrooms

½ cup thawed frozen corn kernels

One 10½-ounce can reduced-calorie condensed mushroom soup

Two 6-ounce cans chunk light water-packed tuna, drained and flaked

½ cup fat-free milk

2 tablespoons minced parsley

½ teaspoon freshly ground pepper

3–4 drops hot red pepper sauce

2 slices reduced-calorie whole-wheat bread, made into crumbs

4 teaspoons grated Parmesan cheese

2 tomatoes, sliced

1. Preheat the oven to 350° F; spray a shallow 2-quart casserole with nonstick cooking spray. Cook the noodles according to package directions; drain.

2. Meanwhile, spray a large nonstick saucepan with nonstick cooking spray; heat. Sauté the onions and celery until tender-crisp, about 2 minutes. Add the bell pepper, mushrooms and corn; cook, stirring, until tender, about 5 minutes longer. Stir in the soup, tuna, milk, parsley, pepper and pepper sauce. Remove from the heat; stir in the noodles. Transfer to the casserole.

3. Sprinkle with the bread crumbs and cheese. Bake until the crumbs are golden brown and crisp, 15–20 minutes. Top with the tomatoes.

**Per serving**: 331 Calories, 5 g Total Fat, 1 g Saturated Fat, 55 mg Cholesterol, 356 mg Sodium, 48 g Total Carbohydrate, 6 g Dietary Fiber, 26 g Protein, 129 mg Calcium. **POINTS** per serving: 6.

# Broiled Tuna with Corn Relish

*Curly endive is a bitter green that also works well in a salad. Mix it with romaine or radicchio and serve with your favorite dressing.*

MAKES 4 SERVINGS

¼ cup balsamic vinegar

1½ teaspoons Dijon mustard

½–1 teaspoon crushed red pepper flakes

¼ teaspoon salt

¼ teaspoon freshly ground pepper

1¼ pounds tuna steaks, cut into 4 pieces

2 cups cooked corn kernels

1 cup chopped roasted red pepper

2 cups torn curly endive

1. To prepare the marinade, in a gallon-size sealable plastic bag, combine the vinegar, mustard, pepper flakes, salt and pepper with 2 tablespoons water; reserve 2 tablespoons of the mixture in a medium bowl. Add the tuna to the bag. Seal the bag, squeezing out the air; turn to coat the tuna. Refrigerate, turning the bag occasionally, 1 hour.

2. Spray a nonstick baking sheet and the broiler rack with nonstick cooking spray; preheat the broiler. Arrange the corn in a thin layer on the baking sheet. Broil 6" from the heat, stirring often, until the corn begins to brown, 2–4 minutes. Add the corn and roasted pepper to the reserved marinade; set aside.

3. Drain and discard the marinade; place the tuna on the broiler rack. Broil 6" from the heat, turning once, until browned on the outside but still juicy inside, 6–7 minutes on each side.

4. Divide the endive among 4 plates; top with the corn relish and tuna.

**Per serving:** 285 Calories, 7 g Total Fat, 2 g Saturated Fat, 43 mg Cholesterol, 236 mg Sodium, 27 g Total Carbohydrate, 5 g Dietary Fiber, 31 g Protein, 95 mg Calcium. **POINTS** per serving: 5.

# Turbot à la Nage

Nage *means swimming in French, and here turbot swims in a lovely poaching broth of white wine flavored with aromatic vegetables, herbs and spices.*

MAKES 4 SERVINGS

1 cup dry white wine

1 carrot, finely diced

2 celery stalks, finely diced

2 leeks, cleaned, split lengthwise and very thinly sliced

2 turnips, finely diced

5 parsley sprigs

4 tarragon sprigs

2 tablespoons white-wine vinegar

2 bay leaves

1 teaspoon salt

1 teaspoon black peppercorns

1¼ pounds turbot fillets, cut into 4 pieces

1 teaspoon Dijon mustard

2 tablespoons chopped chives

1 tablespoon grated lemon zest

1. In a large deep skillet or saucepan, combine the wine, carrot, celery, leeks, turnips, parsley, tarragon, vinegar, bay leaves, salt, peppercorns and 2 cups water; cover and bring to a boil. Reduce the heat and simmer 30 minutes.

2. Add the turbot; poach, covered, over the lowest possible heat until just opaque in the center, 3–5 minutes. With a slotted spatula, transfer the fish to a platter; keep warm.

3. To prepare the sauce, strain the poaching liquid; return to the skillet and boil until reduced to ⅓ cup. Remove from the heat; discard the bay leaves and stir in the mustard. Pour the sauce over the fish; sprinkle with the chives and lemon zest.

**Per serving:** 178 Calories, 4 g Total Fat, 1 g Saturated Fat, 68 mg Cholesterol, 804 mg Sodium, 1 g Total Carbohydrate, 0 g Dietary Fiber, 23 g Protein, 33 mg Calcium. *POINTS* per serving: 4.

# Broiled Stuffed Lobster

*You can buy bouquet garni already made, but it's easy to make your own. Just place parsley, thyme and bay leaf in a small square of cheesecloth; tie the cheesecloth tightly.*

MAKES 4 SERVINGS

2 cups low-fat (1%) milk

½ cup dry white wine

1 bouquet garni

2 cups sliced mushrooms

¼ cup all-purpose flour

3 tablespoons reduced-calorie margarine

1 teaspoon Dijon mustard

1 egg yolk, lightly beaten

2 tablespoons minced parsley

2 teaspoons fresh lemon juice

½ teaspoon salt

½ teaspoon freshly ground pepper

Four 1–1½ pound lobsters

2 slices bread, made into crumbs

4 teaspoons grated Parmesan cheese

4 lemon wedges

1. In a medium nonstick saucepan, combine the milk, wine and bouquet garni; bring to a boil. Remove from the heat; let stand 30 minutes. Discard the bouquet garni.

2. Add the mushrooms, flour, margarine and mustard to the milk; cook over low heat, stirring, until the sauce thickens, about 3 minutes. Remove from the heat; beat in the egg yolk, parsley, lemon juice, salt and pepper.

3. In a very large pot of boiling water, cook the lobsters until bright red, 10–11 minutes. With tongs, transfer to a cutting board; remove the meat from the tails, leaving the shells intact.

4. Preheat the broiler. Cut the lobster meat into 1" cubes. Pour one-fourth of the sauce into the bottom of each lobster's body cavity and tail; fill with the lobster meat. Place the lobsters in a large shallow roasting pan, then sprinkle with the bread crumbs and cheese. Broil 4" from the heat until golden brown and heated through, 3–4 minutes. Place on a platter; garnish with the lemon wedges.

**Per serving:** 310 Calories, 8 g Total Fat, 2 g Saturated Fat, 141 mg Cholesterol, 984 mg Sodium, 21 g Total Carbohydrate, 1 g Dietary Fiber, 31 g Protein, 273 mg Calcium. **POINTS** per serving: 7.

# Classic Steamed Lobster

*Here, the traditional drawn butter gets a healthy makeover. For an even lighter dipping sauce, simmer the parsley and tarragon in ¼ cup of reduced-sodium chicken broth for a few minutes, then stir in the lemon juice.*

MAKES 4 SERVINGS

¼ cup reduced-calorie margarine

1 tablespoon fresh lemon juice

1½ teaspoons minced parsley

1½ teaspoons minced fresh tarragon, or ½ teaspoon dried

1½ teaspoons finely chopped watercress

¼ teaspoon salt

¼ teaspoon freshly ground pepper

Four 1–1½ pound lobsters

4 lemon wedges

1. To prepare the herb butter, in a small skillet over low heat, melt the margarine, lemon juice, parsley, tarragon, watercress, salt and pepper.

2. In a large pot of boiling water, cook the lobsters until bright red, 10–11 minutes. With tongs, transfer to a platter. Serve with the herb butter and lemon wedges.

**Per serving:** 163 Calories, 6 g Total Fat, 1 g Saturated Fat, 81 mg Cholesterol, 712 mg Sodium, 2 g Total Carbohydrate, 0 g Dietary Fiber, 23 g Protein, 73 mg Calcium. **POINTS** per serving: 4.

# Lobster Salad

*Citrus fruits go well with lobster, as this adventurous salad proves.*

MAKES 4 SERVINGS

1 pound cooked lobster meat

1 pink grapefruit, peeled, sectioned, seeded and coarsely chopped

1 navel orange, peeled, sectioned and coarsely chopped

1½ cups cantaloupe balls

1 mango, peeled, pitted and sliced

2 cups watercress leaves, rinsed and drained

½ cup nonfat sour cream

3 tablespoons reduced-calorie mayonnaise

2 teaspoons grated orange zest

¼ cup orange juice

2 tablespoons chopped chives

½ teaspoon freshly ground pepper

1. In a large nonreactive bowl, combine the lobster, grapefruit, orange, cantaloupe and mango.

2. Line a large platter with the watercress; mound the salad in the center.

3. In a small bowl, whisk the sour cream and mayonnaise; whisk in the orange zest and orange juice. Pour over the salad; sprinkle with the chives and pepper.

**Per serving:** 273 Calories, 4 g Total Fat, 1 g Saturated Fat, 81 mg Cholesterol, 558 mg Sodium, 32 g Total Carbohydrate, 3 g Dietary Fiber, 26 g Protein, 165 mg Calcium. **POINTS** per serving: 5.

## Substitution

You can save some money by substituting chunks of cooked monkfish—also called "poor man's lobster"—in this salad, with tasty results.

# Curried Shrimp and Rice Salad

*To give this complex salad even more texture, use brown rice instead of the white or basmati.*

MAKES 4 SERVINGS

2 onions, finely chopped

½ cup low-sodium chicken broth

1 tablespoon curry powder

2 tablespoons golden raisins

2 tablespoons apricot spreadable fruit

2 McIntosh apples, cored and cut into chunks

2 bananas, cut into ¼" slices

1 tablespoon fresh lemon juice

¾ pound cooked medium shrimp, peeled and deveined

2 cups cold cooked white or basmati rice

2 celery stalks, chopped

1½ cups plain nonfat yogurt

3 tablespoons reduced-calorie mayonnaise

½ teaspoon salt

2 cups Boston, Bibb or other lettuce leaves

1. In a small saucepan, combine the onions, broth and curry powder; bring just to a boil. Reduce the heat and simmer until the onions are soft. Stir in the raisins and spreadable fruit; cool completely.

2. In a medium bowl, combine the apples, bananas and lemon juice; stir in the shrimp, rice and celery. In another medium bowl, whisk the broth mixture, yogurt, mayonnaise and salt. Pour over the salad and stir. Serve on a bed of lettuce.

**Per serving**: 419 Calories, 6 g Total Fat, 1 g Saturated Fat, 168 mg Cholesterol, 658 mg Sodium, 66 g Total Carbohydrate, 6 g Dietary Fiber, 27 g Protein, 268 mg Calcium. **POINTS** per serving: 8.

# California Seafood Salad

*By all means, go beyond romaine. Try a mix of spinach and arugula, or red leaf lettuce.*

MAKES 4 SERVINGS

¼ cup clam-tomato juice or tomato juice

¼ cup fresh lemon juice

4 teaspoons olive oil

1 tablespoon Worcestershire sauce

¼ teaspoon salt

¼ teaspoon freshly ground pepper

4 cups romaine or other lettuce, washed and torn into bite-size leaves

¼ pound cooked crab meat, picked through for shells and cartilage

¼ pound cooked shrimp, peeled (tails left on) and deveined

12 cherry tomatoes, halved

¼ medium avocado, sliced

2 navel oranges, peeled and sliced into semicircles

1 cup Croutons (page 20)

1. To make the dressing, in a small bowl, whisk the clam-tomato juice, lemon juice, oil, Worcestershire sauce, salt and pepper. Refrigerate, covered, until ready to use.

2. Line a platter with the lettuce; mound the crab meat in the center. Arrange the shrimp and tomatoes around the crab, then the avocado and oranges around the outside. Pour the dressing over the salad. Serve, sprinkled with the croutons.

**Per serving**: 236 Calories, 9 g Total Fat, 1 g Saturated Fat, 50 mg Cholesterol, 455 mg Sodium, 28 g Total Carbohydrate, 6 g Dietary Fiber, 13 g Protein, 107 mg Calcium. **POINTS** per serving: 4.

# Grilled Shrimp Salad

*If time is a concern, buy shrimp that have been cleaned and deveined.*

MAKES 4 SERVINGS

1 slice whole-wheat bread, cut into ½" cubes

½ cup low-sodium chicken broth

1 tablespoon olive oil

1 tablespoon red-wine vinegar

1 sprig fresh rosemary, or ½ teaspoon dried leaves, crumbled

1 garlic clove, peeled and bruised

¼ teaspoon coarsely ground pepper

½ pound medium shrimp, peeled and deveined

One 10-ounce package triple-washed spinach, rinsed

1. To prepare the croutons, preheat the oven to 300° F. Arrange the bread on a baking sheet; bake until crisp and golden, 20–25 minutes.

2. Meanwhile, in a medium saucepan, combine the broth, oil, vinegar, rosemary, garlic and pepper; bring to a boil. Reduce the heat and simmer 5 minutes; remove from the heat.

3. Spray a baking sheet with nonstick cooking spray; preheat the broiler. Arrange the shrimp on the baking sheet; spray with nonstick cooking spray. Broil 4" from the heat until just pink, about 3 minutes; add to the rosemary mixture. Let stand 5–6 minutes, then discard the rosemary sprig and garlic. Add the croutons; toss to combine. Arrange on a bed of spinach and serve at once.

**Per serving:** 138 Calories, 6 g Total Fat, 1 g Saturated Fat, 70 mg Cholesterol, 210 mg Sodium, 10 g Total Carbohydrate, 4 g Dietary Fiber, 14 g Protein, 147 mg Calcium. **POINTS** per serving: 2.

## Tip

Shrimp are easier to peel and devein when they're raw. The easiest way to devein: Make a shallow slit down the center of the outside of each shrimp. Pull out the vein, then give the shrimp a quick rinse.

# Shrimp and Vegetable Rice

*To make this dish look even more abundant, try slicing the shrimp in half lengthwise, and cook them only 1–2 minutes. It will look as if you have twice as much shrimp!*

MAKES 6 SERVINGS

1¼ cups chicken broth

2 tablespoons cornstarch

1 teaspoon vegetable oil

2 carrots, diced

2 cups snow peas

3 tablespoons reduced-sodium soy sauce

2 teaspoons Asian sesame oil

1¼ pounds large shrimp, peeled and deveined

3 cups hot cooked long-grain rice

1. In a small bowl, combine ¼ cup of the chicken broth and the cornstarch; stir until the cornstarch dissolves.

2. In a large nonstick skillet, heat the vegetable oil. Add the carrots and ⅓ cup of the remaining broth; cook 2 minutes, then stir in the snow peas, ⅓ cup of the remaining broth, the soy sauce and sesame oil. Reduce the heat and simmer, covered, until the snow peas are tender-crisp, about 5 minutes.

3. Add the shrimp and the remaining ⅓ cup of broth; cook, stirring occasionally, just until the shrimp turn pink, 3–4 minutes. Increase the heat and bring to a boil. Stir in the dissolved cornstarch; cook, stirring frequently, until thickened, about 2 minutes. Stir in the rice.

**Per serving**: 284 Calories, 4 g Total Fat, 1 g Saturated Fat, 108 mg Cholesterol, 627 mg Sodium, 40 g Total Carbohydrate, 3 g Dietary Fiber, 20 g Protein, 82 mg Calcium. **POINTS** per serving: 5.

# Jambalaya

*Jambalaya, a Cajun version of paella, has few strict rules beyond requiring rice. Louisiana chefs generally use whatever seafood, meats or sausage they have on hand: If you don't have ham, smoked turkey will do— and oysters make a delicious substitute for the shrimp.*

MAKES 4 SERVINGS

1 tablespoon vegetable oil

2 onions, chopped

10–12 garlic cloves, minced

1⅓ cups white rice

2 cups low-sodium chicken broth

One 14½-ounce can no-salt-added diced tomatoes

½ cup diced lean ham

2 teaspoons minced thyme

½ teaspoon salt

⅛–¼ teaspoon cayenne pepper

¼ teaspoon ground white pepper

1 pound medium shrimp, peeled and deveined

1 tablespoon chopped parsley

In a large nonstick saucepan, heat the oil. Sauté the onions and garlic until softened, about 5 minutes. Add the rice, stirring to coat, about 1 minute. Stir in the broth, tomatoes, ham, thyme, salt, cayenne and pepper; bring to a boil. Reduce the heat and simmer, covered, 15 minutes; add the shrimp and cook until the rice is soft, 5–10 minutes longer. Garnish with the parsley.

**Per serving**: 405 Calories, 7 g Total Fat, 2 g Saturated Fat, 172 mg Cholesterol, 705 mg Sodium, 56 g Total Carbohydrate, 4 g Dietary Fiber, 28 g Protein, 109 mg Calcium. **POINTS** per serving: 8.

# Seafood en Papillote

*For the best appearance, use baking parchment instead of foil, which makes a beautifully puffy, lightly browned package. You can find it in specialty cooking stores and better supermarkets.*

MAKES 4 SERVINGS

¾ pound medium shrimp, peeled and deveined

½ pound medium mussels, scrubbed and debearded

¼ pound sea scallops

½ cup chopped chives

½ cup dry white wine

4 teaspoons olive oil

5–6 garlic cloves, minced

1 teaspoon salt

½ teaspoon freshly ground pepper

8 lemon slices

8 sprigs parsley

1. Preheat the grill. Set the grill rack 5" from the heat. Cut four 12 × 18" pieces of baking parchment or foil. Arrange the shrimp, mussels and scallops in the center of each piece of parchment; sprinkle with the chives, wine, oil, garlic, salt and pepper, then top with the lemon and parsley. Make packets by bringing the sides of the parchment up to meet in the center and folding over the edges, then folding the edge of each end together. Allowing room for the packets to expand, crimp the edges.

2. Grill until the shrimp are pink, the mussels opened and the scallops opaque, about 30 minutes. Transfer the packets to plates; cut open, avoiding the steam. Discard any unopened mussels.

**Per serving:** 166 Calories, 6 g Total Fat, 1 g Saturated Fat, 87 mg Cholesterol, 802 mg Sodium, 3 g Total Carbohydrate, 0 g Dietary Fiber, 19 g Protein, 76 mg Calcium. **POINTS** per serving: 4.

## Catch of the Day

*All fish are not created equal, as you can see at a glance at the chart below. When cooking fish, it is helpful to keep their fat content in mind when planning meals.*

| | CALORIES | PROTEIN (G) | FAT (G) | SODIUM (MG) | CHOLESTEROL (MG) |
|---|---|---|---|---|---|
| Bluefish | 180 | 29 | 6 | 87 | 85 |
| Cod | 118 | 26 | 1 | 88 | 63 |
| Haddock | 127 | 27 | 1 | 99 | 84 |
| Halibut | 159 | 30 | 3 | 79 | 47 |
| Orange Roughy | 100 | 21 | 1 | 92 | 29 |
| Perch, Ocean | 132 | 28 | 1 | 89 | 130 |
| Rockfish (Snapper) | 137 | 27 | 2 | 87 | 51 |
| Salmon, Atlantic | 155 | 22 | 7 | 48 | 60 |
| Sea Bass | 140 | 27 | 3 | 99 | 60 |
| Swordfish | 176 | 29 | 6 | 130 | 57 |
| Tuna, Yellowfin* | 157 | 34 | 1 | 53 | 65 |

*Per 4-ounce cooked, edible portion.*

# Seafood-Vegetable Kebabs

*If you're using bamboo skewers, remember to soak them in water for at least 30 minutes—otherwise they might catch on fire.*

MAKES 4 SERVINGS

½ cup orange juice

¼ cup dry white wine

2 tablespoons reduced-sodium soy sauce

2 tablespoons fresh lemon juice

4 garlic cloves, minced

1 tablespoon Dijon mustard

2 teaspoons olive oil

1 teaspoon ground ginger

¼ teaspoon freshly ground pepper

¼ pound medium shrimp, peeled and deveined

¼ pound sea scallops

½ pound swordfish steak, cut into 1" cubes

24 cherry tomatoes

2 cups bite-size broccoli florets

1½ cups medium mushroom caps

1 medium yellow summer squash or zucchini, cut into 1" cubes

1. Preheat the broiler; spray a nonstick baking sheet or 12 × 18" shallow baking pan and four 18" metal skewers with nonstick cooking spray.

2. To prepare the marinade, in a gallon-size sealable plastic bag, combine the orange juice, wine, soy sauce, lemon juice, garlic, mustard, oil, ginger and pepper; add the shrimp, scallops and swordfish. Seal the bag, squeezing out the air; turn to coat the seafood. With a slotted spoon, transfer the seafood to a medium bowl. Repeat the marinating procedure with the tomatoes, broccoli, mushrooms and squash.

3. Drain the marinade into a small saucepan and bring to a rolling boil. Boil, stirring constantly, 3 minutes. Remove from the heat and let cool to room temperature.

4. Thread the seafood and vegetables onto the skewers, alternating to create a colorful pattern. Place the skewers on the baking sheet; brush with half the marinade. Broil until the shrimp are pink and the other seafood and vegetables are golden, 3–4 minutes; turn and brush with the remaining marinade. Broil until the second side is golden, about 5 minutes.

**Per serving**: 210 Calories, 5 g Total Fat, 1 g Saturated Fat, 81 mg Cholesterol, 529 mg Sodium, 16 g Total Carbohydrate, 4 g Dietary Fiber, 23 g Protein, 75 mg Calcium. **POINTS** per serving: 4.

# Shrimp Creole

*Okra—the immature seed pod of the okra plant—is essential to this dish, because it releases a gummy sap that helps thicken the stew.*

MAKES 4 SERVINGS

4 teaspoons olive oil

2 onions, chopped

1 red bell pepper, seeded and chopped

4 garlic cloves. minced

One 28-ounce can low-sodium stewed tomatoes

¾ pound medium shrimp, peeled and deveined

2 cups sliced fresh or thawed frozen okra

½ teaspoon salt

½ teaspoon chili powder

½ teaspoon freshly ground pepper

½ teaspoon dried thyme leaves, crumbled

⅛ teaspoon ground mace

2 allspice berries

2 whole cloves

1 bay leaf

1 tablespoon cornstarch, dissolved in 2 tablespoons water

2 cups cooked white rice

In a large nonstick saucepan, heat the oil. Sauté the onions, bell pepper and garlic until softened, about 5 minutes. Add the tomatoes, shrimp, okra, salt, chili powder, pepper, thyme, mace, allspice, cloves and bay leaf; simmer, covered, until the flavors are blended, about 20 minutes. Discard the bay leaf. Stir in the dissolved cornstarch; cook, stirring, until thickened, 1–2 minutes. Serve over the rice.

**Per serving**: 268 Calories, 6 g Total Fat, 1 g Saturated Fat, 49 mg Cholesterol, 381 mg Sodium, 45 g Total Carbohydrate, 8 g Dietary Fiber, 12 g Protein, 135 mg Calcium. **POINTS** per serving: 4.

# Shrimp Étouffée

*Étouffée (or smothered) in a recipe title usually signals dietary disaster. In this version, broth and a bit of oil make it deliciously lean. Serve over rice.*

MAKES 4 SERVINGS

6 teaspoons vegetable oil

3 tablespoons all-purpose flour

2 celery stalks, chopped

2 onions, chopped

1 green bell pepper, seeded and chopped

6 scallions, sliced

4–5 garlic cloves, minced

2 cups hot low-sodium chicken broth

1 tablespoon minced parsley

1 teaspoon salt

1 teaspoon fresh lemon juice

¼ teaspoon freshly ground pepper

⅛ teaspoon cayenne pepper

1 pound medium shrimp, peeled and deveined

1. In a heavy small saucepan over low heat, heat 4 teaspoons of the oil. Stir in the flour; cook, stirring constantly, until medium-brown, about 15 minutes.

2. In a large nonstick saucepan, heat the remaining 2 teaspoons of oil. Sauté the celery, onions, bell pepper, scallions and garlic, stirring frequently, until tender, about 15 minutes.

3. Whisk the broth into the flour mixture until smooth, then add to the sautéed vegetables. Stir in the parsley, salt, lemon juice, pepper and cayenne; simmer 5 minutes, then add the shrimp and simmer until the shrimp are opaque, about 5 minutes longer.

**Per serving**: 251 Calories, 10 g Total Fat, 2 g Saturated Fat, 164 mg Cholesterol, 822 mg Sodium, 14 g Total Carbohydrate, 2 g Dietary Fiber, 24 g Protein, 99 mg Calcium. **POINTS** per serving: 5.

# Shrimp Scampi

*This perennially misnamed dish (scampi simply means shrimp in Italian) is everyone's favorite. Deveining the shrimp gives them a better appearance; for best results, use a small, pointed knife blade.*

MAKES 4 SERVINGS

4 teaspoons olive oil

1¼ pounds medium shrimp, peeled (tails left on) and deveined

6–8 garlic cloves, minced

½ cup low-sodium chicken broth

½ cup dry white wine

¼ cup fresh lemon juice

¼ cup + 1 tablespoon minced parsley

¼ teaspoon salt

¼ teaspoon freshly ground pepper

4 lemon slices

1. In a large nonstick skillet, heat the oil. Sauté the shrimp until just pink, 2–3 minutes. Add the garlic and cook, stirring constantly, about 30 seconds. With a slotted spoon, transfer the shrimp to a platter; keep hot.

2. In the skillet, combine the broth, wine, lemon juice, ¼ cup of the parsley, the salt and pepper; bring to a boil. Boil, uncovered, until the sauce is reduced by half; spoon over the shrimp. Serve, garnished with the lemon slices and sprinkled with the remaining tablespoon of parsley.

**Per serving**: 184 Calories, 6 g Total Fat, 1 g Saturated Fat, 219 mg Cholesterol, 404 mg Sodium, 3 g Total Carbohydrate, 0 g Dietary Fiber, 24 g Protein, 58 mg Calcium. *POINTS* per serving: 4.

# Grilled Shrimp Teriyaki

*Too cold out to grill? Try this in the broiler instead, using metal skewers. Spray the broiler rack with non-stick cooking spray and preheat. Broil about 5" from heat about 3 minutes on each side, until the shrimp are opaque.*

MAKES 4 SERVINGS

1¼ pounds large shrimp, peeled (tails left on) and deveined

¼ cup + 2 tablespoons teriyaki sauce

½ medium fresh pineapple, peeled, cored and cut into 1" cubes

2 red bell peppers, seeded and cut into 1" pieces

4 cups cooked white rice

4 scallions, sliced on the diagonal

1. Place the shrimp in a gallon-size sealable plastic bag and pour in ¼ cup of the teriyaki sauce. Seal the bag, squeezing out the air; turn to coat the shrimp. Refrigerate, turning the bag occasionally, at least 2 hours.

2. Spray the grill rack with nonstick cooking spray. If using wooden skewers, soak eight 12" skewers in cold water. Preheat the grill.

3. Drain and discard the teriyaki sauce. Alternately thread the shrimp, pineapple and bell peppers on eight 12" wooden or metal skewers. Grill the kebabs 5" from the heat, turning frequently, until the shrimp are cooked through, 12–15 minutes. Serve over the rice, sprinkled with the remaining 2 tablespoons of teriyaki sauce and the scallions.

**Per serving**: 409 Calories, 2 g Total Fat, 0 g Saturated Fat, 219 mg Cholesterol, 969 mg Sodium, 67 g Total Carbohydrate, 4 g Dietary Fiber, 30 g Protein, 88 mg Calcium. *POINTS* per serving: 8.

# Seafood Risotto

*If you prefer, you can substitute fish or vegetable bouillon for the white wine.*

MAKES 4 SERVINGS

1 fish or vegetable bouillon cube

1 cup dry white wine

4 teaspoons olive oil

2 onions, chopped

4 garlic cloves, minced

1⅓ cups Arborio or other short-grain rice

2 teaspoons dried mixed herbs

¾ pound calamari, cleaned

2 cups sorrel or spinach leaves

1 cup sliced mushrooms

¾ teaspoon salt

½ teaspoon freshly ground pepper

½ pound medium mussels, scrubbed and debearded

½ pound cooked medium shrimp

4 teaspoons grated Parmesan cheese

2 tablespoons minced parsley

1. In a medium saucepan, dissolve the bouillon cube in 3 cups water; bring to a boil. Reduce the heat and simmer. Add the wine.

2. In a large nonstick saucepan, heat the oil. Sauté the onions and garlic until tender, about 5 minutes. Add the rice; cook, stirring to coat, about 1 minute longer.

3. Add 1 cup of the liquid and the mixed herbs; cook, stirring, until the liquid is absorbed. Add ½ cup of the remaining liquid; cook, stirring until the liquid is absorbed. Add the calamari and another ½ cup of the remaining liquid; cook, stirring, until the liquid is absorbed. Add the sorrel, mushrooms, salt, pepper and another ½ cup of the remaining liquid; cook, stirring, until the liquid is absorbed. Add another ½ cup of the remaining liquid; cook, stirring, until it is absorbed.

4. Bring the remaining 1 cup of liquid to a boil. Add the mussels; steam, covered, until their shells open, 3–5 minutes; discard any unopened mussels. Add to the rice mixture with the liquid; stir in the shrimp. Cook, covered, until the liquid is absorbed and shrimp are heated through, 3–5 minutes. Remove from the heat and stir in the cheese and parsley; serve at once.

**Per serving**: 479 Calories, 8 g Total Fat, 2 g Saturated Fat, 285 mg Cholesterol, 966 mg Sodium, 56 g Total Carbohydrate, 3 g Dietary Fiber, 33 g Protein, 109 mg Calcium. **POINTS** per serving: 10.

# Calamari Salad

*Calamari, or squid, is an Italian treat found in most fish markets. If you can't find it cooked, have the fish-monger clean and slice it, then simmer it in a little water until just opaque (1–2 minutes).*

MAKES 4 SERVINGS

¾ pound cooked calamari, cut into ¼" slices

One 7-ounce jar roasted red peppers, drained and cut into 2" strips

1 cup thawed frozen artichoke hearts

6 scallions, sliced

20 small black olives, pitted and halved

8 sun-dried tomato halves (not oil-packed)

½ cup shredded basil

4–5 garlic cloves, minced

½ teaspoon salt

½ teaspoon freshly ground pepper

2 tablespoons red-wine vinegar

2 teaspoons olive oil

2 cups arugula, torn into bite-size pieces

1. In a large bowl, combine the calamari, roasted peppers, artichoke hearts, scallions, olives, tomatoes, basil, garlic, salt and pepper. Add the vinegar and oil; toss to coat. Refrigerate, covered, stirring occasionally, until the flavors are blended, 2–4 hours.

2. Line a large platter with the arugula; mound the salad in the center.

*Per serving*: 216 Calories, 6 g Total Fat, 1 g Saturated Fat, 264 mg Cholesterol, 629 mg Sodium, 21 g Total Carbohydrate, 6 g Dietary Fiber, 23 g Protein, 125 mg Calcium. *POINTS* per serving: 4.

## How We Did It

To shred basil, stack a few leaves on top of one another and roll into a cigar. Cut crosswise into very thin slices.

# New England Steamed Clams

*We've created an easy version of the classic clam bake, complete with corn on the cob and potatoes.*

MAKES 4 SERVINGS

¾ pound medium littleneck or cherrystone clams, scrubbed

1 tablespoon mustard powder

1¼ pounds small new potatoes, scrubbed

4 ears corn on the cob, shucked

3 tablespoons reduced-calorie margarine, melted

1 lemon, cut into wedges

1. In a large pot, combine the clams and mustard with 2¼ cups cold water; let stand 30 minutes to rid the clams of their sand. Rinse well.

2. Place the potatoes in a large saucepan and add cold water to cover; bring to a boil. Reduce the heat and simmer until tender, 15–20 minutes. With a slotted spoon, transfer to a platter; keep warm.

3. In the boiling water, cook the corn on the cob, covered, until tender, about 4 minutes. With a slotted spoon, transfer to the platter; keep warm.

4. In the boiling water, cook the clams, partially covered, until they open, about 4 minutes. Transfer to the platter; discard any unopened clams. Strain the broth and reserve to dunk clams. Drizzle the margarine over the potatoes and corn. Serve with the lemon wedges.

*Per serving*: 284 Calories, 6 g Total Fat, 1 g Saturated Fat, 27 mg Cholesterol, 152 mg Sodium, 45 g Total Carbohydrate, 4 g Dietary Fiber, 15 g Protein, 56 mg Calcium. *POINTS* per serving: 5.

# Roasted Scallops with Fennel

*Bay scallops, generally found on the East Coast, are very small and less plentiful than larger sea scallops. Their meat is also sweeter and juicier, making them more expensive, but worth it.*

MAKES 4 SERVINGS

1¼ pounds bay scallops

1 fennel bulb, finely chopped

Half 10-ounce box frozen artichoke hearts, thawed and chopped

2 slices whole-wheat bread, toasted and made into coarse crumbs

¼ cup dry white wine

2 tablespoons fresh lemon juice

2 teaspoons olive oil

¼ teaspoon salt

¼ teaspoon ground white pepper

1. Preheat the oven to 400° F; spray a 2-quart nonreactive flameproof baking dish with nonstick cooking spray.

2. In a medium bowl, combine the scallops, fennel, artichoke hearts, bread crumbs, wine, lemon juice, oil, salt and pepper; transfer to the baking dish. Bake until lightly browned, about 20 minutes. Remove from the oven and increase the oven temperature to broil. Drain off the liquid from the baking dish. Broil until deep gold, about 5 minutes.

**Per serving:** 219 Calories, 4 g Total Fat, 0 g Saturated Fat, 47 mg Cholesterol, 503 mg Sodium, 16 g Total Carbohydrate, 3 g Dietary Fiber, 27 g Protein, 82 mg Calcium. **POINTS** per serving: 4.

# Scallops Seviche

*Authentic seviche is uncooked—we poach the scallops briefly to help eliminate food-safety problems.*

MAKES 4 SERVINGS

10 ounces sea scallops

2 cups low-sodium chicken broth

½ cup fresh lemon juice

2 tomatoes, peeled, seeded and chopped

6 scallions, minced

4 teaspoons garlic oil

1 tablespoon finely chopped chives

1 tablespoon finely chopped dill

1 tablespoon finely chopped parsley

1 tablespoon finely chopped tarragon

¼ teaspoon finely ground pepper

⅛ teaspoon salt

4 lemon slices

1. Wash the scallops in cold water and pat dry with paper towels. In a medium skillet, bring the broth to a simmer. Add the scallops; poach, covered, until opaque, 2–3 minutes. Transfer to a colander and rinse with cold water. Slice horizontally ¼" thick.

2. Pour the lemon juice into a gallon-size sealable plastic bag; add the scallops. Seal the bag, squeezing out the air; turn to coat the scallops. Refrigerate, turning the bag occasionally, 24 hours.

3. When ready to serve, transfer the scallops to a serving bowl. Stir in the tomatoes, scallions, oil, chives, dill, parsley, tarragon, pepper and salt. Serve with the lemon slices.

**Per serving:** 145 Calories, 7 g Total Fat, 1 g Saturated Fat, 30 mg Cholesterol, 253 mg Sodium, 8 g Total Carbohydrate, 1 g Dietary Fiber, 15 g Protein, 89 mg Calcium. **POINTS** per serving: 3.

*Roasted Scallops with Fennel*

# Scallops with Lime and Herbs

*Bay scallops are considered the best tasting variety, but they can quickly develop an iodine flavor if they're not impeccably fresh. Buy your scallops at a fish market with a high turnover, and select those that have an elastic springiness and cucumber-like aroma.*

MAKES 4 SERVINGS

4 teaspoons Asian sesame oil

¾ pound green beans, cut into 2" lengths

4–5 garlic cloves, minced

2 summer squash, sliced

1 cup thawed frozen green peas

1 tablespoon minced parsley

1 tablespoon minced cilantro

1½ teaspoons minced fresh thyme, or ½ teaspoon dried

1 pound bay scallops

½ cup low-sodium chicken broth

¼ cup fresh lime juice

1 teaspoon salt

½ teaspoon freshly ground pepper

1 lime, sliced

1. In a large nonstick skillet, heat the oil. Sauté the green beans and garlic until the beans begin to soften, about 1 minute. Add the squash, peas, parsley, cilantro and thyme; stir-fry until the beans are almost tender-crisp, 3–4 minutes longer.

2. Add the scallops; cook 1 minute longer. Pour in the broth, lime juice, salt and pepper; bring to a boil. Remove from the heat; add the lime.

**Per serving**: 210 Calories, 7 g Total Fat, 1 g Saturated Fat, 45 mg Cholesterol, 891 mg Sodium, 17 g Total Carbohydrate, 5 g Dietary Fiber, 24 g Protein, 164 mg Calcium. **POINTS** per serving: 4.

# RECIPES

Vegetarian

# Chapter 8

# Vegetarian

Even if you don't call yourself a vegetarian, it's a good idea to eat vegetarian meals at least a few times a week. By planning your meals around vegetables, legumes and grains, you're automatically cutting out fattier sources of protein, like meats—and getting a healthy boost of the fiber, antioxidant vitamins and minerals so abundant in plant foods.

The 12-million-plus Americans who call themselves vegetarians are a varied bunch. There are those who eat dairy products (lactovegetarians) or eggs (ovovegetarians) or both (lacto-ovo), and those who eschew any animal-based foods (vegans). Others, who call themselves semivegetarians, limit their animal food intake but don't eliminate it completely—allowing only fish, or an occasional piece of chicken, for example.

Vegetarians can easily put together a delicious, varied diet that doesn't lack any nutrients; however, going meatless doesn't necessarily mean your diet will be low in fat. If you're going veggie, here are some guidelines to ensure you get the most nutrition with the fewest calories.

## A Healthy Balance

You needn't worry about protein. Animal foods are the best source of high-quality protein, so lacto- or ovovegetarians get plenty in eggs and dairy products. Further, grains, beans (especially soybeans), vegetables, seeds and nuts all contain amino acids, the components of high-quality protein; vegans can get all the protein they need from eating some of these foods daily.

Likewise, iron deficiency is rarely a risk, since many plant foods are good iron sources—especially if you also eat foods that are high in vitamin C, which helps the body absorb iron better. Getting enough calcium doesn't seem to be an issue, either, even for vegans: Studies show they absorb more calcium from foods than nonvegetarians do, so they may need less calcium-rich foods than nonvegetarians do.

One nutrient that does warrant concern is vitamin $B_{12}$, which is found only in animal products. Vegans should include a good source of this vitamin in their diets, preferably from supplements or fortified foods.

To keep the fat down, keep these pointers in mind:

- If you eat dairy products, choose those that are low in fat (1 percent or less) or fat-free.

- Don't eat more than a few servings of full-fat cheese per week. Treat it as a condiment, not a staple.

- Limit your egg intake to 3–4 yolks per week (you can eat as many whites as you like).

- Use light tofu instead of the full-fat version.

**Please note: These recipes may feature eggs, dairy products and, in some instances, chicken broth (which is more flavorful than vegetable broth). If you opt to use vegetable broth, you may need to alter the seasonings.**

# Spinach and Cheese Quiche

*If you'd prefer to use fresh spinach, you'll need about 8 cups of washed trimmed spinach leaves. Cook them in a large saucepan with only the water that clings to them, stirring as needed, until wilted, about 2 minutes. Drain well and finely chop.*

MAKES 12 SERVINGS

One 12-ounce can evaporated skimmed milk

⅓ cup low-fat cottage cheese

¼ cup grated Parmesan cheese

2 eggs

3 egg whites

½ teaspoon salt

¼ teaspoon black pepper

One 10-ounce box frozen chopped spinach, thawed and squeezed dry

Plain Pie Crust, baked and cooled (page 17)

1. Preheat the oven to 425° F. In a medium bowl, whisk the milk, cottage cheese, Parmesan, eggs, egg whites, salt and pepper.

2. Place the pie plate on a jelly-roll pan; spread the spinach over the pie crust, then pour the filling over the spinach. Bake 15 minutes; reduce the oven temperature to 350° F and bake until the filling is set, 20 minutes longer. Let cool 10 minutes before serving.

**Per serving**: 139 Calories, 5 g Total Fat, 2 g Saturated Fat, 40 mg Cholesterol, 359 mg Sodium, 14 g Total Carbohydrate, 1 g Dietary Fiber, 9 g Protein, 188 mg Calcium. *POINTS* per serving: 3.

## How We Did It

It's not unusual to see quiche recipes that call for 3 or so eggs, 1 cup of heavy cream or a cup of cheese. Using 2 or 3 egg whites for one whole egg is a good rule-of-thumb substitution; evaporated skimmed milk, especially combined with creamy cottage cheese, provides the richness of cream at a fraction of the calories. And when it comes to cheese, choose one like extra-sharp cheddar, smoked Gouda, aged or sharp provolone and pecorino or Parmesan—they pack a lot of flavor, so you don't need to use a lot.

# Spanish Tortilla

In Spain, tortilla most commonly refers to an omelet, not the Mexican flatbread we know in the Americas. This variation on the classic adds spinach to the basic egg-and-potato combination. Serve it with a tomato salad and some crusty bread for a perfect brunch menu. Tortillas are just as tasty served at room temperature.

MAKES 4 SERVINGS

2 teaspoons olive oil

2 onions, finely chopped

1 garlic clove, minced

2 medium potatoes, cooked and diced

One 10-ounce box frozen chopped spinach, thawed and squeezed dry

1 cup fat-free egg substitute

2 tablespoons finely chopped parsley

½ teaspoon salt

½ teaspoon freshly ground pepper

¼ teaspoon dried thyme leaves, crumbled

¼ teaspoon ground nutmeg

1. In a large nonstick skillet, heat the oil. Sauté the onions until golden, about 7 minutes. Add the garlic; cook, stirring, 1 minute longer. Stir in the potatoes, spinach, egg substitute, parsley, salt, pepper, thyme and nutmeg. Reduce the heat and cook, covered, until set and browned on bottom, about 10–15 minutes.

2. Loosen the edges with knife and invert onto warm platter, or serve directly from skillet.

**Per serving**: 145 Calories, 3 g Total Fat, 0 g Saturated Fat, 0 mg Cholesterol, 435 mg Sodium, 22 g Total Carbohydrate, 4 g Dietary Fiber, 10 g Protein, 112 mg Calcium. **POINTS** per serving: 2.

# Cheese Soufflé

A soufflé isn't so difficult to make, and it's always guaranteed to impress. A tip: Be sure the egg whites are at room temperature, so they'll fluff up well.

MAKES 4 SERVINGS

1 cup low-fat (1%) milk

3 tablespoons all-purpose flour

1½ cups shredded reduced-fat cheddar cheese

½ teaspoon salt

⅛ teaspoon cayenne pepper

2 eggs, separated

2 egg whites

1. In a medium heavy-bottomed saucepan over low heat, whisk the milk and flour; cook, stirring, until thickened and no longer floury, about 5 minutes. Remove from the heat; stir in the cheese, ¼ teaspoon of the salt and the cayenne.

2. Preheat the oven to 350° F.

3. In a small bowl, stir a small amount of the cheese mixture into the egg yolks, then stir the egg yolk mixture into the cheese mixture.

4. In a large bowl, beat all 4 egg whites until foamy; add the remaining ¼ teaspoon salt and beat until stiff but not dry. Stir one-fourth of the egg whites into the cheese mixture; with a rubber spatula, fold in the remaining egg whites. Scrape into a 3-quart ungreased soufflé dish. Bake until puffed and cooked through, 35 minutes. Serve at once.

**Per serving**: 199 Calories, 10 g Total Fat, 6 g Saturated Fat, 130 mg Cholesterol, 1,028 mg Sodium, 12 g Total Carbohydrate, 0 g Dietary Fiber, 18 g Protein, 413 mg Calcium. **POINTS** per serving: 5.

# Pumpkin Soufflé

*Almost a dessert, this light soufflé is touched with warm spices and sweetened with fruit.*

MAKES 4 SERVINGS

2 eggs, separated

¼ cup currants

2 tablespoons orange juice

One 15-ounce can pumpkin puree

¼ cup grated onion, squeezed dry

4 teaspoons all-purpose flour

1½ teaspoons grated fresh gingerroot

1 teaspoon ground coriander

¼ teaspoon salt

2 egg whites

Pinch cream of tartar

1. Preheat the oven to 325° F; spray a 6-cup soufflé dish with nonstick cooking spray. In a small bowl, lightly beat the egg yolks.

2. In a small saucepan, combine the currants and juice; bring to a boil. Remove from the heat and let stand 10 minutes.

3. In a large bowl, combine the currants and juice, the pumpkin, onion, flour, gingerroot, coriander and salt. Stir in the egg yolks.

4. In a large bowl, with a whisk or a mixer on high speed, beat all 4 egg whites until frothy; add the cream of tartar and continue beating until soft peaks form. Lightly stir one-fourth of the egg whites into the pumpkin mixture; with a rubber spatula, gently fold in the remaining egg whites. Spoon the batter into the soufflé dish. Bake until puffed and golden, 45–50 minutes. Serve at once.

**Per serving:** 115 Calories, 3 g Total Fat, 1 g Saturated Fat, 106 mg Cholesterol, 197 mg Sodium, 17 g Total Carbohydrate, 1 g Dietary Fiber, 7 g Protein, 44 mg Calcium. **POINTS** per serving: 2

# Curried Lentil Salad

*Red lentils need to cook just 5 minutes to reach the right texture in this ginger-orange salad. When you buy fresh gingerroot, choose one that has a smooth skin—if the skin is wrinkled or cracked, the root is old and won't be as flavorful.*

MAKES 4 SERVINGS

1 cup red lentils

2 teaspoons curry powder

3 scallions, minced

¼ cup minced parsley

4 teaspoons olive oil

4 teaspoons red-wine vinegar

2 garlic cloves, minced

1 teaspoon minced peeled gingerroot

1 teaspoon grated orange zest

¼ teaspoon salt

1 cup cooked green peas

1. In a medium saucepan, combine 2½ cups water and the lentils; bring to a boil. Reduce the heat and simmer, covered, until slightly crunchy, about 5 minutes (do not overcook). Drain the lentils into a fine-mesh strainer and rinse under cold water until cool, about 15 seconds; drain well. Transfer to a large bowl.

2. In a small skillet over medium heat, toast the curry powder until fragrant, about 30 seconds. Sprinkle over the lentils. Add the scallions, parsley, oil, vinegar, garlic, gingerroot, orange zest and salt; toss to combine. Add the peas; refrigerate, covered, until the flavors are blended, at least 1 hour.

**Per serving:** 228 Calories, 5 g Total Fat, 1 g Saturated Fat, 0 mg Cholesterol, 144 mg Sodium, 33 g Total Carbohydrate, 5 g Dietary Fiber, 14 g Protein, 51 mg Calcium. **POINTS** per serving: 4.

# Crunchy Lentil Salad

*Lentils are the fast food of beans—they need no soaking and they cook quickly. Just place them in a large quantity of boiling water, return to a boil, reduce the heat and simmer 15–20 minutes.*

MAKES 4 SERVINGS

4 cups hot cooked lentils

½ carrot, finely chopped

½ celery stalk, finely chopped

4 teaspoons extra virgin olive oil

1–2 tablespoons fresh lemon juice

1 garlic clove, finely chopped

¾ cup plain nonfat yogurt

¼ cup finely chopped flat-leaf parsley

¼ cup coarsely chopped walnuts

Salt and freshly ground pepper, to taste

6 cups cleaned curly chicory

1. In a large bowl, combine the lentils, carrot, celery, oil, lemon juice and garlic; cool to room temperature.

2. In a small bowl, combine the yogurt, parsley, walnuts, salt and pepper. Pour over the salad; toss to coat. Serve over the chicory.

**Per serving:** 408 Calories, 10 g Total Fat, 1 g Saturated Fat, 1 mg Cholesterol, 464 mg Sodium, 59 g Total Carbohydrate, 27 g Dietary Fiber, 27 g Protein, 410 mg Calcium. *POINTS* per serving: 6.

## Tip

Cook up a double batch of the lentils—refrigerate them in a covered container for up to a week. Toss them into salads or stir into a rice dish. Use them in place of ground meats in stuffed peppers or even meatloaf—experiment!

# Lentil and Bell Pepper Salad

*Since lentils need no presoaking, a delicious salad like this is less than an hour away. If you have any leftovers, be sure to keep them for the next day—the flavors get even better after a little marinating.*

MAKES 4 SERVINGS

⅔ cup lentils, picked over, rinsed and drained

1 bay leaf

½ medium zucchini, diced

½ red bell pepper, seeded and finely diced

½ green bell pepper, seeded and finely diced

1 red onion, chopped

¼ cup chopped parsley

2 tablespoons red-wine vinegar

4 teaspoons chopped sage

1 tablespoon extra virgin olive oil

½ teaspoon salt

½ teaspoon freshly ground pepper

1. In a large saucepan, bring 4 cups water to a boil; add the lentils and bay leaf. Reduce the heat and simmer, uncovered, until just tender, 15–20 minutes. Drain well; discard the bay leaf.

2. In a large bowl, toss the lentils with the zucchini, bell peppers, onion, parsley, vinegar, sage, oil, salt and pepper. Let cool to room temperature before serving.

**Per serving:** 159 Calories, 4 g Total Fat, 1 g Saturated Fat, 0 mg Cholesterol, 281 mg Sodium, 23 g Total Carbohydrate, 5 g Dietary Fiber, 10 g Protein, 39 mg Calcium. *POINTS* per serving: 3.

# Rice and Lentil Pilaf

*The fresher your spices, the more flavorful this appealing Indian-inspired side dish will be. Try it with basmati or jasmine rice, too.*

MAKES 4 SERVINGS

½ cup lentils, picked over, rinsed and drained

2 teaspoons olive oil

1 onion, chopped

4 garlic cloves, chopped

2 teaspoons curry powder

2 teaspoons grated peeled gingerroot

½ teaspoon ground cumin

1 cup long-grain rice

1¾ cups low-sodium chicken broth

½ teaspoon salt

2 tablespoons chopped cilantro

1½ tablespoons fresh lemon juice

1. In a medium saucepan, bring 4 cups water to a boil; add the lentils. Reduce the heat and simmer until the lentils are almost tender, about 10 minutes; drain well.

2. In a large deep saucepan, heat the oil. Sauté the onion until softened, about 3 minutes. Add the garlic, curry, gingerroot and cumin; cook, stirring, until fragrant, about 1 minute. Stir in the rice and lentils; cook, stirring, until thoroughly coated, 1–2 minutes. Stir in broth and salt; bring to a boil. Reduce the heat and cook, covered, until the liquid is absorbed, about 15 minutes. Let stand 5 minutes, then sprinkle with cilantro and lemon juice; fluff with fork before serving.

**Per serving**: 274 Calories, 4 g Total Fat, 1 g Saturated Fat, 0 mg Cholesterol, 330 mg Sodium, 50 g Total Carbohydrate, 4 g Dietary Fiber, 11 g Protein, 47 mg Calcium. **POINTS** per serving: 5.

# Spinach with Lentils

*This sweet-and-sour vegetable dish is reminiscent of the spinach salad often served with a hot bacon vinaigrette. The lentils add texture—and lots of protein.*

MAKES 4 SERVINGS

½ cup lentils

1 teaspoon mustard seeds

½ teaspoon salt

2 teaspoons olive oil

1 cup red onion, diced

2 tablespoons cider vinegar

1 tablespoon imitation bacon bits

2 teaspoons sugar

One 10-ounce bag triple washed spinach, rinsed

1. In a medium saucepan over high heat, combine the lentils, mustard seeds and salt with 4 cups water; bring to a boil. Reduce the heat and simmer, uncovered, until the lentils are just tender, 15–20 minutes. Drain and rinse under cold water to stop cooking; drain again.

2. In a large skillet, heat the oil. Sauté the onion until softened, about 3 minutes. Stir in the lentils, vinegar, bacon bits and sugar; cook, stirring frequently, until heated through, about 2 minutes. Stir in the spinach; cook, covered, until the spinach begins to wilt, 1–2 minutes. Drain off any liquid. Serve warm.

**Per serving**: 151 Calories, 3 g Total Fat, 1 g Saturated Fat, 1 mg Cholesterol, 419 mg Sodium, 22 g Total Carbohydrate, 10 g Dietary Fiber, 10 g Protein, 95 mg Calcium. **POINTS** per serving: 1.

# Spicy Chickpea Stew

*In this recipe, eggplant is salted to remove some of its bitter juices. You can skip this step if you use baby or Japanese eggplants, which are sweeter.*

MAKES 4 SERVINGS

1 large (1½-pound) eggplant, cut into ½–¾" cubes

1 teaspoon salt

4 teaspoons olive oil

1 tablespoon minced onion

1 tablespoon minced carrot

1 tablespoon minced celery

1 tablespoon grated peeled gingerroot

3 garlic cloves, finely chopped

1 tablespoon raisins

1 teaspoon ground cumin

¼ teaspoon cinnamon

One 14½-ounce can diced tomatoes

¼ teaspoon hot red pepper sauce

One 16-ounce can chickpeas, rinsed and drained

½ cup fresh or thawed frozen green peas

2 tablespoons chopped flat-leaf parsley

1½ cups cooked couscous

1. Toss the eggplant with the salt and place in a strainer or colander in the sink; drain 30 minutes. Press out the excess liquid with the back of a spoon.

2. In a large nonstick skillet, heat the oil. Sauté the onion, carrot and celery until wilted, about 5 minutes. Add the gingerroot and garlic; sauté 30 seconds. Add the eggplant and sauté until it begins to soften, about 5 minutes. Stir in the raisins, cumin and cinnamon; stir well. Add the tomatoes and pepper sauce; bring to a boil. Reduce the heat and simmer, covered, stirring occasionally, until the eggplant is tender, about 15 minutes. If the stew becomes too thick, add hot water gradually, until sufficiently thinned.

3. Stir in the chickpeas and green peas; simmer, stirring occasionally, 10 minutes. Sprinkle with the parsley and serve over the couscous.

**Per serving:** 343 Calories, 7 g Total Fat, 1 g Saturated Fat, 0 mg Cholesterol, 468 mg Sodium, 58 g Total Carbohydrate, 13 g Dietary Fiber, 14 g Protein, 109 mg Calcium. *POINTS* per serving: 5.

## No-Fail Bean Cooking

*Here are the approximate cooking times for the most popular varieties of dried beans (measured after soaking):*

| BEAN | COOKING TIME |
| --- | --- |
| *Black beans* | *1½ hours* |
| *Black-eyed peas* | *1 hour* |
| *Chickpeas* | *2½–3 hours or more* |
| *Great Northern beans* | *1 hour* |
| *Kidney beans* | *1 hour* |
| *Lima beans* | *1½ hours* |
| *Pinto beans* | *1½ hours* |
| *Navy beans* | *45 minutes–1 hour* |

# Vegetarian Bean Chili

*Pinto beans are often used in Mexican dishes because they can stand up to lots of spices. Together with lentils, they make this hearty chili a healthy feast.*

MAKES 4 SERVINGS

4 teaspoons olive oil

2 onions, chopped

1 carrot, chopped

1 red, green or yellow bell pepper, seeded and diced

2 celery stalks, chopped

5–6 garlic cloves, minced

1 jalapeño pepper, seeded, deveined and minced (wear gloves to prevent irritation)

4 teaspoons chili powder

1½ teaspoons ground cumin

1 teaspoon dried oregano leaves, crumbled

¼ teaspoon ground cloves

¾ cup canned pinto or red kidney beans, rinsed and drained

One 14½-ounce can diced tomatoes

1 packet instant vegetable broth and seasoning mix

¼ cup nonfat sour cream

½ red onion, chopped

2 tablespoons chopped cilantro

1. In a large nonstick saucepan, heat the oil. Sauté the onions, carrot, bell pepper, celery, garlic and jalapeño until the vegetables are wilted, about 10 minutes. Stir in the chili powder, cumin, oregano and cloves; cook, stirring, until the vegetables are coated, 1–2 minutes.

2. Stir in the beans. Add the tomatoes, broth mix and 4 cups water; bring to a boil. Reduce the heat and simmer, covered, stirring occasionally, about 30 minutes. Uncover and cook, stirring occasionally, until the beans are falling apart and the chili is thick, about 15 minutes longer. Serve, topped with the sour cream, red onion and cilantro.

**Per serving**: 253 Calories, 6 g Total Fat, 1 g Saturated Fat, 0 mg Cholesterol, 1,061 mg Sodium, 43 g Total Carbohydrate, 11 g Dietary Fiber, 10 g Protein, 130 mg Calcium. *POINTS* per serving: 4.

## Got Leftovers?

**Wrap any leftover chili in tortillas for speedy burritos.**

# Four-Bean Salad

*With a prepared salad dressing, this is a breeze to make! Any combination of beans will do for this classic salad. Try cannellini, adzuki, green or fava beans.*

MAKES 4 SERVINGS

⅓ cup thawed frozen lima beans

¼ cup canned red kidney beans, rinsed and drained

¼ cup canned chickpeas, rinsed and drained

¼ cup canned black beans, rinsed and drained

1 celery stalk, diagonally sliced

½ red onion, slivered

¼ red bell pepper, seeded and diced

2 tablespoons nonfat creamy peppercorn ranch salad dressing

¼ teaspoon cracked black pepper

In a large bowl, combine all the ingredients. Refrigerate, covered, until the flavors are blended, at least 1 hour.

**Per serving:** 107 Calories, 1 g Total Fat, 0 g Saturated Fat, 0 g Cholesterol, 97 mg Sodium, 20 g Total Carbohydrate, 3 g Dietary Fiber, 5 g Protein, 32 mg Calcium. **POINTS** per serving: 2.

# Turkish Bean Salad

*This makes a lovely main-course salad. Use any variety of small white beans.*

MAKES 4 SERVINGS

One 19-ounce can small white beans, rinsed and drained

1 red onion, thinly sliced

½ cup chopped parsley

¼ green bell pepper, seeded and finely chopped

¼ red bell pepper, seeded and finely chopped

3 large black olives (preferably Greek), pitted and chopped

2 tablespoons fresh lemon juice

2 teaspoons olive oil

½ teaspoon salt

Freshly ground pepper, to taste

4 cups torn lettuce leaves

3–4 lemon slices

1. In a medium bowl, combine the beans, onion, parsley, bell peppers, olives, lemon juice, oil, salt and pepper. Let stand, covered, until the flavors are blended, at least 1 hour, tossing several times.

2. Serve the lettuce, topped with the salad and garnished with the lemon slices.

**Per serving:** 190 Calories, 4 g Total Fat, 1 g Saturated Fat, 0 mg Cholesterol, 409 mg Sodium, 30 g Total Carbohydrate, 7 g Dietary Fiber, 10 g Protein, 147 mg Calcium. **POINTS** per serving: 3.

## Got Leftovers?

**Stuff them into a warm pita with chopped cucumber and tomato.**

# Beans with Vegetables

*Keep a can of beans in the cupboard for speedy dishes like this. Vary the vegetables with whatever you have on hand.*

MAKES 4 SERVINGS

4 teaspoons olive oil

1 red bell pepper, seeded and cut into strips

4 garlic cloves, finely chopped

Pinch crushed red pepper flakes (optional)

1 pound broccoli (peel the stem), cut into bite-size pieces and steamed

2 cups cauliflower florets, cut into bite-size pieces and steamed

One 16-ounce can cannellini beans, rinsed and drained

Salt and freshly ground pepper, to taste

In a medium nonstick skillet, heat the oil. Sauté the bell pepper until softened, 4–5 minutes. Add the garlic and pepper flakes (if using); sauté 30 seconds. Add the broccoli and cauliflower; sauté until the garlic is pale gold, 2–3 minutes. Add the beans; cook until heated through, about 4 minutes. Season with the salt and pepper.

**Per serving:** 219 Calories, 6 g Total Fat, 1 g Saturated Fat, 0 mg Cholesterol, 310 mg Sodium, 33 g Total Carbohydrate, 12 g Dietary Fiber, 12 g Protein, 58 mg Calcium. *POINTS* per serving: 2.

# Italian-Style White Beans

*Make this in a large saucepan and add 2 cups of broth with the beans for a delicious soup.*

MAKES 4 SERVINGS

4 teaspoons olive oil

1 garlic clove, finely chopped

2 teaspoons chopped sage

1 teaspoon chopped rosemary

1 cup canned diced tomatoes

One 16-ounce can cannellini beans, rinsed and drained

Salt and freshly ground pepper, to taste

1 tablespoon chopped flat-leaf parsley

1 teaspoon red-wine vinegar

1. In a small heavy saucepan over medium-low heat, heat the oil. Sauté the garlic, sage and rosemary until the garlic turns pale gold, about 5 minutes. Add the tomatoes; raise the heat to medium; cook, stirring occasionally, 5 minutes longer.

2. Add the beans, salt and pepper; reduce the heat and simmer, stirring occasionally, about 5 minutes. Stir in the parsley and vinegar.

**Per serving:** 202 Calories, 5 g Total Fat, 1 g Saturated Fat, 0 mg Cholesterol, 446 mg Sodium, 30 g Total Carbohydrate, 5 g Dietary Fiber, 12 g Protein, 99 mg Calcium. *POINTS* per serving: 3.

## Got Leftovers?

**If you have any leftovers, puree them to make a creamy, flavorful dip.**

# Egyptian Fava Bean Salad

*Fava beans can be found fresh in some supermarkets and Italian or Middle Eastern grocery stores in early spring—and sometimes in the freezer case. To cook them, just shell and simmer the beans in enough water to cover until softened and bright green, about 10–15 minutes.*

MAKES 4 SERVINGS

1 cucumber, peeled, seeded and diced

1 pound cooked fava or red kidney beans

1 tomato, diced

½ cup chopped mint

½ cup chopped flat-leaf parsley

½ red onion, finely chopped

¼ cup tahini (sesame paste), mixed with 1 tablespoon water

¼ cup fresh lemon juice

2 garlic cloves, finely chopped

Dash cayenne pepper

Salt and freshly ground pepper, to taste

Boston lettuce leaves

In a large bowl, combine all the ingredients except the lettuce. Serve at room temperature in the lettuce leaves.

**Per serving**: 285 Calories, 10 g Total Fat, 0 g Saturated Fat, 0 mg Cholesterol, 310 mg Sodium, 35 g Total Carbohydrate, 2 g Dietary Fiber, 16 g Protein, 124 mg Calcium. *POINTS* per serving: 6.

## Tip

Don't bother buying dried favas; they can take an unpredictably long time to soften.

*Egyptian Fava Bean Salad*

# Southwestern Black Bean Salad

*For a piquant twist, use pickled red pepper instead of roasted.*

MAKES 4 SERVINGS

One 16-ounce can black beans, rinsed and drained

1 cup diced roasted red pepper

½ cup cooked corn kernels

1 red onion, finely chopped

½ cup chopped cilantro

4 scallions, thinly sliced

1 jalapeño pepper, seeded, deveined and finely chopped (wear gloves to prevent irritation)

4 teaspoons fresh lime juice

4 teaspoons olive oil

2 garlic cloves, finely chopped

Salt and freshly ground pepper, to taste

In large mixing bowl, combine all the ingredients; toss to combine. Let stand, covered, until the flavors are blended, at least 1 hour.

**Per serving**: 182 Calories, 6 g Total Fat, 1 g Saturated Fat, 0 mg Cholesterol, 356 mg Sodium, 26 g Total Carbohydrate, 8 g Dietary Fiber, 8 g Protein, 52 mg Calcium. *POINTS* per serving: 4.

# Black Beans and Rice

*This makes a very satisfying dinner when you add a simple salad.*

MAKES 4 SERVINGS

4 teaspoons olive oil

1 green bell pepper, seeded and finely chopped

1 onion, finely chopped

5–6 garlic cloves, finely chopped

One 16-ounce can black beans, rinsed and drained

One 14½-ounce can diced tomatoes

1 cup low-sodium chicken broth

4 teaspoons dry sherry

1 teaspoon chopped thyme

1 bay leaf

¼ teaspoon dried oregano leaves

¼ teaspoon hot red pepper sauce

1 tablespoon chopped cilantro

Salt and freshly ground pepper, to taste

4 cups cooked white rice

1. In a medium nonstick saucepan, heat the oil. Sauté the bell pepper, onion and garlic until very soft, about 15 minutes. Stir in the beans, tomatoes, broth, sherry, thyme, bay leaf, oregano, pepper sauce and ½ cup water; bring to a boil. Reduce the heat and simmer, stirring occasionally, until the sauce thickens and vegetables are tender, about 45 minutes. If the mixture becomes too thick, add hot water to thin to desired consistency.

2. Stir in the cilantro and season with the salt and pepper; discard the bay leaf. Serve over the rice.

**Per serving**: 457 Calories, 6 g Total Fat, 1 g Saturated Fat, 0 mg Cholesterol, 532 mg Sodium, 82 g Total Carbohydrate, 13 g Dietary Fiber, 17 g Protein, 97 mg Calcium. *POINTS* per serving: 7.

# Broccoli and Bulgur in Spicy Peanut Sauce

*With definite Asian ancestry, this is a hearty and filling meal in a bowl, best served warm.*

MAKES 6 SERVINGS

1 cup bulgur

½ cup loosely packed cilantro leaves

3 tablespoons chunky peanut butter

2 tablespoons reduced-sodium soy sauce

1 tablespoon white-wine vinegar

1 teaspoon sugar

⅛ teaspoon cayenne pepper

3 cups small broccoli florets, steamed until tender-crisp

1. In a medium saucepan, bring 3 cups water to a boil; stir in the bulgur. Reduce the heat and simmer until the liquid is absorbed, 10–15 minutes.

2. In a food processor or blender, combine the cilantro, peanut butter, soy sauce, vinegar, sugar and cayenne; puree. Pour the peanut sauce over the bulgur; stir to combine. Add the broccoli; gently stir to combine. Cook, stirring occasionally, until heated through, 3–5 minutes.

**Per serving**: 174 Calories, 5 g Total Fat, 1 g Saturated Fat, 0 mg Cholesterol, 460 mg Sodium, 29 g Total Carbohydrate, 8 g Dietary Fiber, 8 g Protein, 44 mg Calcium. *POINTS* per serving: 2.

# Marinated Tofu-Vegetable Kebabs

*If you have time, press the tofu before cutting it to make it even firmer: Place it between two plates and weight the top plate with 2–3 soup cans. Let stand 1 hour, then pour off the water.*

MAKES 4 SERVINGS

¼ cup fresh lemon juice

2 tablespoons reduced-sodium soy sauce

4 teaspoons Asian sesame oil

1 tablespoon grated peeled gingerroot

5–6 garlic cloves, finely chopped

½ teaspoon crushed red pepper flakes

1 pound firm tofu, cut into 24 cubes

2 medium zucchini, cut into 1" cubes

1 red or yellow bell pepper, seeded and cut into 1" pieces

1 onion, cut into 8 wedges (leave root end intact)

8 small mushrooms

8 cherry tomatoes

1. In a shallow bowl, combine the lemon juice, soy sauce, oil, gingerroot, garlic and pepper flakes; add the tofu, zucchini, bell pepper, onion and mushrooms. Let stand at room temperature, stirring occasionally, at least 2 hours.

2. If you are using bamboo or wooden skewers, soak eight 12" skewers in cold water about 1 hour.

3. Preheat the broiler. Beginning and ending with an onion, alternately thread the marinated vegetables, tofu and tomatoes onto the skewers; place the kebabs on the broiler rack. Broil, basting with the marinade, until the vegetables are slightly charred and the tofu is browned, about 5 minutes on each side. Brush with any remaining marinade before serving.

**Per serving**: 263 Calories, 15 g Total Fat, 2 g Saturated Fat, 0 mg Cholesterol, 329 mg Sodium, 17 g Total Carbohydrate, 6 g Dietary Fiber, 21 g Protein, 265 mg Calcium. POINTS per serving: 5.

## Tip

**If you find reduced-fat tofu, use it to save on fat grams.**

## Soy, Oh Boy

*Soybeans provide high-quality protein and a health boost, as well: Studies suggest eating soy foods daily can reduce your risk of heart disease and, perhaps, some cancers. Compounds in soy foods may also help relieve the symptoms of menopause. Here are some ways to add soy to your plate:*

*Soy milk: Made by pressing the liquid from ground soy beans, soy milk can be used interchangeably with milk. Look for low-fat brands that are fortified with calcium and vitamin D, and for flavored varieties like vanilla and carob. Use them in smoothies, or drink them chilled.*

*Tofu: A mild-tasting, cheese-like food made from pressed curdled soy milk. Soft tofu can be pureed and mashed into sauces, dips and creamy desserts; firm tofu makes a good meat substitute, as it can be crumbled, grilled, baked or simmered.*

*Miso: A salty condiment made from fermented ground soybeans, sometimes with rice or barley added. Thinned with water, it's a staple soup base in Japan; it can also flavor sauces, dressings and marinades.*

*Tempeh: A cake of fermented whole soybeans, sometimes with rice, barley or other grains added. It has a nutty taste and meaty texture, and works well crumbled into dishes as a ground meat substitute. Tempeh can also be marinated and grilled, or simmered in stews.*

# Vegetable Quesadillas

*These tasty Mexican treats beg for your favorite tongue-searing fresh salsa. Serve with a dollop of non-fat sour cream to cool back down.*

MAKES 4 SERVINGS

2 cups small broccoli florets

1½ cups fat-free milk

¼ cup + 2 tablespoons all-purpose flour

½ cup thawed frozen corn kernels

¼ red bell pepper, seeded and chopped

¼ cup coarsely chopped green chiles

½ teaspoon salt

⅛ teaspoon cayenne pepper

¼ cup chopped cilantro

Four 6" flour tortillas

1. In a large pot of boiling water, cook the broccoli 2 minutes; drain.

2. Preheat the oven to 425° F; spray a baking sheet with nonstick cooking spray.

3. In a small nonstick saucepan over medium heat, whisk the milk and flour; cook, stirring frequently, 4–5 minutes. Stir in the corn, bell pepper, chiles, salt and cayenne; remove from the heat and stir in the broccoli and cilantro.

4. Spoon the vegetable mixture over the bottom half of the tortillas, leaving a ½" border; fold the top half over the vegetables. Place the quesadillas on the baking sheet; bake until hot and bubbling, about 8 minutes. Serve at once.

**Per serving:** 184 Calories, 2 g Total Fat, 0 g Saturated Fat, 2 mg Cholesterol, 436 mg Sodium, 33 g Total Carbohydrate, 4 g Dietary Fiber, 9 g Protein, 173 mg Calcium. *POINTS* per serving: 3.

# Stuffed Potatoes

*To speed up the prep time of this recipe, microwave the potatoes instead of baking them.*

MAKES 4 SERVINGS

2 large baking potatoes, scrubbed

2 teaspoons olive oil

2 onions, chopped

1 cup chopped broccoli

1 carrot, chopped

4 garlic cloves, minced

½ cup nonfat cottage cheese

¼ cup chopped parsley

2 tablespoons grated Parmesan cheese

½ teaspoon freshly ground pepper

¼ teaspoon salt

1. Preheat the oven to 400° F. Pierce the potatoes several times with a fork; bake until tender, about 1 hour. Reduce the oven temperature to 350° F.

2. In a medium nonstick skillet, heat the oil. Sauté the onions until softened, about 5 minutes. Add the broccoli, carrot and garlic; cook, stirring as needed, until softened, about 5 minutes. Reduce the heat and cook, covered, 4 minutes.

3. Halve the potatoes lengthwise; scoop out the pulp, leaving the skins intact. In a large bowl, combine the potato pulp, sautéed vegetables, cottage cheese, parsley, Parmesan, pepper and salt, stirring and mashing potatoes with a fork to the desired texture. Spoon the stuffing back into the potato skins. Place on a baking sheet and bake until heated through, about 15 minutes.

**Per serving:** 196 Calories, 3 g Total Fat, 1 g Saturated Fat, 4 mg Cholesterol, 311 mg Sodium, 34 g Total Carbohydrate, 5 g Dietary Fiber, 9 g Protein, 103 mg Calcium. *POINTS* per serving: 3.

# Twice-Baked Potatoes

*Next time you're baking a batch of potatoes, throw in a few extra to have on hand in the fridge for tasty meals like this one.*

MAKES 4 SERVINGS

4 medium baking potatoes, scrubbed

1 cup shredded extra-sharp cheddar cheese

¼ cup light sour cream

¼ cup fat-free milk

4 teaspoons olive oil

1 teaspoon Dijon mustard

¾ teaspoon salt

⅛ teaspoon cayenne pepper

3 cups chopped broccoli florets, steamed

1. Preheat the oven to 425° F. Pierce the potatoes in several places with a fork; bake until the skin cracks slightly when pressed, about 1 hour. Reduce the oven temperature to 375° F.

2. Halve the potatoes lengthwise. Scoop out the pulp, leaving about ¼" shell intact. In a medium bowl, combine the potato pulp, cheese, sour cream, milk, oil, mustard, salt and cayenne; fold in the broccoli. Spoon the mixture into the potato shells; place on a baking sheet. Bake until hot and bubbling, about 10 minutes.

**Per serving**: 354 Calories, 16 g Total Fat, 8 g Saturated Fat, 35 mg Cholesterol, 676 mg Sodium, 42 g Total Carbohydrate, 5 g Dietary Fiber, 14 g Protein, 291 mg Calcium. *POINTS* per serving: 7.

# Celeriac Milanese

*Don't be intimidated by celeriac's hairy brown exterior. Peel it away and you'll find a delicately flavored vegetable that tastes like a cross between a strong celery and parsley. This simple yet hearty dish works well as a main course or side dish.*

MAKES 4 SERVINGS

4 tablespoons white vinegar

1 pound celeriac (celery root)

½ teaspoon olive oil

4 cups whole mushrooms

1½ cups low-sodium tomato sauce

¼ teaspoon cayenne pepper

¼ cup grated Parmesan cheese

3 tablespoons plain dried bread crumbs

1. In a large bowl, combine 2 tablespoons of the vinegar with 4 cups water. Peel the celeriac and cut into ⅛" slices, dropping the slices into the acidulated water mixture as you cut them.

2. In a medium saucepan, bring 4 cups water to a boil; stir in the remaining 2 tablespoons vinegar. Drain the celeriac; add to the boiling water. Reduce the heat and simmer until celeriac is just tender, about 15 minutes; drain.

3. Preheat the oven to 400° F. In a large ovenproof skillet, heat the oil. Sauté the mushrooms, stirring occasionally, until the mushroom liquid has evaporated, 7–10 minutes. Remove from heat, stir in the tomato sauce, cayenne and celeriac. In a small bowl, combine the cheese and bread crumbs; sprinkle over the celeriac mixture. Bake until browned and bubbling, 15–20 minutes.

**Per serving**: 135 Calories, 3 g Total Fat, 1 g Saturated Fat, 4 mg Cholesterol, 256 mg Sodium, 23 g Total Carbohydrate, 4 g Dietary Fiber, 7 g Protein, 126 mg Calcium. *POINTS* per serving: 2.

# Eggplant Rollatini

*Fontina, a mild cheese with a honey-like flavor, can be found in most supermarkets and gourmet cheese shops. When using parsley, don't tear or cut into it until ready to use—cutting a food rich in vitamin C releases ascorbic acid oxidase, which decreases the food's vitamin C and reduces the food's nutritional value.*

MAKES 4 SERVINGS

2 large eggplants (3 pounds total), peeled and cut lengthwise into 4 slices each

1 teaspoon olive oil

2 onions, finely chopped

1 celery stalk, finely chopped

1 cup nonfat ricotta cheese

2 tablespoons finely chopped parsley

¾ teaspoon dried oregano leaves, crumbled

½ teaspoon freshly ground pepper

⅛ teaspoon ground nutmeg

1 cup low-sodium tomato sauce

¼ teaspoon cayenne pepper

⅓ cup shredded fontina cheese

1 tablespoon grated Parmesan cheese

1. Preheat the broiler; line 2 baking sheets with foil, then spray with nonstick cooking spray. Arrange the eggplant slices in a single layer on the baking sheet. Broil until deep golden brown on one side only; let cool.

2. Reduce the oven temperature to 375° F; spray a 9 × 13" baking dish with nonstick cooking spray. In a medium nonstick skillet, heat the oil. Sauté the onions and celery until softened, about 4 minutes.

3. In a medium bowl, combine the ricotta, parsley, ¼ teaspoon of the oregano, ¼ teaspoon of the pepper and the nutmeg; stir in the sautéed vegetables. Divide the mixture over the eggplant slices and roll up; place the eggplant rolls, seam-side down, in the baking dish.

4. In a small bowl, combine the tomato sauce with the remaining ½ teaspoon of oregano, the remaining ¼ teaspoon pepper and the cayenne; pour over the eggplant rolls, then sprinkle with the fontina and Parmesan. Bake until browned and bubbling, about 30 minutes.

**Per serving**: 234 Calories, 6 g Total Fat, 2 g Saturated Fat, 18 mg Cholesterol, 207 mg Sodium, 31 g Total Carbohydrate, 6 g Dietary Fiber, 18 g Protein, 517 mg Calcium. **POINTS** per serving: 4.

# Brussels Sprouts with Chestnuts

*Store fresh chestnuts in a plastic bag in the refrigerator for up to two weeks—or freeze for up to four months.*

MAKES 4 SERVINGS

1 pound Brussels sprouts (about 4 cups), trimmed and blanched

½ pound chestnuts, cooked, peeled and finely chopped

¾ cup low-sodium vegetable broth

¾ cup evaporated skimmed milk

2 tablespoons finely chopped onion

1 tablespoon cornstarch

3 tablespoons shredded Gruyère cheese

½ teaspoon caraway seeds

¼ teaspoon dried rosemary leaves, crumbled

¼ teaspoon dried tarragon leaves

¼ teaspoon salt

Pinch freshly ground pepper

Pinch cayenne pepper

2 tablespoons plain dried bread crumbs

1 tablespoon grated Parmesan cheese

1. Preheat the oven to 375° F; spray a shallow 1-quart baking dish with nonstick cooking spray. In the baking dish, combine the Brussels sprouts and chestnuts.

2. To prepare the sauce, in a medium saucepan over medium heat, whisk the broth, milk, onion and cornstarch; cook, whisking constantly, until the mixture comes to a boil and thickens. Remove from the heat; stir in the Gruyère, caraway, rosemary, tarragon, salt, pepper and cayenne. Pour over the Brussels sprouts.

3. In a small bowl, combine the bread crumbs and Parmesan; sprinkle over the sauce. Bake until browned and bubbling, about 15 minutes.

**Per serving**: 307 Calories, 5 g Total Fat, 2 g Saturated Fat, 9 mg Cholesterol, 413 mg Sodium, 55 g Total Carbohydrate, 6 g Dietary Fiber, 12 g Protein, 299 mg Calcium. **POINTS** per serving: 5.

## Tip

To blanch the Brussels sprouts, bring 2 cups water to a boil in a medium saucepan. Add the sprouts and cook 1 minute; drain and rinse in cold water.

# Pan Bagnat

*Great bread makes all the difference in this simply delicious recipe from southern France; its name (pronounced* pan ban-YAH) *means soaked bread. Get the crustiest loaf you can find—ideally, a long, slim French baguette.*

MAKES 4 SERVINGS

2 very ripe tomatoes, peeled

One 8-ounce loaf day-old French or Italian bread, halved lengthwise

⅓ cup shredded part-skim mozzarella cheese

¼ cup finely chopped flat-leaf parsley

2 scallions, thinly sliced

2 tablespoons white-wine vinegar

2 teaspoons extra virgin olive oil

Freshly ground pepper, to taste

1. Halve each tomato horizontally; with a spoon, scoop out and discard the seeds and pulp. Dice the tomato shells.

2. Pull out the soft insides of the bread and tear into pea-size pieces. Transfer to a medium bowl; stir in the tomatoes, cheese, parsley, scallions, vinegar, oil and pepper.

3. Fill the bread loaf with the tomato mixture; close the bread and wrap tightly in plastic wrap. Refrigerate overnight; just before serving, cut into 4 sandwiches.

**Per serving**: 222 Calories, 6 g Total Fat, 2 g Saturated Fat, 6 mg Cholesterol, 404 mg Sodium, 34 g Total Carbohydrate, 3 g Dietary Fiber, 8 g Protein, 122 mg Calcium. **POINTS** per serving: 4.

## How We Did It

To peel tomatoes, cut an × on the bottom, just deep enough to cut the skin. In a medium saucepan, bring 4" water to a boil. Drop in the tomatoes and boil just until the skins split, 10–15 seconds. With a slotted spoon, remove the tomatoes and hold under cold running water; rub off the skins.

# Cannellini Bean–Stuffed Peppers

*These fiber-rich peppers can stand alone as an entrée; just make sure you choose evenly shaped round peppers. Use orange, yellow and even purple bell peppers for a variety of color.*

MAKES 4 SERVINGS

One 16-ounce can cannellini beans, rinsed and drained

2 celery stalks, finely chopped

1 onion, finely chopped

2 tablespoons dry white wine

1 tablespoon balsamic vinegar

1 tablespoon red-wine vinegar

2 teaspoons olive oil

1 teaspoon dried oregano leaves, crumbled

1 teaspoon dried thyme leaves, crumbled

1 teaspoon dried basil leaves, crumbled

¼ teaspoon salt

¼ teaspoon freshly ground pepper

4 red bell peppers

Chopped parsley, to garnish

1. In a medium bowl, combine the beans, celery, onion, wine, balsamic vinegar, wine vinegar, oil, oregano, thyme, basil, salt and pepper. Let stand covered, until the flavors are blended, about 2 hours.

2. Meanwhile, preheat the oven to 425° F. Line a 9 × 13" baking dish with foil.

3. Cut off the stem ends of the bell peppers; remove the seeds and membranes, then rinse under cold running water. Halve lengthwise and place in the baking dish. Cover with foil and roast until tender-crisp, 20 minutes; uncover and roast 15 minutes longer. Drain, cover, and let cool to room temperature. Fill the peppers with the bean mixture; garnish with the parsley and serve at room temperature.

**Per serving:** 211 Calories, 3 g Total Fat, 0 g Saturated Fat, 0 mg Cholesterol, 167 mg Sodium, 36 g Total Carbohydrate, 6 g Dietary Fiber, 11 g Protein, 79 mg Calcium. **POINTS** per serving: 3.

# Risotto with Swiss Chard

*The slightly bitter Swiss chard is a nice contrast to the creamy risotto in this Northern Italian comfort food. Experiment with other bitter greens—try spinach, kale or escarole.*

MAKES 4 SERVINGS

3½ cups low-sodium chicken broth

1 tablespoon olive oil

2 onions, finely chopped

1⅓ cup Arborio rice

1 cup dry white wine

1 bunch Swiss chard, cleaned and chopped

2 tablespoons freshly grated Parmesan cheese

¼ teaspoon ground pepper

¼ teaspoon ground nutmeg

1. In a medium saucepan, bring the broth to a boil. Reduce the heat and simmer.

2. In a medium nonstick saucepan, heat the oil. Sauté the onions until softened, about 5 minutes. Add the rice; cook, stirring to coat, about 1 minute.

3. Add 1 cup of the broth; cook, stirring, until the broth is absorbed. Add the wine; cook, stirring, until the wine is absorbed. Stir in a handful of the chard. Alternate adding the remaining broth, ½ cup at a time, with the chard, a handful at a time, stirring until the broth is absorbed before adding more, until the rice and chard are just tender. The total cooking time should be about 25–30 minutes. Stir in the cheese, pepper and nutmeg. Serve at once.

**Per serving**: 329 Calories, 7 g Total Fat, 2 g Saturated Fat, 2 mg Cholesterol, 351 mg Sodium, 55 g Total Carbohydrate, 3 g Dietary Fiber, 10 g Protein, 113 mg Calcium. **POINTS** per serving: 7.

# Zucchini Risotto with Sun-Dried Tomatoes

*Zesty sun-dried tomatoes perk up the rice and zucchini in this delicious dish. Snip the tomatoes with sharp kitchen shears instead of using a knife to chop—they'll be less likely to fly off your cutting board.*

MAKES 4 SERVINGS

$3\frac{1}{2}$ cups reduced-sodium vegetable broth

$\frac{1}{2}$ cup tomato juice

1 tablespoon olive oil

6 shallots, chopped

4 medium zucchini, chopped

$\frac{1}{2}$ cup dry white wine

$1\frac{1}{3}$ cups Arborio rice

16 sun-dried tomato halves (not oil-packed), finely chopped

$\frac{1}{2}$ cup chopped parsley

1 tablespoon chopped fresh marjoram, or $\frac{1}{2}$ teaspoon dried

2 tablespoons grated Parmesan cheese

$\frac{1}{4}$ teaspoon freshly ground pepper

Chopped parsley, to garnish

1. In a medium saucepan, combine the broth and tomato juice; bring to a boil. Reduce the heat and simmer.

2. In a medium nonstick saucepan, heat the oil. Sauté the shallots until soft, about 2 minutes. Add the zucchini and wine; cook until the zucchini is softened, about 5 minutes longer. Add the rice; cook, stirring, about 1 minute.

3. Add 1 cup of the broth mixture, the sun-dried tomatoes, parsley and marjoram; cook, stirring, until the liquid is absorbed. Continue adding broth, $\frac{1}{2}$ cup at a time, stirring until the broth is absorbed before adding more, until the rice is just tender. The total cooking time should be about 25–30 minutes. Stir in the cheese and pepper; serve at once, garnished with the parsley.

**Per serving:** 368 Calories, 5 g Total Fat, 1 g Saturated Fat, 2 mg Cholesterol, 412 mg Sodium, 69 g Total Carbohydrate, 4 g Dietary Fiber, 11 g Protein, 105 mg Calcium. *POINTS* per serving: 7.

*Zucchini Risotto with Sun-Dried Tomatoes*

# Stuffed Swiss Chard

*The sweetness of raisins and figs in the filling makes a nice contrast to the slightly bitter chard wrapper. Serve this hot, cold or at room temperature.*

MAKES 4 SERVINGS

2 tablespoons golden raisins

1 cup lukewarm (105–115° F) water

⅔ cup long-grain rice

4 teaspoons olive oil

1 onion, chopped

1 bunch Swiss chard

½ cup low-sodium chicken broth

3 large dried figs, finely chopped

1 egg white

¼ teaspoon salt

¼ teaspoon ground white pepper

1. Preheat the oven to 325° F. In a small bowl, soak the raisins in the lukewarm water until plumped, about 15 minutes; drain.

2. Meanwhile, cook the rice according to package directions.

3. In a small nonstick skillet, heat 2 teaspoons of the oil. Sauté the onion until it starts to turn golden, 5–7 minutes. Remove from the heat.

4. Rinse the chard under cold running water. Being careful not to tear the leaves, separate them from the stems; finely chop the stems. Add the stems and broth to the onion; cook until the liquid evaporates, about 5 minutes. Stir in the raisins, rice, figs and egg white.

5. Place 1½ tablespoons of the rice mixture on each chard leaf; gently wrap, envelope-style, and secure with toothpick, if necessary. Place the chard bundles seam-side down and close together in a 9 × 13" baking dish. With a pastry brush, coat the chard bundles with the remaining 2 teaspoons of oil, then sprinkle with the salt and pepper. Add ¼" water to the baking dish. Bake until heated through and tender, about 35 minutes.

**Per serving**: 223 Calories, 5 g Total Fat, 1 g Saturated Fat, 0 mg Cholesterol, 282 mg Sodium, 69 g Total Carbohydrate, 3 g Dietary Fiber, 5 g Protein, 67 mg Calcium. **POINTS** per serving: 4.

# RECIPES

# Chapter 9

# Pasta

Now that everyone's wild about pasta, it's hard to believe that Americans once eyed this Italian immigrants' staple food with suspicion. In fact, carbohydrate-rich pasta is a healthy foundation for a meal—as long as it isn't doused in heavy sauces. Choose whole-wheat pasta, and you're getting an extra boost of vitamins, minerals and fiber.

## Fresh versus Dry

With freshly made pasta displays in every gourmet shop, it's easy to think that fresh pasta is superior to dry—but Italians don't look at it that way. They simply use the two types differently in their cooking. Dried pasta has a firm texture and robust flavor that stands up to a variety of cooking methods and sauces. Fresh pasta, more delicately textured and flavored, calls for simpler preparations.

In most cases, you can use fresh or dried pasta interchangeably in these recipes, but for dishes where the texture of the pasta is important, such as lasagna or noodles in broth, you'll get better results using dried pasta, which is sturdier.

Consider 3 ounces of fresh, uncooked pasta noodles to be equivalent to 2 ounces of dried; both will make about 1 cup when cooked. Fresh pasta takes only a minute or two to cook after the water returns to a boil. Taste for doneness; it should be tender, with no raw floury taste. See "Perfect Pasta," page 254, for cooking recommendations.

## Reheating the Right Way

Pasta purists insist that pasta must be prepared fresh every time you use it, but you can break the rules a little for the sake of convenience. For example, you can prepare a double batch of pasta and keep the extra in the refrigerator for up to a week, to toss into salads or reheat quickly for other meals. Rinse the leftover pasta in a colander to prevent sticking, and refrigerate it, unsauced, in a covered container.

Pasta is best reheated in the microwave, where its texture is changed the least. Evenly spread the pasta in a microwavable covered container, and sprinkle with a few tablespoons of water. Microwave on High, stirring often, until just heated through; drain and serve immediately.

You can also reheat pasta on the stove, in a nonstick saucepan with a few tablespoons of water. Cook over moderate heat, tossing gently, just until heated through; drain and serve immediately.

# Capellini with Fresh Tomato Sauce

*Although capellini (sometimes called "angel hair" pasta) is traditionally used in broths, it also works nicely with this uncooked pasta sauce. You can also use thin spaghetti or spaghettini, if you prefer.*

MAKES 6 SERVINGS

5–6 tomatoes, chopped

1 onion, chopped

½ cup chopped basil

¼ cup red-wine vinegar

2 tablespoons olive oil

3 garlic cloves, minced

1 teaspoon sugar

¼ pound capellini

¼ cup grated Parmesan cheese

1. In a large nonreactive bowl, combine the tomatoes, onion, basil, vinegar, oil, garlic and sugar. Let stand, covered, at least 4 hours.

2. Meanwhile, cook the capellini according to package directions; drain and place in a large serving bowl. Top with the sauce; toss to combine. Serve, sprinkled with the cheese.

**Per serving:** 159 Calories, 7 g Total Fat, 2 Saturated Fat, 3 mg Cholesterol, 155 mg Sodium, 21 g Carbohydrate, 3 g Dietary Fiber, 6 g Protein, 79 mg Calcium. *POINTS* per serving: 3.

## Perfect Pasta

*You can make perfect pasta every time by following these pointers:*

- *Use at least a quart of water for every ¼ pound of dry pasta.*

- *Bring the water to a rapid boil. Add the pasta in small amounts—be sure the water remains boiling at all times.*

- *Cook uncovered, and stir frequently for even cooking.*

- *Test for doneness according to package directions. Pasta should be tender but still firm when you eat it, what the Italians call al dente.*

- *Fresh pasta cooks in approximately 2–3 minutes, so check it frequently to be sure it does not overcook.*

- *When the pasta is al dente, drain immediately and serve.*

# Cavatelli with Broccoli

*You can freeze garden-fresh basil and other herbs to enjoy year-round. First, bring a pot of water to a boil; plunge in 2–3 sprigs of herbs at a time for about 30 seconds, then hold them under cold running water for 10 seconds. Pat the herbs dry, chop the leaves (discard the stems). Place in a single layer on a plate; cover with plastic and freeze 2 hours, then transfer to an airtight container and return to the freezer.*

MAKES 4 SERVINGS

2 cups cavatelli or rotelle

4 teaspoons olive oil

4 garlic cloves, minced

2 cups broccoli florets

¼ cup chopped basil

½ teaspoon salt

2 tablespoons grated Parmesan cheese

Coarsely ground black pepper, to taste

1. Cook the cavatelli according to package directions. Drain, reserving ¼ cup of the pasta cooking water, and keep warm.

2. In a large nonstick skillet, heat the oil. Sauté the garlic until fragrant, about 30 seconds. Add the broccoli; cook, stirring, until tender-crisp, 3–4 minutes. Add the sautéed vegetables, basil and salt to the pasta; toss, adding just enough of the pasta water to moisten. Sprinkle with the cheese and pepper.

**Per serving:** 247 Calories, 7 g Total Fat, 2 g Saturated Fat, 4 mg Cholesterol, 391 mg Sodium, 37 g Total Carbohydrate, 3 g Dietary Fiber, 10 g Protein, 136 mg Calcium. **POINTS** per serving: 5.

## How We Did It

You can buy cracked or coarsely ground pepper, or you can adjust your pepper mill to the coarsest grind. Another method—it leaves the peppercorns fairly large, so it's the method pepper-lovers should use—is to crush the peppercorns between two spoons.

# Noodles in Sesame-Soy Sauce

*Use dark, or Asian, rather than light sesame oil to make this Chinese restaurant favorite. Its intense flavor allows you to use just a little.*

MAKES 6 SERVINGS

2 tablespoons reduced-sodium soy sauce

1 tablespoon Asian sesame oil

1 teaspoon sugar

1 teaspoon white-wine vinegar

4 cucumbers, peeled and julienned

3 cups hot cooked vermicelli or rice noodles

6 scallions (green part only), chopped

1. To prepare the sauce, in a small bowl, combine the soy sauce, oil, sugar and vinegar.

2. In a large bowl, combine the cucumbers, vermicelli and the sauce; toss to coat. Transfer to a platter; sprinkle with the scallions.

**Per serving**: 140 Calories, 3 g Total Fat, 0 g Saturated Fat, 0 mg Cholesterol, 208 mg Sodium, 25 g Total Carbohydrate, 2 g Dietary Fiber, 4 g Protein, 28 mg Calcium. *POINTS* per serving: 3.

# Orzo with Garlic-Ginger Vegetables

*Orzo, sometimes labeled rosa marina, is a tiny, rice-shaped pasta—a perfect pair with brilliant spring vegetables. Or, make this delicious dish with 3 cups of cooked brown or jasmine rice instead of orzo.*

MAKES 6 SERVINGS

1 tablespoon olive oil

2 tablespoons minced peeled gingerroot

3 garlic cloves, crushed

2 cups sliced baby carrots

2 cups sliced baby zucchini

1 red bell pepper, seeded and chopped

1 yellow bell pepper, seeded and chopped

1 teaspoon chicken bouillon granules, dissolved in $^3/_4$ cup boiling water

$2^1/_2$ cups cooked orzo

$^1/_8$ teaspoon freshly ground pepper, or to taste

1. In a wok or large skillet over low heat, heat the oil. Sauté the gingerroot and garlic until deep brown, 4–5 minutes; keep the heat low so they don't burn.

2. Increase the heat to high; add the carrots. Stir-fry, adding the zucchini, bell peppers and dissolved bouillon, until the vegetables are tender-crisp, about 3 minutes.

3. Add the orzo and pepper; toss to combine. Serve immediately.

**Per serving**: 134 Calories, 3 g Total Fat, 0 g Saturated Fat, 0 mg Cholesterol, 177 mg Sodium, 24 g Total Carbohydrate, 2 g Dietary Fiber, 4 g Protein, 26 mg Calcium. *POINTS* per serving: 3.

*Orzo with Garlic-Ginger Vegetables*

# Rosemary-Zucchini Pasta

*Fresh rosemary leaves, with their piney scent, are essential to this dish. Use any leftover sprigs to chop and sprinkle over roast pork or poultry, or hang them up to air dry and use later.*

MAKES 6 SERVINGS

   1 tablespoon margarine

   3 garlic cloves, minced

   2 medium zucchini, sliced

   2 medium yellow squash, sliced

   1 red bell pepper, seeded and cut into strips

   1 cup canned crushed tomatoes

   ½ cup orange juice

   1 tablespoon chopped rosemary

   2 teaspoons chicken bouillon granules

   3 cups hot cooked rotelle

   ¼ cup chopped parsley

1. In a large nonstick saucepan over low heat; melt the margarine. Sauté the garlic until deep brown, 4–5 minutes; keep the heat low so it doesn't burn. Add the zucchini, squash and bell pepper; sauté 2–3 minutes. Stir in the tomatoes, orange juice, rosemary, bouillon and ½ cup water; bring to a boil. Reduce the heat and simmer until the vegetables are tender-crisp, about 5 minutes.

2. Stir in the pasta; transfer to a large serving bowl. Serve, sprinkled with the parsley.

**Per serving**: 159 Calories, 3 g Total Fat, 0 g Saturated Fat, 1 mg Cholesterol, 393 mg Sodium, 29 g Total Carbohydrate, 3 g Dietary Fiber, 5 g Protein, 49 mg Calcium. **POINTS** per serving: 3.

# Spaghetti with Kale and Garlic

*If ever there were a nutritional powerhouse, it's kale. This cooking green provides ample amounts of vitamins A, C and E, as well as folic acid, calcium and potassium. Best of all, it's delicious sautéed with garlic.*

MAKES 4 SERVINGS

   6 ounces spaghetti

   2 teaspoons extra virgin olive oil

   2 Spanish onions, thinly sliced

   1 bunch kale, cleaned and chopped

   6 garlic cloves, chopped

   3 plum tomatoes, diced

   ½ teaspoon freshly ground pepper

   ¼ teaspoon salt

   2 tablespoons grated Parmesan cheese

1. Cook the spaghetti according to package directions. Drain, reserving ½ cup of the pasta cooking liquid. Return the spaghetti to the pot; keep warm.

2. In a large nonstick saucepan, heat the oil. Sauté the onions until light golden, 7–8 minutes. Add the kale and garlic; cook, stirring, until the kale is wilted, about 1 minute. Stir in ½ cup water; reduce the heat and simmer, covered, until the kale is tender, 8–10 minutes.

3. Add the tomatoes, the pasta cooking liquid, pepper and salt; heat through. Add the spaghetti and cook, stirring, 1 minute. Stir in the cheese.

**Per serving**: 245 Calories, 4 g Total Fat, 1 g Saturated Fat, 2 mg Cholesterol, 225 mg Sodium, 43 g Total Carbohydrate, 6 g Dietary Fiber, 9 g Protein, 138 mg Calcium. **POINTS** per serving: 4.

# Spaghetti with Pesto and Tomatoes

*The traditional pesto ingredients of basil and Parmesan cheese combine with arugula and fresh tomatoes to make this flavorful pasta dish.*

MAKES 4 SERVINGS

4 teaspoons olive oil

4 plum tomatoes, chopped

8 sun-dried tomato halves (not oil-packed), chopped

⅛ teaspoon crushed red pepper flakes

6 ounces spaghetti

1 cup packed arugula leaves

1 cup packed basil leaves

½ cup packed parsley leaves

1 tablespoon chopped mint

2 garlic cloves, chopped

¼ teaspoon salt

⅛ teaspoon freshly ground pepper

1 tablespoon grated Parmesan cheese

1. In a medium nonstick skillet, heat 2 teaspoons of the oil. Add the tomatoes, sun-dried tomatoes and pepper flakes; cook, stirring frequently, until the sauce thickens, about 10 minutes.

2. Cook the spaghetti according to package instructions; drain and place in a serving bowl.

3. Meanwhile, to prepare the pesto, in a food processor or blender, combine the arugula, basil, parsley, mint, the remaining 2 teaspoons of oil and the garlic; puree. Pulse in the salt and pepper. Add the tomato sauce, pesto and cheese to the pasta; toss to combine.

**Per serving:** 249 Calories, 6 g Total Fat, 1 g Saturated Fat, 1 mg Cholesterol, 186 mg Sodium, 42 g Total Carbohydrate, 3 g Dietary Fiber, 8 g Protein, 157 mg Calcium. **POINTS** per serving: 5.

# Vegetable Lasagna

*You can cut cooking time even more by using no-boil lasagna noodles, now widely available in supermarkets.*

MAKES 6 SERVINGS

Two 10-ounce boxes frozen chopped spinach, thawed and squeezed dry

3 medium zucchini, sliced

3 cups nonfat unsalted cottage cheese

2 cups sliced mushrooms

2 carrots, finely grated

2 onions, chopped

2 eggs, lightly beaten

¼ cup grated Parmesan cheese

3½ cups low-sodium tomato sauce

½ pound lasagna noodles, cooked

1 cup shredded part-skim mozzarella cheese

1. Preheat the oven to 350° F; spray a 9 × 13" baking dish with nonstick cooking spray.

2. In a large bowl, combine the spinach, zucchini, cottage cheese, mushrooms, carrots, onions, eggs and Parmesan.

3. Spread ½ cup of the tomato sauce in the baking dish; arrange a layer of lasagna noodles over the sauce. Spread with half of the vegetable mixture; top with 1 cup of the remaining sauce.

Repeat the layers, ending with lasagna noodles; top with the remaining 1 cup of sauce. Cover with foil and bake 45 minutes. Sprinkle with the mozzarella; bake, uncovered, until the cheese melts, about 15 minutes longer. Let stand 10–15 minutes before cutting.

**Per serving:** 363 Calories, 8 g Total Fat, 3 g Saturated Fat, 86 mg Cholesterol, 300 mg Sodium, 55 g Total Carbohydrate, 7 g Dietary Fiber, 20 g Protein, 330 mg Calcium. *POINTS* per serving: 7.

## Tip

**If you have time, try salting the zucchini before you use it to drain off some of its liquid. To salt, layer the zucchini slices in a large, nonreactive bowl, sprinkling with salt between each layer. Top with a plate and weight with soup cans. Let stand 30 minutes, then pour off the accumulated liquid. Rinse the zucchini well and pat dry with a paper towel. Proceed with the recipe at Step 1.**

# Cheese-Stuffed Manicotti

*Manicotti shells—wide pasta tubes—can be found in better supermarkets and Italian grocery stores. Or, substitute 12 large pasta shells.*

MAKES 6 SERVINGS

1 teaspoon olive oil

3 garlic cloves, crushed

Three 8-ounce cans low-sodium tomato sauce

1 tablespoon Italian herb seasoning

¼ teaspoon freshly ground pepper

1½ cups part-skim ricotta cheese

1¼ cups shredded part-skim mozzarella cheese

¾ cup grated Parmesan cheese

1 egg, lightly beaten

¼ cup chopped flat-leaf parsley

12 manicotti shells, cooked

1. In a large nonstick skillet, heat the oil. Sauté the garlic until golden, about 2 minutes. Stir in the tomato sauce, Italian seasoning and pepper; bring to a boil. Reduce the heat and simmer, covered, stirring occasionally, about 15 minutes.

2. Meanwhile, preheat the oven to 350° F; spray a 9 × 13" baking dish with nonstick cooking spray.

3. In a medium bowl, combine the ricotta, mozzarella, Parmesan, egg and parsley. Fill the manicotti shells with the cheese mixture; place in the baking dish. Pour the sauce over the shells. Bake until browned and bubbling, 30–40 minutes.

**Per serving**: 409 Calories, 14 g Total Fat, 8 g Saturated Fat, 75 mg Cholesterol, 410 mg Sodium, 46 g Total Carbohydrate, 3 g Dietary Fiber, 24 g Protein, 460 mg Calcium. *POINTS* per serving: 9.

# Four-Cheese Macaroni

*Got a mac-and-cheese craving? This quick recipe will work with any mixture of cheeses you have on hand, but be sure that at least one of them is a processed cheese (like American). This ensures the sauce melts smoothly.*

MAKES 6 SERVINGS

2¼ cups elbow macaroni

1 cup fat-free milk

¾ cup shredded reduced-fat sharp cheddar cheese

¾ cup shredded reduced-fat Monterey Jack cheese

⅓ cup shredded American cheese

⅓ cup shredded part-skim mozzarella cheese

½ teaspoon ground white pepper

1. Cook the macaroni according to package directions; drain and return to the pot.

2. Add the milk, cheddar, Monterey Jack, American cheese, mozzarella and pepper. Cook over low heat, stirring constantly, until the cheeses melt, about 5 minutes.

**Per serving:** 299 Calories, 9 g Total Fat, 5 g Saturated Fat, 30 mg Cholesterol, 353 mg Sodium, 35 g Total Carbohydrate, 1 g Dietary Fiber, 18 g Protein, 402 mg Calcium. *POINTS* per serving: 7.

# Pasta Primavera with Provolone

*To avoid a mess on your counter when grating cheese, wrap a piece of plastic wrap around the bottom of your grater and secure it with a rubber band to catch the freshly grated cheese.*

MAKES 4 SERVINGS

1 teaspoon olive oil

2 onions, sliced

1 green or red bell pepper, seeded and diced

1 medium zucchini, diced

1 garlic clove, minced

1 cup stewed tomatoes, coarsely chopped

½ cup low-sodium chicken broth

2 tablespoons finely chopped parsley

¼ teaspoon dried oregano leaves, crumbled

¼ teaspoon crushed red pepper flakes

3 cups hot cooked penne, farfalle or medium pasta shells

⅓ cup shredded smoked provolone or other smoked cheese

1 tablespoon grated Parmesan cheese

1. In a large nonstick skillet, heat the oil. Sauté the onions, bell pepper and zucchini until the onions are golden, about 5 minutes. Add the garlic; cook, stirring, 1 minute longer.

2. Stir in the tomatoes, broth, parsley, oregano and pepper flakes; bring to a boil. Reduce the heat and simmer until thickened, about 10 minutes. Pour over the penne, then stir in the provolone and Parmesan.

**Per serving:** 255 Calories, 5 g Total Fat, 3 g Saturated Fat, 11 mg Cholesterol, 280 mg Sodium, 41 g Total Carbohydrate, 4 g Dietary Fiber, 11 g Protein, 150 mg Calcium. *POINTS* per serving: 5.

*Four-Cheese Macaroni*

# Spinach Fettuccine in Cheese Sauce

*Does eating spinach pasta count toward your daily vegetable quota? Sadly, no—there's only enough spinach for color. But in this recipe you'll get your spinach both ways.*

MAKES 6 SERVINGS

1¼ cups part-skim ricotta cheese

1 cup fat-free milk

1½ cups shredded part-skim mozzarella cheese

¼ cup grated nonfat Parmesan cheese

2 tablespoons margarine

4 garlic cloves, crushed

Two 10-ounce boxes frozen chopped spinach, thawed and squeezed dry

3 cups hot cooked spinach fettuccine

1. In a food processor or blender, combine the ricotta, milk, mozzarella and Parmesan; puree.

2. In a large nonstick skillet over low heat, melt the margarine. Sauté the garlic until deep brown, 4–5 minutes; keep the heat low so it doesn't burn.

3. Add the cheese mixture and spinach to the garlic; cook, stirring, until heated through. Add the fettuccine; toss gently to coat.

**Per serving**: 335 Calories, 13 g Total Fat, 6 g Saturated Fat, 57 mg Cholesterol, 462 mg Sodium, 30 g Total Carbohydrate, 2 g Dietary Fiber, 26 g Protein, 627 mg Calcium. **POINTS** per serving: 7.

# Linguine Alfredo

*This creamy, rich sauce envelops a mélange of vegetables and pasta.*

MAKES 4 SERVINGS

1 tablespoon reduced-calorie margarine

2 garlic cloves, minced

1 tablespoon all-purpose flour

1 cup fat-free milk

¼ cup nonfat cream cheese

¼ cup grated Asiago or Parmesan cheese

1 cup broccoli florets

1 medium red bell pepper, seeded and cut into 1" pieces

½ carrot, thinly sliced

1 celery stalk, sliced

4 cups hot cooked linguine

1. In a medium nonstick saucepan, melt the margarine. Sauté the garlic until fragrant, about 30 seconds. Whisk in the flour, then gradually whisk in the milk; cook, stirring constantly, until slightly thickened, about 2 minutes. Whisk in the cream cheese and Asiago; cook, stirring, until smooth, 1–2 minutes. Remove from the heat and cover to keep warm.

2. Meanwhile, place the broccoli, bell pepper, carrot and celery in a steamer basket; set in a saucepan over 1" of boiling water. Cover and steam until tender-crisp, about 3 minutes.

3. In a large bowl, combine the pasta and steamed vegetables. Add the cheese sauce; toss to coat thoroughly. Serve at once.

**Per serving**: 276 Calories, 5 g Total Fat, 3 g Saturated Fat, 10 mg Cholesterol, 250 mg Sodium, 42 g Total Carbohydrate, 3 g Dietary Fiber, 13 g Protein, 223 mg Calcium. **POINTS** per serving: 5.

# Chickpeas and Pasta

Chickpeas, also called garbanzo beans, and pasta are a classic Italian combination. You'll love the speed of this pasta dish when you want to make dinner quickly.

MAKES 4 SERVINGS

4 teaspoons olive oil

1 red bell pepper, seeded and diced

5–6 garlic cloves, finely chopped

1 tablespoon finely chopped rosemary

2 tablespoons chopped flat-leaf parsley

Pinch crushed red pepper flakes

One 14½-ounce can diced tomatoes

One 16-ounce can chickpeas, rinsed and drained

Freshly ground pepper, to taste

2 cups cooked ditalini or macaroni

¼ cup Parmesan cheese

1. In a medium nonstick saucepan, heat the oil. Sauté the bell pepper, garlic, rosemary, 1 tablespoon of the parsley and the pepper flakes until the garlic turns pale gold, about 5 minutes.

2. Add the tomatoes; bring to a boil. Reduce the heat and simmer, stirring frequently, 10 minutes. Add the chickpeas and season with the pepper; cook, stirring occasionally, until heated through, about 5 minutes. Stir in the ditalini, cheese and the remaining tablespoon of parsley.

**Per serving**: 361 Calories, 11 g Total Fat, 3 g Saturated Fat, 8 mg Cholesterol, 471 mg Sodium, 51 g Total Carbohydrate, 10 g Dietary Fiber, 17 g Protein, 227 mg Calcium. **POINTS** per serving: 6.

# Pasta e Fagioli

This soupy stew is a homey classic. Unlike most stews, it does not improve with age; serve it immediately with a coarse bread to sop up the juices.

MAKES 4 SERVINGS

2 teaspoons olive oil

4 onions, chopped

1 carrot, chopped

1 celery stalk, chopped

2 large garlic cloves, minced

⅔ cup dried Great Northern beans, picked over, soaked overnight and drained

1½ cups boiling water

1 cup canned plum tomatoes in juice

½ teaspoon dried rosemary

½ cup small pasta shells, cooked al dente, drained and rinsed with cold water

¼ cup finely chopped parsley

¼ teaspoon salt

¼ teaspoon freshly ground pepper

2 tablespoons grated Parmesan cheese

1. In a medium saucepan, heat the oil. Sauté the onions, carrot, celery and garlic until soft, about 8 minutes.

2. Add the beans, boiling water, tomatoes and their juice and rosemary; bring to a boil. Reduce the heat and simmer, covered, until the beans are tender, about 2 hours.

3. Stir in the pasta, parsley, salt and pepper; simmer, covered about 5 minutes. Serve at once, sprinkled with the cheese.

**Per serving**: 264 Calories, 4 g Total Fat, 1 g Saturated Fat, 2 mg Cholesterol, 322 mg Sodium, 46 g Total Carbohydrate, 14 g Dietary Fiber, 12 g Protein, 149 mg Calcium. **POINTS** per serving: 3.

Pasta **269**

# Fettuccine with Chicken and Broccoli Rabe

*To clean broccoli rabe thoroughly, wash it under running water, then trim the ends.*

MAKES 4 SERVINGS

1 bunch broccoli rabe, cleaned and chopped

6 ounces spinach fettuccine

4 teaspoons olive oil

Four 4-ounce skinless boneless chicken breasts

½ teaspoon salt-free garlic and herb seasoning

1 red onion, thinly sliced and separated into rings

4 garlic cloves, minced

1 head radicchio, shredded

2 tablespoons grated Parmesan cheese

¼ teaspoon freshly ground pepper

¼ cup chopped basil

1. In a large pot of boiling water, cook the broccoli rabe 2 minutes. With a slotted spoon, transfer to a bowl. In the boiling water, cook the fettuccine according to package directions; drain.

2. In a large nonstick skillet, heat 2 teaspoons of the oil. Add the chicken and sprinkle with the herb seasoning; sauté until cooked through, 4–5 minutes on each side. Transfer to plates.

3. In the skillet, heat the remaining 2 teaspoons of oil; sauté the onion and garlic until tender, 3–4 minutes. Stir in the broccoli rabe and radicchio; cook, stirring frequently, until tender, 4–5 minutes. Add the fettuccine, then sprinkle with the cheese and pepper. Serve alongside the chicken, sprinkled with the basil.

**Per serving**: 339 Calories, 8 g Total Fat, 2 g Saturated Fat, 92 mg Cholesterol, 156 mg Sodium, 37 g Total Carbohydrate, 5 g Dietary Fiber, 29 g Protein, 147 mg Calcium. *POINTS* per serving: 6.

*Fettuccine with Chicken and Broccoli Rabe*

# Penne with Sausage and Prosciutto

*This 20-minute skillet supper combines everyone's favorite Italian flavors. Serve with an escarole salad and garlic bread for an authentic trattoria meal.*

MAKES 4 SERVINGS

2 cups penne

2½ cups broccoli florets

½ pound hot Italian turkey sausage, cut into ½" slices

4 teaspoons olive oil

1 red bell pepper, seeded and cut into strips

1 yellow bell pepper, seeded and cut into strips

1 red onion, thinly sliced and separated into rings

1 cup thinly sliced mushrooms

2 ounces prosciutto, cut into thin strips

2 garlic cloves, minced

¼ teaspoon crushed red pepper flakes

¼ cup chopped basil

1 tablespoon grated Parmesan cheese

1. In a large pot of boiling water, cook the penne 6 minutes; add the broccoli and cook until the penne is al dente and the broccoli is tender, 2–4 minutes longer. Drain and transfer to a serving bowl.

2. Meanwhile, spray a large nonstick skillet with nonstick cooking spray; heat. Sauté the sausage until cooked through, 6–8 minutes. Add to the penne.

3. In the skillet, heat 2 teaspoons of the oil. Sauté the bell peppers and onion until softened, about 5 minutes. Add the mushrooms, prosciutto, garlic and pepper flakes; sauté until tender, 3–4 minutes. Add to the penne, then add the remaining 2 teaspoons of oil, the basil and cheese; toss to combine.

**Per serving**: 368 Calories, 13 g Total Fat, 1 g Saturated Fat, 57 mg Cholesterol, 572 mg Sodium, 44 g Total Carbohydrate, 5 g Dietary Fiber, 21 g Protein, 97 mg Calcium. **POINTS** per serving: 7.

## Matching Pasta Shapes to Sauces

*Those myriad pasta shapes aren't just for fun; they serve a purpose. Various types work best when they're paired with certain types of sauces. Here are some general guidelines:*

- *String or ribbon pasta (spaghetti, linguine, fettuccine): These long shapes work best with smooth or oil-based sauces; meat sauces tend to fall off the strands unless the meat is finely ground. Seafood and finely chopped vegetable sauces are also a good match.*

- *Angel-hair pasta: This fine-stranded pasta is best used in soups; unless the sauces are very smooth (think vegetable purees), they tend to fall to the sides of the strands.*

- *Short pasta shapes (bow ties, elbows, fusilli, radiatori) are best with thick, creamy sauces that can coat them.*

- *Tubular shapes (ziti, penne) work well with sauces containing meats and beans, which can easily slip inside their channels.*

# Fettuccine with Smoked Salmon

*If you prefer, substitute ½ cup reduced-sodium chicken broth for the wine.*

MAKES 4 SERVINGS

6 ounces fettuccine

1 cup clam-tomato juice

½ cup dry white wine

2 red onions, finely chopped

2 tomatoes, peeled, seeded and chopped

¼ cup light cream cheese

2 teaspoons pink or mixed peppercorns, bruised

¼ teaspoon salt

½ pound smoked salmon, flaked

2 tablespoons chopped dill

1. Cook the fettuccine according to package directions; drain and place in serving bowl.

2. In a medium saucepan, combine the clam-tomato juice and wine; bring to a boil. Add the onions; reduce the heat and simmer until soft, about 3 minutes. Stir in the tomatoes, cream cheese, peppercorns and salt; cook, stirring constantly, until well blended, about 2 minutes.

3. Sprinkle the salmon over the fettuccine; add the sauce and toss to coat. Serve, sprinkled with the dill.

**Per serving**: 344 Calories, 6 g Total Fat, 2 g Saturated Fat, 21 mg Cholesterol, 921 mg Sodium, 48 g Total Carbohydrate, 3 g Dietary Fiber, 19 g Protein, 61 mg Calcium. **POINTS** per serving: 7.

# Penne with Salmon and Asparagus

*Make this dish in the spring, when salmon and asparagus are abundant.*

MAKES 4 SERVINGS

2 cups penne

1 chicken bouillon cube

½ cup dry white wine

1 pound asparagus, cut into 1" lengths

¾ pound salmon fillets, skinned and cut into 4 pieces

1 cup nonfat sour cream

3 tablespoons whole-grain mustard

¾ teaspoon salt

½ teaspoon freshly ground pepper

4 tablespooons chopped chives

1. Cook the penne according to package directions; drain and place in serving bowl.

2. In a large skillet, bring ½ cup water to a boil. Add the bouillon cube; stir until dissolved, then add the wine. Add the asparagus and salmon; poach until the fish is just opaque in the center and the asparagus is tender-crisp, 5–6 minutes. With a slotted spoon, transfer the salmon and asparagus to the serving bowl; reserve the cooking liquid. Flake the salmon into bite-size pieces.

3. In a medium bowl, beat the sour cream, mustard, salt, pepper, 3 tablespoons of the chives and the cooking liquid. Pour over the penne mixture; toss to coat. Sprinkle with the remaining 1 tablespoon of chives.

**Per serving**: 382 Calories, 7 g Total Fat, 1 g Saturated Fat, 46 mg Cholesterol, 811 mg Sodium, 45 g Total Carbohydrate, 3 g Dietary Fiber, 26 g Protein, 109 mg Calcium. **POINTS** per serving: 8.

# Capellini with Sole and Vegetables

*If you don't see sole in your market, you'll probably find flounder: The fish are closely related and can be substituted for one another.*

MAKES 4 SERVINGS

Four 5-ounce sole fillets

1 cup fish or vegetable broth

6 ounces capellini

2 cups broccoli florets

1 cucumber, peeled, seeded and cut into strips

1 teaspoon grated lemon zest

2 tablespoons fresh lemon juice

4–5 drops hot red pepper sauce

½ teaspoon salt

½ teaspoon freshly ground pepper

4 teaspoons cornstarch, dissolved in 1 tablespoon water

1½ cups plain nonfat yogurt

1 tablespoon chopped parsley

1. Cut each fillet diagonally into 4 pieces. Roll into 16 pinwheels; secure with toothpicks.

2. In a large saucepan, bring the broth to a boil; add the pinwheels. Reduce the heat and poach until just opaque in the center, 3–4 minutes. With a slotted spoon, transfer to a plate; reserve the broth.

3. In a large pot of boiling water, cook the capellini and broccoli until tender, about 3 minutes; drain and place in a shallow serving bowl.

4. In the saucepan, bring the broth to a boil; add the cucumber, lemon zest, lemon juice, pepper sauce, salt and pepper. Whisk in the dissolved cornstarch. Reduce the heat and simmer, stirring constantly, until thickened, about 3 minutes. Whisk in the yogurt; cook until heated through (do not boil), 3–5 minutes.

5. Arrange the pinwheels on top of the capellini; remove the toothpicks. Pour the sauce over the pinwheels; sprinkle with the parsley.

**Per serving:** 378 Calories, 3 g Total Fat, 1 g Saturated Fat, 76 mg Cholesterol, 509 mg Sodium, 48 g Total Carbohydrate, 3 g Dietary Fiber, 39 g Protein, 231 mg Calcium. *POINTS* per serving: 7.

# Linguine with Clams and Red Peppers

*Here is a very flavorful and low-fat version of the classic. You can cook the clams, onions and peppers ahead of time; then cook the pasta and finish the sauce just before serving.*

### MAKES 4 SERVINGS

36 medium or 24 large clams, scrubbed

6 ounces whole-wheat linguine

2 teaspoons olive oil

2 onions, chopped

1 red bell pepper, seeded and thinly sliced

6 garlic cloves, chopped

¼ cup dry white wine

¼ cup chopped basil

Freshly ground pepper, to taste

1. Place the clams and ½ cup water in a large pot. Steam, covered, over high heat until the clams open, 5–7 minutes; discard any unopened clams. Carefully strain the cooking liquid into a small bowl, discarding any sand. Remove half of the clams from the shells; chop.

2. Cook the linguine according to package directions; drain.

3. Meanwhile, in a large nonstick skillet, heat the oil. Sauté the onions, bell pepper and about one-third of the garlic until the onions are softened, about 5 minutes. Transfer to a plate.

4. In the skillet, combine the wine, the clam liquid and the remaining garlic; bring to a boil and cook, stirring frequently, until reduced to ¾ cup, 4–5 minutes. Stir in the linguine, then stir in the sautéed vegetables and chopped clams; cook until heated through, 3–5 minutes. Transfer to a serving bowl; sprinkle with the basil and arrange the whole clams on top. Serve, seasoned with pepper.

**Per serving**: 269 Calories, 4 g Total Fat, 0 g Saturated Fat, 29 mg Cholesterol, 54 mg Sodium, 41 g Total Carbohydrate, 6 g Dietary Fiber, 18 g Protein, 95 mg Calcium. **POINTS** per serving: 5.

# Pappardelle with Shrimp

*Pappardelle are long, flat egg noodles cut with a pretty crimped edge; in the photo, we used mafalda, which look like mini lasagna noodles. If you like, you can substitute egg noodles for either.*

MAKES 4 SERVINGS

6 ounces pappardelle

3 tablespoons reduced-calorie margarine

1 pound medium shrimp, peeled and deveined

1½ teaspoons curry powder

¼ cup dry white wine

¾ cup low-sodium chicken broth

2 eggs

2 tablespoons grated Parmesan cheese

3 tablespoons finely chopped mint

½ teaspoon salt

¼ teaspoon freshly ground pepper

1. Cook the pappardelle according to package directions; drain.

2. In a large nonstick skillet, melt the margarine. Cook the shrimp and curry powder until the shrimp just begin to turn opaque, 2–3 minutes. Add the wine; bring to a boil, then add the broth.

3. In a small bowl, beat the eggs and cheese; gradually whisk ½ cup of the hot broth into the egg mixture. Pour the egg mixture into the skillet, whisking constantly. Reduce the heat and stir in the pappardelle; cook, stirring, until the sauce thickens and the pasta is heated through, 2–3 minutes. Remove from the heat and sprinkle with the mint, salt and pepper; toss to combine.

**Per serving:** 345 Calories, 10 g Total Fat, 3 g Saturated Fat, 252 mg Cholesterol, 686 mg Sodium, 33 g Total Carbohydrate, 1 g Dietary Fiber, 26 g Protein, 133 mg Calcium. *POINTS* per serving: 8.

*Pappardelle with Shrimp*

# Seafood Lasagna

*Depending on what looks good at the fish market, you could substitute cod, whiting or perch for the haddock and bay scallops for the shrimp.*

MAKES 4 SERVINGS

½ pound lasagna noodles

One 28-ounce can plum tomatoes, well drained

1½ cups chopped watercress

1 cup sliced mushrooms

2 onions, chopped

2 tablespoons low-sodium tomato paste

¾ teaspoon salt

½ teaspoon freshly ground pepper

½ pound haddock fillet, cubed

¼ pound medium shrimp, peeled and deveined

1½ cups plain nonfat yogurt

⅔ cup low-fat cottage cheese

1 egg, lightly beaten

¼ teaspoon ground nutmeg

3 tablespoons grated Parmesan cheese

½ cup watercress leaves

1 tomato, sliced

1. Preheat the oven to 375° F; spray a 9" baking dish with nonstick cooking spray. Cook the lasagna noodles according to package directions. Rinse with cold water; lay flat on paper towels to drain.

2. In a medium saucepan, combine the canned tomatoes, chopped watercress, mushrooms, onions, tomato paste, ½ teaspoon of the salt and ¼ teaspoon of the pepper; bring to a boil. Reduce the heat and simmer 5 minutes. Add the haddock and shrimp; cook until the shrimp just turn opaque, 3–4 minutes longer.

3. In a medium bowl, beat the yogurt, cottage cheese, egg, the remaining ¼ teaspoon of salt, the remaining ¼ teaspoon of pepper and the nutmeg.

4. In the baking dish, layer one-third of the fish sauce, one-third of the yogurt-cheese mixture and one-third of the lasagna noodles; repeat 2 times, ending with the lasagna noodles; sprinkle with the Parmesan. Bake until the top is browned and the sauce is bubbling, about 1 hour. Serve, topped with the watercress and tomato.

**Per serving**: 366 Calories, 5 g Total Fat, 2 g Saturated Fat, 115 mg Cholesterol, 1,091 mg Sodium, 44 g Total Carbohydrate, 4 g Dietary Fiber, 34 g Protein, 328 mg Calcium. *POINTS* per serving: 7.

# Spaghetti Vongole

*When using fresh clams, be sure the shells are tightly closed. If the shell is slightly open, it should close when you tap it.*

MAKES 4 SERVINGS

4 teaspoons olive oil

One 14½-ounce can stewed tomatoes

2 onions, chopped

2 tablespoons tomato paste

4–5 garlic cloves, minced

½ teaspoon dried basil leaves, crumbled

½ teaspoon dried oregano leaves, crumbled

½ teaspoon dried parsley leaves, crumbled

1 pound minced shelled fresh clams or
12 ounces drained canned minced clams

½ teaspoon freshly ground pepper

¼ teaspoon salt

6 ounces spaghetti

1. In a large nonstick skillet, heat the oil. Add the tomatoes, onions, tomato paste, garlic, basil, oregano and parsley; cook, stirring frequently, about 5 minutes. Reduce the heat and simmer, uncovered, until thick, 20–30 minutes. Stir in the clams, then season with the pepper and salt; cook 5 minutes longer.

2. Meanwhile, cook the spaghetti according to package directions; drain and place on a platter. Spoon the sauce over the spaghetti.

**Per serving:** 353 Calories, 7 g Total Fat, 1 g Saturated Fat, 36 mg Cholesterol, 540 mg Sodium, 51 g Total Carbohydrate, 4 g Dietary Fiber, 21 g Protein, 120 mg Calcium. **POINTS** per serving: 7.

# Tagliatelle with Scallops

*Tagliatelle is a long, thin, flat pasta; you can substitute fettuccine.*

MAKES 4 SERVINGS

¾ pound bay scallops

6 ounces tagliatelle

3 tablespoons reduced-calorie margarine

2 onions, finely chopped

1 cup low-sodium chicken broth

½ cup evaporated skimmed milk

½ teaspoon salt

Freshly ground pepper, to taste

1 tablespoon cornstarch, dissolved in
1 tablespoon water

2 tomatoes, peeled, seeded and chopped

2 tablespoons minced chervil

1. Cut each scallop horizontally into 3 thin slices. Cook the tagliatelle according to package directions; drain and place in a serving bowl.

2. In a large nonstick skillet, melt the margarine. Sauté the onions until softened, about 5 minutes. Add the scallops and broth; simmer until opaque, 1–2 minutes. With a slotted spoon, transfer the scallops to the bowl; discard the liquid.

3. In the skillet, mix the milk, saffron with soaking water, salt and pepper, then add the dissolved cornstarch; bring to a boil. Stir in the tomatoes; simmer, stirring constantly, until thickened, about 3 minutes. Pour the sauce over the pasta and scallops; toss to coat. Serve, sprinkled with the chervil.

**Per serving:** 242 Calories, 5 g Total Fat, 1 g Saturated Fat, 30 mg Cholesterol, 552 mg Sodium, 29 g Total Carbohydrate, 3 g Dietary Fiber, 21 g Protein, 135 mg Calcium. **POINTS** per serving: 5.

# Lemon-Dilled Pasta Salad

*Nonfat yogurt is a wonderful ally in the low-fat kitchen, but its somewhat sharp flavor often needs to be tamed. Here, fresh dill helps round out the flavor deliciously.*

MAKES 6 SERVINGS

¾ cup plain nonfat yogurt

¼ cup + 2 tablespoons fresh lemon juice

¼ cup finely chopped dill

3 cups cooked pasta shells

3 cups small broccoli florets, steamed until tender-crisp

3 cups small cauliflower florets, steamed until tender-crisp

1. In a small bowl, combine the yogurt, lemon juice and dill.

2. In a large serving bowl, combine the pasta, broccoli and cauliflower. Drizzle with the dressing; toss to coat. Refrigerate, covered, until chilled, at least 1 hour.

**Per serving**: 137 Calories, 1 g Total Fat, 0 g Saturated Fat, 1 mg Cholesterol, 47 mg Sodium, 27 g Total Carbohydrate, 4 g Dietary Fiber, 8 g Protein, 117 mg Calcium. *POINTS* per serving: 2.

# Pasta Salad Primavera

*This is a low-in-fat yet rich-tasting pasta salad studded with vibrant vegetables and tossed with a yogurt-based dressing. It makes a perfect pot-luck dish.*

MAKES 4 SERVINGS

⅓ cup plain nonfat yogurt

2 tablespoons grated Parmesan cheese

1 tablespoon red-wine vinegar

1 teaspoon grated lemon zest

1 teaspoon olive oil

1 garlic clove, minced

¼ teaspoon freshly ground pepper

2 cups cooked rotelle

1 cup small broccoli florets, steamed until tender-crisp

1 cup small cauliflower florets, steamed until tender-crisp

12 cherry tomatoes, halved

¼ cup shredded basil

½ red onion, chopped

1. To prepare dressing, in small bowl, combine the yogurt, cheese, vinegar, lemon zest, oil, garlic and pepper.

2. In a large bowl, combine the pasta, broccoli, cauliflower, tomatoes, basil and onion. Drizzle with the dressing; toss to coat. Refrigerate, covered, until chilled, at least 1 hour.

**Per serving**: 158 Calories, 3 g Total Fat, 1 g Saturated Fat, 2 mg Cholesterol, 77 mg Sodium, 27 g Total Carbohydrate, 3 g Dietary Fiber, 7 g Protein, 128 mg Calcium. *POINTS* per serving: 3.

# Tricolor Pasta Salad

*For this deliciously easy salad, try an interesting pasta shape with lots of curves and grooves to catch the dressing, like farfalle (also called bow ties or butterflies), radiatore (radiators) or fusilli (short twists).*

MAKES 6 SERVINGS

3 cups cooked tricolor fusilli

1 green bell pepper, seeded and chopped

1 red bell pepper, seeded and chopped

1 yellow bell pepper, seeded and chopped

½ onion, chopped

3 scallions, sliced

½ cup fat-free ranch dressing

8 green-leaf lettuce leaves

1. In a large bowl, combine the fusilli, the bell peppers, onion and scallions. Drizzle with the ranch dressing; toss to coat. Refrigerate, covered, until chilled, at least 1 hour.

2. Line a serving bowl with the lettuce; top with the pasta salad.

**Per serving**: 142 Calories, 1 g Total Fat, 0 g Saturated Fat, 0 mg Cholesterol, 204 mg Sodium, 28 g Total Carbohydrate, 2 g Dietary Fiber, 4 g Protein, 20 mg Calcium. *POINTS* per serving: 3.

## Low-Fat Pasta

*Pasta has always been a low-fat favorite, but the sauce on pasta can be a high-fat trap. To keep your pasta high in flavor and low in fat, follow these tasty sauce suggestions.*

- *Make tomato or vegetable-based sauces.*

- *In cream sauces, use low-fat milk or evaporated skimmed milk; nonfat yogurt; fat-free mayonnaise; or low-fat or nonfat sour cream—see Lemon-Dilled Pasta Salad (page 278).*

- *Top pasta with herbs and spices and a light sprinkle of Parmesan cheese.*

- *When preparing a meaty pasta dish, choose skinless poultry, lean cuts of meat or fish.*

- *Add beans or lentils to pasta for a protein punch.*

# Chapter 10

# Vegetable Side Dishes

Although side dishes are often an afterthought, when they're vegetable-based, like the ones in this chapter, they're worth planning your meals around. Why not make the side dish the star of your next supper? The idea isn't so far-fetched, since you're probably used to turning salad into a main-dish meal.

Since vegetables play starring roles in these recipes, it's important that you cook them properly to preserve nutrients, texture and color. Steam them or cook in a very small amount of water, to help preserve water-soluble nutrients like vitamin C. Don't add the vegetable until the water is boiling, so cooking time is shorter (and the opportunity for nutrient loss is less). Remove the vegetables when their color has intensified and they're tender-crisp. A microwave is ideal for cooking vegetables. It requires only a tiny amount of water and only the briefest of cooking times.

Don't add anything acid or alkaline to the cooking water until the vegetables are fully cooked. Acids (like those found in tomatoes, lemon juice or vinegar) will make the vegetables resist softening longer and will turn green vegetables an unappetizing gray. Alkaline ingredients, like baking soda, brighten the color of greens and speed up the softening of vegetables (that's why some people add it to the pot when they make beans). But baking soda also leeches out vitamin C, and can quickly turn a crisp veggie to mush.

## Frozen and Canned— a Compromise?

Of course, it's best to eat fresh vegetables. But sometimes convenience, season and price make that difficult. Indeed, canned or frozen vegetables—picked at their height of ripeness and processed immediately after picking—may retain more nutrients than the "fresh" vegetables in the produce aisle that may have been trucked cross-country two weeks ago. Besides, it's important to have vegetables every day, no matter where they come from. This is a stronger possibility if your freezer and pantry are always stocked with options.

When buying frozen, make sure the box doesn't have ice crystals on the outside, or that the bagged vegetables are frozen in a solid block. Both are signs of thawing and refreezing, so taste, texture and nutritional value will be compromised. Look for canned vegetables with no added salt or sugar.

# Herb-Stuffed Artichokes

*Lots of work but worth it—an artichoke is almost like a meal—eating each individual leaf forces you to slow down, too. When selecting artichokes, look for those with tight leaves and a good weight.*

MAKES 4 SERVINGS

4 medium (¾-pound each) artichokes

½ lemon

¾ cup plain dried bread crumbs

1 tomato, chopped

2 tablespoons chopped parsley

2 tablespoons chopped basil

2 tablespoons chopped tarragon

1 teaspoon grated lemon zest

2 tablespoons fresh lemon juice

½ teaspoon chopped rosemary

½ teaspoon salt

¼ teaspoon freshly ground pepper

1. With a large stainless-steel knife, cut off the stem of each artichoke flush with base so that artichokes will stand upright; remove and discard the center leaves and choke. With scissors, trim 1" from the top of each artichoke; rub the cut ends with the lemon.

2. Fill a large nonreactive saucepan with 8 cups of water, then add the artichokes and lemon; bring to a boil. Reduce the heat and simmer until tender, 15–20 minutes.

3. Meanwhile, preheat the oven to 350° F. Sprinkle the bread crumbs on a nonstick baking sheet; bake until toasted, 15–20 minutes, then transfer to a large bowl. Add the tomato, parsley, basil, tarragon, lemon zest, lemon juice, rosemary, salt and pepper; toss to combine.

4. Fill the center of the artichokes with the breadcrumb mixture; place on the baking sheet. Bake until the bread crumbs are nicely browned, 25–30 minutes.

**Per serving**: 160 Calories, 2 g Total Fat, 0 g Saturated Fat, 0 mg Cholesterol, 583 mg Sodium, 33 g Total Carbohydrate, 9 g Dietary Fiber, 8 g Protein, 134 mg Calcium. **POINTS** per serving: 2.

## Tip

Like apples and pears, artichokes will turn brown if they're not dropped in acidulated water or rubbed with lemon. Adding what's left of the lemon to the cooking water helps to retain their color.

# Broccoli Rabe and Potato Cake

*This is a classic Italian dish—and it's just as delicious with kale. Try making this with Yukon gold potatoes—their buttery flavor makes it even tastier.*

MAKES 4 SERVINGS

4 teaspoons olive oil

2 medium all-purpose potatoes, peeled and thinly sliced

1 teaspoon paprika

¼ teaspoon salt

1 cup reduced-sodium vegetable broth

1 bunch broccoli rabe, cleaned and chopped

4 garlic cloves, thinly sliced

¼ teaspoon crushed red pepper flakes

Fresh lemon juice

Lemon wedges, to garnish

1. In a large nonstick skillet, heat the oil. Arrange the potato slices in a spiral in the pan, overlapping if necessary, then sprinkle with the paprika and salt; cook until they begin to brown, about 10 minutes. Add ½ cup of the broth; reduce the heat and cook, covered, checking frequently that the potatoes don't burn, until the liquid evaporates and the potatoes are tender, about 10 minutes longer.

2. Meanwhile, steam the broccoli rabe until bright green and tender, about 7 minutes. Transfer to a bowl; toss with the garlic and pepper flakes. Spread the broccoli rabe over the potatoes, then add the remaining ½ cup broth; cook, covered, 5 minutes. Uncover and cook until the liquid evaporates, about 5 minutes longer. With a spatula, gently loosen the potatoes from the bottom of the pan; slide the cake onto a large plate. Cut into 4 wedges and serve, sprinkled with the lemon juice and garnished with the lemon wedges.

**Per serving**: 126 Calories, 5 g Total Fat, 1 g Saturated Fat, 0 mg Cholesterol, 237 mg Sodium, 18 g Total Carbohydrate, 3 g Dietary Fiber, 4 g Protein, 61 mg Calcium. *POINTS* per serving: 2.

## Roasting Peppers

*Roasted peppers add wonderful flavor to salads, sandwiches and soups. Choose any color of pepper that you wish. Red peppers will give a slightly milder flavor than green.*

- *Preheat the broiler. On the broiler rack, broil peppers as close to the heat as possible, turning several times as the skin on top blackens and chars.*

- *When the peppers are entirely blackened, place in a paper bag for 5–10 minutes to cool. (Steam created as the peppers cool will make the skin easier to remove.)*

- *With a small, sharp knife, carefully scrape away the charred skin; run the peppers under cold water to wash away any remaining bits of skin.*

# Braised Endive with Lemon

*You can identify fresh Belgian endive by its tightly packed head and pale yellowish tip.*

MAKES 4 SERVINGS

4 medium heads endive, trimmed

½ cup chicken broth

1 tablespoon fresh lemon juice

2 teaspoons chopped parsley

¼ teaspoon grated lemon zest

¼ teaspoon salt

¼ teaspoon freshly ground pepper

Preheat the oven to 350° F. Arrange the endive in a 9 × 13" baking dish; add the broth and lemon juice. Cover with foil and bake until fork-tender, about 25 minutes. Remove the foil; bake 5 minutes longer. Serve, sprinkled with the parsley, lemon zest, salt and pepper.

**Per serving**: 20 Calories, 0 g Total Fat, 0 g Saturated Fat, 0 mg Cholesterol, 266 mg Sodium, 4 g Total Carbohydrate, 2 g Dietary Fiber, 1 g Protein, 4 mg Calcium. **POINTS** per serving: 0.

# Oven-Roasted Beets and Garlic

*Be sure to use fresh, not canned, beets in this recipe—the flavor is incomparable. Serve alongside a roast chicken for a perfect family supper.*

MAKES 4 SERVINGS

4 large beets (2½" diameter), trimmed, peeled and quartered (about 2 cups)

6 garlic cloves, quartered

1 tablespoon minced thyme

2 teaspoons olive oil

¼ cup + 1 tablespoon orange juice

1. Preheat the oven to 375° F. In a 9 × 13" baking pan, combine the beets, garlic, half of the thyme and the oil.

2. In a small bowl, combine the orange juice and 2 tablespoons water; pour over the beets. Cover with foil and roast until tender, 45–50 minutes. Remove the foil; roast 10 minutes longer. Serve, sprinkled with the remaining thyme.

**Per serving**: 65 Calories, 2 g Total Fat, 0 g Saturated Fat, 0 mg Cholesterol, 43 mg Sodium, 10 g Total Carbohydrate, 2 g Dietary Fiber, 1 g Protein, 26 mg Calcium. **POINTS** per serving: 1.

# Broccoli with Garlic

*If you love the taste of broccoli and cheese together, stir in 1/2 cup shredded reduced-fat cheddar with the bell pepper—for only 1 added* **POINT**.

MAKES 4 SERVINGS

2 teaspoons olive oil

1 pound broccoli, chopped and steamed until tender-crisp

3 garlic cloves, minced

1/4 teaspoon dried oregano leaves, crumbled

1/4 cup julienned roasted red bell pepper

In a large nonstick skillet, heat the oil. Sauté the broccoli, garlic and oregano until the garlic is golden, about 3 minutes. Stir in the roasted pepper; cook, stirring frequently, until heated through, about 2 minutes.

**Per serving:** 51 Calories, 3 g Total Fat, 0 g Saturated Fat, 0 mg Cholesterol, 24 mg Sodium, 6 g Total Carbohydrate, 3 g Dietary Fiber, 3 g Protein, 49 mg Calcium. **POINTS** per serving: 1.

# Brussels Sprouts Sauté

*If the mere mention of Brussels sprouts conjures up images from childhood you'd rather not recall, take heart in this dish. Minimal cooking releases all of their flavor and little of their sometimes off-putting odor.*

MAKES 4 SERVINGS

2 teaspoons olive oil

1/2 red onion, chopped

1/2 cup julienned boiled ham

2 cups Brussels sprouts, steamed until tender-crisp and quartered

1/3 cup orange sections

1 tablespoon cider vinegar

1 teaspoon caraway seeds

In a large nonstick skillet, heat the oil. Sauté the onion until translucent, 3–4 minutes. Add the ham; cook, stirring frequently, 2 minutes. Stir in the Brussels sprouts, orange sections, vinegar and caraway seeds; sauté, stirring, until heated through, about 1 minute.

**Per serving:** 73 Calories, 3 g Total Fat, 1 g Saturated Fat, 8 mg Cholesterol, 183 mg Sodium, 7 g Total Carbohydrate, 3 g Dietary Fiber, 5 g Protein, 33 mg Calcium. **POINTS** per serving: 1.

# Stir-Fried Asparagus

*Seek out thinner asparagus—they're more tender than thicker spears. Also avoid those with dry-looking ends; they tend to be woody and, often, inedible.*

MAKES 4 SERVINGS

⅓ cup low-sodium chicken broth

2 teaspoons reduced-sodium soy sauce

1 teaspoon cornstarch

½ teaspoon sugar

1 teaspoon vegetable oil

½ pound asparagus, cut into ½" diagonal pieces

½ carrot, thinly sliced

1. In a small bowl, combine the broth, soy sauce, cornstarch and sugar, stirring to dissolve the cornstarch and sugar.

2. In a large nonstick skillet over high heat, heat the oil. Sauté the asparagus until bright green, about 2 minutes. Add the broth mixture and carrot; cook, stirring constantly, until the asparagus is tender and the sauce is thickened, about 3 minutes.

**Per serving:** 43 Calories, 1 g Total Fat, 0 g Saturated Fat, 0 mg Cholesterol, 111 mg Sodium, 6 g Total Carbohydrate, 1 g Dietary Fiber, 3 g Protein, 23 mg Calcium. *POINTS* per serving: 1.

# Dilled Carrots

*Check out your local farmers' market for organic carrots. This dish looks especially pretty when garnished with their brilliant green, coarsely chopped tops.*

MAKES 4 SERVINGS

4 carrots, cut into ¼" slices

2 bay leaves

1 cinnamon stick

½ teaspoon salt

¼ cup fresh lemon juice

2 tablespoons chopped fresh dill

4 teaspoons olive oil

1 teaspoon sugar

⅛ teaspoon cayenne pepper

1. In a large skillet, combine the carrots, bay leaves, cinnamon stick and salt; add water to cover and bring to a boil. Reduce the heat and simmer until tender, about 10 minutes. Drain well; discard the bay leaves and cinnamon stick.

2. In a medium bowl, whisk the lemon juice, dill, oil, sugar and cayenne. Add the carrots; toss to coat. Refrigerate, covered, until the flavors are blended, about 1 hour. Serve at room temperature.

**Per serving:** 98 Calories, 5 g Total Fat, 1 g Saturated Fat, 0 mg Cholesterol, 313 mg Sodium, 14 g Total Carbohydrate, 4 g Dietary Fiber, 1 g Protein, 47 mg Calcium. *POINTS* per serving: 2.

# Fennel and Pears

*What a difference a leaf makes: The peppery bite of dark green watercress is an ideal contrast to the sweetness of pears.*

MAKES 4 SERVINGS

1½ teaspoons reduced-calorie margarine

2 fennel bulbs, trimmed and thinly sliced

⅛ teaspoon salt

4 pears, cored and thinly sliced

1 teaspoon grated lemon zest

1 bunch watercress, cleaned

1. In a large nonstick skillet, melt the margarine. Add the fennel and salt; cook, stirring occasionally, until fragrant, about 2 minutes. Stir in the pears; reduce the heat and cook, covered, until the fennel is tender, about 5 minutes. Remove from the heat; add the lemon zest and toss.

2. Divide the watercress among 4 plates, top with the fennel mixture.

**Per serving:** 166 Calories, 3 g Total Fat, 0 g Saturated Fat, 0 mg Cholesterol, 180 mg Sodium, 36 g Total Carbohydrate, 5 g Dietary Fiber, 2 g Protein, 56 mg Calcium. *POINTS* per serving: 3.

# Red Cabbage with Ginger

*Braising is one of the best ways to prepare red cabbage, since this method retains lots of flavor. But be sure to serve it immediately to retain the rich burgundy color.*

MAKES 4 SERVINGS

2 teaspoons olive oil

½ onion, thinly sliced

2 tablespoons grated peeled gingerroot

4 cups thinly sliced red cabbage

⅔ cup chicken broth

In a medium saucepan, heat the oil. Sauté the onion and gingerroot until just fragrant, about 1 minute; stir in the cabbage and broth. Reduce the heat and simmer, covered, stirring occasionally, until the cabbage is tender, about 20 minutes.

**Per serving:** 53 Calories, 3 g Total Fat, 0 g Saturated Fat, 0 mg Cholesterol, 174 mg Sodium, 7 g Total Carbohydrate, 2 g Dietary Fiber, 2 g Protein, 42 mg Calcium. *POINTS* per serving: 1.

# Cauliflower with Tomato-Curry Sauce

*Try serving this as an Indian-inspired appetizer—scoop up the spicy sauce and chunks of cauliflower with pieces of warm Naan (page 60). Cutting the cauliflower florets into bite-size pieces makes it easier to eat.*

MAKES 4 SERVINGS

1 teaspoon olive oil

1 onion, finely chopped

2 teaspoons grated peeled gingerroot

2 teaspoons curry powder

½ teaspoon ground cumin

1 cup canned tomato puree

1 pound cauliflower florets, cut into bite-size pieces and steamed

1 tablespoon chopped parsley

1. In a large nonstick skillet, heat the oil. Sauté the onion and gingerroot until the onion is translucent, 4–5 minutes. Stir in the curry powder and cumin; cook 1 minute.

2. Stir in the tomato puree and ½ cup water. Reduce the heat and simmer, covered, stirring occasionally, 15 minutes. Remove from the heat; cool slightly. Transfer to a blender or food processor; puree.

3. Place the cauliflower in serving bowl; top with the sauce and sprinkle with the parsley.

**Per serving:** 73 Calories, 2 g Total Fat, 0 g Saturated Fat, 0 mg Cholesterol, 266 mg Sodium, 14 g Total Carbohydrate, 5 g Dietary Fiber, 3 g Protein, 51 mg Calcium. **POINTS** per serving: 1.

## Tip

Once you've trimmed off the tough end of the stem and the florets, don't throw out the core of the cauliflower; it's perfectly good eating! Simply cut it into chunks about 2" long and ½" wide, and steam them with the florets.

# Lemon-Sautéed Green Beans with Parsley

*To make this dish even more delectable, use haricots verts, the long, thin green beans that are commonplace in French kitchens. They are exquisitely tender and make a truly elegant presentation.*

MAKES 4 SERVINGS

1 teaspoon olive oil

1 pound green beans, cut into 2" lengths

2 tablespoons chopped parsley

1 tablespoon fresh lemon juice

In a large nonstick skillet, heat the oil. Sauté the beans until bright green, about 3 minutes; add the parsley. Cook, stirring frequently, 3 minutes. Stir in the lemon juice and 2 tablespoons water. Reduce the heat and cook, covered, 2–3 minutes. Uncover and cook, stirring frequently, until the beans are tender-crisp, 2–3 minutes longer.

**Per serving:** 37 Calories, 1 g Total Fat, 0 g Saturated Fat, 0 mg Cholesterol, 6 mg Sodium, 6 g Total Carbohydrate, 2 g Dietary Fiber, 2 g Protein, 33 mg Calcium. **POINTS** per serving: 0.

# Broiled Eggplant

*When eggplant is fried, it becomes a sponge for oil. Here, it's baked with tomato sauce for just 33 calories a serving. Choose a firm, heavy eggplant with a shiny skin.*

MAKES 4 SERVINGS

1 plum tomato, finely chopped

3 tablespoons balsamic vinegar

2 tablespoons chopped basil

1 garlic clove, crushed

1 small (¾-pound) eggplant, cut into ½" slices

¼ teaspoon salt

¼ teaspoon freshly ground pepper

1. Spray the broiler rack with nonstick cooking spray; preheat the broiler.

2. In a small bowl, whisk the tomato, vinegar, basil and garlic. Place the eggplant slices on the broiler rack and brush with some of the tomato mixture. Broil 5–6" from heat until lightly browned on one side, about 8 minutes. Turn the slices over; brush with a little more of the tomato mixture. Broil until lightly browned, 3–5 minutes longer. Transfer to a platter.

3. Add the salt and pepper to the remaining tomato mixture; pour over the eggplant.

**Per serving**: 33 Calories, 0 g Total Fat, 0 g Saturated Fat, 0 mg Cholesterol, 143 mg Sodium, 7 g Total Carbohydrate, 2 g Dietary Fiber, 1 g Protein, 46 mg Calcium. *POINTS* per serving: 0.

## Tip

Eggplant is also delicious when grilled. Spray the grill rack with nonstick cooking spray, then preheat the grill. Follow Steps 2 and 3 above, grilling the eggplant 5–6" from the coals.

# Kale with Balsamic Vinaigrette

*Look for kale that's deep, almost bluish-green; avoid bunches with thick stalks. Store it in a perforated plastic bag in the fridge for up to five days.*

MAKES 4 SERVINGS

2 teaspoons olive oil

6 shallots, finely chopped

1 tablespoon balsamic vinegar

½ teaspoon Dijon mustard

4 cups chopped cleaned kale, steamed until just wilted

⅛ teaspoon salt

⅛ teaspoon freshly ground pepper

In a large nonstick skillet, heat the oil. Sauté the shallots until translucent, about 5 minutes. Add ¼ cup water, the vinegar and mustard; bring to a boil. Cook, stirring constantly, 1 minute. Stir in the kale; toss to combine. Sprinkle with the salt and pepper.

**Per serving**: 70 Calories, 3 g Total Fat, 0 g Saturated Fat, 0 mg Cholesterol, 120 mg Sodium, 10 g Total Carbohydrate, 5 g Dietary Fiber, 3 g Protein, 100 mg Calcium. *POINTS* per serving: 1.

# Creole-Style Okra

*Okra releases a sticky substance when it's cooked, which helps to thicken stews and gumbo. Cook it briefly to avoid the sticky texture.*

MAKES 6 SERVINGS

2 teaspoons vegetable oil

1 onion, chopped

1 celery stalk, chopped

4½ cups fresh or thawed frozen okra, trimmed

One 14½-ounce can crushed tomatoes

2 strips bacon, crisp-cooked and crumbled

⅛ teaspoon cayenne pepper

⅛ teaspoon freshly ground pepper

1 bay leaf

⅛ teaspoon filé powder

In a large nonstick skillet, heat the oil. Sauté the onion and celery until golden, 6–8 minutes. Stir in the okra, tomatoes, bacon, cayenne, pepper, bay leaf and ¾ cup water; bring to a boil. Reduce the heat and simmer, covered, until the okra is tender, 12–15 minutes. Remove from the heat; discard the bay leaf and stir in the filé powder.

**Per serving:** 67 Calories, 3 g Total Fat, 1 g Saturated Fat, 2 mg Cholesterol, 177 mg Sodium, 9 g Total Carbohydrate, 3 g Dietary Fiber, 3 g Protein, 69 mg Calcium. *POINTS* per serving: 1.

## Tip

Filé powder is made from dried sassafras leaves; it flavors and thickens many creole and Cajun dishes. Always stir in after you remove the pot from the heat, since filé powder can become tough if cooked too long or over heat that's too high.

# Mushroom and Bell Pepper Sauté

*If you prefer less liquid, cook this dish uncovered— keep a close eye on it, though, to make sure too much liquid doesn't evaporate.*

MAKES 4 SERVINGS

1 teaspoon olive oil

4 cups sliced mushrooms

1 red bell pepper, seeded and julienned

2 sun-dried tomato halves (not oil-packed), julienned

2 tablespoons dry white wine

1 tablespoon chopped chives

1 teaspoon chopped rosemary

⅛ teaspoon freshly ground pepper

In a large nonstick skillet, heat the oil. Sauté the mushrooms and bell pepper until golden, 4–5 minutes. Stir in the tomatoes, wine, chives, rosemary and pepper. Cook, covered, until heated through, about 2 minutes.

**Per serving:** 44 Calories, 2 g Total Fat, 0 g Saturated Fat, 0 mg Cholesterol, 5 mg Sodium, 6 g Total Carbohydrate, 2 g Dietary Fiber, 2 g Protein, 10 mg Calcium. *POINTS* per serving: 1.

## Got Leftovers?

This nutritious side dish serves as an excellent filling for omelets the next day.

# Oven-Baked Onion Rings

*Team these pub-style rings with a lean, mean Monterey Jack Turkey Burger (page 146) and all the burger fixin's. Pass the ketchup, please!*

MAKES 6 SERVINGS

¼ cup + 2 tablespoons all-purpose flour

½ teaspoon salt

⅛ teaspoon cayenne pepper

1 large Spanish onion, cut into ¼" slices

3 egg whites, lightly beaten

¾ cup plain dried bread crumbs

1. Preheat the oven to 400° F; spray a nonstick baking sheet with nonstick cooking spray. On a sheet of wax paper, combine the flour, salt and cayenne.

2. Separate the onion slices in rings, but keep them in groups of two, one ring inside another. Dredge the rings in the seasoned flour, then dip in the egg whites and then coat in the bread crumbs; place on the baking sheet. Bake on the top oven rack until browned, about 10 minutes. Turn the onion rings over and bake until browned, 5–10 minutes.

**Per serving:** 108 Calories, 1 g Total Fat, 0 g Saturated Fat, 0 mg Cholesterol, 330 mg Sodium, 20 g Total Carbohydrate, 1 g Dietary Fiber, 5 g Protein, 46 mg Calcium. **POINTS** per serving: 2.

# Oven-Roasted Corn on the Cob

*When selecting fresh corn, check the silk strands at the top of corn husks: They should be smooth and shiny, not dry.*

MAKES 4 SERVINGS

2 tablespoons finely chopped cilantro

2 tablespoons fresh lime juice

4 teaspoons reduced-calorie margarine, melted

4 ears corn on the cob, shucked

1. Preheat the oven to 450° F. Tear off four 12" square sheets of foil.

2. In a shallow bowl, combine the cilantro, lime juice, and margarine with 1 tablespoon water. Roll the corn in the cilantro butter, then place on the foil; brush with any remaining cilantro butter. Wrap the foil around the corn securely, then place directly on oven rack. Bake, turning occasionally, until tender, about 35 minutes.

**Per serving:** 208 Calories, 4 g Total Fat, 1 g Saturated Fat, 0 mg Cholesterol, 44 mg Sodium, 46 g Total Carbohydrate, 6 g Dietary Fiber, 6 g Protein, 9 mg Calcium. **POINTS** per serving: 3.

## Got Leftovers?

**Cut fresh corn from the cob and toss into soup or a favorite cornbread recipe for super flavor.**

*Oven-Roasted Corn on the Cob*

# Sautéed Summer Squash

*Zucchini and yellow squash both fall under the category of summer squash. Feel free to use either—or a combination of both—in this recipe.*

MAKES 4 SERVINGS

2 teaspoons olive oil

3 medium yellow squash, diagonally sliced

½ teaspoon grated lemon zest

1 tablespoon fresh lemon juice

1 teaspoon minced thyme

⅛ teaspoon salt

⅛ teaspoon freshly ground pepper

In a large nonstick skillet, heat the oil. Sauté the squash, turning occasionally, until golden brown, about 5 minutes. Sprinkle with the lemon zest, lemon juice, thyme, salt and pepper; cook, stirring occasionally, until heated through, about 3 minutes longer.

**Per serving**: 40 Calories, 2 g Total Fat, 0 g Saturated Fat, 0 mg Cholesterol, 71 mg Sodium, 4 g Total Carbohydrate, 1 g Dietary Fiber, 1 g Protein, 23 mg Calcium. **POINTS** per serving: 1.

# Pumpkin Pancakes

*These fragrant colorful pancakes make a perfect accompaniment to a pork or beef roast.*

MAKES 4 SERVINGS

¾ cup + 2 tablespoons all-purpose flour

¼ cup whole-wheat flour

¼ cup packed dark brown sugar

½ teaspoon baking powder

½ teaspoon baking soda

½ teaspoon pumpkin pie spice

Pinch salt

½ cup currants

½ cup canned pumpkin puree

½ cup fat-free milk

2 eggs

2 apples, peeled, cored and diced

1. Sift the flours, brown sugar, baking powder, baking soda, pumpkin pie spice and salt into a medium bowl; stir in the currants.

2. In another medium bowl, combine the pumpkin puree, milk and eggs; beat until smooth. Add to the flour mixture, stirring just until combined.

3. Spray a large nonstick skillet with nonstick cooking spray; heat. Pour the batter by ¼-cup measures into the skillet, making 4 pancakes. Cook until bubbles appear on the surface, 2–3 minutes; turn and cook 2 minutes longer. With a spatula, transfer the pancakes to a plate; keep warm. Repeat to make 4 more pancakes.

4. In a small microwavable dish, microwave the apples on High until tender, 1 minute. Serve the pancakes, topped with the apples.

**Per serving**: 318 Calories, 4 g Total Fat, 1 g Saturated Fat, 107 mg Cholesterol, 307 mg Sodium, 65 g Total Carbohydrate, 4 g Dietary Fiber, 9 g Protein, 129 mg Calcium. **POINTS** per serving: 6.

# Ratatouille Casserole

*This dish will surely become a favorite—it's so versatile! Try it wrapped in a tomato-flavored tortilla or as a topping for your favorite grilled fish.*

MAKES 6 SERVINGS

1 small (about ¾-pound) eggplant, peeled and cut into ¼" slices

4 teaspoons olive oil

1 large yellow squash, cut into ¼" diagonal slices

1 medium zucchini, cut into ¼" diagonal slices

1 red bell pepper, seeded and julienned

1 onion, very thinly sliced

3 garlic cloves, very thinly sliced

¼ cup tomato paste

2 tablespoons chopped parsley

2 tablespoons chopped basil

2 teaspoons minced thyme

¼ teaspoon salt

¼ teaspoon freshly ground pepper

1 tomato, thinly sliced

1. Preheat the oven to 400° F; spray nonstick baking sheets and a 1-quart casserole with nonstick cooking spray. In a medium bowl, combine the eggplant and 1 teaspoon of the oil; toss to coat. Transfer to a baking sheet in a single layer. Repeat with the squash, then the zucchini, tossing each with 1 teaspoon of the oil and placing each in a single layer on the baking sheets (depending on their size, you may need 2 or 3). Bake 12 minutes; then turn the vegetables over and bake 8 minutes longer. Reduce the oven temperature to 350° F.

2. In a large nonstick skillet, heat the remaining 1 teaspoon of oil; Sauté the bell pepper, onion and garlic until softened, about 5 minutes. Cook, covered, shaking the skillet occasionally, 5 minutes longer.

3. In a small bowl, combine the tomato paste and ½ cup water. In another small bowl, combine the parsley, basil, thyme, salt and pepper.

4. In the casserole, arrange half of the eggplant; sprinkle with 1 teaspoon of the herbs. Continue layering with half of the tomato, squash, sautéed vegetables and zucchini, sprinkling 1 teaspoon of the herbs between each layer. Repeat the layers, ending with the zucchini. Pour the tomato paste over the vegetables. Cover with foil and bake until the vegetables are tender, about 50 minutes. Uncover; bake until browned on top, about 15 minutes longer.

**Per serving:** 80 Calories, 4 g Total Fat, 0 g Saturated Fat, 0 mg Cholesterol, 184 mg Sodium, 12 g Total Carbohydrate, 3 g Dietary Fiber, 2 g Protein, 58 mg Calcium. **POINTS** per serving: 1.

## Got Leftovers?

**Ratatouille is delicious cold; toss any leftovers with cold cooked pasta for a quick pasta salad.**

# "Creamed" Spinach

*For the ultimate comfort-food supper, serve this with our homestyle meatloaf (page 145) and mashed potatoes (page 318).*

MAKES 4 SERVINGS

⅔ cup low-fat (1%) cottage cheese

¼ cup low-fat (1%) milk

1 tablespoon grated Parmesan cheese

½ garlic clove, minced

¼ teaspoon salt

⅛ teaspoon freshly ground pepper

Two 10-ounce bags triple-washed spinach, steamed until tender and chopped

1. In a food processor or blender, combine the cottage cheese, milk, Parmesan, garlic, salt and pepper; puree. Add one-fourth of the spinach; puree until smooth.

2. In a large nonstick skillet, combine the remaining spinach with the cottage cheese mixture. Cook, stirring occasionally, until heated through, about 5 minutes.

**Per serving:** 71 Calories, 1 g Total Fat, 1 g Saturated Fat, 3 mg Cholesterol, 432 mg Sodium, 7 g Total Carbohydrate, 4 g Dietary Fiber, 10 g Protein, 201 mg Calcium. **POINTS** per serving: 1.

## How We Did It

A pureed mixture of cottage cheese and milk stands in for the heavy cream and butter traditionally used in this classic dish. If you like cream sauces on your veggies, simply combine all the ingredients (except the spinach) and heat through for 5 minutes. Serve over cooked cauliflower or broccoli.

## The Greatness of Greens

*Make a list of the most nutritious foods, and you'll find leafy greens on top. From spinach and chard to dandelion greens, almost all are good sources of heart-healthy fiber, folic acid (think "foliage") and vitamin C, and many, like kale, turnip greens and mustard greens, also contain calcium and iron. You should have at least one serving of greens every day.*

*Luckily, it's easy to sneak greens into foods, so you can add them to your diet in all kinds of ways. Steam a batch, chop them fine and keep them in the refrigerator to sprinkle into soup or stews, layer on a sandwich or pizza, or throw into a salad. They're also delicious cold, tossed with a little salad dressing or sprinkled with grated cheese.*

# Spaghetti Squash Primavera

*To speed up preparation, cook the squash in the microwave. Pierce with a fork, place on a paper towel and microwave on High until softened, 8–12 minutes, turning it over and rotating a quarter turn every 3 minutes. Let stand 5 minutes, then cut open and discard the seeds; scoop the pulp into a bowl.*

MAKES 4 SERVINGS

One 2-pound spaghetti squash

2 teaspoons olive oil

2 scallions, thinly sliced

2 garlic cloves, minced

½ cup chicken broth

½ teaspoon dried marjoram

½ teaspoon grated lemon zest

¼ teaspoon salt

12 thin asparagus spears, cut into 2" diagonal lengths

1 cup thawed frozen green peas

2 teaspoons fresh lemon juice

1. Preheat the oven to 350° F. Cut the squash in half lengthwise; scoop out the seeds. Place the squash, cut-side down, in a 7 × 11" baking dish; add water to a depth of about ½". Cover with foil and bake until tender, about 45 minutes. Remove the squash from the water; let stand until cool enough to handle. With a fork, scoop out the pulp; transfer to a medium bowl.

2. In a large nonstick skillet, heat the oil. Sauté the scallions and garlic until fragrant, about 1 minute. Add the broth, marjoram, lemon zest and salt; bring to a boil, then add the asparagus and peas. Reduce the heat and simmer, covered, 2 minutes. Stir in the squash and lemon juice; cook, stirring occasionally, until heated through, about 3 minutes.

**Per serving:** 117 Calories, 4 g Total Fat, 1 g Saturated Fat, 0 mg Cholesterol, 328 mg Sodium, 19 g Total Carbohydrate, 2 g Dietary Fiber, 5 g Protein, 63 mg Calcium. **POINTS** per serving: 2.

## Tip

**If it's difficult to cut the spaghetti squash in half, try softening it first in the microwave. Pierce the skin with a fork in a few places. Place the squash on a paper towel and microwave on High, turning every 30 seconds or so, until it is soft enough to slice easily.**

# Broiled Tomatoes

*Serve these hot tomatoes, bursting with flavor, as the British do, alongside eggs, bacon and toast.*

MAKES 4 SERVINGS

¼ cup chopped basil

2 garlic cloves, minced

1 teaspoon grated lemon zest

¼ teaspoon freshly ground pepper

1 teaspoon extra virgin olive oil

⅛ teaspoon salt

2 large tomatoes, halved crosswise

1. Spray the broiler rack with nonstick cooking spray; preheat the broiler.

2. Chop the basil, garlic, lemon zest and pepper together, making a paste. Transfer to a small bowl; stir in the oil and salt. Spread on the cut side of the tomatoes; place the tomatoes on the rack. Broil 5–6" from the heat until lightly browned, 4–5 minutes.

**Per serving**: 45 Calories, 2 g Total Fat, 0 g Saturated Fat, 0 mg Cholesterol, 82 mg Sodium, 7 g Total Carbohydrate, 2 g Dietary Fiber, 1 g Protein, 35 mg Calcium. *POINTS* per serving: 1.

## Tip

If you like, use plum tomatoes; figure one per person, and halve them lengthwise.

# Stewed Tomatoes

*At a loss about what to do with a bumper crop of tomatoes? This tasty recipe is the answer—double or triple the recipe if you like.*

MAKES 4 SERVINGS

4 tomatoes, blanched, peeled, seeded and quartered

3 scallions, thinly sliced

1 teaspoon chopped basil

½ teaspoon sugar

¼ teaspoon paprika

In a medium saucepan, combine the tomatoes, scallions, basil, sugar, paprika and 2 tablespoons water; bring to a boil. Reduce the heat and simmer, covered, until the tomatoes are very soft, about 15 minutes.

**Per serving**: 37 Calories, 1 g Total Fat, 0 g Saturated Fat, 0 mg Cholesterol, 15 mg Sodium, 8 g Total Carbohydrate, 2 g Dietary Fiber, 1 g Protein, 14 mg Calcium. *POINTS* per serving: 0.

## Grilling Tips

*Leaping from the ranks of the maligned to the sublime, vegetables have finally come into their own. One of the most popular ways to enjoy them is grilled.*

- *Use a grilling basket for small or soft vegetables to make turning easier.*

- *When grilling root vegetables, shorten the cooking time by parboiling them in the microwave for a few minutes.*

- *Cooking times will vary according to the vegetables and the intensity of the heat. To determine doneness, test with a skewer—it should be easy to insert when the veggies are done.*

# Swiss Chard au Gratin

*Swiss chard is widely available from spring through fall. Like spinach, it freezes well—simply drop cleaned leaves into boiling water for about 2 minutes, then chill in ice water. Drain the leaves and put into an airtight container in your freezer.*

MAKES 4 SERVINGS

1 teaspoon salt

2 cups cut Swiss chard stalks (2" lengths)

4½ cups shredded Swiss chard leaves

⅓ cup shredded reduced-fat Jarlsberg cheese

1 tablespoon grated Parmesan cheese

1 garlic clove, minced

¼ teaspoon freshly ground pepper

1. Preheat the oven to 400° F; spray a 1-quart casserole with nonstick cooking spray.

2. In a large saucepan, bring the salt and 8 cups water to a boil; add the chard stalks. Boil 5 minutes, then add the chard leaves; cook until tender, about 3 minutes. Drain.

3. Place half of the chard in the casserole; top with half each of the Jarlsberg, Parmesan, garlic and pepper. Repeat the layers, ending with the pepper. Bake on the top rack until the cheese is melted and bubbling, about 20 minutes.

**Per serving**: 50 Calories, 2 g Total Fat, 1 g Saturated Fat, 7 mg Cholesterol, 736 mg Sodium, 3 g Total Carbohydrate, 0 g Dietary Fiber, 5 g Protein, 53 mg Calcium. **POINTS** per serving: 1.

# Roasted Zucchini Provençal

*Serve this on toasted Italian or French bread for an appealing variation on bruschetta.*

MAKES 4 SERVINGS

4 medium zucchini, quartered lengthwise and sliced

2 teaspoons olive oil

5 small niçoise olives, pitted

3 anchovy fillets, rinsed

1 large garlic clove

½ teaspoon grated lemon zest

2 tablespoons plain dried bread crumbs

2 teaspoons minced thyme

⅛ teaspoon freshly ground pepper

1. Preheat the oven to 425° F; spray a nonstick baking sheet with nonstick cooking spray.

2. In a medium bowl, combine the zucchini and oil. Transfer to the baking sheet. Roast until golden, about 10 minutes; turn and roast until golden, about 5 minutes longer. Transfer to a 1-quart baking dish.

3. Meanwhile, chop the olives, anchovies, garlic and lemon zest together. Transfer to a small bowl; stir in the bread crumbs, thyme and pepper. Sprinkle over the zucchini. Bake until the crumbs are browned, 8–10 minutes.

**Per serving**: 71 Calories, 4 g Total Fat, 1 g Saturated Fat, 2 mg Cholesterol, 175 mg Sodium, 8 g Total Carbohydrate, 1 g Dietary Fiber, 3 g Protein, 49 mg Calcium. **POINTS** per serving: 2.

# Cucumbers with Dilled Buttermilk Dressing

*A warm-weather favorite, try this cold salad with a hot, grilled London broil and roasted corn on the cob. The dressing will keep for about a week in the refrigerator—drizzle it over your favorite mixed greens.*

MAKES 4 SERVINGS

½ cup low-fat buttermilk

⅓ cup chopped fresh dill

½ teaspoon white-wine vinegar

¼ teaspoon mustard powder

¼ teaspoon salt

⅛ teaspoon freshly ground pepper (optional)

Pinch ground white pepper

2 cucumbers, seeded and thinly sliced

1. To prepare the dressing, in a small bowl, combine the buttermilk, dill, vinegar, mustard, salt, black pepper (if using) and white pepper. Refrigerate, covered, until the flavors are blended, 2–3 hours.

2. Place the cucumbers in a medium bowl. Drizzle with the dressing; toss to coat. Serve at once.

**Per serving:** 26 Calories, 1 g Total Fat, 0 g Saturated Fat, 2 mg Cholesterol, 170 mg Sodium, 4 g Total Carbohydrate, 1 g Dietary Fiber, 2 g Protein, 31 mg Calcium. **POINTS** per serving: 0.

# Tomato Salad with Red Onion and Basil

*The showcase for summer's garden bounty, best enjoyed at the height of the season, when tomatoes are ripe and juicy and fresh basil is plentiful.*

MAKES 4 SERVINGS

3 tablespoons red-wine vinegar

4 teaspoons olive oil

½ teaspoon sugar

½ teaspoon salt

½ teaspoon Dijon mustard

¼ teaspoon freshly ground pepper

4 tomatoes, cut into wedges

1 red onion, thinly sliced

⅓ cup tightly packed fresh basil leaves, shredded

1. To prepare the dressing, in a small bowl, whisk the vinegar, oil, sugar, salt, mustard and pepper.

2. In a large salad bowl, combine the tomatoes, onions and basil. Drizzle with the dressing; toss to coat. Refrigerate, covered, tossing once, until the flavors are blended, at least 1 hour.

**Per serving:** 92 Calories, 5 g Total Fat, 1 g Saturated Fat, 0 mg Cholesterol, 299 mg Sodium, 12 g Total Carbohydrate, 3 g Dietary Fiber, 2 g Protein, 51 mg Calcium. **POINTS** per serving: 2.

# Zucchini-Carrot Salad with Cumin Dressing

*For a more slaw-like texture, grate the zucchini and carrots—if you use a food processor, you'll save time, too.*

MAKES 4 SERVINGS

1 teaspoon ground cumin

3 tablespoons reduced-calorie mayonnaise

½ teaspoon grated lime zest

1 tablespoon fresh lime juice

1 teaspoon chopped cilantro

¼ teaspoon salt

⅛ teaspoon freshly ground pepper

2 carrots, julienned

1 medium zucchini, julienned

1. To prepare the dressing, in a small skillet, toast the cumin over low heat, stirring frequently, until fragrant, about 1 minute. Transfer to a small bowl; stir in the mayonnaise, lime zest, lime juice, cilantro, salt and pepper.

2. In a medium bowl, combine the carrots and zucchini. Drizzle with the dressing; toss to coat.

**Per serving**: 58 Calories, 3 g Total Fat, 1 g Saturated Fat, 3 mg Cholesterol, 210 mg Sodium, 8 g Total Carbohydrate, 2 g Dietary Fiber, 1 g Protein, 27 mg Calcium. *POINTS* per serving: 1.

# Coleslaw with Caraway-Mint Dressing

*To shred cabbage, cut the head in half lengthwise and cut out the core. Place the cabbage, flat-side down, on a work surface. Using a sharp knife, cut the cabbage crosswise into long slices.*

MAKES 4 SERVINGS

3 tablespoons reduced-calorie mayonnaise

2 tablespoons cider vinegar

1 tablespoon caraway seeds

1 teaspoon sugar

¼ teaspoon freshly ground pepper

1 small head green cabbage, shredded

2 carrots, shredded

1 onion, grated

2 tablespoons chopped mint

1. To prepare the dressing, in a small bowl, mix the mayonnaise, vinegar, caraway seeds, sugar and pepper.

2. In a large bowl, combine the cabbage, carrots, onion and mint. Drizzle with the dressing; toss to coat. Refrigerate, covered, until chilled, 2–3 hours.

**Per serving**: 68 Calories, 3 g Total Fat, 1 g Saturated Fat, 3 mg Cholesterol, 74 mg Sodium, 10 g Total Carbohydrate, 2 g Dietary Fiber, 2 g Protein, 48 mg Calcium. *POINTS* per serving: 1.

# Radicchio, Cabbage and Jicama Slaw

*Jicama (pronounced HEE-cah-mah) is a crispy tuberous vegetable similar to water chestnuts in taste and texture. Look for it in most supermarkets and Latino grocery stores.*

MAKES 4 SERVINGS

2 cups shredded savoy or green cabbage

1 cup shredded radicchio or red cabbage

1 cup julienned jicama

½ yellow bell pepper, seeded and julienned

1 celery stalk, sliced

2 tablespoons plain nonfat yogurt

2 tablespoons fat-free mayonnaise

1 tablespoon raspberry vinegar

½ teaspoon grated lemon or lime zest

Pinch salt

1. In a large bowl, combine the cabbages, radicchio, jicama, bell pepper and celery.

2. In a small bowl, whisk the yogurt, mayonnaise, vinegar, lemon zest and salt. Pour over the vegetables; toss to coat. Refrigerate, covered, until the flavors are blended, at least 1 hour.

**Per serving:** 42 Calories, 0 g Total Fat, 0 g Saturated Fat, 0 mg Cholesterol, 118 mg Sodium, 10 g Total Carbohydrate, 4 g Dietary Fiber, 2 g Protein, 45 mg Calcium. *POINTS* per serving: 0.

*Radicchio, Cabbage and Jicama Slaw*

# Cabbage Slaw

*The surprises in this slaw are vanilla yogurt and fennel—together, they add a slightly sweet, creamy and crunchy tang. If you prefer, use plain nonfat yogurt instead of vanilla.*

MAKES 4 SERVINGS

4 cups shredded green cabbage

1 fennel bulb, trimmed and chopped

1 carrot, shredded

½ onion, finely chopped

2 tablespoons dry white wine

2 tablespoons white-wine vinegar

2 tablespoons aspartame-sweetened vanilla nonfat yogurt

2 teaspoons sugar

2 teaspoons vegetable or olive oil

2 teaspoons reduced-calorie mayonnaise

1 teaspoon fennel seeds

1 teaspoon grainy mustard

1 teaspoon drained horseradish

½ teaspoon celery seeds

¼ teaspoon salt

¼ teaspoon freshly ground pepper

1. In a large bowl, combine the cabbage, fennel, carrot and onion.

2. In a small bowl, whisk the wine, vinegar, yogurt, sugar, oil, mayonnaise, fennel seeds, mustard, horseradish, celery seeds, salt and pepper. Pour over the vegetables; toss to coat. Serve at room temperature, or refrigerate, covered, several hours and serve chilled.

**Per serving:** 79 Calories, 3 g Total Fat, 0 g Saturated Fat, 1 mg Cholesterol, 220 mg Sodium, 10 g Total Carbohydrate, 3 g Dietary Fiber, 2 g Protein, 78 mg Calcium. *POINTS* per serving: 1.

# Marinated Three-Bean Salad

*This is a great picnic salad—make it the night before so the flavors can blend. Be sure to mix the salad with still-warm green beans and wax beans so they'll absorb the flavors of the dressing better.*

MAKES 4 SERVINGS

2 tablespoons cider vinegar

2 tablespoons apple juice

2 teaspoons grated peeled gingerroot

1 cup cut green beans (2" lengths), steamed until tender-crisp

1 cup cut wax beans (2" lengths), steamed until tender-crisp

½ cup canned red kidney beans, rinsed and drained

1 onion, minced

¼ red bell pepper, seeded and finely diced

2 tablespoons chopped basil

In a large bowl, mix the vinegar, apple juice and gingerroot. Add the green beans, wax beans, kidney beans, onion, bell pepper and basil; toss to coat. Refrigerate, covered, until chilled, at least 3 hours.

**Per serving**: 65 Calories, 0 g Total Fat, 0 g Saturated Fat, 0 mg Cholesterol, 5 mg Sodium, 13 g Total Carbohydrate, 2 g Dietary Fiber, 4 g Protein, 44 mg Calcium. *POINTS* per serving: 1.

# Yucatan Salad

*Jicama, a knobby root vegetable frequently found in Mexican dishes, is very sweet and crunchy; its texture is similar to water chestnuts. It is delicious raw, as in this salad, and turns sweeter when cooked. Steer clear of large jicamas, which tend to be dry and tough.*

MAKES 4 SERVINGS

1 small jicama, peeled and julienned

1 navel orange, peeled and sectioned

¾ cup orange juice

½ red bell pepper, seeded and finely diced

6 scallions, including some greens, sliced

2 tablespoons fresh lime juice

1 teaspoon chili powder

½ teaspoon salt

2 cups soft lettuce leaves, such as Bibb or butter lettuce

1. In a large nonreactive bowl, combine all the ingredients except the lettuce. Refrigerate, covered, stirring several times, at least 4 hours or overnight.

2. Line four salad plates with the lettuce leaves; top with the jicama mixture.

**Per serving**: 75 Calories, 0 g Total Fat, 0 g Saturated Fat, 0 mg Cholesterol, 289 mg Sodium, 17 g Total Carbohydrate, 3 g Dietary Fiber, 2 g Protein, 59 mg Calcium. *POINTS* per serving: 1.

# Mesclun, Orange and Walnut Salad

## (*pictured on page 210*)

*Mesclun is a mixture of small, tender young lettuce leaves; it usually includes frisée (or curly endive), mâche (or lamb's lettuce), arugula and radicchio, along with Bibb and red and green oak leaf.*

MAKES 4 SERVINGS

2 tablespoons orange juice

2 teaspoons walnut oil

¼ teaspoon salt

Pinch cayenne pepper

6 cups mesclun

1 navel orange, peeled and sectioned

½ red onion, thinly sliced

¼ cup walnuts, chopped and toasted

1. To prepare the dressing, in a small bowl, whisk the orange juice, oil, salt and cayenne.

2. In a large salad bowl, combine the mesclun, orange, onion and walnuts. Drizzle with the dressing; toss to coat. Serve at once.

**Per serving:** 109 Calories, 7 g Total Fat, 1 g Saturated Fat, 0 mg Cholesterol, 144 mg Sodium, 11 g Total Carbohydrate, 2 g Dietary Fiber, 3 g Protein, 85 mg Calcium. **POINTS** per serving: 2.

# Pear Salad with Blue Cheese Dressing

*Unusual and refreshing, the cheese is in the dressing, coating the pears with a creamy tang. Look for red Bartlett pears—they make this salad especially pretty.*

MAKES 4 SERVINGS

¼ cup part-skim ricotta cheese

⅓ cup crumbled blue cheese

2 large pears, cored and cut into thin wedges

4 celery stalks, cut into 3" sticks

2 teaspoons white-wine vinegar

¼ cup golden raisins

1. To prepare the dressing, in a mini food processor or blender, combine the ricotta and 2 tablespoons water; puree. Transfer to a small bowl; add the blue cheese. Stir, mashing the blue cheese against the sides of the bowl.

2. Arrange the pears and celery on 4 salad plates; sprinkle with the vinegar. Drizzle with the dressing, then top with the raisins.

**Per serving:** 184 Calories, 5 g Total Fat, 3 g Saturated Fat, 13 mg Cholesterol, 195 mg Sodium, 33 g Total Carbohydrate, 5 g Dietary Fiber, 5 g Protein, 132 mg Calcium. **POINTS** per serving: 3.

# Minted Quinoa Fruit Salad

*Pronounced KEEN-wah, this grain was cultivated by the Incas. Be sure to rinse the quinoa well—it has a coating that, if not rinsed off, can make it bitter.*

MAKES 6 SERVINGS

¼ teaspoon salt

1 cup quinoa, rinsed thoroughly

⅓ cup chopped mint

¼ cup aspartame-sweetened vanilla-flavored nonfat yogurt

2 tablespoons orange juice

1½ cups sliced strawberries

2 kiwi fruits, peeled and sliced

One 11-ounce can mandarin orange sections, drained

1. In a medium saucepan, bring the salt and 2 cups water to a boil; add the quinoa. Reduce the heat and simmer, covered, until the quinoa is translucent, about 15 minutes.

2. In mini food processor or blender, combine the mint, yogurt and orange juice; puree.

3. Set aside 6 strawberry slices and 3 kiwi slices for garnish. In a large serving bowl, combine the remaining strawberries, the remaining kiwi and the orange sections. Drizzle with the yogurt sauce; toss to coat. Add the quinoa; toss gently to combine. Garnish with the reserved fruit. Refrigerate, covered, until well chilled, 1–2 hours.

**Per serving:** 160 Calories, 2 g Total Fat, 0 g Saturated Fat, 0 mg Cholesterol, 117 mg Sodium, 32 g Total Carbohydrate, 6 g Dietary Fiber, 5 g Protein, 51 mg Calcium. **POINTS** per serving: 2.

# Orange–Red Onion Salad with Citrus Dressing

*The zest of a citrus fruit refers to the peel without any of the pith (white membrane). To remove the zest, use a zester or vegetable peeler. To sliver the zest, use a sharp knife to cut into very thin strips.*

MAKES 4 SERVINGS

1 tablespoon slivered orange zest

¼ cup + 2 tablespoons orange juice

4 teaspoons fresh lemon juice

4 teaspoons fresh lime juice

1 tablespoon balsamic vinegar

½ teaspoon Dijon mustard

Pinch salt

1 teaspoon olive oil

2 cups torn chicory leaves or escarole

1 carrot, finely grated

2 navel oranges, peeled and sectioned

½ red onion, sliced into paper-thin rings

1. To prepare the dressing, in a blender or food processor, combine the orange zest, orange juice, lemon juice, lime juice, vinegar, mustard and salt; pulse to blend. With the machine running, gradually drizzle in the oil; blend thoroughly.

2. Divide the chicory among 4 salad plates. Top with the carrot, orange sections and onion rings, then drizzle with the dressing.

**Per serving:** 90 Calories, 2 g Total Fat, 0 g Saturated Fat, 0 mg Cholesterol, 101 mg Sodium, 19 g Total Carbohydrate, 4 g Dietary Fiber, 3 g Protein, 132 mg Calcium. **POINTS** per serving: 1.

*Minted Quinoa Fruit Salad*

# Baked Beans

*Classic baked beans were a Colonial staple. Our updated version keeps the nutrition and the taste, minus the salt pork and without a lot of extra sweetening.*

MAKES 4 SERVINGS

1 onion, finely chopped

2 tablespoons ketchup

1 tablespoon packed dark brown sugar

1 tablespoon cider vinegar

1 tablespoon maple syrup

2 teaspoons molasses

¾ teaspoon mustard powder

¼ teaspoon ground ginger

¼ teaspoon freshly ground pepper

Pinch ground cloves

One 16-ounce can navy or great Northern beans, rinsed and drained

Salt, to taste

1. Preheat the oven to 275° F. In 2½-quart flame-proof casserole, combine all ingredients except the beans and salt. Stir in 1 cup water; bring to a boil. Reduce the heat and simmer, stirring occasionally, until thickened, about 20 minutes.

2. Stir in the beans and salt. Bake, covered, stirring occasionally, 1 hour; add a tablespoon or two of water if the beans look dry. If there is too much liquid after 1 hour, uncover and continue to bake, stirring occasionally, until the beans absorb the excess liquid.

**Per serving**: 211 Calories, 1 g Total Fat, 0 g Saturated Fat, 0 mg Cholesterol, 385 mg Sodium, 42 g Total Carbohydrate, 4 g Dietary Fiber, 10 g Protein, 102 mg Calcium. *POINTS* per serving: 4.

# Mexican Baked Beans

*The addition of molasses in this recipe helps tame the heat of jalapeños and pepper flakes without mellowing their flavor.*

MAKES 4 SERVINGS

1 cup canned pinto beans, rinsed and drained (reserve 2 tablespoons liquid)

½ cup low-sodium tomato sauce

½ onion, finely chopped

¼ cup Mexican beer

3 tablespoons molasses

1½ teaspoons mustard powder

½ jalapeño pepper, seeded, deveined and minced (wear gloves to prevent irritation)

¾ teaspoon Worcestershire sauce

¼ teaspoon crushed red pepper flakes, or to taste

1 tablespoon minced cilantro

Preheat the oven to 350° F. In a large bowl, combine the beans, tomato sauce, onion, beer, molasses, mustard, jalapeño, Worcestershire sauce and pepper flakes. Transfer to a 1-quart casserole. Bake until most of the liquid is absorbed, 45–50 minutes. Stir in the cilantro just before serving.

**Per serving**: 126 Calories, 1 g Total Fat, 0 g Saturated Fat, 0 mg Cholesterol, 221 mg Sodium, 25 g Total Carbohydrate, 3 g Dietary Fiber, 5 g Protein, 59 mg Calcium. *POINTS* per serving: 2.

# Braised Lima Beans with Tomato and Parsley

*Parsley isn't just a garnish! Its clean taste adds freshness to any dish. With one of the highest levels of chlorophyll (the active ingredient in breath fresheners) of any food, parsley can also freshen your breath—chew on a sprig to see for yourself.*

MAKES 4 SERVINGS

2 teaspoons reduced-calorie margarine

2 onions, chopped

2¼ cups thawed frozen baby lima beans

2 teaspoons chopped thyme leaves

¼ teaspoon salt

¼ teaspoon freshly ground pepper

2 plum tomatoes, diced

¼ cup chopped flat-leaf parsley

1. In a medium nonstick skillet, melt the margarine. Sauté the onions until softened, about 5 minutes.

2. Stir in the lima beans, thyme, salt, pepper and 1 cup water. Simmer, covered, until the beans are very tender, about 15 minutes. Add the tomatoes and cook until heated through; stir in the parsley just before serving.

**Per serving:** 152 Calories, 2 g Total Fat, 0 g Saturated Fat, 0 mg Cholesterol, 206 mg Sodium, 28 g Total Carbohydrate, 6 g Dietary Fiber, 8 g Protein, 51 mg Calcium. **POINTS** per serving: 2.

## Got Leftovers?

Stir in cooked rice for a meal-in-a-bowl lunch.

# Succotash
### *(pictured on page 144)*

*Succotash comes from the native American word msíckquatash. Created by the Narragansett, the dish originally included chicken or meat as well as vegetables. Our version is a hearty vegetarian one.*

MAKES 4 SERVINGS

4 teaspoons olive oil

1 red bell pepper, seeded and diced

½ medium zucchini, diced

½ onion, diced

1 garlic clove, finely chopped

1 tomato, seeded and diced

1 cup cooked green lima beans

1 cup fresh or thawed frozen corn kernels

2 tablespoons chopped flat-leaf parsley

1 teaspoon paprika

½ teaspoon salt

½ teaspoon freshly ground pepper

¼ teaspoon dried marjoram

1. In a medium nonstick skillet, heat the oil. Sauté the bell pepper, zucchini, onion and garlic until wilted, about 8 minutes. Add the tomato; sauté 2 minutes.

2. Stir in the lima beans, corn, parsley, paprika, salt, pepper and marjoram. Reduce the heat and simmer, covered, until the flavors are blended, about 10 minutes.

**Per serving:** 154 Calories, 5 g Total Fat, 1 g Saturated Fat, 0 mg Cholesterol, 327 mg Sodium, 24 g Total Carbohydrate, 6 g Dietary Fiber, 6 g Protein, 32 mg Calcium. **POINTS** per serving: 2.

## Got Leftovers?

Spoon this mixture into a pita for an effortless vegetarian lunch.

Grain and Potato Side Dishes

# Chapter 11

# Grain and Potato Side Dishes

The world's healthiest cuisines have grains and potatoes at their core, and one reason they've endured over the centuries is that they're just plain delicious. After you've expanded your gastronomic repertoire to include more of these traditional ingredients, you'll use them again and again, so here's some know-how that will come in handy.

## Potato Smarts

You'll find all shapes and sizes of potatoes in the supermarket, but they fall into two categories: baking and waxy potatoes. Baking potatoes, like Idaho and russet Burbank, are higher in starch, so they have a fluffier, mealier texture ideal for baking. They also brown well without burning, so they're often used for frying. Waxy potatoes, like red-skinned new potatoes, are lower in starch and less flaky; they're the best choice for boiling or mashing. (All-purpose potatoes—a blend of both characteristics—are suitable for any cooking method, but with less dazzling results.)

No matter what type of potato you buy, don't try to freeze it; its texture won't survive. Commercially frozen potatoes are made using special dehydration processes to preserve texture, and even they are a compromise.

Likewise, don't try to mash a cooked potato in a food processor or blender; the pulverizing action will cause a gummy protein, gluten, to be activated. You'll end up with a gray, sticky mass. Instead, use a potato masher or ricer, then stir in the milk and flavorings. If you want them extra creamy, whip them afterward with a fork, heavy whisk or electric mixer.

## Grain Glossary

When you choose whole grains, you're getting the entire kernel of a grain—its fiber-rich outer shell layers, or *bran*; its inner *germ*, which contains the protein, fat and B vitamins necessary for the plant to grow; and the *endosperm*, the starchy material that makes up most of the kernel. "Refined" grains, like white rice or white flour, contain only the endosperm component, so they're missing the nutrients and fiber of the bran and germ. Refined grains are enriched during processing to replace some of the missing nutrients, but the fiber is still lost.

Whole grains aren't quite as convenient to use as refined grains: Because they contain the tougher bran layers, they generally take longer to cook. And since the germ contains fat that can become rancid, they tend to be more perishable than refined grains. Store them in the refrigerator for the short term, and in the freezer for longer periods (up to a year). The nuttier taste, interesting texture and nutritional benefits make whole grains worth the extra trouble.

# German Potato Salad

*Serve this dish alongside the lower-in-fat flavored sausages now available in supermarkets—they're packed with flavor but low on fat and calories.*

MAKES 4 SERVINGS

4 medium all-purpose potatoes, cooked and diced

1 onion, chopped

1 celery stalk, chopped

½ green bell pepper, seeded and chopped

3 slices bacon, crisp-cooked and crumbled

½ cup apple juice

¼ cup cider vinegar

1 tablespoon all-purpose flour

½ teaspoon salt

¼ teaspoon freshly ground pepper

1. In a large bowl, combine the potatoes, onion, celery, bell pepper and bacon; set aside.

2. In a small saucepan, whisk the apple juice, vinegar and flour; bring to a boil, whisking constantly. Boil, whisking constantly, until thickened, about 4 minutes; stir in the salt and pepper. Drizzle over the vegetables; toss to coat. Serve at once.

**Per serving:** 163 Calories, 3 g Total Fat, 1 g Saturated Fat, 4 mg Cholesterol, 370 mg Sodium, 32 g Total Carbohydrate, 3 g Dietary Fiber, 4 g Protein, 26 mg Calcium. **POINTS** per serving: 3.

# Potato and Bean Salad with Walnut Vinaigrette

*If you're using red potatoes, cut them into chunks after they've cooled (no need to chop new potatoes since they're already bite-size). To add even more flavor and crunch to this elegant salad, toast the walnuts.*

MAKES 4 SERVINGS

3 tablespoons balsamic vinegar

1 tablespoon dry white wine

1 teaspoon Dijon mustard

Salt and freshly ground pepper, to taste

2 teaspoons extra virgin olive oil

2 teaspoons canola oil

2 shallots or 1 scallion, finely chopped

¼ cup walnuts, finely chopped

1 pound new or small red potatoes, cooked and cooled

1¼ cups cut green beans (1" lengths), steamed until tender-crisp

½ cup canned red kidney beans, rinsed and drained

1. In a small bowl, whisk the vinegar, wine, mustard, salt and pepper. Add the olive oil and canola oil, a little at a time, whisking constantly. Mix in shallots and walnuts.

2. In a large bowl, combine the potatoes, green beans and kidney beans. Drizzle with the dressing; toss to coat. Let stand at room temperature until the flavors are blended, about 1 hour. Toss again before serving.

**Per serving:** 186 Calories, 5 g Total Fat, 1 g Saturated Fat, 0 mg Cholesterol, 177 mg Sodium, 34 g Total Carbohydrate, 5 g Dietary Fiber, 4 g Protein, 66 mg Calcium. **POINTS** per serving: 3.

# Hash Brown Potatoes

*Though purists do not approve, you can also toss in a handful of cooked chopped carrots for a pretty, healthy variation.*

MAKES 4 SERVINGS

1 teaspoon vegetable oil

1 teaspoon unsalted margarine

1¼ pounds all-purpose potatoes, peeled, cooked and cut into ½" cubes

2 onions, minced

½ cup chicken broth

½ teaspoon salt

⅛ teaspoon freshly ground pepper

In a large nonstick skillet, heat the oil and margarine. Sauté the potatoes and onions until lightly browned, about 5 minutes. Add the broth, salt and pepper. Reduce the heat and cook, patting the mixture down and turning it over as it forms a crust, about 15 minutes longer.

**Per serving:** 159 Calories, 3 g Total Fat, 0 g Saturated Fat, 0 mg Cholesterol, 304 mg Sodium, 32 g Total Carbohydrate, 3 g Dietary Fiber, 3 g Protein, 21 mg Calcium. **POINTS** per serving: 3.

# Colcannon

*This traditional Irish dish is particularly nice on cold evenings when you'd like a hearty side dish with your entrée.*

MAKES 6 SERVINGS

3 medium all-purpose potatoes, peeled, cooked, and cubed

½ cup plain nonfat yogurt

4 cups chopped green cabbage, steamed until tender

3–4 leeks, cleaned, chopped and steamed until tender

3 tablespoons chopped chives

¾ teaspoon salt

¼ teaspoon ground white pepper

Pinch ground nutmeg

2 teaspoons reduced-calorie margarine

Preheat the oven to 350° F; spray a 1½-quart casserole with nonstick cooking spray. In a large bowl, combine the potatoes and yogurt. With an electric mixer at low speed, beat until the potatoes are fairly smooth; stir in the cabbage, leeks, chives, salt, pepper and nutmeg, mixing well. Transfer to the casserole; dot with the margarine. Bake until lightly browned, about 30 minutes.

**Per serving:** 95 Calories, 1 g Total Fat, 0 g Saturated Fat, 1 mg Cholesterol, 320 mg Sodium, 19 g Total Carbohydrate, 2 g Dietary Fiber, 3 g Protein, 87 mg Calcium. **POINTS** per serving: 2.

## Got Leftovers?

Don't throw out those leek tops—they provide a wonderful, oniony flavoring for soups and stews. Keep them whole and let them simmer with the broth while the other ingredients cook, then remove them just before serving.

# Garlic Mashed Potatoes

---

*For extra bite, add ½ cup sautéed diced onions just before serving.*

MAKES 4 SERVINGS

1¼ pounds all-purpose potatoes, peeled and thinly sliced

8 garlic cloves, peeled

1 bay leaf

½ teaspoon salt

3 tablespoons fat-free buttermilk

1. In a large pot, combine the potatoes, garlic, bay leaf, ¼ teaspoon of the salt and cold water to cover; bring to a boil. Reduce the heat and simmer and cook until the potatoes are tender, 10–15 minutes. Drain, reserving the cooking liquid; discard the bay leaf.

2. With a potato masher or an electric mixer at low speed, mash the potatoes and garlic with the buttermilk and the remaining ¼ teaspoon salt; thin with the cooking liquid, if needed.

**Per serving:** 135 Calories, 0 g Total Fat, 0 g Saturated Fat, 0 mg Cholesterol, 311 mg Sodium, 31 g Total Carbohydrate, 3 g Dietary Fiber, 3 g Protein, 36 mg Calcium. *POINTS* per serving: 2.

## How We Did It

Garlic and buttermilk combine to make these mashed potatoes so luscious you won't even notice they don't have a drop of fat!

# Herbed Mashed Potatoes

---

*Nobody doesn't like mashed potatoes—especially when they're this creamy. Try a dollop in your favorite homemade soup.*

MAKES 4 SERVINGS

4 medium baking potatoes, scrubbed

½ cup plain nonfat yogurt, at room temperature

2 tablespoons chopped parsley

¾ teaspoon chopped rosemary leaves

½ teaspoon salt

¼ teaspoon freshly ground pepper

1. Preheat the oven to 400° F. Pierce the potatoes in several places with a fork; bake until tender, about 1 hour. Let cool slightly.

2. Peel and halve the potatoes lengthwise; discard the skins and coarsely chop the pulp. In a medium bowl, combine the potatoes, yogurt, parsley, rosemary, salt and pepper, mashing and whipping with a potato masher or spoon until smooth. Serve at once.

**Per serving:** 132 Calories, 0 g Total Fat, 0 g Saturated Fat, 1 g Cholesterol, 307 mg Sodium, 29 g Total Carbohydrate, 3 g Dietary Fiber, 4 g Protein, 79 mg Calcium. *POINTS* per serving: 2.

## Tip

Keep a toothbrush or nail brush near the sink and use it to scrub farm-fresh veggies, like potatoes and carrots, clean.

# Mexican-Style Baked Potatoes

*Monterey pepperjack cheese—spiked with cayenne or chopped jalapeños—makes a deliciously spicy potato topping. Other delicious options are reduced-fat sharp cheddar, with or without hot pepper, or pepato, a provolone-type cheese with black peppercorns. Check your supermarket's dairy case!*

MAKES 4 SERVINGS

4 medium baking potatoes, scrubbed

¾ cup shredded Monterey pepperjack cheese

⅔ cup low-fat (1%) cottage cheese

½ cup thawed frozen corn kernels

¼ cup salsa

¼ cup plain low-fat yogurt

4 sprigs cilantro

1. Preheat the oven to 425° F. Pierce the potatoes in several places with a fork; bake until the skins crack slightly when pressed, about 1 hour.

2. In a small bowl, combine the pepperjack, cottage cheese and corn. Split the potatoes lengthwise and spoon the cheese mixture over each; top with the salsa, yogurt and cilantro.

**Per serving**: 294 Calories, 8 g Total Fat, 5 g Saturated Fat, 25 mg Cholesterol, 371 mg Sodium, 43 g Total Carbohydrate, 4 g Dietary Fiber, 15 g Protein, 215 mg Calcium. **POINTS** per serving: 6.

## Grain Guide

| GRAIN (1 CUP DRY) | WATER NEEDED | COOKING INSTRUCTIONS |
| --- | --- | --- |
| *Bulgur wheat* | *2 cups* | *Bring water to a boil and pour over the bulgur; cover and let stand 30 minutes. Fluff with a fork.* |
| *Brown rice* | *2½ cups* | *Bring water to a boil. Gradually stir in the rice, keeping water at a boil; cover, lower heat and simmer 35 minutes without lifting the lid.* |
| *Millet* | *2½ cups* | *Toast in a dry pan over high heat, stirring constantly, until fragrant. Then prepare as directed for brown rice.* |
| *Quinoa* | *2 cups* | *Toast in a dry pan over high heat, stirring constantly, until fragrant. Rinse in a fine sieve. Bring water to a boil, stir in quinoa and return to a boil. Reduce heat and simmer, covered, 15 minutes.* |
| *Whole-wheat couscous\** | *2 cups* | *Follow instructions for preparing bulgur wheat, but steep it 15 minutes.* |

*\*Look for whole-wheat couscous in health-food stores.*

# Oven "Fries"

*Soaking the potatoes in a salt-sugar solution draws out some of their water. This way they brown in the oven rather than steam.*

MAKES 4 SERVINGS

1¼ pounds baking potatoes, peeled and cut into ½" strips

¾ teaspoon salt

½ teaspoon sugar

4 teaspoons oil

1 teaspoon paprika

1. Preheat the oven to 450° F; spray a nonstick baking sheet with nonstick cooking spray.

2. In a large bowl, combine the potatoes, ¼ teaspoon of the salt and the sugar with cold water to cover. Soak 15 minutes; drain and blot dry.

3. In another large bowl, toss the potatoes with the oil and paprika. Place in a single layer on the baking sheet. Bake, turning the potatoes over as they brown, until cooked through and crisp, about 45 minutes. Sprinkle with the remaining ½ teaspoon of salt.

**Per serving:** 159 Calories, 5 g Total Fat, 1 g Saturated Fat, 0 mg Cholesterol, 442 mg Sodium, 28 g Total Carbohydrate, 3 g Dietary Fiber, 2 g Protein, 7 mg Calcium. *POINTS* per serving: 3.

## How We Did It

Sugar on French fries? The sugar (and the salt) serve to drain the liquid from the potatoes, giving them a crisper bite. Since the potatoes don't get crisped by frying, this extra step helps a lot.

# Lyonnaise Potatoes

*Sacre bleu! Could this classic French dish be made without lots of butter? Absolutely.*

MAKES 4 SERVINGS

1 tablespoon + 1 teaspoon olive oil

1¼ pounds all-purpose potatoes, peeled, sliced ¼" thick and boiled

½ teaspoon salt

¼ teaspoon dried marjoram

⅛ teaspoon freshly ground pepper

2 onions, thinly sliced

2 garlic cloves, slivered

¼ cup chicken broth

1. In a large nonstick skillet, heat 1 tablespoon of the oil. Add the potatoes and sprinkle with the salt, marjoram and pepper; cook, turning as they color, 10–15 minutes.

2. Meanwhile, in another large nonstick skillet, heat the remaining teaspoon of oil. Sauté the onions until softened, about 5 minutes. Add the garlic and cook 2 minutes. Stir in the broth; cook until the onions are very tender and browned, 5–7 minutes longer. Add the onions to the potatoes; toss to combine.

**Per serving:** 182 Calories, 5 g Total Fat, 1 g Saturated Fat, 1 mg Cholesterol, 360 mg Sodium, 33 g Total Carbohydrate, 3 g Dietary Fiber, 3 g Protein, 19 mg Calcium. *POINTS* per serving: 3.

*Oven "Fries"*

# Mixed Potato Pancakes

*Never wash potatoes prior to storing them—this accelerates their deterioration. To maximize freshness, remove potatoes from their plastic grocery bag and store them in a vegetable bin in a dark, dry place.*

MAKES 4 SERVINGS

2 small sweet potatoes, peeled and quartered

2 medium all-purpose potatoes, peeled and quartered

2 onions, chopped

1 garlic clove, minced

1/4 teaspoon freshly ground pepper

1/8 teaspoon salt

1. Combine both kinds of potatoes in a medium saucepan and and add cold water to cover; bring to a boil. Reduce the heat and simmer, covered, until barely tender, about 8 minutes. Drain the potatoes and let cool; with a grater, shred into a medium bowl.

2. Spray a medium nonstick skillet with nonstick cooking spray; heat. Sauté the onions and garlic until light brown, 3–4 minutes. Add to the shredded potatoes, then sprinkle with the pepper and salt; toss gently to combine. Let cool slightly, then divide into 8 pancakes.

3. Wipe out the skillet with a paper towel and spray with more nonstick cooking spray; heat. Cook the pancakes, 4 at a time; until lightly browned, about 4 minutes on each side. Repeat with the remaining pancakes. Serve at once.

**Per serving**: 134 Calories, 1 g Total Fat, 0 g Saturated Fat, 0 mg Cholesterol, 82 mg Sodium, 30 g Total Carbohydrate, 3 g Dietary Fiber, 3 g Protein, 26 mg Calcium. *POINTS* per serving: 2.

# Potato Pancakes

*In this recipe, it's critical to use starchy baking potatoes like russet Burbanks or Idahos. Waxy, or boiling, potatoes will brown and burn too easily.*

MAKES 4 SERVINGS

1 1/4 pounds baking potatoes, peeled and shredded

2 egg whites

3 tablespoons all-purpose flour

2 scallions, minced

3/4 teaspoon salt

4 teaspoons vegetable oil

1. Soak the potatoes in cold water 30 minutes; drain and blot dry. Preheat the oven to 375° F.

2. In a medium bowl, combine the potatoes, egg whites, flour, scallions and salt. Form into 12 pancakes.

3. In a large nonstick skillet over medium heat, heat one-third of the oil. Cook the pancakes, 4 at a time, until just golden, about 2 minutes on each side; transfer to a baking sheet. Repeat with the remaining oil and pancakes. Bake until crisp and cooked through, 5–7 minutes.

**Per serving**: 160 Calories, 5 g Total Fat, 1 g Saturated Fat, 0 mg Cholesterol, 469 mg Sodium, 26 g Total Carbohydrate, 2 g Dietary Fiber, 4 g Protein, 13 mg Calcium. *POINTS* per serving: 3.

# Potato Chips

*Starchy baking potatoes like russet Burbanks are perfect for these crispy chips; alternatively, try Idahos.*

MAKES 4 SERVINGS

1¼ pounds baking potatoes, peeled and very thinly sliced

¾ teaspoon salt

1. In a medium bowl, combine the potatoes, ¼ teaspoon of the salt and cold water to cover. Soak 30 minutes; drain and blot dry.

2. Preheat the oven to 350° F; spray 2 nonstick baking sheets with nonstick cooking spray. Place the potatoes in a single layer on the baking sheets. Bake, turning the potatoes over frequently so that they color and crisp evenly, 30–45 minutes. Sprinkle with the remaining ½ teaspoon of salt.

**Per serving:** 115 Calories, 0 g Total Fat, 0 g Saturated Fat, 0 mg Cholesterol, 442 mg Sodium, 27 g Total Carbohydrate, 2 g Dietary Fiber, 2 g Protein, 6 mg Calcium. **POINTS** per serving: 2.

## Tip

Flavor homemade chips with herbs or spices (such as dill, paprika or rosemary) or sprays (like Cajun, butter-flavored or garlic).

# Sweet Potato Chips

*Don't worry if the chips aren't perfectly crisp by the end of the cooking time; they'll continue crisping as they cool.*

MAKES 4 SERVINGS

1 pound sweet potatoes, peeled and very thinly sliced

½ teaspoon sugar

¾ teaspoon salt

1. In a medium bowl, combine the potatoes, sugar, ¼ teaspoon of the salt and cold water to cover. Soak 30 minutes; drain and blot dry.

2. Preheat the oven to 350° F; spray 2 nonstick baking sheets with nonstick cooking spray. Place the potatoes in a single layer on the baking sheets. Bake, turning the potatoes over frequently so that they color and crisp evenly, 35–40 minutes. Sprinkle with the remaining ½ teaspoon of salt.

**Per serving:** 118 Calories, 0 g Total Fat, 0 g Saturated Fat, 0 mg Cholesterol, 447 mg Sodium, 28 g Total Carbohydrate, 3 g Dietary Fiber, 2 g Protein, 32 mg Calcium. **POINTS** per serving: 2.

# Roasted Sweet Potatoes

*Sweet potatoes are one of nature's great nutrition bargains, packed with heart-healthy carotenoids and fiber. They're also satisfyingly sweet.*

MAKES 4 SERVINGS

4 teaspoons olive oil

4 garlic cloves (do not peel)

1 teaspoon fresh rosemary leaves, or ½ teaspoon dried

1 pound sweet potatoes, peeled and cut into ¾" chunks

¼ cup chicken broth

½ teaspoon salt

1. Preheat the oven to 350° F. In an 8" square baking dish, combine the oil, garlic and rosemary. Bake until the oil is hot, about 7 minutes; add the potatoes and stir to coat. Roast, turning the potatoes occasionally, 30 minutes.

2. Add the broth; cook, turning the potatoes occasionally, until browned and cooked through, about 15 minutes longer. Serve, sprinkled with the salt.

**Per serving:** 163 Calories, 5 g Total Fat, 1 g Saturated Fat, 1 mg Cholesterol, 364 mg Sodium, 29 g Total Carbohydrate, 3 g Dietary Fiber, 2 g Protein, 39 mg Calcium. **POINTS** per serving: 3.

# Sweet Potato Casserole

*Rescued from under a marshmallow topping, this sweet potato casserole is just right for holiday meals— or anytime you're looking for a tantalizing side dish.*

MAKES 4 SERVINGS

2 apples, peeled, cored and thinly sliced

1 pound sweet potatoes, peeled and thinly sliced

¾ teaspoon finely chopped crystallized ginger

½ teaspoon salt

¼ cup thawed frozen apple juice concentrate

2 tablespoons packed dark brown sugar

2 teaspoons fresh lemon juice

¼ teaspoon cinnamon

⅛ teaspoon ground cloves

2 teaspoons margarine, diced

1. Preheat the oven to 375° F; spray an 8" square baking dish with nonstick cooking spray. Arrange half of the apples in the baking dish; top with half of the sweet potatoes, then sprinkle with half the ginger and half the salt. Repeat the layers.

2. In a small bowl, combine the juice concentrate, brown sugar, lemon juice, cinnamon, cloves and ¼ cup water. Pour over the potatoes. Cover with foil and bake 45 minutes; dot with the margarine. Bake, uncovered, until tender, bubbling and lightly browned, about 15 minutes longer.

**Per serving:** 220 Calories, 2 g Total Fat, 0 g Saturated Fat, 0 mg Cholesterol, 332 mg Sodium, 50 g Total Carbohydrate, 4 g Dietary Fiber, 2 g Protein, 48 mg Calcium. **POINTS** per serving: 4.

# Sweet Potatoes with Fruit Topping

*Cooking the dried fruit in orange juice in this recipe adds to the natural sweetness of the sweet potato. It's a perfect complement when served with a savory chicken dish.*

MAKES 4 SERVINGS

1 cup orange juice

¾ cup coarsely chopped mixed dried fruit

1 tablespoon slivered orange zest

2 teaspoons sugar

4 small sweet potatoes, cooked

1. In a small nonreactive saucepan, combine the orange juice, dried fruit, orange zest and sugar; bring to a boil. Reduce the heat and simmer, covered, 5 minutes. Uncover and simmer until the liquid is slightly syrupy, 10–15 minutes.

2. With a fork, pierce an × across each potato and squeeze the sides to puff out the insides; spoon the fruit mixture over each.

**Per serving:** 203 Calories, 0 g Total Fat, 0 g Saturated Fat, 0 mg Cholesterol, 15 mg Sodium, 50 g Total Carbohydrate, 3 g Dietary Fiber, 3 g Protein, 44 mg Calcium. *POINTS* per serving: 3.

# Mashed Sweet Potatoes

*Next time you need a side dish for roasted meats or poultry, why not try this creatively seasoned, easy treat?*

MAKES 4 SERVINGS

1 pound sweet potatoes, peeled and thinly sliced

¾ teaspoon salt

2 teaspoons unsalted margarine

¼ teaspoon ground ginger

⅛ teaspoon ground cardamom

⅛ teaspoon freshly ground pepper

⅛ teaspoon ground nutmeg

1. Place the sweet potatoes in a medium saucepan; add cold water to cover and ½ teaspoon of the salt; bring to a boil. Reduce the heat and simmer until tender, 15–20 minutes. Drain, reserving 2 tablespoons of the cooking liquid.

2. With a potato masher or an electric mixer on low speed, mash the potatoes with the cooking liquid, margarine, ginger, cardamom, pepper, nutmeg and the remaining ¼ teaspoon of salt; serve at once.

**Per serving:** 137 Calories, 2 g Total Fat, 0 g Saturated Fat, 0 mg Cholesterol, 451 mg Sodium, 28 g Total Carbohydrate, 3 g Dietary Fiber, 2 g Protein, 25 mg Calcium. *POINTS* per serving: 2.

# Root Vegetable Bake

*Don't fear the root vegetable! Make this dish in winter when they are at their best.*

MAKES 4 SERVINGS

1 small butternut squash, peeled, seeded and cubed

1 small celeriac (celery root), peeled and cubed

1 carrot, chopped

1 medium all-purpose potato, peeled and cubed

½ cup chopped peeled yellow turnip or rutabaga

1 onion, chopped

½ cup low-sodium chicken broth

1 tablespoon + 1 teaspoon reduced-calorie margarine

2 tablespoons fat-free milk

¼ teaspoon salt

¼ teaspoon ground white pepper

1. In a large saucepan, combine the squash, celeriac, carrot, potato and turnip and cold water to cover; bring to a boil. Reduce the heat and simmer, covered, until all the vegetables are very tender, 30 minutes. Drain and return to the saucepan.

2. Meanwhile, preheat the oven to 425° F; spray a 1½-quart casserole with nonstick cooking spray. In a small nonstick skillet, combine the onion, broth and 1 teaspoon of the margarine; cook, stirring as needed, until the liquid evaporates and the onion begins to turn golden, about 15 minutes.

3. Add the milk, the remaining tablespoon of margarine, the salt and pepper to the root vegetables; with an electric mixer, beat until smooth. Transfer to the casserole and top with the onions. Bake until crusty, about 25 minutes.

**Per serving:** 155 Calories, 3 g Total Fat, 0 g Saturated Fat, 0 mg Cholesterol, 258 mg Sodium, 32 g Total Carbohydrate, 5 g Dietary Fiber, 4 g Protein, 115 mg Calcium. **POINTS** per serving: 2.

# Turnip Puree

*If you like, substitute an equal amount of parsnips, which lend a slightly sweet flavor, for the turnips.*

MAKES 4 SERVINGS

4–5 turnips, peeled and diced

2 medium all-purpose potatoes, peeled and diced

2 tablespoons light sour cream

½ teaspoon salt

½ teaspoon freshly ground pepper

⅛ teaspoon ground nutmeg

1. In a large saucepan, combine the turnips, potatoes and cold water to cover; bring to a boil. Reduce the heat and simmer until tender, 15–20 minutes. Drain and return to the saucepan.

2. Add the sour cream, salt, pepper and nutmeg; with a potato masher or an electric mixer, puree. Transfer to a serving bowl; serve at once.

**Per serving:** 89 Calories, 1 g Total Fat, 1 g Saturated Fat, 3 mg Cholesterol, 342 mg Sodium, 18 g Total Carbohydrate, 3 g Dietary Fiber, 2 g Protein, 37 mg Calcium. **POINTS** per serving: 1.

## Got Leftovers?

**Leftover turnip puree, thinned with a little water or broth, makes a delicious, creamy soup. Throw in some chopped cooked vegetables—say, carrots or broccoli—for color and crunch.**

# Corn Pudding

*In a 1-quart soufflé dish, this bakes spectacularly high and puffy, but it tastes just as delicious in a 9" square baking dish.*

MAKES 4 SERVINGS

2 cups fresh or frozen corn kernels

1 teaspoon corn oil

1 onion, finely chopped

¼ green bell pepper, seeded and finely chopped

¼ red bell pepper, seeded and finely chopped

½ cup evaporated skimmed milk

2 tablespoons all-purpose flour

⅓ cup shredded Gruyère cheese

1 tablespoon grated Parmesan cheese

⅛ teaspoon ground nutmeg

⅛ teaspoon cayenne pepper

3 egg whites

1. Adjust the racks to divide the oven into thirds. Preheat the oven to 350° F; spray a 1-quart soufflé dish or 9" square baking dish with nonstick cooking spray.

2. In a small saucepan, cook the corn in 1 cup water. Drain, reserving the liquid. Set each aside.

3. In a medium nonstick saucepan, heat the oil. Sauté the onion and bell peppers until softened, about 5 minutes. Remove from the heat. Add the corn cooking liquid, the milk and flour, whisking until smooth. Cook over medium heat, stirring, until the mixture boils and thickens slightly, about 5 minutes. Remove from the heat; stir in the Gruyère, Parmesan, nutmeg, cayenne and corn.

4. In a large bowl, beat the egg whites until stiff but not dry. With a rubber spatula, fold into the corn mixture; pour into the baking dish. Bake on the bottom rack until the pudding is brown and puffy, and a knife inserted near center comes out almost clean, about 1 hour in the soufflé dish, or 45 minutes in the baking dish. Serve at once.

**Per serving**: 191 Calories, 6 g Total Fat, 3 g Saturated Fat, 14 mg Cholesterol, 149 mg Sodium, 24 g Total Carbohydrate, 3 g Dietary Fiber, 12 g Protein, 226 mg Calcium. *POINTS* per serving: 4.

# Spanish-Style Hominy

*Though hominy is usually breakfast fare down South or made into a porridge in Mexico (where it's called pozole), it makes a delicious casserole, too.*

MAKES 6 SERVINGS

3 cups drained canned golden hominy

1 green bell pepper, seeded and finely chopped

1 cup sliced mushrooms

2 onions, finely chopped

One 8-ounce can tomato sauce

½ cup tomato paste

2½ teaspoons chili powder

1 teaspoon ground cumin

⅛ teaspoon freshly ground pepper

¾ cup shredded reduced-fat Monterey Jack cheese

¾ cup shredded reduced-fat sharp cheddar cheese

Preheat the oven to 350° F; spray a 2-quart casserole with nonstick cooking spray. In the casserole, combine the hominy, bell pepper, mushrooms, onions, tomato sauce, tomato paste, chili powder, cumin and pepper; sprinkle with the Monterey Jack and cheddar. Bake until the cheeses are bubbling, about 30 minutes.

**Per serving:** 196 Calories, 6 g Total Fat, 3 g Saturated Fat, 20 mg Cholesterol, 789 mg Sodium, 24 g Total Carbohydrate, 5 g Dietary Fiber, 11 g Protein, 285 mg Calcium. *POINTS* per serving: 3.

## Tip

Hominy is dried corn that has had its outer hull and inner germ removed by soaking in lye or soda. With cooking, it plumps up into delicious juicy kernels. Hominy can also be ground into grits—another Southern staple.

# Polenta with Fontinella-Mushroom Sauce

*Fontinella is a semifirm Italian cheese; if you can't find it, substitute ½ cup grated pecorino Romano. You'll need a 4-ounce chunk of fontinella to get 1 cup when grated.*

MAKES 6 SERVINGS

1 cup instant polenta

⅛ teaspoon salt

2 tablespoons margarine

⅛ teaspoon freshly ground pepper

2 tablespoons all-purpose flour

1½ cups fat-free milk

1 cup grated fontinella cheese

½ cup grated Parmesan cheese

3 cups sliced mushrooms

1. Spray a tall, round 1-quart container (a clean 4-cup yogurt or cottage cheese container is ideal) and a 9 × 13" baking dish with nonstick cooking spray.

2. In a small saucepan, bring 2½ cups water to a boil. Whisking constantly, gradually add the polenta in a thin stream; add the salt. Reduce the heat and cook, whisking constantly, 5 minutes. Transfer to the 1-quart container; refrigerate, covered, until chilled, about 1 hour.

3. Preheat the oven to 350° F. Unmold the polenta. Cut into 6 rounds; place in the baking dish.

4. In a medium saucepan, melt the margarine. Stir in the pepper, then sprinkle with the flour; whisk quickly to combine. Whisk in the milk, fontinella and Parmesan; stir in the mushrooms. Pour the mushroom sauce over the polenta. Bake until heated through, about 30 minutes.

**Per serving**: 267 Calories, 13 g Total Fat, 2 g Saturated Fat, 29 mg Cholesterol, 504 mg Sodium, 24 g Total Carbohydrate, 2 g Dietary Fiber, 14 g Protein, 398 mg Calcium. *POINTS* per serving: 6.

## Got Leftovers?

**Instant polenta reduces the cooking and stirring time to just 5 minutes, but why not make a double batch of the polenta and serve the rest as a breakfast treat? Slice into rounds, cook in a nonstick skillet with a little margarine until crisped on both sides, and serve with syrup or fresh fruit.**

# Bulgur Pilaf

*Best known for its use in Middle Eastern tabbouleh, bulgur lends a mild wheaty taste to this pilaf, where it stands in for rice.*

MAKES 6 SERVINGS

2 cups sliced mushrooms

2 onions, chopped

1 cup bulgur

½ cup chopped dried apricots

½ cup chopped parsley

¼ cup raisins

¼ cup slivered almonds

In a medium saucepan, combine the mushrooms, onions, bulgur, apricots, parsley, raisins and 3 cups water; bring to a boil. Reduce the heat and simmer, covered, until the liquid is absorbed and the bulgur is tender, 15–20 minutes. Stir in the almonds.

**Per serving**: 253 Calories, 8 g Total Fat, 1 g Saturated Fat, 0 mg Cholesterol, 12 mg Sodium, 42 g Total Carbohydrate, 8 g Dietary Fiber, 8 g Protein, 70 mg Calcium. *POINTS* per serving: 4.

# Tabbouleh

*For a festive touch, serve this Middle Eastern salad in hollowed-out tomatoes or lightly steamed bell pepper cups.*

MAKES 6 SERVINGS

½ cup fresh lemon juice

1 cup bulgur

1 tablespoon olive oil

1 teaspoon freshly ground pepper, or to taste

¼ teaspoon salt

3 tomatoes, chopped

1 cup chopped flat-leaf parsley

1 red onion, chopped

3 scallions (green part only), sliced

2 garlic cloves, crushed

1 lemon, sliced

1. In a medium saucepan, bring the juice and 1½ cups water to a boil. Stir in the bulgur, oil, pepper and salt. Remove from the heat; cover and let stand until the water is absorbed, 20–25 minutes.

2. In a large bowl, combine the tomatoes, parsley, onion, scallions and garlic. Add the bulgur; toss to combine. Refrigerate, covered, until well chilled, at least 3 hours. Serve, garnished with the lemon slices.

**Per serving**: 150 Calories, 3 g Total Fat, 0 g Saturated Fat, 0 mg Cholesterol, 106 mg Sodium, 29 g Total Carbohydrate, 7 g Dietary Fiber, 5 g Protein, 29 mg Calcium. *POINTS* per serving: 2.

*Tabbouleh*

# Wheat Berry, Orange and Mint Salad

*Wheat berries, also called whole-grain wheat or whole-grain wheat kernels, are available at health-food stores. If you are unable to find wheat berries, substitute brown rice or bulgur; reduce the cooking time accordingly.*

MAKES 4 SERVINGS

1 cup wheat berries

2 navel oranges, peeled and sectioned

½ carrot, diced

½ red onion, minced

½ cup chopped mint

3 tablespoons fresh lemon juice

2 teaspoons olive oil

¼ teaspoon salt

¼ teaspoon freshly ground pepper

1. In a medium saucepan, bring 2¼ cups water to a boil. Add the wheat berries; reduce the heat and simmer, covered, until the grain is tender and the water is absorbed, 1½–2 hours. Fluff with a fork, then let stand 5 minutes.

2. In a large bowl, combine the wheat berries, orange sections, carrot, onion, mint, lemon juice, oil, salt and pepper; toss to combine. Refrigerate, covered, 1 hour before serving.

**Per serving:** 212 Calories, 3 g Total Fat, 0 g Saturated Fat, 0 mg Cholesterol, 142 mg Sodium, 43 g Total Carbohydrate, 9 g Dietary Fiber, 6 g Protein, 61 mg Calcium. *POINTS* per serving: 3.

# Kasha Varnishkes

*The classic combination of buckwheat groats and farfalle comes into a health-conscious age, without chicken fat.*

MAKES 6 SERVINGS

½ cup buckwheat groats (kasha)

1 egg, lightly beaten

1 tablespoon vegetable oil

1 onion, thinly sliced

1 teaspoon chicken bouillon granules, dissolved in 2 tablespoons water

2 cups thinly sliced mushrooms

1½ cups cooked farfalle

1 teaspoon paprika

⅛ teaspoon freshly ground pepper

1. In a small bowl, combine the groats and egg; stir to coat.

2. In a small nonstick saucepan over low heat, heat the oil. Add the groats; cook, stirring constantly, until the groats are dry and the grains are separated, about 5 minutes.

3. Add ½ cup water; bring to a boil. Reduce the heat and simmer, covered, 5–10 minutes.

4. Meanwhile, spray a large nonstick skillet with nonstick cooking spray; heat. Add the onion and dissolved bouillon granules; cook, stirring constantly, adding water if needed, until the onion is browned, about 5 minutes. Add the mushrooms; sauté 2–3 minutes. Reduce the heat and stir in the groats, farfalle, ¾ teaspoon of the paprika and the pepper. Serve, sprinkled with the remaining ¼ teaspoon paprika.

**Per serving:** 147 Calories, 4 g Total Fat, 1 g Saturated Fat, 174 mg Sodium, 35 mg Cholesterol, 24 g Total Carbohydrate, 3 g Dietary Fiber, 5 g Protein, 15 mg Calcium. *POINTS* per serving: 3.

# Couscous with Lime-Ginger Sauce

*Couscous is the ultimate convenience food: Just pour boiling water or broth over the couscous and let it stand 5 minutes.*

MAKES 6 SERVINGS

1 cup couscous

1 teaspoon Asian sesame oil

1/4 teaspoon salt

1 red bell pepper, seeded and finely chopped

1 carrot, scrubbed and finely chopped

8 scallions, thinly sliced

1/2 cup fresh lime juice

1/4 cup minced parsley

1/4 teaspoon ground ginger

1/8 teaspoon freshly ground pepper

1. In a medium saucepan, bring 1 1/2 cups water to a boil; add the couscous, oil and salt. Remove from the heat; let stand until the water is absorbed, about 5 minutes. Fluff with a fork.

2. In a large bowl, combine the bell pepper, carrot, scallions, lime juice, parsley, ginger and pepper. Add the couscous; toss to combine. Refrigerate, covered, until chilled, at least 3 hours.

**Per serving:** 138 Calories, 1 g Total Fat, 0 g Saturated Fat, 0 mg Cholesterol, 103 mg Sodium, 28 g Total Carbohydrate, 1 g Dietary Fiber, 4 g Protein, 31 mg Calcium. *POINTS* per serving: 3.

# Curried Basmati Rice

*Considered a luxury food in India and Pakistan, where it was originally cultivated, this aromatic rice was named basmati, which means "queen of fragrance."*

MAKES 6 SERVINGS

1 cup sliced mushrooms

2 onions, chopped

1/2 red bell pepper, seeded and chopped

1/2 green bell pepper, seeded and chopped

1 cup basmati rice

1 1/2 teaspoons curry powder

1/4 teaspoon salt

1. Spray a large nonstick saucepan with nonstick cooking spray, heat. Combine the mushrooms, onions and bell peppers; sauté until softened, 3–4 minutes.

2. Stir in the rice, curry powder, salt and 1 1/2 cups water; bring to a boil. Reduce the heat and simmer, covered, 15–20 minutes.

**Per serving:** 117 Calories, 1 g Total Fat, 0 g Saturated Fat, 0 mg Cholesterol, 104 mg Sodium, 26 g Total Carbohydrate, 1 g Dietary Fiber, 4 g Protein, 10 mg Calcium. *POINTS* per serving: 2.

## Tip

Not all curry powders are created equal. Experiment with various "heats," from mild to superhot.

# Herbed Instant Brown Rice

*In this speedy but special dish, you can enjoy in short order the nutritious benefits of brown rice enhanced with vegetables and herbs.*

MAKES 6 SERVINGS

1 tablespoon margarine

1 onion, chopped

3 garlic cloves, minced

1 red bell pepper, seeded and finely chopped

1 celery stalk, finely chopped

1 cup instant brown rice

¼ teaspoon ground marjoram

½ cup chopped flat-leaf parsley

In a large nonstick saucepan, melt the margarine. Sauté the onions and garlic until the garlic is lightly browned, 2–3 minutes. Add the bell pepper and celery; sauté 2–3 minutes. Add the rice, marjoram and 1½ cups water; bring to a boil. Reduce the heat and simmer, covered, 5 minutes. Remove from the heat; stir in the parsley. Let stand 5 minutes.

**Per serving:** 128 Calories, 3 g Total Fat, 0 g Saturated Fat, 0 mg Cholesterol, 46 mg Sodium, 26 g Total Carbohydrate, 2 g Dietary Fiber, 3 g Protein, 19 mg Calcium. **POINTS** per serving: 2.

# Microwave Risotto

*With a food processor and microwave oven, you can make this savory risotto in less than 30 minutes!*

MAKES 6 SERVINGS

1 cup packed basil leaves

⅓ cup pine nuts

¾ cup dry white wine

4 garlic cloves

1 tablespoon + 2 teaspoons olive oil

1 cup Arborio or other short-grain rice

3 cups chicken broth

12 sun-dried tomato halves (not oil-packed), diced

¼ cup grated Parmesan cheese

1. To prepare the pesto, in a food processor, combine the basil, pine nuts, ¼ cup of the wine, the garlic and 2 teaspoons of the oil; process 4–5 minutes, stopping occasionally to scrape the sides of the bowl.

2. In a 2½-quart microwavable casserole, microwave the remaining tablespoon of oil on High 1 minute; stir in the rice. Stir in 2 cups of the broth, the remaining ½ cup of wine and ½ cup water. Microwave on High 12 minutes.

3. Add the pesto, the remaining cup of broth and the tomatoes to the rice; stir to combine. Microwave on High until the rice and tomatoes are tender and the liquid is absorbed, 8–10 minutes. Sprinkle with the cheese.

**Per serving:** 259 Calories, 11 g Total Fat, 2 g Saturated Fat, 3 mg Cholesterol, 566 mg Sodium, 31 g Total Carbohydrate, 1 g Dietary Fiber, 8 g Protein, 129 mg Calcium. **POINTS** per serving: 6.

# Moroccan Rice Salad

*Cumin and fresh cilantro, also called coriander or Chinese parsley, lend exotic overtones to this very easy-to-prepare, healthful salad. If all you can find is hot paprika, start with ½ teaspoon.*

MAKES 4 SERVINGS

¼ cup chopped parsley

2 tablespoons chopped cilantro

2 tablespoons fresh lemon juice

2 teaspoons sweet paprika

2 teaspoons olive oil

1 teaspoon ground cumin

½ teaspoon freshly ground pepper

¼ teaspoon salt

4 cups cooked brown rice

½ carrot, finely diced

½ cup cooked green peas

½ red bell pepper, seeded and diced

1. To prepare the dressing, in a small bowl, combine the parsley, cilantro, lemon juice, paprika, oil, cumin, pepper and salt.

2. In a large bowl, combine the rice, carrot, peas and bell pepper. Drizzle with the dressing; toss to coat.

**Per serving:** 272 Calories, 4 g Total Fat, 1 g Saturated Fat, 0 mg Cholesterol, 153 mg Sodium, 52 g Total Carbohydrate, 5 g Dietary Fiber, 7 g Protein, 44 mg Calcium. **POINTS** per serving: 5.

# Vegetable Fried Rice

*If you don't have time to do the slicing, many of these ingredients can be picked up at your supermarket's salad bar.*

MAKES 6 SERVINGS

1 cup thinly sliced baby carrots

12 scallions, thinly sliced

1 cup sliced mushrooms

1 cup bean sprouts

1 tablespoon chicken bouillon granules, dissolved in ¾ cup boiling water

3 eggs, slightly beaten

¼ cup dry sherry

3 cups hot cooked long-grain rice

1. Spray a large nonstick skillet or wok with nonstick cooking spray; heat. Stir-fry the carrots, scallions, mushrooms, bean sprouts and dissolved bouillon granules until the vegetables are tender-crisp, 2–3 minutes. Transfer to a bowl.

2. Spray the skillet with more nonstick cooking spray. Add the eggs and sherry; cook, stirring to break up the eggs until the eggs are set, about 2 minutes. Add the vegetables and rice to the eggs; toss to combine. Cook, stirring frequently, until heated through, 1–2 minutes.

**Per serving:** 198 Calories, 3 g Total Fat, 1 g Saturated Fat, 106 mg Cholesterol, 525 mg Sodium, 35 g Total Carbohydrate, 2 g Dietary Fiber, 7 g Protein, 43 mg Calcium. **POINTS** per serving: 4.

# Rice, Black Bean and Corn Salad

*Roasted or grilled corn adds a wonderful flavor to this colorful salad. Next time you're grilling, shuck a few ears of corn and place them around the edge of the grill for a few minutes. Turn them often and remove when they are lightly browned. Save an ear and cut the kernels off to use in this salad.*

MAKES 4 SERVINGS

1 cup cold cooked brown rice

½ cup cooked corn kernels

½ green bell pepper, seeded and chopped

1 celery stalk, chopped

⅓ cup canned black beans, rinsed and drained

½ red onion, minced

2 tablespoons minced cilantro

½ jalapeño pepper, seeded, deveined and minced (wear gloves to prevent irritation)

2 tablespoons red-wine vinegar

1½ tablespoons fresh lime juice

1 tablespoon extra virgin olive oil

¼ teaspoon salt

1. In a large bowl, combine the rice, corn, bell pepper, celery, beans, onion, cilantro and jalapeño.

2. In a small bowl, whisk the vinegar, lime juice, oil and salt. Pour over the rice mixture; toss to coat. Refrigerate, covered, until the flavors are blended, at least 1 hour.

**Per serving:** 119 Calories, 4 g Total Fat, 1 g Saturated Fat, 0 mg Cholesterol, 197 mg Sodium, 19 g Total Carbohydrate, 3 g Dietary Fiber, 3 g Protein, 21 mg Calcium. **POINTS** per serving: 2.

# Wild Rice– Asparagus Salad

*Wild rice—which is actually a grass—has a chewy texture and nutty flavor. It's somewhat expensive, but worth its slightly higher price.*

MAKES 6 SERVINGS

2 teaspoons chicken bouillon granules

½ cup regular long-grain rice

½ cup wild rice, rinsed

1 pound asparagus, cut into 1" lengths and steamed until tender-crisp

1 red bell pepper, seeded and chopped

1 red onion, chopped

½ cup chopped parsley

⅓ cup white-wine vinegar

1 tablespoon olive oil

1 teaspoon sugar

⅛ teaspoon freshly ground pepper

12 red leaf lettuce leaves

1. In a medium saucepan, combine 2¾ cups water and the bouillon granules; bring to a boil. Add both kinds of rice. Reduce the heat and simmer, covered, until tender, 45–50 minutes. Remove from the heat.

2. In a large bowl, combine the asparagus, bell pepper, onion, parsley, vinegar, oil, sugar and pepper. Add the rice; toss to combine.

3. Line a platter with the lettuce leaves; top with the rice mixture. Refrigerate, covered, until chilled, at least 3 hours.

**Per serving:** 172 Calories, 3 g Total Fat, 0 g Saturated Fat, 1 mg Cholesterol, 311 mg Sodium, 32 g Total Carbohydrate, 3 g Dietary Fiber, 7 g Protein, 55 mg Calcium. **POINTS** per serving: 2.

*Wild Rice–Asparagus Salad*

# Wild Rice–
# Mushroom Stuffing

*Serve this elegant stuffing with roast pork or veal.*

MAKES 4 SERVINGS

1 cup low-sodium chicken broth

⅔ cup wild rice, rinsed

4 teaspoons reduced-calorie margarine

2 cups thinly sliced shiitake mushrooms

1 red bell pepper, seeded and cut into strips

1 celery stalk, chopped

6 shallots, chopped

1 teaspoon dried thyme leaves

¼ teaspoon salt

¼ teaspoon freshly ground pepper

¼ cup dry red wine

1 cup chopped cleaned spinach

1. In a small saucepan, combine the broth and 1 cup water; bring to a boil. Add the rice. Reduce the heat and simmer, covered, until tender, 45–50 minutes.

2. Preheat the oven to 325° F; spray a 2-quart casserole with nonstick cooking spray. Meanwhile, in a large nonstick skillet, melt the margarine. Sauté the mushrooms, bell pepper, celery, shallots, thyme, salt and pepper until the vegetables are softened, 5–7 minutes; stir in the wine. Reduce the heat and simmer until the liquid evaporates, 2–3 minutes. Remove from the heat. Stir in the spinach and rice; transfer to the casserole. Bake until heated through, 30–40 minutes.

**Per serving:** 174 Calories, 3 g Total Fat, 0 g Saturated Fat, 0 mg Cholesterol, 216 mg Sodium, 30 g Total Carbohydrate, 3 g Dietary Fiber, 7 g Protein, 46 mg Calcium. **POINTS** per serving: 3.

## Microwave Magic

*Rice cooks very nicely in a microwave—try our Microwave Risotto, page 334. Use the instructions below to cook basic rice.*

- *Combine 1 cup rice and liquid (see chart on page 340) in a 2-to-3-quart microwavable baking dish.*

- *Cover and cook on High for 5 minutes, or until boiling.*

- *Reduce setting to Medium and cook 15 minutes for regular white rice, 20 minutes for parboiled rice and 30 minutes for brown rice.*

# Cornbread-Cranberry Dressing

**(pictured on page 103)**

*Try this with your turkey dinner—it's sure to become your family's new favorite. The dried cranberries add a tart hint to the slightly sweet cornbread. Make the cornbread (Step 1) a day or so ahead to cut down on holiday chaos.*

MAKES 12 SERVINGS

½ cup + 2 tablespoons yellow cornmeal

½ cup + 1 tablespoon all-purpose flour

3 scallions, thinly sliced

2 tablespoons minced dill

1 tablespoon sugar

½ teaspoon baking powder

½ teaspoon baking soda

¼ teaspoon salt

3 egg whites

½ cup fat-free milk

2 tablespoons canola oil

1 cup apple juice

½ cup chopped dried apricots

¼ cup dried cranberries

1 cinnamon stick

4 slices stale whole-wheat bread, cut into cubes

1. Preheat the oven to 425° F; spray an 8" baking dish with nonstick cooking spray. To prepare the cornbread, in a medium bowl, combine the cornmeal, flour, scallions, dill, sugar, baking powder, baking soda and salt. In another medium bowl, combine 2 of the egg whites, the milk and oil; pour over the cornmeal mixture. With a wooden spoon, beat 30 seconds. Spoon the batter into the baking dish. Bake until the edges are golden and toothpick inserted in center comes out clean, 12–15 minutes. Cool in the pan 10 minutes; remove from the pan and cool completely on rack.

2. In a small saucepan, combine the apple juice, apricots, cranberries and cinnamon stick; bring to a boil. Reduce the heat and simmer until the liquid is reduced by half, 5–10 minutes; discard the cinnamon stick.

3. Preheat the oven to 325° F; spray a 2-quart casserole with nonstick cooking spray. Crumble the cornbread into a large bowl; add the juice mixture, the remaining egg white and the bread cubes; mix until just combined. Transfer to the casserole. Bake until golden, 40–50 minutes.

**Per serving:** 137 Calories, 3 g Total Fat, 0 g Saturated Fat, 0 mg Cholesterol, 188 mg Sodium, 24 g Total Carbohydrate, 2 g Dietary Fiber, 4 g Protein, 41 mg Calcium. **POINTS** per serving: 3.

# Sausage and Rice Dressing

*Although this is wonderful as a side dish, it may also be used to stuff a chicken—bake any that's leftover in a lightly oiled baking dish alongside the chicken.*

MAKES 4 SERVINGS

¼ pound turkey sausage, casings removed

1 tablespoon reduced-calorie margarine

2 celery stalks, chopped

1 onion, chopped

½ cup chopped trimmed fennel

2 garlic cloves, minced

3 cups cooked brown rice

¼ cup low-sodium chicken broth

2 tablespoons chopped fresh sage

1 tablespoon grated lemon zest

¼ teaspoon freshly ground pepper

1. Preheat the oven to 325° F; spray a 2-quart casserole with nonstick cooking spray. In a large nonstick skillet, cook the sausage, breaking apart the meat with a wooden spoon, until browned, 5–7 minutes. With a slotted spoon, transfer the sausage to a plate.

2. In the skillet, melt the margarine. Sauté the celery, onion, fennel and garlic until softened, about 5 minutes. Stir in the sausage, rice, broth, sage, lemon zest and pepper. Reduce the heat to low and simmer until the liquid evaporates, about 5 minutes. Transfer to the casserole. Bake until heated through and golden, 45–50 minutes.

**Per serving**: 260 Calories, 8 g Total Fat, 1 g Saturated Fat, 25 mg Cholesterol, 335 mg Sodium, 38 g Total Carbohydrate, 3 g Dietary Fiber, 11 g Protein, 47 mg Calcium. *POINTS* per serving: 5.

## Rice Rules

*Below are the basic guidelines for cooking rice. (If you are cooking a specialty rice, however, be sure to follow the directions on the package.)*

*Combine 1 cup of rice and the amount of water listed in the chart below in a 2- to 3-quart saucepan. Bring to a boil; stir once or twice. Reduce the heat to simmer; cook, covered, for the time specified in the chart. If the rice is not quite tender, or if the liquid is not absorbed, replace the lid and cook 2–4 minutes longer. Fluff with a fork before serving.*

| UNCOOKED RICE (1 CUP) | LIQUID | COOKING TIME |
|---|---|---|
| Regular-milled long-grain | 1¾–2 cups | 15 minutes |
| Regular-milled medium- or short-grain | 1½ cups | 15 minutes |
| Brown | 2–2½ cups | 45–50 minutes |

Desserts

# Chapter 12

# Desserts

Here's a startling thought: If you're trying to lose weight, don't skip this chapter. That's because an occasional dessert not only makes life sweeter but also it can help you stay on a healthy eating plan without feeling deprived. So let yourself have a treat once in a while, and make it worthwhile; a little bit of something real will satisfy you more than a tasteless, fat-free "treat."

These recipes celebrate the natural sweetness of fresh fruits, while keeping rich ingredients to a minimum. They also employ some skillful fat-cutting techniques worth learning, like the following:

- Fruit juice concentrates and fruit purees (applesauce, canned prune puree and baby-food prunes are ideal) serve as a partial substitute for fat and sugar. Try substituting them for half the fat called for in a conventional recipe, and adjust as needed.

- When nuts are used in a recipe, they are toasted first to intensify the flavor, so fewer will go a longer way. In baked goods, try sprinkling on the nuts at the end of baking time rather than stirring them into the dough; you'll get more crunch with fewer nuts.

- Reduced-fat ingredients are used liberally, but with care. Before you use a reduced-fat product, read its label carefully to make sure it's appropriate for the recipe. Reduced-calorie margarine doesn't melt properly for frying, for example, and fat-free cream cheese separates when it's beaten.

# Chocolate Layer Cake

*Instant espresso powder makes the chocolate flavor more intense and rich tasting. If you're concerned about caffeine, use decaf.*

## MAKES 12 SERVINGS

1 cup + 2 tablespoons all-purpose flour

⅓ cup unsweetened cocoa powder

1 teaspoon espresso powder or instant-coffee granules

1 teaspoon baking powder

1 teaspoon baking soda

¼ teaspoon salt

¼ cup + 2 tablespoons granulated sugar

2 tablespoons + 2 teaspoons reduced-calorie tub margarine

1 egg

1 teaspoon vanilla extract

1 cup fat-free buttermilk

½ cup apricot spreadable fruit

1 tablespoon confectioners' sugar

1. Preheat the oven to 350° F; spray two 8" square baking pans with nonstick cooking spray.

2. In a small bowl, combine the flour, cocoa powder, espresso powder, baking powder, baking soda and salt.

3. In a medium bowl, with an electric mixer on high speed, cream the granulated sugar and margarine; add the egg and vanilla, beating until smooth. Gradually beat in the flour mixture alternately with the buttermilk, until the batter is smooth. Divide the batter between the pans. Bake until a toothpick inserted in center comes out clean, 15–20 minutes. Cool completely in the pans on a rack. Insert a sharp knife around edges of each pan; remove the cakes from the pans. Transfer 1 cake to a platter, flat-side up.

4. Meanwhile, in a small saucepan over low heat, melt the spreadable fruit 2–3 minutes. Brush ¼ cup of the spreadable fruit on top of the cake on the platter; top with the other cake; brush with the remaining spreadable fruit. Sprinkle with the confectioners' sugar.

**Per serving**: 119 Calories, 3 g Total Fat, 1 g Saturated Fat, 19 mg Cholesterol, 243 mg Sodium, 22 g Total Carbohydrate, 1 g Dietary Fiber, 3 g Protein, 54 mg Calcium. *POINTS* per serving: 2.

# Vanilla Layer Cake with Chocolate-Ginger Frosting

*Part-skim ricotta cheese is a wonderfully versatile staple; here, it's the basis for a creamy frosting. Don't try to substitute nonfat ricotta—its grainy texture won't work as well.*

MAKES 12 SERVINGS

1 cup + 2 tablespoons cake flour

1 teaspoon baking soda

¼ teaspoon salt

¼ cup + 2 tablespoons granulated sugar

2 tablespoons + 2 teaspoons reduced-calorie tub margarine

1 egg

2½ teaspoons vanilla extract

½ cup fat-free milk

1¼ cups part-skim ricotta cheese

¼ cup unsweetened cocoa powder

¼ cup packed dark brown sugar

2 teaspoons unsalted butter, softened

¾ teaspoon ground ginger

1. Preheat the oven to 350° F; spray two 8" round cake pans with nonstick cooking spray.

2. To prepare the cake, in a small bowl, combine the cake flour, baking soda and salt.

3. In a medium bowl, with an electric mixer on high speed, cream the granulated sugar and margarine; add the egg and 2 teaspoons of the vanilla, beating until smooth. Gradually beat in the flour mixture alternately with the milk, until the batter is smooth. Divide the batter between the pans. Bake until a toothpick inserted in the center comes out clean, 15–20 minutes. Cool in the pans 5 minutes; remove from the pans and cool completely on a rack. Transfer 1 cake to a platter.

4. Meanwhile, to prepare the frosting, in a food processor or blender, combine the ricotta, cocoa powder, brown sugar, butter, ginger and the remaining ½ teaspoon of vanilla; blend until smooth. Spread a thin layer of frosting over the cake on the platter; top with the remaining cake. Spread the remaining frosting over the top and sides of the cake.

**Per serving:** 149 Calories, 5 g Total Fat, 2 g Saturated Fat, 28 mg Cholesterol, 220 mg Sodium, 22 g Total Carbohydrate, 1 g Dietary Fiber, 5 g Protein, 93 mg Calcium. **POINTS** per serving: 3.

# Caramel Cake with Bourbon-Pear Sauce

*Caramel syrup is quite easy to make, and it adds incomparable flavor without any fat.*

MAKES 12 SERVINGS

½ cup granulated sugar

½ cup boiling water

2¼ cups all-purpose flour

1 teaspoon baking powder

1 teaspoon baking soda

¼ teaspoon salt

¼ cup reduced-calorie tub margarine

¾ cup fat-free buttermilk, at room temperature

½ cup packed dark brown sugar

½ cup egg substitute, at room temperature

½ teaspoon vanilla extract

3 large Bosc pears, peeled, cored and cubed

2 teaspoons bourbon

1. To prepare the caramel syrup, in a medium saucepan over medium heat, combine the granulated sugar and 1 tablespoon water; cook, washing down the sides of the pan with a brush dipped in cold water and swirling the pan to keep the sugar moving, until it turns amber, 6–7 minutes (do not stir). Remove from the heat and carefully stir in the boiling water; cook, stirring constantly, until the sugar dissolves completely. Let cool.

2. Preheat the oven to 350° F; spray a 9" round cake pan with nonstick cooking spray.

3. In a medium bowl, combine the flour, baking powder, baking soda and salt.

4. In a large bowl, with an electric mixer on high speed, beat the margarine until creamy; add the buttermilk, brown sugar, egg substitute, vanilla and ¼ cup of the caramel syrup, beating until well blended. Gradually add the flour mixture, stirring just until combined. Scrape the batter into the pan. Bake until a toothpick inserted in the center comes out clean, 25–30 minutes. Cool in the pan 5 minutes; remove from the pan and cool completely on a rack.

5. Meanwhile, add the pears to the remaining caramel syrup in the medium saucepan; bring to a boil. Reduce the heat and simmer, covered, 15 minutes. Remove from the heat; with a fork or potato masher, lightly mash the pears until they resemble a chunky applesauce; stir in the bourbon. Pour into a medium serving bowl; let cool slightly. Serve the cake, topping each piece with the pear sauce.

**Per serving**: 228 Calories, 3 g Total Fat, 0 g Saturated Fat, 1 mg Cholesterol, 261 mg Sodium, 48 g Total Carbohydrate, 3 g Dietary Fiber, 4 g Protein, 64 mg Calcium. *POINTS* per serving: 4.

*Caramel Cake with Bourbon-Pear Sauce*

# Frosted Carrot Cake

*We've re-created the ever-popular carrot cake, down to the cream cheese frosting, in a newer, lighter version.*

MAKES 8 SERVINGS

¾ cup all-purpose flour

½ cup yellow cornmeal

1½ teaspoons baking powder

½ teaspoon cinnamon

¼ teaspoon salt

¼ teaspoon ground ginger

½ cup thawed frozen apple juice concentrate

1 egg

¼ cup fat-free milk

2 tablespoons + 2 teaspoons vegetable oil

2 tablespoons packed dark brown sugar

1 cup shredded carrots

½ cup golden raisins

½ cup light cream cheese

1 tablespoon honey

1. Preheat the oven to 375° F; spray a 9" Bundt pan with nonstick cooking spray.

2. In a medium bowl, combine the flour, cornmeal, baking powder, cinnamon, salt and ginger.

3. In a medium bowl, with an electric mixer on medium speed, beat the apple juice concentrate, egg, milk, oil and brown sugar; stir in the carrots and raisins. Gradually add the flour mixture, stirring just until combined. Scrape the batter into the pan. Bake until a toothpick inserted in the center comes out clean, 35–40 minutes. Cool completely in the pan on a rack.

4. Meanwhile, to prepare the frosting, in a food processor or blender, combine the cream cheese and honey; blend until smooth. Invert the cake onto serving platter; spread the frosting over top and sides.

**Per serving**: 243 Calories, 8 g Total Fat, 2 g Saturated Fat, 34 mg Cholesterol, 263 mg Sodium, 39 g Total Carbohydrate, 2 g Dietary Fiber, 5 g Protein, 103 mg Calcium. *POINTS* per serving: 5.

## Perfect Baking Everytime

*Baking is a pleasure with these no-fail baking tips:*

- *Always follow directions to preheat the oven.*

- *When several dry ingredients, such as baking powder, salt and spices are added together, measure them into a small cup. For a clean-up short-cut, use paper cups or muffin liners and toss them away once you have added the ingredients.*

- *Do the same for larger quantities like flour mixtures: Sift them onto a sheet of wax paper or a paper plate, then use the paper or plate to hold the spatula after you've scraped the mixing bowl. That way, you'll have fewer bowls to wash, and your counter will stay clean as well.*

- *If your stationary mixer head lifts up or your mixer is handheld, at the end of the mixing process, lift beaters slowly at the lowest setting, allowing the batter to spin off the mixing blades into the bowl.*

- *Most baked goods freeze well. Use moisture- and vapor-proof wrapping; press out all of the air and then seal. Label containers with the name, date and portion size. Use within 2–3 months.*

# Brandied Fruit Cake

*Though the ingredients list seems long, this holiday staple is a breeze to make—and gets results even fruit cake loathers will love.*

MAKES 12 SERVINGS

1¼ cups all-purpose flour

1 cup whole-wheat flour

1 teaspoon baking powder

1 teaspoon baking soda

¼ teaspoon salt

¼ cup reduced-calorie tub margarine

½ cup packed dark brown sugar

1 tablespoon grated peeled gingerroot

1 teaspoon cinnamon

½ teaspoon ground nutmeg

¼ teaspoon ground cloves

1 cup fat-free buttermilk

½ cup egg substitute

1 teaspoon grated orange zest

1 teaspoon grated lemon zest

1 teaspoon vanilla extract

12 dried apricot halves, chopped

½ cup golden raisins

6 large pitted prunes, chopped

6 dried dates, pitted and chopped

3 tablespoons brandy, bourbon or rum

1. Preheat the oven to 350° F; spray a 9" Bundt pan with nonstick cooking spray.

2. Sift the all-purpose flour, whole-wheat flour, baking powder, baking soda and salt into a medium bowl.

3. In a large bowl, with an electric mixer on high speed, beat the margarine until creamy; add the brown sugar, gingerroot, cinnamon, nutmeg and cloves, beating until fluffy. Add the buttermilk, egg substitute, orange zest, lemon zest and vanilla, beating until well blended. Gradually add the flour mixture, stirring just until combined. Gently stir in the apricots, raisins, prunes, dates and brandy. Scrape the batter into the pan. Bake until a toothpick inserted in the center comes out clean, 35–40 minutes. Cool in the pan 5 minutes, then remove from the pan and cool completely on a rack.

**Per serving**: 212 Calories, 3 g Total Fat, 1 g Saturated Fat, 1 mg Cholesterol, 268 mg Sodium, 42 g Total Carbohydrate, 3 g Dietary Fiber, 5 g Protein, 76 mg Calcium. *POINTS* per serving: 4.

## Tip

If you have the time, soak the dried fruit in the brandy for a few hours—or a few days—in a tightly covered container.

# Rolled Orange Sponge Cake

*Here's one recipe guaranteed to dazzle—and it's practically foolproof. When you beat the egg whites, be sure to start with a squeaky-clean and dry bowl and beaters for best results.*

MAKES 10 SERVINGS

2 tablespoons confectioners' sugar

4 eggs, separated

3 egg whites, at room temperature

$\frac{3}{4}$ cup granulated sugar

2 tablespoons finely grated orange zest

1 tablespoon fresh lemon juice

$\frac{1}{8}$ teaspoon salt

$\frac{3}{4}$ cup + 3 tablespoons sifted cake flour

$\frac{1}{2}$ cup + 2 tablespoons orange spreadable fruit

1. Preheat the oven to 350° F. Line a $15\frac{1}{2} \times 10\frac{1}{2} \times 1$" jelly-roll pan with wax paper; dust a clean dish towel with 1 tablespoon of the confectioners' sugar.

2. In a medium bowl, with an electric mixer on medium speed, beat all 7 of the egg whites until soft peaks form.

3. In a large bowl, with a whisk, beat the egg yolks until thick; gradually whisk in the granulated sugar, beating until thick and light. Add the orange zest, lemon juice and salt; beat to combine. Gradually stir in the cake flour, mixing well. Stir one-fourth of the egg whites into the batter; with a rubber spatula, gently fold in the remaining whites. Spread the batter in the pan. Bake until golden and the top springs back when touched lightly with finger, 12–15 minutes.

4. Run a knife around the edge of the pan; invert the cake onto the dish towel. Peel the wax paper off the cake. Starting at the narrow end, roll up the cake with the towel. Transfer to a rack and cool completely.

5. Unroll the cake and remove the towel. Spread the spreadable fruit over the cake; reroll. Place the cake, seam-side down, on a platter; sprinkle with the remaining tablespoon of confectioners' sugar.

**Per serving:** 175 Calories, 2 g Total Fat, 1 g Saturated Fat, 85 mg Cholesterol, 70 mg Sodium, 35 g Total Carbohydrate, 0 g Dietary Fiber, 4 g Protein, 14 mg Calcium. **POINTS** per serving: 4.

# Banana Cupcakes

*Save your extra-ripe bananas for this recipe. They'll keep in the refrigerator for 2–3 days, though their skins will turn black.*

MAKES 12 SERVINGS

2¼ cups all-purpose flour

1 teaspoon baking powder

½ teaspoon baking soda

⅛ teaspoon salt

4 ripe bananas, cut into chunks

1 cup fat-free buttermilk

½ cup reduced-calorie tub margarine

¼ cup + 3 tablespoons packed light brown sugar

1 egg, at room temperature

½ cup currants

1¼ cups part-skim ricotta cheese

2 tablespoons unsweetened cocoa powder

1 tablespoon rum

1. Preheat the oven to 350° F; line a 12-cup muffin tin with double papers.

2. Sift the flour, baking powder, baking soda and salt into a medium bowl.

3. In a large bowl, with an electric mixer on medium speed, beat the bananas, buttermilk, margarine, ¼ cup of the brown sugar and the egg. Stir in the flour mixture just until blended. Stir in the currants. Fill the muffin cups two-thirds full with the batter. Bake until a toothpick inserted in center comes out clean, about 30 minutes. Cool completely in the pan on a rack.

4. Meanwhile, to prepare the frosting, in a food processor or blender, combine the ricotta, the remaining 3 tablespoons of brown sugar, the cocoa powder and rum; blend until smooth. Spread the frosting on the cooled cupcakes.

**Per serving**: 254 Calories, 7 g Total Fat, 2 g Saturated Fat, 26 mg Cholesterol, 253 mg Sodium, 42 g Total Carbohydrate, 2 g Dietary Fiber, 7 g Protein, 137 mg Calcium. **POINTS** per serving: 5.

# Lemon Angel Food Cake with Berries

*Who says a fat-free dessert can't be delicious and elegant? Try using orange-flavored liqueur instead of raspberry for a tempting variation.*

MAKES 12 SERVINGS

1½ cups sugar

1 cup + 2 tablespoons sifted cake flour

¼ teaspoon salt

12 egg whites, at room temperature

1¼ teaspoons cream of tartar

1 tablespoon + 1 teaspoon grated lemon zest

1 teaspoon vanilla extract

2¼ cups raspberries

2¼ cups sliced strawberries

2 tablespoons raspberry liqueur (framboise)

1. Preheat the oven to 375° F; arrange an oven rack in the lower third of the oven. Sift ¾ cup of the sugar, the cake flour and salt onto a sheet of wax paper.

2. In a large bowl, with an electric mixer on low speed, beat the egg whites until small bubbles appear and the surface is frothy, 1–2 minutes. Sprinkle with the cream of tartar; with the mixer on medium speed, add the remaining ¾ cup of sugar in a slow, steady stream, beating until all the sugar is incorporated. With a rubber spatula, scrape the sides and bottom of the bowl. Add 1 tablespoon of the lemon zest and the vanilla; beat until the egg whites are stiff but not dry.

3. Sift one-third of the flour mixture over the egg whites; with the rubber spatula, quickly fold into the whites, being careful to scrape the sides and bottom of the bowl. Repeat with the remaining flour mixture, making sure all the flour is blended into the whites. Scrape the batter into an ungreased 9" or 10" tube pan; with the spatula, smooth the surface. Bake in the lower third of the oven until a toothpick inserted in center of the cake comes out clean, 25–30 minutes. Run a knife around the edge of the pan; invert the cake onto a platter and cool completely.

4. Meanwhile, in a large bowl, combine the raspberries, strawberries, liqueur and the remaining 1 teaspoon of lemon zest; let stand 30 minutes. Serve the cake, topping each slice with the berries.

**Per serving:** 175 Calories, 0 g Total Fat, 0 g Saturated Fat, 0 mg Cholesterol, 101 mg Sodium, 38 g Total Carbohydrate, 2 g Dietary Fiber, 5 g Protein, 14 mg Calcium. *POINTS* per serving: 3.

## Tip

**To get the fluffiest egg whites, start with the whites at room temperature, and use a metal bowl (copper is ideal). Clean the bowl and beaters until they're scrupulously clean, and wipe them absolutely dry with a paper towel (any grease or water hinders foaming).**

# Mocha-Cinnamon Angel Food Cake

*Cream of tartar—essential to making angel food cakes—is a powder derived from the acid deposits that form on the inside of wine barrels. It helps make egg whites more stable, and hold more air when they are beaten.*

MAKES 12 SERVINGS

1½ cups granulated sugar

½ cup + 1 tablespoon sifted cake flour

½ cup unsweetened cocoa powder

1 teaspoon cinnamon

1 teaspoon espresso powder or instant-coffee granules

¼ teaspoon salt

12 egg whites, at room temperature

1¼ teaspoons cream of tartar

2 teaspoons vanilla extract

1 tablespoon confectioners' sugar (optional)

1. Preheat the oven to 375° F; arrange an oven rack in the lower third of the oven. Sift ¾ cup of the sugar, the cake flour, cocoa powder, cinnamon, espresso powder and salt onto a sheet of wax paper.

2. In a medium bowl, with an electric mixer on low speed, beat the egg whites until frothy and small bubbles appear, 1–2 minutes. Sprinkle with the cream of tartar; with the mixer on medium speed, add the remaining ¾ cup sugar in a slow, steady stream, beating until all the sugar is incorporated. With a rubber spatula, scrape the sides and bottom of bowl. Add the vanilla; beat until the egg whites are stiff but not dry.

3. Sift one-third of the flour mixture over the egg whites; with the rubber spatula, quickly fold into the whites, being careful to scrape the sides and bottom of the bowl. Repeat with the remaining flour mixture, making sure all the flour is blended into the whites. Scrape the batter into an ungreased 9" or 10" tube pan; with the spatula, smooth the surface. Bake in the lower third of the oven until a toothpick inserted in the center of the cake comes out clean, 25–30 minutes. Run a knife around the edge of the pan; invert the cake onto a platter and cool completely. Dust with the confectioners' sugar (if using).

**Per serving**: 144 Calories, 1 g Total Fat, 0 g Saturated Fat, 0 mg Cholesterol, 101 mg Sodium, 32 g Total Carbohydrate, 1 g Dietary Fiber, 5 g Protein, 10 mg Calcium. **POINTS** per serving: 3.

# Pumpkin Cheesecake

*An amazingly rich-tasting cheesecake, just right to serve as the finale to a holiday meal.*

MAKES 6 SERVINGS

9 graham crackers (2½" squares), made into crumbs

1 cup low-fat (1%) cottage cheese

¾ cup part-skim ricotta cheese

¾ cup egg substitute

½ cup sugar

1 teaspoon ground ginger

1 teaspoon vanilla extract

½ teaspoon ground nutmeg

½ teaspoon cinnamon

⅛ teaspoon salt

One 15-ounce canned pumpkin puree

1. Preheat the oven to 350° F; spray a 9" glass pie plate with nonstick cooking spray. Sprinkle the graham cracker crumbs over the bottom of the pie plate.

2. In a food processor or blender, combine the cottage cheese and ricotta; process until smooth, about 1 minute. Transfer to a large bowl; stir in the egg substitute, sugar, ginger, vanilla, nutmeg, cinnamon and salt. Reserve ¼ cup of the batter. Add the pumpkin to the batter; stir until blended.

Scrape the batter into the pie plate, then drizzle the reserved batter in 3 concentric circles over the pumpkin batter. With a knife, lightly draw a line through the batter from the center toward the outer edge; about 2" from that line, lightly draw the knife through the batter from the outer edge toward the center. Repeat around the pie, alternating directions, to make a spiderweb.

3. Bake until a knife inserted in the center comes out clean, 45–50 minutes. Cool completely on rack. Refrigerate, covered, until ready to serve.

**Per serving**: 218 Calories, 4 g Total Fat, 2 g Saturated Fat, 11 mg Cholesterol, 344 mg Sodium, 33 g Total Carbohydrate, 1 g Dietary Fiber, 12 g Protein, 138 mg Calcium. *POINTS* per serving: 4.

*Pumpkin Cheesecake*

# Cheesecake

*Thanks to light cream cheese and nonfat sour cream, you can still enjoy your favorite creamy dessert.*

MAKES 16 SERVINGS

12 graham crackers (2½" squares), made into crumbs

2 cups light cream cheese

1 cup nonfat sour cream

½ cup sugar

2 teaspoons vanilla extract

2 eggs

2 teaspoons grated lemon zest

1. Preheat the oven to 325° F; wrap the outside of a 10" springform pan with heavy-duty foil; then spray the inside entirely with nonstick cooking spray. Sprinkle the graham cracker crumbs over the bottom and partially up the sides of the pan.

2. In a large bowl, with an electric mixer on medium speed, beat the cream cheese, sour cream, sugar and vanilla until smooth. Add the eggs, one at a time, beating on low speed until blended; stir in the lemon zest. Pour the batter into the pan. Set the springform pan into a large roasting pan; pour boiling water into the roasting pan to come halfway up the sides of the springform pan. Bake until almost completely set, 30–35 minutes. Turn off the oven and prop open the door with a wooden spoon; leave the cake in the oven 30 minutes. Transfer to a rack and run a knife around the edge of the pan to release the cake. Cool completely, then refrigerate, covered, until ready to serve.

**Per serving**: 128 Calories, 6 g Total Fat, 3 g Saturated Fat, 42 mg Cholesterol, 210 mg Sodium, 14 g Total Carbohydrate, 0 g Dietary Fiber, 5 g Protein, 64 mg Calcium. **POINTS** per serving: 3.

## Just Desserts

*Be sure to get your just desserts by following these tips to bake the best cakes and cookies!*

- *Cakes and cookies bake best in shiny aluminum, tin or stainless-steel pans which allow for the most even distribution of heat. Check the pans for smooth seams to make cleaning easier.*

- *Use a cold baking sheet for each batch of cookies; the batter will begin to spread and melt on a warm sheet.*

- *Cookies are done when they are a little brown around the edges and an imprint remains when gently pressed in the center. Adjust the baking time if the first batch comes out over- or underdone.*

- *As a general rule, cake and muffin batter should fill a pan by no more than two-thirds. During baking, the batter will rise just to or slightly above the rim. If you use a larger pan than called for, the cake will end up flat; if your pan is smaller than called for, the batter might overflow, causing a cracked or wrinkled surface—and a messy oven.*

- *Because heat rises, oven temperatures are not uniform throughout. For best results, place baking pans in the center of the oven, and do not place one pan directly over another. If necessary, stagger pans on the same rack so they don't touch each other or the sides of the oven. If you're baking two sheets of cookies or two cake pans simultaneously, reverse the pans top and bottom halfway through the baking time for more even baking and browning.*

# Double Apple Strudel

*Like Grandmother's, but better! Keep phyllo dough covered with a slightly damp towel while you work, as it dries out quickly.*

MAKES 12 SERVINGS

3 apples, peeled, cored and diced

18 slices dried apple, coarsely chopped

¼ cup + 2 tablespoons dark raisins

⅓ cup sugar

2 tablespoons cornstarch

½ teaspoon cinnamon

1 teaspoon vanilla extract

¾ cup walnuts

4 gingersnap cookies

¼ cup reduced-calorie tub margarine, melted

Twelve 12 × 17" sheets phyllo dough, at room temperature

1. To prepare the filling, in a large nonstick skillet, combine the apples, dried apple, raisins, sugar, cornstarch, cinnamon and ½ cup water. Cook, covered, stirring occasionally, until the apples are very tender and the mixture thickens. Stir in the vanilla; cool completely.

2. In a food processor, combine the walnuts and gingersnaps; pulse to form crumbs.

3. Preheat the oven to 375° F; spray a jelly-roll pan with nonstick cooking spray. Reserve 2 teaspoons of the margarine. To assemble the strudel, place a sheet of phyllo on a clean, dry towel, keeping the remaining phyllo covered with a damp towel; lightly brush with some of the margarine. Top with another sheet of the phyllo; lightly brush with some more margarine and sprinkle with 1 tablespoon of the crumbs. Repeat using all of the phyllo, crumb mixture and margarine, ending with the phyllo.

4. Spoon the apple filling over the phyllo, leaving a 2" border. Using the towel to lift the edges and starting at the wide end, roll the strudel, jelly-roll style, enclosing filling. Place, seam-side down, on the pan; brush the top with the 2 teaspoons of margarine. Make 11 shallow cuts through the top layers of phyllo (do not cut into filling). Bake until golden, 40–45 minutes. Cool 10 minutes, then cut at scored sections.

**Per serving**: 210 Calories, 8 g Total Fat, 1 g Saturated Fat, 0 mg Cholesterol, 154 mg Sodium, 34 g Total Carbohydrate, 1 g Dietary Fiber, 3 g Protein, 16 mg Calcium. *POINTS* per serving: 5.

# Baked Apples with Caramel Sauce

*For microwave "baked" apples, stuff the apples as described but place in a microwavable dish, covered and vented, with 1–2 tablespoons of water. Microwave on High for about 5–7 minutes.*

MAKES 4 SERVINGS

### Apples

24 dried apricot halves, chopped

4 teaspoons packed dark brown sugar

1 teaspoon vanilla extract

4 small Granny Smith apples, cored

### Caramel Sauce

½ cup evaporated skimmed milk

4 teaspoons packed dark brown sugar

1 teaspoon cornstarch

Pinch salt

½ teaspoon vanilla extract

1. Preheat the oven to 350° F. In a small bowl, combine the apricots, brown sugar and vanilla. Pack into the apple cavities, then wrap each apple in foil. Bake until soft, 40–45 minutes.

2. Meanwhile, to prepare the caramel sauce, in a small saucepan over medium heat, combine ¼ cup of the milk, the brown sugar, cornstarch and salt, stirring until smooth, then stir in the remaining milk; bring just to a boil, stirring constantly. Reduce the heat and cook 1 minute longer. Remove from the heat and stir in the vanilla. Serve the apples, drizzled with the caramel sauce.

**Per serving:** 180 Calories, 1 g Total Fat, 0 g Saturated Fat, 1 mg Cholesterol, 75 mg Sodium, 43 g Total Carbohydrate, 4 g Dietary Fiber, 3 g Protein, 117 g Calcium. **POINTS** per serving: 3.

# Apple Betty

*This low-fat take on the traditional crumb-topped cake is a snap to make. It can easily be halved—or even quartered, for solitary sumptuousness! Try combining varieties of apples like Fuji, Braeburn and Granny Smith.*

MAKES 4 SERVINGS

4 apples, peeled, cored and sliced

4 slices reduced-calorie whole-wheat or multigrain bread, lightly toasted

2 tablespoons packed light brown sugar

1 teaspoon cinnamon

2 teaspoons reduced-calorie margarine

1. Preheat the oven to 375° F; spray a 1½-quart shallow casserole with nonstick cooking spray. Place half of the apples in the casserole.

2. In a food processor or blender, process the toast to coarse crumbs. Transfer to a small bowl; combine with the brown sugar and cinnamon. Sprinkle half the mixture over the apples, then layer the remaining apples and crumb mixture. Dot with the margarine; add ⅓ cup water. Bake until the top is crisp and the fruit is bubbling, about 45 minutes.

**Per serving:** 175 Calories, 2 g Total Fat, 0 g Saturated Fat, 0 mg Cholesterol, 139 mg Sodium, 41 g Total Carbohydrate, 7 g Dietary Fiber, 3 g Protein, 48 mg Calcium. **POINTS** per serving: 2.

# Apple Cobbler

*Use the reduced-fat version of buttermilk baking mix if you can find it; you'll cut fat without sacrificing any goodness in this homey dessert.*

MAKES 4 SERVINGS

4 apples, peeled, cored and sliced

2 tablespoons sugar

1 tablespoon fresh lemon juice

¾ cup buttermilk baking mix

¼ cup low-fat buttermilk

½ teaspoon ground cardamom

1. Preheat the oven to 350° F; spray a 1-quart baking dish with nonstick cooking spray.

2. In a medium saucepan, combine the apples, 1 tablespoon of the sugar and the lemon juice; bring to a boil. Reduce the heat and simmer, stirring constantly, until the apples are soft, about 5 minutes. Pour into the baking dish.

3. In a small bowl, combine the baking mix, buttermilk, the remaining tablespoon of sugar and the cardamom; stir until smooth. With a spoon, drop the batter over the fruit. Bake until browned, 20–25 minutes. Serve warm.

**Per serving**: 191 Calories, 4 g Total Fat, 1 g Saturated Fat, 1 mg Cholesterol, 304 mg Sodium, 38 g Total Carbohydrate, 3 g Dietary Fiber, 4 g Protein, 43 mg Calcium. *POINTS* per serving: 4.

# Apple-Cranberry Crisp

*For a variation, use pears instead of apples, or a combination of both. Serve with a dollop of nonfat vanilla frozen yogurt or nondairy topping.*

MAKES 4 SERVINGS

½ cup quick-cooking rolled oats

4 tablespoons packed light brown sugar

1 tablespoon all-purpose flour

4 teaspoons cold reduced-calorie tub margarine

6 Empire or other firm cooking apples, peeled, cored and thinly sliced

1 cup fresh or frozen cranberries

1 tablespoon fresh lemon juice

¼ teaspoon cinnamon

⅛ teaspoon ground nutmeg

1. Preheat the oven to 375° F, spray an 8" square baking dish with nonstick cooking spray.

2. In a small bowl, combine the oats, 2 tablespoons of the brown sugar and the flour; with two knives or your fingers; work in the margarine until crumbly.

3. In a large bowl, combine the apples, cranberries, the remaining 2 tablespoons of brown sugar, the lemon juice, cinnamon and nutmeg; toss to combine. Spoon into the pan; sprinkle with the oats mixture. Bake until the filling is bubbling and the topping is golden brown, 35–40 minutes.

**Per serving**: 190 Calories, 3 g Total Fat, 1 g Saturated Fat, 0 mg Cholesterol, 44 mg Sodium, 41 g Total Carbohydrate, 3 g Dietary Fiber, 2 g Protein, 26 mg Calcium. *POINTS* per serving: 3.

# Peach Bars

*Thanks to peach spreadable fruit, these bars have all the goodness of peaches without any extra sugar.*

## MAKES 24 SERVINGS

2¼ cups all-purpose flour, sifted

½ teaspoon baking powder

¼ teaspoon salt

1 cup packed light brown sugar

1 cup reduced-calorie tub margarine, at room temperature

1 egg, at room temperature

½ teaspoon almond extract

¼ cup + 2 tablespoons peach spreadable fruit

1. Preheat the oven to 350° F; spray a 9" square baking pan with nonstick cooking spray.

2. In a medium bowl, combine the flour, baking powder and salt.

3. In a large bowl, with an electric mixer on medium-high speed, cream the brown sugar and margarine until pale and fluffy; beat in the egg and almond extract. With the mixer on low speed, gradually beat in the flour mixture, beating until blended. Scrape the batter into the pan, smoothing the surface with a rubber spatula. With a spoon, drop the spreadable fruit over the batter. Bake until lightly browned and the batter begins to pull away from the sides of the pan, 25–30 minutes. Cool completely on a rack.

**Per serving:** 125 Calories, 4 g Total Fat, 1 g Saturated Fat, 9 mg Cholesterol, 112 mg Sodium, 21 g Total Carbohydrate, 0 g Dietary Fiber, 1 g Protein, 16 mg Calcium. *POINTS* per serving: 3.

# Quick Pear Tartlets

*To ripen pears at home, simply keep them in a bowl or basket at room temperature for a few days—when the skin near the stem yields to gentle pressure, they're ripe. If you like, chop a few pieces of crystallized ginger; add to the filling with the currants and sugar.*

## MAKES 4 SERVINGS

### Crust

¼ cup wheat-and-barley cereal nuggets

2 tablespoons currants

1 teaspoon packed dark brown sugar

¼ teaspoon unsweetened cocoa powder

¼ teaspoon vanilla extract

### Filling

3 large pears, peeled, cored and diced

2 tablespoons currants

2 tablespoons packed dark brown sugar

¼ cup light frozen nondairy whipped topping, thawed

1. In a mini food processor or blender, combine the crust ingredients; process until well blended.

2. To prepare the filling, in a small saucepan over low heat, combine the pears and ½ cup water; cook, covered, until the pears just begin to soften, 4–5 minutes. Stir in the currants and brown sugar; cook 5 minutes longer.

3. Divide the crust mixture among four 4" tartlet pans, pressing it over the bottom and up the sides to form a crust. Divide the filling among the crusts; let cool slightly, then top with the whipped topping.

**Per serving:** 230 Calories, 2 g Total Fat, 0 g Saturated Fat, 0 mg Cholesterol, 51 mg Sodium, 56 g Total Carbohydrate, 7 g Dietary Fiber, 2 g Protein, 43 mg Calcium. *POINTS* per serving: 3.

# Strawberry-Rhubarb Tartlets

*When buying rhubarb, choose brightly colored stalks with fresh-looking leaves—but never eat the leaves, since they can be toxic. The tartness of rhubarb and the sweetness of strawberries make a truly sweet tart!*

MAKES 4 SERVINGS

6 graham crackers (2½" squares)

2 teaspoons reduced-calorie margarine, melted

3 cups chopped rhubarb

⅓ cup sugar

Pinch salt

1 teaspoon cornstarch, dissolved in 1 teaspoon water

1½ cups sliced strawberries

¼ cup + 2 tablespoons nonfat cream cheese

2 tablespoons nonfat sour cream

¾ teaspoon vanilla extract

1. To prepare the crust, in a food processor or blender, whirl the graham crackers until finely crushed. Add the margarine and process until well blended. Divide the crust among four 4" tartlet pans, pressing it over the bottom and up the sides to form a crust.

2. To prepare the filling, in a medium saucepan over low heat, combine the rhubarb, all but 1 teaspoon of the sugar and the salt with ¼ cup water. Cook, stirring occasionally, until the rhubarb is soft, about 15 minutes. Stir in the dissolved cornstarch; bring to a boil over medium-high heat. Reduce the heat and cook, stirring constantly, 30 seconds longer. Remove from the heat and stir in the strawberries. Divide among the tartlet pans; refrigerate, covered, until chilled, 1–2 hours.

3. To prepare the topping, in a small bowl, combine the cream cheese, sour cream, the remaining teaspoon of sugar and the vanilla; stir until smooth. Spread over the tartlets; cover and refrigerate until firm, 2–3 hours.

**Per serving**: 194 Calories, 2 g Total Fat, 0 g Saturated Fat, 2 mg Cholesterol, 226 mg Sodium, 39 g Total Carbohydrate, 3 g Dietary Fiber, 5 g Protein, 159 mg Calcium. **POINTS** per serving: 3.

# Peach Soufflé

*Soufflés were meant to fall, so be sure to time this dish to make its appearance just before serving.*

MAKES 4 SERVINGS

5 tablespoons granulated sugar

2 peaches, peeled, pitted and sliced

1½ teaspoons fresh lemon juice

4 eggs, separated, at room temperature

2 egg whites, at room temperature

4 tablespoons confectioners' sugar

1. Preheat the oven to 450° F. Spray a 6-cup soufflé dish with nonstick cooking spray, then coat the bottom and sides of the dish with 2 tablespoons of the granulated sugar; refrigerate.

2. In a blender or food processor, combine the remaining 3 tablespoons of granulated sugar, the peaches and lemon juice; puree. Add the egg yolks and blend; transfer to a large bowl.

3. In a medium bowl, with an electric mixer on medium speed, beat all of the egg whites until stiff peaks form. Sprinkle with 3 tablespoons of the confectioners' sugar; beat until stiff peaks form again. Stir one-fourth of the egg whites into the peach mixture; with a rubber spatula, fold in the remaining whites.

4. Scrape the batter into the soufflé dish; place in a small roasting pan. Pour hot (not boiling) water halfway up the sides of the roasting pan. Bake 10 minutes. Put the remaining tablespoon of confectioners' sugar in a small sieve; shake over the soufflé as you remove it from the oven. Serve at once.

**Per serving**: 202 Calories, 5 g Total Fat, 2 g Saturated Fat, 213 mg Cholesterol, 91 mg Sodium, 31 g Total Carbohydrate, 1 g Dietary Fiber, 8 g Protein, 29 mg Calcium. *POINTS* per serving: 4.

## Tip

**To make a nectarine soufflé, substitute 2 small nectarines for the peaches.**

# Peaches in Red Wine

*If you prefer, peel the skin from the peaches. Cut a shallow × in the bottom of the peaches, then plunge them into boiling water for 30 seconds; submerge in ice water—the skin will peel off effortlessly.*

MAKES 4 SERVINGS

6 medium peaches, pitted and sliced

1 cup dry red wine

2 teaspoons sugar

Fresh mint sprigs, to garnish

In a medium bowl, combine the peaches, wine and sugar; let stand at room temperature 30 minutes. Spoon into 4 dessert dishes and serve garnished with the mint.

**Per serving:** 127 Calories, 0 g Total Fat, 0 g Saturated Fat, 0 mg Cholesterol, 3 mg Sodium, 23 g Total Carbohydrate, 3 g Dietary Fiber, 2 g Protein, 14 mg Calcium. **POINTS** per serving: 2.

## Get the Brown Out

*To keep cut-up fresh fruit from turning brown, try this tip.*

- *Peel, core and slice the fruit. Dip the fruit into a bowl of acidulated water or lemon juice (you can also use a bowl of ascorbic-acid color keeper). Drain the fruit on a paper towel.*

# Apple-Oatmeal Cookies

*Toast the oats to bring out their nutty flavor.*

MAKES 12 SERVINGS

1½ cups quick-cooking rolled oats, toasted until lightly browned

½ cup all-purpose flour

½ teaspoon cinnamon

¼ teaspoon baking soda

¼ teaspoon salt

¼ cup packed light brown sugar

¼ cup reduced-calorie tub margarine

1 apple, peeled, cored and coarsely grated

1 egg

½ teaspoon vanilla extract

¼ cup + 2 tablespoons dark raisins

1. Preheat the oven to 350° F; spray 2 baking sheets with nonstick cooking spray.

2. In a large bowl, combine the oats, flour, cinnamon, baking soda and salt.

3. In a medium bowl, with an electric mixer on high speed, cream the brown sugar and margarine until pale and fluffy. Add the apple, egg and vanilla; beat until combined. Add the oats mixture; stir to blend, then stir in the raisins.

4. Drop the dough by tablespoons onto the baking sheets, forming 12 cookies on each sheet; flatten with the back of a spoon. Bake until lightly browned, 12–15 minutes. Cool completely on a rack. Store in an airtight container.

**Per serving:** 125 Calories, 3 g Total Fat, 1 g Saturated Fat, 18 mg Cholesterol, 116 mg Sodium, 22 g Total Carbohydrate, 1 g Dietary Fiber, 3 g Protein, 16 mg Calcium. **POINTS** per serving: 3.

# Fruity Oatmeal Cookies

*Dried apricots make a tasty, tangy alternative to raisins in these giant, chewy cookies that are full of good old-fashioned flavor. Double the recipe if you like; they freeze well.*

MAKES 8 SERVINGS

6 medium pitted prunes

½ cup rolled oats

¼ cup + 2 tablespoons all-purpose flour

2 tablespoons whole-wheat flour

1 teaspoon cinnamon

¾ teaspoon ground ginger

½ teaspoon baking powder

½ teaspoon salt

¼ cup + 1 tablespoon packed dark brown sugar

4 teaspoons reduced-calorie margarine

1 egg, lightly beaten

1 tablespoon light molasses

24 dried apricot halves, chopped

1. Preheat the oven to 350° F; spray a nonstick baking sheet with nonstick cooking spray. In blender or mini food processor, combine the prunes with 2 teaspoons water; puree.

2. In a large bowl, combine the oats, all-purpose flour, whole-wheat flour, cinnamon, ginger, baking powder and salt. In a medium bowl, beat the brown sugar and margarine until smooth; beat in the prune puree, egg and molasses. Add to the oats mixture, stirring just until combined; stir in the apricots.

3. Drop the batter by ¼ cup measures onto the baking sheet, forming 4 cookies; flatten with the back of a spoon. Bake until firm and lightly browned, 25 minutes. Cool completely on a rack.

**Per serving:** 145 Calories, 3 g Total Fat, 0 g Saturated Fat, 26 mg Cholesterol, 200 mg Sodium, 30 g Total Carbohydrate, 2 g Dietary Fiber, 3 g Protein, 49 mg Calcium. **POINTS** per serving: 3.

*Clockwise from upper right: Fruity Oatmeal Cookies, Double Chocolate Hazelnut Biscotti (page 364), Peanut Butter Cookies (page 366), Lemon Poppy Seed Crisps (page 365)*

# Double Chocolate Hazelnut Biscotti

*(pictured on page 363)*

---

*These taste like crispy brownies; they are perfect for dipping into a cup of hazelnut coffee.*

MAKES 40 SERVINGS

¾ cup hazelnuts, chopped

1¾ cups all-purpose flour

¾ cup mini semisweet chocolate chips

½ cup unsweetened Dutch-process cocoa powder

1 tablespoon instant espresso or coffee powder

1 teaspoon baking soda

¼ teaspoon salt

1 cup sugar

2 eggs

2 egg whites

1 tablespoon vanilla extract

1. Preheat the oven to 350° F. Adjust the oven racks to divide the oven into thirds. Place the hazelnuts on a baking sheet; bake until light brown, about 8 minutes. Let cool slightly. Line 2 large baking sheets with foil and spray the foil with nonstick cooking spray.

2. In a food processor, combine 2 tablespoons of the hazelnuts, the flour, 2 tablespoons of the chocolate chips, the cocoa, espresso powder, baking soda and salt. Process until the nuts are finely ground; transfer the dry ingredients to a large bowl. In the food processor (no need to clean), combine the sugar, eggs, egg whites and vanilla; whirl until slightly thickened, about 2 minutes. Add to the dry ingredients. Stir in the remaining hazelnuts and chocolate chips.

3. Spoon one-fourth of the batter (about ¾ cup) into a long log, about 14" long and 1½" wide, on one side of the baking sheet; repeat with the remaining batter, making 2 logs on each baking sheet, with space in between. Bake, reversing the baking sheets once, until firm, about 15 minutes; cool on the pans on racks 10 minutes. Reduce the oven temperature to 300° F.

4. Place the logs on a cutting board. Cut with a serrated knife on the diagonal into ½" thick slices, making 80 biscotti. Place the slices upright on the baking sheets, 1" apart. Bake until the cut sides feel dry to the touch, 20–25 minutes. Cool completely on wire racks. Store in an airtight container.

**Per serving:** 75 Calories, 3 g Total Fat, 1 g Saturated Fat, 11 mg Cholesterol, 53 mg Sodium, 12 g Total Carbohydrate, 1 g Dietary Fiber, 2 g Protein, 8 mg Calcium. **POINTS** per serving: 2.

# Lemon–Poppy Seed Crisps

*(pictured on page 363)*

---

*These pretty crisps are delicious on their own, or spread them with a little light cream cheese.*

MAKES 8 SERVINGS

¾ cup all-purpose flour

1 tablespoon poppy seeds

¼ cup sugar

3 tablespoons reduced-calorie tub margarine

1 teaspoon grated lemon zest

Pinch salt

1. Preheat the oven to 350° F; spray a nonstick baking sheet with nonstick cooking spray.

2. In a small bowl, combine the flour and poppy seeds.

3. In a large bowl, with an electric mixer on medium-high speed, beat the sugar, margarine, lemon zest and salt until pale and fluffy. With the mixer at low speed, beat in the flour mixture just until combined. Gather the dough into a ball; wrap half in plastic wrap and refrigerate.

4. Roll out the remaining dough between 2 sheets of wax paper, forming a 7" circle. With a fluted pastry wheel or pizza cutter, cut into 16 equal wedges. With a spatula, transfer the wedges to the baking sheet. Repeat with the refrigerated dough. Bake until just golden, 10–12 minutes. Cool completely on a rack.

**Per serving**: 90 Calories, 3 g Total Fat, 0 g Saturated Fat, 0 mg Cholesterol, 54 mg Sodium, 15 g Total Carbohydrate, 0 g Dietary Fiber, 1 g Protein, 18 mg Calcium. *POINTS* per serving: 2.

## Tip

**If the dough is too soft to transfer the wedges to the baking sheet, replace the top sheet of wax paper and refrigerate the dough until it's easier to handle, 15–30 minutes.**

# Peanut Butter Cookies

*(pictured on page 363)*

---

*To make these cookies even more nutritious, substitute ½ cup whole-wheat pastry flour for ½ cup of the all-purpose flour.*

MAKES 12 SERVINGS

  1 cup + 2 tablespoons all-purpose flour

  ½ teaspoon baking soda

  ½ teaspoon salt

  ¼ cup reduced-calorie tub margarine

  ¼ cup natural chunky peanut butter

  ¼ cup + 2 tablespoons packed dark brown sugar

  1 egg

  ½ teaspoon vanilla extract

  ½ cup peanut butter chips

1. Preheat the oven to 350° F; spray 2 baking sheets with nonstick cooking spray.

2. In a medium bowl, combine the flour, baking soda and salt. In another medium bowl, with an electric mixer on high speed, cream the margarine and peanut butter. Gradually beat in the brown sugar; add the egg and vanilla, beating until fluffy. With the mixer on low speed, gradually beat in the flour mixture until blended. Stir in the peanut butter chips.

3. Drop the dough by generous tablespoons onto the baking sheets, forming 12 cookies on each sheet; with the back of a fork, lightly press each cookie to flatten in a checkerboard pattern. Bake until browned on bottom, 12–15 minutes. Cool completely on a rack. Store in an airtight container.

**Per serving:** 152 Calories, 7 g Total Fat, 1 g Saturated Fat, 18 mg Cholesterol, 219 mg Sodium, 19 g Total Carbohydrate, 0 g Dietary Fiber, 4 g Protein, 15 mg Calcium. *POINTS* per serving: 4.

# Raspberry Brownies

*Chocolate can be melted in a microwave oven, if you prefer. In a 1-quart glass bowl, microwave the chocolate chips on High 1½ minutes, stirring halfway through cooking.*

MAKES 8 SERVINGS

¾ cup semisweet chocolate chips

4 eggs, at room temperature

½ cup sugar

1 teaspoon vanilla extract

¼ teaspoon salt

½ cup reduced-calorie tub margarine, melted and cooled to room temperature

¾ cup all-purpose flour

½ cup raspberry spreadable fruit

1. Preheat the oven to 350° F; spray an 8" square baking pan with nonstick cooking spray.

2. In a double boiler over simmering water, melt the chocolate chips; remove from the heat and stir until smooth. Let cool to room temperature.

3. In a large bowl, with an electric mixer on high speed, beat the eggs and sugar until pale yellow and tripled in volume, about 7 minutes; beat in the vanilla and salt. Add the margarine; stir to blend. Stir in the flour, mixing well.

4. Pour half the mixture into a medium bowl. Stir the melted chocolate into one half and the spreadable fruit into the other. Scrape the chocolate batter into the pan, reserving ½ cup. Scrape the raspberry batter over the chocolate batter; scatter spoonfuls of the reserved chocolate batter over the raspberry batter. With a knife, cut through the batter to create a marbled effect. Bake until a toothpick inserted in center comes out almost clean, 20–25 minutes. Cool completely in the pan on a rack.

**Per serving**: 274 Calories, 12 g Total Fat, 4 g Saturated Fat, 106 mg Cholesterol, 211 mg Sodium, 39 g Total Carbohydrate, 0 g Dietary Fiber, 5 g Protein, 18 mg Calcium. *POINTS* per serving: 6.

## Tip

**If you don't have a microwave or a double boiler, here's a way to fashion a double boiler to melt the chocolate: Put an inch or so of water in a saucepan. Find a bowl that's slightly wider than the saucepan—the bowl should rest on the rim of the pan and should *not* touch the water.**

# Triple-Ginger Gingerbread

*Crystallized ginger is the surprise ingredient in this ginger trio; serve gingerbread warm with a cup of herbal tea.*

MAKES 12 SERVINGS

1¼ cups all-purpose flour

1 cup whole-wheat flour

1 teaspoon baking powder

1 teaspoon baking soda

¼ teaspoon salt

¼ cup reduced-calorie tub margarine

½ cup packed dark brown sugar

1 tablespoon grated peeled gingerroot

2 teaspoons ground ginger

¼ teaspoon ground cloves

1 cup fat-free buttermilk

½ cup egg substitute

2 tablespoons crystallized ginger, chopped

1 teaspoon vanilla extract

¼ cup + 2 tablespoons golden raisins

1. Preheat the oven to 350° F; spray an 8" square baking pan with nonstick cooking spray.

2. In a medium bowl, combine the all-purpose flour, whole-wheat flour, baking powder, baking soda and salt.

3. In a large bowl, with an electric mixer on high speed, beat the margarine until creamy; add the brown sugar, gingerroot, ground ginger and cloves, beating until fluffy. Stir in the buttermilk, egg substitute, crystallized ginger and vanilla; stir in the flour mixture, then fold in raisins. Scrape the batter into the pan. Bake until a toothpick inserted in the center comes out clean, 25–30 minutes. Cool completely in the pan on a rack.

**Per serving:** 171 Calories, 3 g Total Fat, 0 g Saturated Fat, 1 mg Cholesterol, 269 mg Sodium, 34 g Total Carbohydrate, 2 g Dietary Fiber, 4 g Protein, 72 mg Calcium. **POINTS** per serving: 3.

# Gingerbread Bars

*Glaze these bars with orange-flavored frosting—whisk together 1 cup confectioners' sugar and 2 tablespoons orange juice—to make them even more irresistible.*

MAKES 6 SERVINGS

1 cup + 2 tablespoons whole-wheat flour

1 cup + 2 tablespoons all-purpose flour

1 tablespoon finely minced orange zest

2¼ teaspoons ground ginger

1 teaspoon cinnamon

1 teaspoon baking powder

1 teaspoon baking soda

¼ teaspoon salt

⅛ teaspoon ground white pepper

¼ cup packed brown sugar

¼ cup reduced-calorie margarine

¼ cup unsweetened applesauce

1 cup low-fat buttermilk

3 egg whites

1. Preheat the oven to 350° F; spray an 8" square baking pan with nonstick cooking spray.

2. In a medium bowl, combine the whole-wheat flour, all-purpose flour, orange zest, ginger, cinnamon, baking powder, baking soda, salt and pepper.

3. In a large bowl, with an electric mixer on high speed, beat the brown sugar, margarine and applesauce until smooth; beat in the buttermilk and egg whites. Reduce the mixer speed to low; gradually beat in the flour mixture until blended.

4. Spread the batter into the baking pan. Bake until a toothpick inserted in the center comes out clean, 25–30 minutes. Cool completely in the pan on a rack.

**Per serving**: 265 Calories, 5 g Total Fat, 1 g Saturated Fat, 2 mg Cholesterol, 531 mg Sodium, 48 g Total Carbohydrate, 4 g Dietary Fiber, 9 g Protein, 120 mg Calcium. **POINTS** per serving: 5.

# Bread Pudding with Anise

*The strong licorice flavor of anise is treasured in Italian and Scandinavian baking. It makes this simple bread pudding something special.*

MAKES 4 SERVINGS

4 slices 2-day-old white bread

8 teaspoons reduced-calorie tub margarine

6 tablespoons golden raisins

2 cups low-fat (1%) milk

2 eggs

3 tablespoons honey

½ teaspoon anise seeds, lightly crushed

½ teaspoon vanilla extract

Pinch salt

1. Spray a 1½-quart casserole with nonstick cooking spray. Spread both sides of the bread with the margarine; cut each into quarters. Arrange 8 pieces in the casserole; sprinkle with 3 tablespoons of the raisins. Repeat with the remaining bread and raisins.

2. In a medium bowl, whisk the milk, eggs, honey, anise seeds, vanilla and salt; pour over the bread mixture. Let stand at room temperature 1 hour.

3. Preheat the oven to 350° F. Place the casserole in a roasting pan; pour hot (not boiling) water halfway up the sides of the roasting pan. Bake until a knife inserted in center of the egg mixture comes out clean, about 1 hour. Serve warm.

**Per serving**: 283 Calories, 9 g Total Fat, 2 g Saturated Fat, 111 mg Cholesterol, 336 mg Sodium, 43 g Total Carbohydrate, 1 g Dietary Fiber, 10 g Protein, 199 mg Calcium. *POINTS* per serving: 6.

## Got Leftovers?

**Around the holidays, try this recipe with a festive holiday bread like panettone or stollen. Or use whole-wheat or oatmeal bread for a fiber-rich variation.**

# Chocolate-Orange Pudding

*This rich tasting pudding gets most of its creaminess from naturally fat-free gelatin. When heating the gelatin, take care to heat just enough to dissolve, but no more. Otherwise, it will lose its gelling ability.*

MAKES 4 SERVINGS

1 envelope unflavored gelatin

1 cup low-fat (1%) milk

⅓ cup packed dark brown sugar

¾ cup part-skim ricotta cheese

¼ cup unsweetened cocoa powder

4 teaspoons orange liqueur

1 teaspoon vanilla extract

1. In a small saucepan, sprinkle the gelatin over the milk; let stand until softened, about 1 minute. Stir in the brown sugar; cook over medium-low heat, stirring constantly, until the gelatin completely dissolves, about 2 minutes (do not boil).

2. In blender, combine the ricotta, cocoa powder, orange liqueur and vanilla; puree on medium speed about 1 minute, scraping down the sides of the container as necessary. Reduce the speed to low and remove the knob in the lid; gradually add the milk mixture, blending until combined. Pour the pudding into each of four 6-ounce custard cups. Refrigerate, covered, until set, at least 2 hours.

**Per serving**: 193 Calories, 5 g Total Fat, 3 g Saturated Fat, 17 mg Cholesterol, 100 mg Sodium, 28 g Carbohydrate, 2 g Dietary Fiber, 10 g Protein, 224 mg Calcium. *POINTS* per serving: 4.

## Substitution

For a delicious twist on this recipe, use another flavored liqueur instead, such as framboise (raspberry), amaretto (almond) or hazelnut.

# Rice Pudding with Golden Raisins

*Arborio rice, the short-grain rice used to make risotto, is the key to the creaminess of this pudding with a homey, old-fashioned taste.*

MAKES 4 SERVINGS

2 cups fat-free milk

¼ cup sugar

1⅓ cups Arborio or other short-grain rice

2 eggs

¼ cup golden raisins

1 teaspoon vanilla extract

Pinch cinnamon

4 teaspoons reduced-calorie tub margarine

1. In a small saucepan, bring 1 cup of the milk, the sugar and 2 tablespoons water to a boil; stir in the rice. Reduce the heat and simmer, stirring occasionally, 30 minutes.

2. Preheat the oven to 325° F; spray a 1½-quart baking dish with nonstick cooking spray.

3. In a medium bowl, combine the remaining cup of milk, the eggs, raisins, vanilla and cinnamon; stir in the rice. Pour into the baking dish; dot with the margarine. Bake, stirring twice, about 25 minutes.

**Per serving**: 280 Calories, 5 g Total Fat, 1 g Saturated Fat, 109 mg Cholesterol, 133 mg Sodium, 49 g Total Carbohydrate, 1 g Dietary Fiber, 9 g Protein, 169 mg Calcium. *POINTS* per serving: 6.

# Banana "Cream" Pie

*An old-fashioned favorite with a new profile: A non-fat yogurt base replaces the traditional cream filling.*

MAKES 8 SERVINGS

12 graham crackers (2½" squares), made into crumbs

4 teaspoons margarine

4 bananas, thinly sliced on the diagonal

2 tablespoons fresh lime juice

1 envelope unflavored gelatin

⅓ cup sugar

1½ cups plain nonfat yogurt

1 teaspoon vanilla extract

Grated lime zest

1. Preheat the oven to 350° F; spray a 9" pie plate with nonstick cooking spray.

2. In a medium bowl, combine the graham cracker crumbs and margarine with a fork. Press into the bottom and up the sides of the pie plate. Bake until firm, 3–5 minutes; cool.

3. In another medium bowl, toss the bananas with the lime juice; reserve 1 cup. Arrange the remaining bananas over the crust.

4. In a small saucepan, sprinkle the gelatin over ½ cup cold water; let stand 2 minutes. Add the sugar; cook over medium-high heat, stirring constantly, until the mixture boils and the gelatin and sugar dissolve, 2–3 minutes. Remove from the heat; whisk in the yogurt and vanilla. Pour into the pie plate. Arrange the reserved bananas over the pie; sprinkle with the lime zest. Refrigerate, covered with plastic wrap, until chilled, 2–3 hours.

**Per serving**: 175 Calories, 3 g Total Fat, 1 g Saturated Fat, 1 mg Cholesterol, 120 mg Sodium, 33 g Total Carbohydrate, 1 g Dietary Fiber, 4 g Protein, 92 mg Calcium. *POINTS* per serving: 4.

*Banana "Cream" Pie*

# Toasted Coconut Custard

*Though coconut is high in saturated fat, you can still enjoy its flavor by using coconut extract (it's fat-free) and a sprinkle of real coconut, toasted to enhance its flavor.*

MAKES 4 SERVINGS

1 cup low-fat (1%) milk

⅓ cup instant nonfat dry milk powder

2 tablespoons sugar

1 teaspoon coconut extract

2 eggs

½ teaspoon vanilla extract

4 teaspoons shredded coconut, toasted until golden

1. Preheat the oven to 350° F; spray four 6-ounce custard cups with nonstick cooking spray.

2. In a medium saucepan over medium-high heat, combine the milk, dry milk, sugar and coconut extract; cook, stirring frequently, until the mixture boils and the sugar dissolves, 3–4 minutes.

3. In a medium bowl, whisk the eggs until light; gradually whisk in the hot milk mixture and vanilla. Pour into the custard cups; sprinkle with the coconut. Place the cups in a shallow roasting pan; pour hot (not boiling) water halfway up the sides of the pan. Bake until the custards are set and a knife inserted in center comes out clean, 20–25 minutes. Refrigerate, covered, until chilled.

**Per serving:** 121 Calories, 4 g Total Fat, 2 g Saturated Fat, 110 mg Cholesterol, 97 mg Sodium, 14 g Total Carbohydrate, 0 g Dietary Fiber, 7 g Protein, 157 mg Calcium. *POINTS* per serving: 3.

## How We Did It

Stirring nonfat dry milk powder into low-fat milk gives it a creamy richness and body, so there's no need to use the whole milk called for in traditional custard recipes. The bonus: a calcium boost and a big fat savings.

# Buttermilk Pie

*This Southern specialty makes the most of buttermilk, which, despite its name, is lower in fat than whole milk.*

MAKES 12 SERVINGS

¼ cup cold reduced-calorie tub margarine

¾ cup + 2 tablespoons sugar

4 eggs

1⅓ cups all-purpose flour

2 cups low-fat buttermilk, at room temperature

¼ cup reduced-calorie tub margarine, melted, at room temperature

1 tablespoon grated lemon zest

¼ cup fresh lemon juice

Pinch salt

1. Preheat the oven to 350° F.

2. To prepare the crust, in a food processor, combine the cold margarine and 2 tablespoons of the sugar; pulse to blend. Add 1 egg; pulse to blend. Add 1 cup + 2 tablespoons of the flour and pulse several times, until a soft dough forms. Press the dough over the bottom and up the sides of a 10" pie plate; with a fork, prick the dough. Line the crust with foil; fill with dried beans or pie weights. Bake 10 minutes; remove the pie weights and foil. Bake until golden, 10–12 minutes longer; cool on a rack. Increase the oven temperature to 425° F.

3. To prepare the filling, combine the remaining ¾ cup sugar and the remaining flour. With a whisk, beat in the remaining 3 eggs, the buttermilk, melted margarine, lemon zest, lemon juice and salt. Pour into the pie crust. Bake 10 minutes; cover the edges of the crust with foil. Reduce the oven temperature to 350° F; bake until a knife inserted in the center comes out clean, about 30 minutes longer. Serve slightly warm or at room temperature.

**Per serving**: 187 Calories, 6 g Total Fat, 1 g Saturated Fat, 73 mg Cholesterol, 148 mg Sodium, 28 g Total Carbohydrate, 0 g Dietary Fiber, 5 g Protein, 17 mg Calcium. **POINTS** per serving: 4.

# Sweet Potato Pie

*Mace is the lacy membrane that covers nutmeg; its flavor is similar to, but somewhat stronger than, nutmeg's. If you don't have any on hand, substitute ¼ teaspoon ground nutmeg.*

MAKES 12 SERVINGS

**Crust**

¾ cup all-purpose flour

¼ cup + 1 tablespoon whole-wheat flour

2 tablespoons sugar

½ teaspoon salt

½ teaspoon cinnamon

¼ cup vegetable oil

3 tablespoons ice water

**Filling**

2 pounds sweet potatoes, cooked, peeled and mashed

1½ cups low-fat (1%) milk

½ cup fat-free egg substitute

¼ cup sugar

1 teaspoon vanilla extract

½ teaspoon cinnamon

½ teaspoon brandy

⅛ teaspoon ground mace

1. To prepare the crust, in a small bowl, whisk the all-purpose flour, whole-wheat flour, sugar, salt and cinnamon. Add the oil; with your fingers, work in until the mixture resembles coarse crumbs. Stir in the ice water, 1 tablespoon at a time, until the mixture forms a soft dough. Gather the dough into a ball and wrap in plastic wrap; refrigerate until chilled, at least 1 hour.

2. Preheat the oven to 400° F. Place the dough between 2 sheets of wax paper; roll into a 9" circle. Transfer to an 8" pie plate, pressing to form a rim. Refrigerate while you make filling.

3. To prepare the filling, in a large bowl, combine the filling ingredients; spoon into the crust. Bake 10 minutes, then reduce the oven temperature to 325° F. Bake until the filling is firm, 80–90 minutes. Cool on a wire rack for at least 1 hour.

**Per serving:** 190 Calories, 5 g Total Fat, 1 g Saturated Fat, 1 mg Cholesterol, 132 mg Sodium, 32 g Total Carbohydrate, 3 g Dietary Fiber, 4 g Protein, 59 mg Calcium. **POINTS** per serving: 4.

# Frozen Mango-Lime Mousse

*The tropical flavors of mango and lime make this the perfect choice to follow a spicy Mexican or Caribbean entrée.*

MAKES 4 SERVINGS

2 mangoes, peeled and cut into ½" cubes

½ cup part-skim ricotta cheese

¼ cup sugar

1 teaspoon grated lime zest

2 tablespoons fresh lime juice

1 envelope unflavored gelatin

1 cup low-fat (1%) milk

1. In a food processor or blender, combine the mangoes, ricotta, sugar, lime zest and lime juice.

2. Sprinkle the gelatin over ¼ cup cold water; let stand until softened, about 2 minutes, then pour into the food processor.

3. In a small saucepan, bring the milk just to a boil. Pour into the food processor with the mango mixture; puree. Pour the mousse into four 8-ounce freezer-safe dishes; cover with plastic wrap. Freeze until set, about 2 hours.

**Per serving**: 189 Calories, 3 g Total Fat, 2 g Saturated Fat, 12 mg Cholesterol, 75 mg Sodium, 35 g Total Carbohydrate, 1 g Dietary Fiber, 8 g Protein, 172 mg Calcium. **POINTS** per serving: 4.

# Blueberry Sherbet

*Buttermilk and lime add just the right touch of acidity to this pretty dessert.*

MAKES 8 SERVINGS

3 cups thawed frozen blueberries

½ cup sugar

1 tablespoon fresh lime juice

1 envelope unflavored gelatin

2 cups low-fat buttermilk

1. In a large saucepan, combine the blueberries, sugar and lime juice; sprinkle with the gelatin. Let stand 2 minutes. Simmer over medium-low heat, stirring constantly, until the sugar and gelatin completely dissolve, about 3 minutes. Remove from the heat; stir in the buttermilk. Transfer to a 2½-quart freezer-safe container with a tight-fitting lid; freeze, covered, until mixture resembles set gelatin, 4–6 hours.

2. In two batches, puree the berry mixture in a blender or food processor; return to the container. Freeze, covered, overnight. Let stand at room temperature 5 minutes before serving.

**Per serving**: 114 Calories, 1 g Total Fat, 0 g Saturated Fat, 4 mg Cholesterol, 69 mg Sodium, 23 g Total Carbohydrate, 1 g Dietary Fiber, 3 g Protein, 12 mg Calcium. **POINTS** per serving: 2.

# Mocha Semifreddo

*Semifreddo is literally translated as half-frozen. This Italian treat has the flavor of a creamy cappuccino. Be sure to use freshly ground, not instant, coffee.*

MAKES 4 SERVINGS

One 16-ounce container chocolate nonfat frozen yogurt

Half 16-ounce container (1 cup) coffee nonfat frozen yogurt

3 teaspoons freshly ground coffee beans

2 teaspoons sugar

1 teaspoon unsweetened cocoa powder

1. Spray an $8\frac{1}{2} \times 5"$ disposable foil loaf pan with nonstick cooking spray. Let the yogurts soften at room temperature 10 minutes. In a small bowl, combine 2 teaspoons of the ground coffee, the sugar and cocoa powder.

2. Spread the chocolate yogurt in the loaf pan; sprinkle with the cocoa mixture, then spread with the coffee yogurt. Cover with plastic wrap; freeze at least 8 hours or overnight.

3. To serve, let stand at room temperature 10 minutes. Invert onto a platter; unmold by cutting away the foil pan. Cut into 4 slices and serve, sprinkled with remaining ground coffee.

**Per serving**: 141 Calories, 1 g Total Fat, 0 g Saturated Fat, 1 mg Cholesterol, 81 mg Sodium, 30 g Total Carbohydrate, 1 g Dietary Fiber, 6 g Protein, 187 mg Calcium. **POINTS** per serving: 3.

# Peach Melba

*Melba sauce gets its name from the Australian opera singer Dame Nellie Melba, for whom the sauce was originally made. A quick zap in the microwave turns this melba into a hot sundae with oomph!*

MAKES 4 SERVINGS

2 medium peaches, peeled, halved and pitted

2 teaspoons fresh lemon juice

3 cups raspberries

2 teaspoons sugar

One 16-ounce container sugar-free vanilla nonfat frozen yogurt

1. In a medium bowl, toss the peaches with the lemon juice; set aside.

2. In a small bowl, crush half the raspberries; toss with the sugar. If desired, microwave on High $1–1\frac{1}{2}$ minutes.

3. Divide the frozen yogurt among 4 dessert dishes. Top with the crushed raspberries, then cap with a peach half; sprinkle with the whole raspberries. Serve at once.

**Per serving**: 155 Calories, 1 g Total Fat, 0 g Saturated Fat, 0 mg Cholesterol, 66 mg Sodium, 39 g Total Carbohydrate, 5 g Dietary Fiber, 5 g Protein, 174 mg Calcium. **POINTS** per serving: 2.

# Watermelon Sorbet

*Superfine sugar dissolves quickly, even when chilled—an essential quality when making this refreshing sorbet. If unavailable, you can process granulated sugar in the blender for about 30 seconds, until it has a superfine texture.*

MAKES 4 SERVINGS

4 cups seeded watermelon chunks

¼ cup superfine sugar

2 tablespoons fresh lime juice

1. In a blender or food processor, combine the watermelon, sugar and lime juice; puree. Transfer to a 2-quart freezer-safe container with a tight-fitting lid; freeze, covered, until the mixture resembles set gelatin, 4–6 hours.

2. In two batches, puree the watermelon mixture in the blender or food processor; return to the container. Freeze, covered, overnight. Let the sorbet stand at room temperature 5 minutes before serving.

**Per serving:** 102 Calories, 1 g Total Fat, 0 g Saturated Fat, 0 mg Cholesterol, 3 mg Sodium, 25 g Total Carbohydrate, 1 g Dietary Fiber, 1 g Protein, 14 mg Calcium. *POINTS* per serving: 2.

## Granita, Sorbet—What's the Difference?

*Both granita and sorbet are made from frozen fruit juices and sugar, but it's their textures that make them different. While sorbet is beaten or pureed to a velvety smooth consistency, granita, as its name implies, is supposed to have a granular texture. Fork-stirring as the granita hardens keeps the ice crystals large, so they form crunchy "grains."*

# Double-Chocolate Sorbet

*If you loved those fudge ice pops when you were a kid, this is the dessert for you.*

MAKES 4 SERVINGS

½ cup sugar

⅓ cup unsweetened cocoa powder

¼ cup honey

½ teaspoon instant espresso or coffee powder

½ ounce (½ square) unsweetened chocolate, chopped

1. In a medium saucepan, combine the sugar, cocoa powder, honey, espresso powder, chocolate and ½ cup water. Bring to a simmer and cook until the sugar is dissolved, 2–3 minutes. Remove from the heat and stir in 1½ cups water.

2. Transfer to a 9 × 13" baking pan. Freeze until just frozen, 2–3 hours.

3. Transfer to a food processor; puree. Scrape into a quart-size container with a tight-fitting lid; freeze until firm. If the sorbet loses its velvety texture, reprocess right before serving.

**Per serving:** 194 Calories, 3 g Total Fat, 1 g Saturated Fat, 0 mg Cholesterol, 1 g Dietary Fiber, 2 g Protein, 15 mg Calcium. *POINTS* per serving: 4.

# Pink Grapefruit and Raspberry Granita

*Besides looking prettier, pink grapefruit is actually healthier than yellow grapefruit because it's richer in heart-healthy carotenoids.*

MAKES 6 SERVINGS

2 cups pink grapefruit juice

1½ cups fresh or drained thawed frozen raspberries

½ cup superfine sugar

1. In a medium bowl, combine the grapefruit juice and raspberries; stir to mix well. Set a fine-mesh sieve over a 2-quart freezer-safe container with a tight-fitting lid. Pour the raspberry mixture through the sieve; press the raspberries to extract as much juice as possible, discarding the seeds.

2. Add the sugar to the raspberry puree; stir to mix well. Freeze, covered, stirring with a fork every 30 minutes until frozen, about 6 hours.

**Per serving:** 112 Calories, 0 g Total Fat, 0 g Saturated Fat, 0 mg Cholesterol, 1 mg Sodium, 28 g Total Carbohydrate, 1 g Dietary Fiber, 1 g Protein, 14 mg Calcium. **POINTS** per serving: 2.

## Tip

If you don't have superfine sugar on hand, process granulated sugar in a blender until it's very fine.

# Almond-Fudge Truffles

*Make these at holiday time and pack them in a pretty tin with the recipe attached for a wonderful, personal gift.*

MAKES 24 SERVINGS

½ cup + 2 tablespoons unsweetened cocoa powder

1 cup sifted confectioners' sugar

½ cup light cream cheese, at room temperature

½ teaspoon almond extract

1. Reserve 2 tablespoons of the cocoa powder on a sheet of wax paper. In a food processor or in a medium bowl, with an electric mixer on high speed, blend the remaining ½ cup of of cocoa powder, the confectioners' sugar, cream cheese and almond extract.

2. Drop the cream cheese mixture by rounded teaspoons into the reserved cocoa powder, making 24 truffles; roll into balls and refrigerate until firm, 1–2 hours.

**Per serving:** 45 Calories, 1 g Total Fat, 1 g Saturated Fat, 2 mg Cholesterol, 27 mg Sodium, 6 g Total Carbohydrate, 1 g Dietary Fiber, 1 g Protein, 10 mg Calcium. **POINTS** per serving: 1.

*Pink Grapefruit and Raspberry Granita*
*with a Coconut-Macadamia Kiss (page 384)*

# Black and White Strawberries

*You've probably seen chocolate-dipped fruit in elegant restaurants and expensive gourmet shops, but did you know how easy it is to make? Our version uses semi-sweet and white chocolate for a dramatic presentation.*

MAKES 4 SERVINGS

¼ cup + 2 tablespoons semisweet chocolate chips

1½ teaspoons raspberry liqueur (framboise)

½ ounce white chocolate, chopped, or 2 tablespoons white chocolate chips

2 cups whole strawberries

1. Line a large baking sheet with wax paper. In a small microwavable bowl, combine the chocolate chips, liqueur and 1½ teaspoons water; microwave on High, stirring twice, until melted and smooth, about 1½ minutes. Holding a berry by the hull, dip the berry halfway into the chocolate; set on the wax paper. Repeat with the remaining berries and chocolate.

2. In another small microwavable bowl, melt the white chocolate in the microwave on High, stirring once, until melted and smooth, about 1 minute. Dip a fork in the white chocolate; drizzle over the strawberries. Refrigerate until the chocolate hardens. Serve chilled.

**Per serving**: 97 Calories, 4 g Total Fat, 2 g Saturated Fat, 0 mg Cholesterol, 4 mg Sodium, 15 g Total Carbohydrate, 2 g Dietary Fiber, 1 g Protein, 21 mg Calcium. *POINTS* per serving: 2.

## Tip

**Try this with other fruits, too: Grapes, orange sections, apple or pear wedges, or banana chunks (dip the apples, pears or bananas in a mixture of lemon juice and water to prevent browning). It's also delicious with fat-free pretzels.**

## Sectioning Grapefruit and Oranges

*Here's the easy way to section fresh grapefruit and oranges:*

- *Begin by cutting off the peel and the white membrane with a very sharp utility knife or a serrated knife for peeling citrus fruits. Remove the sections by cutting into the center of the fruit between one section and the membrane. Then turn the knife and slide it down the other side of the section, next to the membrane. Remove any seeds. Allow the grapefruit or orange sections to fall into a bowl along with any juice.*

# Coconut-Macadamia Kisses

*(pictured on page 380)*

---

*Light, sweet, studded with the rich taste of macadamia nuts, these kisses are a very special treat. They keep well, stored in an airtight container.*

MAKES 18 SERVINGS

3 egg whites, at room temperature

Pinch salt

½ cup sugar

¼ cup shredded coconut

1 teaspoon coconut extract

18 macadamia nuts, halved

1. Preheat the oven to 250° F. Line a baking sheet with parchment paper or foil.

2. In a medium bowl, with an electric mixer on medium speed, combine the egg whites and salt; beat until foamy. Gradually beat in the sugar, beating until the egg whites are shiny and stiff peaks form. With a rubber spatula, fold in the coconut and coconut extract.

3. Spoon the meringue into a pastry bag fitted with a large star tip. Pipe 36 rosettes onto the baking sheet. Place a macadamia half in the center of each. Bake until the edges begin to dry and the kisses are lightly browned, about 40 minutes. Turn off the oven; let the kisses dry completely in the oven until crisp, at least 3 hours or overnight. Peel the paper or foil from the kisses. Store in an airtight container.

**Per serving**: 46 Calories, 2 g Total Fat, 1 g Saturated Fat, 0 mg Cholesterol, 19 mg Sodium, 6 g Total Carbohydrate, 0 g Dietary Fiber, 1 g Protein, 2 mg Calcium. **POINTS** per serving: 1.

# Minted Grapefruit and Oranges

---

*Mint creates the illusion of sweetness, so it's a perfect complement to tart grapefruit.*

MAKES 4 SERVINGS

½ cup chopped mint

2 tablespoons sugar

1 grapefruit

2 oranges

Mint leaves, to garnish

1. To prepare the mint syrup, in a small saucepan, combine the mint, sugar and ¼ cup water; bring to a boil. Reduce the heat and simmer 3 minutes. Remove from the heat; let cool 10 minutes.

2. Meanwhile, remove the skin and membranes from the grapefruit. Over a medium bowl, cut the grapefruit into sections. Remove the skin and membranes from the oranges. Cut each crosswise into 4 slices; combine with the grapefruit sections.

3. Strain the mint syrup over the fruit, squeezing any juice from the leaves. Refrigerate, covered, until chilled. Serve, garnished with the mint leaves.

**Per serving**: 73 Calories, 0 g Total Fat, 0 g Saturated Fat, 0 mg Cholesterol, 0 mg Sodium, 18 g Total Carbohydrate, 2 g Dietary Fiber, 1 g Protein, 40 mg Calcium. **POINTS** per serving: 1.

# RECITES

New American Cooking

# Chapter 13

# New American Cooking

The United States is a country of immigrants; only Native Americans can stake any claim to a true American cuisine. So our favorite ethnic cuisines—Italian, Chinese and Mexican—really aren't so foreign at all.

Being a cultural melting pot allows for culinary excitement that is impossible to find in most other countries. Where else would a Mexican flour tortilla be stuffed with a Chinese stir-fry and served with Italian biscotti for dessert? This openness to experimentation, and the fusion of different cultures in a single dish, is something uniquely North American. The recipes in this chapter are delicious proof.

With just a few ingredients, you can capture some of the flavor of various ethnic cuisines in your own cooking. Use this chart as a starting point for seasoning your own creations.

| Cuisine Type | Key Seasonings Used |
| --- | --- |
| Italian | Olive oil, garlic, basil, tomato, oregano, rosemary, anchovy |
| Chinese | Gingerroot, garlic, scallion, soy sauce, Asian sesame oil, black bean sauce |
| Mexican | Cumin, lime, chile, tomato, garlic, onion |
| Provençal | Olive oil, thyme, rosemary, sage, garlic, onion |
| Thai | Fish sauce, chile, curry, coconut, lemongrass |
| Indian | Cumin, ginger, garlic, curry, coconut, tamarind |
| Japanese | Soy sauce, sake, sugar, scallion |
| Scandinavian | Sour cream, dill, onion, allspice, caraway |

# Squash Soup

*When most people think of squash in Italian cooking, they think of zucchini. But in Mantua, near Venice and Verona, the yellow winter squash* zucca gialla *is a staple. One favorite preparation is a thick, rich soup, where pureed squash is delicately flavored with sage; instead of prosciutto, we use Canadian bacon.*

MAKES 4 SERVINGS

One 2–2½-pound butternut squash, peeled, seeded and coarsely chopped

4 teaspoons olive oil

1 onion, chopped

1 slice Canadian bacon, diced

3 cups low-sodium chicken broth

Freshly ground pepper, to taste

4 teaspoons minced fresh sage, or 1¼ teaspoons dried

1. Place the squash in a steamer basket; set in a large saucepan, over 1" of boiling water. Cover and steam until tender, about 15 minutes.

2. In a large nonstick saucepan or Dutch oven, heat the oil. Sauté the onion and bacon until the onion is light golden, about 5 minutes. Add the squash and broth; bring to a boil. Reduce the heat and simmer, covered, until the squash is very soft, 10–15 minutes.

3. Transfer the squash mixture to a food processor; puree. Return to the saucepan and add the pepper; heat to serving temperature. Serve, sprinkled with the sage.

Per serving: 185 Calories, 7 g Total Fat, 1 g Saturated Fat, 4 mg Cholesterol, 196 mg Sodium, 31 g Total Carbohydrate, 5 g Dietary Fiber, 7 g Protein, 135 mg Calcium. **POINTS** per serving: 3.

# Chickpea Soup

*A subtle blend of several spices gives this soup rich, complex flavor—but only a touch of heat.*

MAKES 4 SERVINGS

2 roasted red peppers, coarsely chopped

2¼ cups reduced-sodium chicken broth

4 teaspoons extra virgin olive oil

2 teaspoons fresh lemon juice

¼–½ teaspoon hot red pepper sauce

1 onion, chopped

One 1" piece peeled gingerroot, minced

¼ teaspoon ground cumin

Two 15-ounce cans chickpeas, rinsed and drained

2 carrots, chopped

2 tablespoons tomato paste

1. In a blender or food processor, combine the peppers, ¼ cup of the broth, 3 teaspoons of the oil, the lemon juice and pepper sauce; puree. Pour into a small serving bowl.

2. In a large nonstick saucepan or Dutch oven, heat the remaining teaspoon of oil. Sauté the onion, gingerroot and cumin until the onion is soft, 3–4 minutes. Stir in the chickpeas, the remaining 2 cups of broth, the carrots and tomato paste; bring to a boil. Reduce the heat and simmer 10 minutes. Remove 1 cup of the chickpeas and carrots with a slotted spoon and set aside.

3. Transfer the remaining soup to the blender or food processor (no need to wash); puree. Return to the saucepan with the reserved chickpeas and carrots; heat to serving temperature. Serve, topped with a dollop of the red pepper puree.

**Per serving:** 278 Calories, 9 g Total Fat, 1 g Saturated Fat, 0 mg Cholesterol, 326 mg Sodium, 38 g Total Carbohydrate, 12 g Dietary Fiber, 13 g Protein, 83 mg Calcium. **POINTS** per serving: 4.

# Vietnamese Ginger Chicken Soup

*The secret to this subtly flavored, heavenly soup is blackening the ginger first, as the street vendors do in Vietnam. It only takes a minute, but makes all the difference!*

MAKES 4 SERVINGS

Two 2" pieces peeled gingerroot

2 onions, halved

4 cups reduced-sodium chicken broth

One 5-ounce skinless boneless chicken breast

1 tablespoon Vietnamese fish sauce*

1 teaspoon black peppercorns

3 ounces rice sticks† or thin spaghetti

2 scallions (white part only), thinly sliced

1½ cups bean sprouts

¼ cup chopped cilantro

¼ cup chopped mint

Lime wedges

1. To blacken the gingerroot and onions, thread each on a metal skewer and hold over a gas-burner flame, turning, until scorched on all sides, 1–2 minutes (or, blacken in a cast-iron skillet over high heat, turning frequently, 3–4 minutes). Leave one piece of gingerroot whole; when cool, finely chop the second piece.

2. In a large saucepan or Dutch oven, combine the broth, chicken, fish sauce, peppercorns and the blackened onions and whole ginger piece; bring to a boil. Reduce the heat and simmer, covered, until the chicken is cooked through, about 5 minutes. Remove the chicken and, when cool enough to handle, shred into bite-size pieces. Continue simmering the broth until the flavors are blended, about 20 minutes.

3. Meanwhile, place the rice sticks in a large bowl; add enough warm water to cover and let soak until softened through, about 10 minutes. (Or, cook the spaghetti according to package directions.) Drain and set aside.

4. Strain the broth, discarding the solids, and return to a boil. Add the chopped ginger and scallions; reduce the heat and simmer 5 minutes longer.

5. To serve, divide the rice sticks among 4 bowls. Top each with the bean sprouts and shredded chicken, then ladle over the broth. Serve with cilantro, mint and lime wedges on the side.

**Per serving:** 167 Calories, 4 g Total Fat, 1 g Saturated Fat, 22 mg Cholesterol, 293 mg Sodium, 22 g Total Carbohydrate, 1 g Dietary Fiber, 12 g Protein, 51 mg Calcium. **POINTS** per serving: 3.

*Fish sauce (also called nuoc cham or nuoc mam), a thin brown sauce made from salted and fermented fish, is available in Asian groceries and some supermarkets. In a pinch, reduced-sodium soy or teriyaki sauce is an acceptable substitute.*

†Rice sticks or rice vermicelli are thin noodles made from rice flour. They can be found in Asian markets and some supermarkets.

# Yogurt Soup with Lamb Meatballs

*Complex flavorings give this satisfying soup a wonderful bite. If you're restricting your sodium, substitute a packet of low-sodium chicken broth and seasoning mix for the bouillon.*

MAKES 4 SERVINGS

1 onion

5 ounces lean ground lamb

1 egg, separated

3 tablespoons plain dried bread crumbs

¼ teaspoon ground cumin

¼ teaspoon ground coriander

4 teaspoons olive oil

3 cups reduced-sodium chicken broth

2 cups thin egg noodles

1 teaspoon instant chicken bouillon granules

1 medium zucchini, sliced into ¼" cubes

3 cups plain nonfat yogurt

1 tablespoon all-purpose flour

2 tablespoons slivered fresh mint leaves, or 2 teaspoons dried

Freshly ground pepper, to taste

1. Grate a small piece of the onion to make 2 tablespoons; finely chop the rest and set aside.

2. In a medium bowl, combine the lamb, grated onion, egg white, bread crumbs, cumin and coriander. Shape the mixture into 16 meatballs, about 1" each.

3. In a large nonstick saucepan or Dutch oven, cook the meatballs until browned on all sides, about 3 minutes. Transfer to a plate; pour off any fat remaining in the pan.

4. In the saucepan, heat the oil. Sauté the chopped onion until tender, 2–3 minutes. Stir in the broth and bring to a boil. Add the meatballs, noodles and bouillon; cook until the noodles are nearly tender, 4–5 minutes. Add the zucchini; simmer until tender, 3 minutes.

5. In a medium bowl, whisk the yogurt, egg yolk and flour; gradually stir into the soup and bring to a boil, stirring constantly. Simmer until slightly thickened, 1 minute. Stir in the mint and sprinkle with pepper just before serving.

**Per serving:** 368 Calories, 12 g Total Fat, 3 g Saturated Fat, 107 mg Cholesterol, 514 mg Sodium, 36 g Total Carbohydrate, 2 g Dietary Fiber, 27 g Protein, 392 mg Calcium. *POINTS* per serving: 8.

# Chicken Avgolemono Soup

*Creamy, lemon-and-egg-based avgolemono sauce is one of the masterpieces of Greek cuisine. Here, it's interpreted in an easy soup form—minus a lot of the fat.*

MAKES 4 SERVINGS

4 cups reduced-sodium chicken broth

½ pound skinless boneless chicken breast

2 eggs

¼ cup fresh lemon juice

One 10-ounce box frozen chopped spinach, thawed and squeezed dry

2 cups hot cooked rice

Freshly ground pepper, to taste

1. In a large saucepan or Dutch oven, bring the broth and chicken to a boil; reduce the heat and simmer until the chicken is cooked through, 5–7 minutes. Remove the chicken and, when cool enough to handle, shred into bite-size pieces.

2. In a medium bowl, whisk the eggs and lemon juice until frothy; gradually whisk in 1 cup of the hot broth.

3. Add the spinach to the broth in the saucepan; bring to a boil. Reduce the heat to low; stir in the rice. Slowly add the egg-broth mixture, whisking constantly to avoid curdling; continue whisking until thickened, 3 minutes (do not boil). Stir in the chicken and heat to serving temperature. Season with the pepper and serve at once.

**Per serving:** 261 Calories, 7 g Total Fat, 2 g Saturated Fat, 140 mg Cholesterol, 163 mg Sodium, 28 g Total Carbohydrate, 2 g Dietary Fiber, 22 g Protein, 141 mg Calcium. **POINTS** per serving: 5.

# Senegalese Peanut Soup

*If you're craving the rich taste of peanuts but not the fat and calories, this unusual soup fills the bill. Make it a day ahead of time, if possible, to let the flavors develop even more.*

MAKES 4 SERVINGS

One 15-ounce can chickpeas, rinsed and drained

3 cups reduced-sodium chicken broth

3 tablespoons natural creamy peanut butter

1 teaspoon peanut oil

2 onions, chopped

One 1" piece peeled gingerroot, minced

1½ teaspoons curry powder

½ teaspoon ground cumin

One 14½-ounce can diced tomatoes

¼ teaspoon cayenne pepper, or to taste

Chopped cilantro

1. In a blender or food processor, combine the chickpeas, ½ cup of the broth and the peanut butter; puree.

2. In a large nonstick saucepan or Dutch oven, heat the oil. Sauté the onions and gingerroot until the onions are soft, 7–8 minutes. Stir in the curry powder and cumin; sauté 1 minute longer. Add the remaining 2½ cups of broth, the tomatoes and the chickpea mixture; simmer 5 minutes to blend the flavors. Season with the cayenne. Serve, sprinkled with the cilantro.

**Per serving:** 215 Calories, 11 g Total Fat, 2 g Saturated Fat, 0 mg Cholesterol, 217 mg Sodium, 20 g Total Carbohydrate, 6 g Dietary Fiber, 10 g Protein, 61 mg Calcium. *POINTS* per serving: 4.

## How We Did It

**Chickpeas have a slightly nutty taste and a thick, creamy texture when pureed—making them an excellent stand-in for some of the peanut butter.**

*Senegalese Peanut Soup*

# Creamy Potato Soup with Roast Garlic

*This hearty soup is a meal in itself, but you can also skip the ham and string beans if you'd like to serve it as a first course. Don't worry about too much garlic; roasting makes it sweet and mild.*

MAKES 4 SERVINGS

1 garlic bulb, cloves separated

2 cups reduced-sodium chicken broth

4 teaspoons olive oil

1 onion

1¼ pounds russet potatoes, peeled and cubed

1 bay leaf

2 cups low-fat (1.5%) or fat-free buttermilk

One 10-ounce box frozen chopped green beans, thawed

½ cup chopped lean ham

Freshly ground pepper, to taste

1. To roast the garlic, preheat the oven or toaster oven to 350° F; line a small shallow baking pan with foil. In the pan, combine the garlic, ¼ cup of the broth and 2 teaspoons of the oil. Cover with foil and bake until the cloves are soft and have absorbed all the liquid, about 1 hour.

2. When the cloves are cool enough to handle, squeeze their pulp out of their papery skins and reserve.

3. To prepare the soup, in a large nonstick saucepan or Dutch oven, heat the remaining 2 teaspoons of oil. Sauté the onion until softened, about 5 minutes. Add the remaining 1¾ cups of broth, the potatoes, roasted garlic pulp and the bay leaf; bring to a boil. Reduce the heat and simmer, covered, until the potatoes are soft, 15–20 minutes. Discard the bay leaf, remove 1 cup of the cooked potatoes with a slotted spoon and set aside.

4. Transfer the remaining potato-onion mixture to a blender or food processor; puree. Return to the saucepan and stir in the reserved potato chunks, the buttermilk, green beans and ham; heat to serving temperature. Serve, sprinkled with the pepper.

**Per serving:** 210 Calories, 8 g Total Fat, 2 g Saturated Fat, 14 mg Cholesterol, 373 mg Sodium, 24 g Total Carbohydrate, 4 g Dietary Fiber, 11 g Protein, 208 mg Calcium. **POINTS** per serving: 4.

## How We Did It

Roasted garlic adds a nutty, rich flavor to dishes, creating an illusion of fat without the calories. And, since roasting tames its strong flavor, even garlic avoiders will love it. Try adding a few roasted cloves to salad dressings, creamy sauces or soups. If you like, you can roast the garlic up to two days ahead. Squeeze the pulp into a glass jar (which doesn't absorb odors the way plastic can) and refrigerate.

# Spinach-Stuffed Focaccia

*Spinach, anchovies and capers are a classic Neapolitan combination even fish haters will love—gentle cooking renders the flavors nutty, not fishy. Serve this as a side dish with grilled seafood or poultry, or as an appetizer to serve eight.*

## MAKES 4 SERVINGS

One 10-ounce tube refrigerated pizza dough

4 teaspoons extra virgin olive oil

4 anchovy fillets, rinsed and patted dry

1 garlic clove, minced

One 10-ounce box frozen chopped spinach, thawed and squeezed dry

1 teaspoon capers, rinsed and drained

1 teaspoon dried rosemary

Freshly ground pepper, to taste

1. Preheat the oven to 400° F; spray a 9" pie plate with nonstick cooking spray.

2. On a lightly floured surface, turn out the dough; divide it into 2 equal pieces. Roll each into a 9" round, cover with plastic wrap and let the dough stand 10 minutes.

3. Meanwhile, in a medium nonstick skillet over low heat, heat the oil. Add the anchovies and garlic; cook, stirring gently, until the anchovies have fallen apart, 1–2 minutes. Stir in the spinach and capers; sauté until the mixture is dry, 2–3 minutes. Remove from the heat and let cool slightly.

4. Line the pie plate with one of the dough rounds. Top evenly with the spinach mixture, leaving a 1" border along the edges. Cover with the second dough round, pinching the edges together and rolling over to seal. With your finger, make several indentations in the dough; sprinkle evenly with the rosemary and pepper. Bake until golden brown and crisp along the edges, 12–15 minutes.

**Per serving:** 233 Calories, 6 g Total Fat, 1 g Saturated Fat, 3 mg Cholesterol, 442 mg Sodium, 37 g Total Carbohydrate, 2 g Dietary Fiber, 10 g Protein, 127 mg Calcium. **POINTS** per serving: 5.

## Got Leftovers?

You'll find all kinds of uses for leftover anchovies. Toss them with chunks of roasted red pepper, chopped celery and black olives for a quick antipasto. Chop a few and cook them gently in a little oil and garlic until they're golden; from there, you can toss them with pasta for a simple and satisfying supper. Or fold them into beaten eggs and make a wonderfully flavored omelet.

## Five Healthy Ways to Top a Prebaked Pizza Crust

- *Sautéed broccoli florets and garlic with crumbled feta cheese*
- *Flaked tuna, chopped tomatoes and sliced black olives*
- *Sautéed Swiss chard with a sprinkling of chopped turkey ham*
- *Sautéed mushrooms, onions and zucchini with a dusting of grated Parmesan cheese and oregano*
- *Steamed asparagus tips and shredded light Jarlsberg cheese*

# Stromboli

*A favorite at Italian-American street fairs, stromboli is something like a rolled pizza. Thanks to store-bought pizza dough, found near the biscuits in the refrigerator case at your supermarket, it's easy to re-create at home. You can use just about any pizza topping as a filling, but this hero sandwich-style recipe wins our vote.*

MAKES 4 SERVINGS

One 10-ounce tube refrigerated pizza dough

⅓ cup shredded part-skim mozzarella cheese

½ cup thinly sliced artichoke hearts

3 roasted red peppers, sliced into thin strips

½ cup thinly sliced turkey salami

1. Preheat the oven to 375° F; line a baking sheet with foil and spray with nonstick cooking spray.

2. On a lightly floured surface, turn out the dough; press into a 8 × 12" rectangle. Sprinkle with the cheese, leaving a 1" border along the edges. Top with the artichoke hearts, peppers and salami. Starting on a short end, roll up the dough jelly-roll style to enclose the filling. Crimp the edges to seal.

3. Place the stromboli, seam-side down, on the baking sheet. Bake until golden brown and crusty, 20–25 minutes. Cut into quarters and serve piping hot.

**Per serving:** 262 Calories, 5 g Total Fat, 2 g Saturated Fat, 17 mg Cholesterol, 418 mg Sodium, 44 g Total Carbohydrate, 5 g Dietary Fiber, 14 g Protein, 92 mg Calcium. **POINTS** per serving: 5.

# Cuban Sandwiches

*These simple sandwiches are good with just about any sliced meat filling; try turkey breast or roast beef for a variation. According to Cuban-sandwich aficionados, the meat, cheese and pickles must be sliced paper thin.*

MAKES 4 SERVINGS

4 teaspoons Dijon mustard

Four 2-ounce sandwich rolls, split

½ pound thinly sliced lean deli ham

8 thin slices Monterey Jack cheese (6–8 ounces)

4 gherkin pickles, thinly sliced

1. To assemble the sandwiches, spread the mustard on the bottom halves of the rolls. Layer them with the ham, cheese and pickles, then cover with the top roll halves.

2. Spray a medium nonstick skillet with nonstick cooking spray; heat. Cook the sandwiches on both sides, flattening them with a pot lid as they cook, until lightly browned on both sides.

**Per serving:** 444 Calories, 20 g Total Fat, 10 g Saturated Fat, 72 mg Cholesterol, 1,399 mg Sodium, 38 g Total Carbohydrate, 0 g Dietary Fiber, 28 g Protein, 433 mg Calcium. **POINTS** per serving: 11.

# Tuscan Panzanella

*The Tuscans are equally proud of their crusty bread and their frugality. This savory salad puts both to good use; it's perfect for days when the garden is brimming and the bread is on the stale side. Use only the ripest, in-season tomatoes.*

MAKES 4 SERVINGS

One 8-ounce loaf 1- or 2-day-old crusty Italian bread, coarsely chopped

4 tomatoes, peeled and chopped

4 celery stalks, finely chopped

2 red onions, chopped

½ cup minced parsley

2 tablespoons red-wine vinegar

4 teaspoons extra virgin olive oil

2 garlic cloves, minced

¼ teaspoon salt

¼ teaspoon freshly ground pepper

¼ cup minced basil

1. In a medium bowl, soak the bread in water until soggy, 3 minutes. Drain and squeeze dry; discard the water. Return the bread to the bowl; with a fork, break it into small pieces.

2. In a large bowl, combine the tomatoes, celery, onions, parsley, vinegar, oil, garlic, salt and pepper. Let stand until the tomatoes have released some of their juice, about 30 minutes. Stir in the bread; sprinkle with the basil. Serve at room temperature.

**Per serving:** 257 Calories, 7 g Total Fat, 1 g Saturated Fat, 0 mg Cholesterol, 514 mg Sodium, 43 g Total Carbohydrate, 5 g Dietary Fiber, 8 g Protein, 114 mg Calcium. *POINTS* per serving: 5.

# Danish Smørbrod with Salmon, Eggs and Asparagus

*The name of these pretty open-face sandwiches translates as buttered bread. The Danes put almost anything on their bread and call it lunch, but there are a few rules: First, don't heap on the toppings, overwhelming the bread; second, eat your sandwich with a knife and fork.*

MAKES 4 SERVINGS

4 slices pumpernickel or other dark bread

2 tablespoons light cream cheese

¼ pound thinly sliced smoked salmon

12 steamed asparagus tips (hot or cold)

3 eggs

⅓ cup low-fat (1%) cottage cheese

1 teaspoon minced chives (optional)

2 teaspoons margarine

Freshly ground pepper, to taste

1. Spread each slice of bread with ½ tablespoon cream cheese; layer with the salmon. Top each with 3 asparagus tips, set on the diagonal.

2. In a medium bowl, whisk together the eggs, cottage cheese and chives (if using).

3. In a medium nonstick skillet, melt the margarine. Pour in the egg mixture and cook, stirring as needed, until firm, 1–2 minutes. Spoon a thin layer of eggs between the asparagus tips on each sandwich and sprinkle with pepper.

**Per serving:** 226 Calories, 9 g Total Fat, 3 g Saturated Fat, 170 mg Cholesterol, 621 mg Sodium, 18 g Total Carbohydrate, 3 g Dietary Fiber, 17 g Protein, 76 mg Calcium. **POINTS** per serving: 5.

## Substitutions

**Ready for other smørbrod toppings? Try one— or all—of these: smoked turkey with sliced cornichon pickles and lemon; roast beef with sliced radishes; turkey salami with sliced potato and capers; cucumber with light cream cheese– horseradish spread, topped with salmon caviar**

# Tuna Pan Bagnat

*Translated from the Italian-influenced southern French dialect, pan bagnat means soaked bread—referring to the moist filling that seeps into the bread as it's pressed. Because the sandwiches need to be made at least a half-hour ahead of time, they're ideal picnic fare.*

MAKES 4 SERVINGS

One 8-ounce loaf day-old coarse peasant-style bread, halved lengthwise

1 garlic clove, halved

One 6-ounce can water-packed solid white tuna, drained

1 pickled red bell pepper, chopped

½ cup thawed frozen artichoke hearts, chopped

2 scallions, sliced

1 tablespoon red-wine vinegar

4 teaspoons olive oil

1. Rub the inside of the bread with the cut side of the garlic; discard any remaining garlic.

2. In a small bowl, combine the remaining ingredients; layer onto the bottom half of the bread. Cover with the top half of the bread. Cover the sandwich with a weighted flat object (such as a skillet, weighted with soup cans) and let stand for 30 minutes. Cut the sandwich crosswise into 4 servings.

**Per serving:** 284 Calories, 8 g Total Fat, 1 g Saturated Fat, 18 mg Cholesterol, 1,357 mg Sodium, 35 g Total Carbohydrate, 3 g Dietary Fiber, 17 g Protein, 59 mg Calcium. *POINTS* per serving: 6.

# Tuna Salad Sandwiches Latino

*Tired of the same old tuna salad? A little creative seasoning makes it a tropical delight. The recipe halves easily if you're not serving the whole family.*

MAKES 4 SERVINGS

½ cup plain nonfat yogurt

4 medium scallions, sliced

2–3 teaspoons prepared horseradish

¼ teaspoon ground ginger

¼ teaspoon imitation coconut extract

Two 6-ounce cans water-packed solid white tuna, drained

8 large lettuce leaves

1 tomato, cut into 4 thick slices

8 slices whole-wheat bread

In a medium bowl, combine the yogurt, scallions, horseradish, ginger and coconut extract; stir in the tuna and blend well. Layer the tuna mixture, lettuce and tomato evenly onto 4 slices of the bread, then top each with a slice of the remaining bread.

**Per serving:** 295 Calories, 5 g Total Fat, 2 g Saturated Fat, 38 mg Cholesterol, 733 mg Sodium, 32 g Total Carbohydrate, 8 g Dietary Fiber, 31 g Protein, 121 mg Calcium. *POINTS* per serving: 5.

# Chicken Couscous

*Don't fret about the number of ingredients in this special-occasion dish; most are common items.*

### MAKES 6 SERVINGS

### Red Pepper (Harissa) Sauce

½ cup reduced-sodium chicken broth

2 jarred roasted red peppers, chopped

1 tablespoon olive oil

2 teaspoons fresh lemon juice

¼–½ teaspoon red chile paste*

¼ teaspoon ground cumin

1 teaspoon chopped flat-leaf parsley

1 teaspoon chopped cilantro

### Couscous Topping

2 teaspoons unsalted butter

1 pound chicken parts, skinned

One 14½-ounce can diced tomatoes

2 medium onions, quartered

2 sprigs flat-leaf parsley

2 sprigs cilantro

1 cinnamon stick

½ teaspoon turmeric

2 carrots, cut into 1" lengths

2 turnips, cut into 2" chunks

One 15-ounce can chickpeas, rinsed and drained

1 medium zucchini, quartered lengthwise and cut into 2" lengths

2 baby eggplants, halved

1 mild chile pepper (try poblano or Anaheim), seeded and quartered

2 tablespoons raisins

### Couscous

One 10-ounce box couscous

3 cups boiling water

¼ cup chopped flat-leaf parsley

¼ cup chopped cilantro

1. To prepare the harissa sauce, in a blender or food processor, puree the sauce ingredients; set aside.

2. To prepare the couscous topping, in a large saucepan or Dutch oven over medium heat, melt the butter until it turns golden brown (do not burn), about 2 minutes. Stir in 6 cups water, the chicken, tomatoes, onions, parsley and cilantro sprigs, cinnamon and turmeric. Bring to a boil; reduce the heat and simmer, covered, 1 hour. Add the carrots and turnips; simmer 10 minutes. Add the chickpeas, zucchini, eggplants, chile and raisins; simmer until all the vegetables are soft, about 10 minutes. Discard the parsley and cilantro sprigs and cinnamon stick. Set aside and keep warm.

3. To prepare the couscous, in a medium heat-proof bowl, cover the couscous with the boiling water and let stand, covered, 5 minutes. Fluff the couscous with a fork and mound in a large serving bowl, leaving a well in the center. With a slotted spoon, transfer the chicken and vegetables to the well in the center of the couscous, leaving the broth behind. Sprinkle the couscous with the chopped parsley and cilantro, and serve with the red pepper sauce and broth on the side.

**Per serving:** 428 Calories, 8 g Total Fat, 2 g Saturated Fat, 42 mg Cholesterol, 163 mg Sodium, 63 g Total Carbohydrate, 10 g Dietary Fiber, 26 g Protein, 83 mg Calcium. **POINTS** per serving: 7.

*\* Made from mashed red hot chile peppers, vinegar and seasonings, this pungent condiment adds fiery zest to many dishes. Find it in Asian markets and gourmet grocery stores; if unavailable, substitute crushed red pepper flakes.*

## Tip

**If you prefer, you can substitute store-bought harissa paste; just thin it with a little lemon juice and water to make a spoonable consistency. Harissa paste can be found in tubes or jars, in Middle Eastern markets or gourmet grocery stores.**

# Farfalle with Cauliflower and Hot Pepper

*Turn humble cauliflower into something wonderful, with this southern Italian specialty. The secrets are to cook the anchovies gently (it gets rid of fishiness) and to avoid overcooking the cauliflower. It should be al dente, or just tender.*

MAKES 4 SERVINGS

4 teaspoons olive oil

8 anchovies, rinsed and patted dry

½ cup reduced-sodium chicken broth

1 small cauliflower head, chopped into bite-size pieces

3 cups farfalle

¼ cup chopped flat-leaf parsley

Pinch crushed red pepper flakes

1. In a small nonstick skillet over low heat, heat the oil. Add the anchovies and cook, stirring gently, until they have fallen apart, 1–2 minutes. Stir in the broth; bring to a boil. Reduce the heat and simmer until the mixture is reduced by half, about 5 minutes. Remove from the heat.

2. Cook the farfalle according to package directions. Drain and place in a serving bowl; keep warm.

3. In the microwave or on the stove, steam the cauliflower until tender, 8–10 minutes. Add to the pasta with the anchovy mixture, parsley and pepper flakes; toss to combine.

**Per serving:** 406 Calories, 8 g Total Fat, 1 g Saturated Fat, 7 mg Cholesterol, 341 mg Sodium, 68 g Total Carbohydrate, 8 g Dietary Fiber, 17 g Protein, 75 mg Calcium. *POINTS* per serving: 7.

# Fettuccine with Walnut Sauce

*A creamy walnut sauce with flecks of parsley makes this a festive dish. Gorgonzola is the Italian version of blue cheese. Its flavor is slightly milder than Roquefort's, and its texture is more crumbly.*

MAKES 4 SERVINGS

½ cup part-skim ricotta cheese

¼ cup low-sodium chicken broth

1 teaspoon grated lemon zest

6 ounces fettuccine

¼ cup walnuts, chopped

¼ cup crumbled Gorgonzola cheese

2 tablespoons minced flat-leaf parsley

1. In a small bowl, combine the ricotta, broth and lemon zest; mix until smooth.

2. Cook the fettuccine according to package directions; drain and place in a serving bowl. Top with the ricotta mixture, then sprinkle with walnuts, Gorgonzola and parsley; toss to coat.

**Per serving:** 271 Calories, 10 g Total Fat, 3 g Saturated Fat, 55 mg Cholesterol, 129 mg Sodium, 33 g Total Carbohydrate, 2 g Dietary Fiber, 12 g Protein, 136 mg Calcium. *POINTS* per serving: 6.

# Orzo with Zucchini and Feta

*This simple pasta dish only uses six ingredients, yet never fails to please. Next time you're asked to bring a pasta salad to a party, take along a double or triple batch.*

MAKES 4 SERVINGS

1 cup orzo

1 medium zucchini, quartered lengthwise and cut into ¼" wedges

¾ cup crumbled feta cheese

2 tablespoons fresh oregano leaves, or 2 teaspoons dried

4 teaspoons extra virgin olive oil

Freshly ground pepper, to taste

1. Cook the orzo according to package directions. Drain and place in a serving bowl; keep warm.

2. In a medium microwavable casserole, combine the zucchini and 2 tablespoons water; microwave on High until the zucchini is just starting to lose its white color, 1 minute. Drain and add to the pasta, along with the remaining ingredients. Toss gently and serve hot or cold.

**Per serving:** 283 Calories, 11 g Total Fat, 5 g Saturated Fat, 25 mg Cholesterol, 318 mg Sodium, 35 g Total Carbohydrate, 2 g Dietary Fiber, 10 g Protein, 165 mg Calcium. **POINTS** per serving: 3.

# Peasant Pasta

*Here's an easy and delicious way to get your dark green leafies—garlic and lemon give the whole dish real pizazz. Use any combination of broccoli rabe, spinach, Swiss chard or kale.*

MAKES 4 SERVINGS

4 teaspoons olive oil

2 onions, chopped

1 garlic clove, chopped

½ cup low-sodium chicken broth

One 10-ounce bag triple-washed spinach, rinsed and coarsely chopped

2 cups coarsely chopped cleaned Swiss chard

¼ teaspoon salt

Freshly ground pepper, to taste

2 cups rotelle

½ tablespoon fresh lemon juice

1. In a large nonstick skillet, heat the oil. Sauté the onions and garlic until softened, about 5 minutes. Add the broth; cook until most of the broth evaporates, 3–4 minutes.

2. Place the spinach and chard in a steamer basket; set in a large saucepan over 1" boiling water. Cover and steam until the greens are tender, 5–6 minutes.

3. Remove the greens from the steamer; squeeze out any excess moisture. Stir into the onion mixture and season with salt and pepper. Cook, stirring frequently, 1 minute. Set aside and keep warm.

4. Meanwhile, cook the rotelle according to package directions; drain and place in a large serving bowl. Add the greens and sprinkle with the lemon juice; toss to combine.

**Per serving:** 246 Calories, 6 g Total Fat, 1 g Saturated Fat, 0 mg Cholesterol, 281 mg Sodium, 41 g Total Carbohydrate, 5 g Dietary Fiber, 10 g Protein, 141 mg Calcium. **POINTS** per serving: 4.

# Pastitsio

*Pastitsio (known in some Greek restaurants as Greek Lasagna) is normally a fat trap, loaded with ground beef, cheese and elbow macaroni, with an eggy cream sauce to bind it all.*

MAKES 6 SERVINGS

½ pound lean ground beef (10% or less fat)

2 medium onions, chopped

One 10-ounce box frozen chopped spinach, thawed and squeezed dry

One 14½-ounce can diced tomatoes

¼ teaspoon nutmeg

¼ teaspoon cinnamon

Freshly ground pepper, to taste

1½ cups cooked ziti

One 12-ounce can evaporated skimmed milk

2 eggs

2 egg whites

⅓ cup crumbled feta cheese

1. Preheat the oven to 350° F; spray a 2-quart casserole dish with nonstick cooking spray.

2. Spray a large nonstick skillet with nonstick cooking spray; heat. Sauté the beef and onions, breaking apart the beef with a wooden spoon, until the beef is cooked through and the onions are soft, 5–8 minutes. Stir in the spinach, tomatoes, nutmeg, cinnamon and pepper; heat through. Stir in the ziti; transfer to the baking dish.

3. In a medium saucepan, heat the milk to just below a boil. Whisk in the eggs and egg whites until frothy. Pour over the beef mixture; sprinkle with the cheese and more of the pepper. Bake until golden brown, about 45 minutes.

**Per serving:** 235 Calories, 7 g Total Fat, 3 g Saturated Fat, 103 mg Cholesterol, 273 mg Sodium, 24 g Total Carbohydrate, 3 g Dietary Fiber, 20 g Protein, 316 mg Calcium. *POINTS* per serving: 5.

## How We Did It

We've worked a little magic to lighten this dish, using spinach to beef up the filling, evaporated skimmed milk to add creaminess and the larger ziti pasta to create more volume.

# "Salad Bar" Pad Thai

*If you've had pad Thai in a restaurant, you probably think it's a complicated dish—but like most Asian street-food dishes, it's meant to be assembled quickly and to vary with what you have on hand. This version can be put together with ingredients you've found at your supermarket's salad bar.*

MAKES 4 SERVINGS

¼ pound rice sticks* or thin spaghetti

¼ cup rice or cider vinegar

3 tablespoons fish sauce* or soy sauce

1 tablespoon sugar

¼ teaspoon red chile paste* or crushed red pepper flakes

2 teaspoons peanut oil

8 scallions, sliced

1 garlic clove, coarsely chopped

1½ cups cooked snow peas, halved

1 tomato, sliced into bite-size chunks

1 cup bean sprouts

3 hard-cooked eggs, peeled and finely chopped

½ cup chopped cilantro

½ cup chopped mint

½ cup chopped basil

3 tablespoons unsalted dry-roasted peanuts, coarsely chopped

1. Place the rice sticks in a large bowl; add enough warm water to cover and let soak until softened through, about 10 minutes. (Or, prepare the spaghetti according to package directions.) Drain and set aside.

2. In a small bowl, whisk the vinegar, fish sauce, sugar and chile paste.

3. In a large nonstick skillet or wok, heat the oil. Sauté the scallions and garlic until the scallions just begin to soften (do not brown), about 3 minutes. Add the rice sticks and toss to coat. Stir in the vinegar mixture and cook, tossing gently, until heated through, about 2 minutes; add the snow peas, tomato and bean sprouts; cook, tossing gently, 1 minute. Sprinkle with the eggs, cilantro, mint, basil and peanuts just before serving.

**Per serving:** 298 Calories, 10 g Total Fat, 2 g Saturated Fat, 160 mg Cholesterol, 742 mg Sodium, 41 g Total Carbohydrate, 4 g Dietary Fiber, 11 g Protein, 140 mg Calcium. *POINTS* per serving: 6.

*\* The following ingredients can be found in Asian groceries and some supermarkets: Rice sticks or rice vermicelli are thin noodles made from rice flour. Fish sauce (also called nuoc cham or nuoc mam) is a thin brown sauce made from salted and fermented fish. Red chile paste is made from mashed red hot chile peppers, vinegar and seasonings (often including garlic).*

# Soba Noodles with Miso-Glazed Vegetables

*In Japan, soba noodles—made from buckwheat flour—are usually served cold, with a flavorful dipping sauce on the side. But they're also delicious topped with this creamy miso dressing, and any steamed veggies you have on hand (such as the combination we've created here). Miso, a fermented soybean paste with a rich, earthy flavor, is available in Asian markets and natural-food stores.*

MAKES 4 SERVINGS

2 tablespoons rice vinegar

4 teaspoons vegetable oil

1 tablespoon Dijon mustard

1 tablespoon miso (try golden yellow or barley miso)

6 ounces soba noodles

1 carrot, sliced into thin rounds

1 cup broccoli florets

6 asparagus spears, cut into 3" lengths

6 radishes, thinly sliced

1 scallion, minced

1. To prepare the glaze, in a blender or food processor, combine the vinegar, oil, mustard and miso; puree.

2. Cook the soba noodles according to package directions. Rinse in cold water until chilled; drain and place in a serving bowl.

3. In the microwave or on the stove, steam the carrot 5 minutes, then add the broccoli and steam 3 minutes longer. Add the asparagus; steam 2 minutes, then add the radishes and scallion and steam 1 minute longer. Rinse the vegetables in the steamer rack or a colander with cold water until chilled. Combine with the noodles and glaze; toss to coat.

**Per serving:** 220 Calories, 6 g Total Fat, 1 g Saturated Fat, 0 mg Cholesterol, 530 mg Sodium, 38 g Total Carbohydrate, 2 g Dietary Fiber, 8 g Protein, 46 mg Calcium. **POINTS** per serving: 5.

## Tip

Add a little zip by stirring ¼ teaspoon of hot chili paste into the glaze.

*Soba Noodles with Miso-Glazed Vegetables*

# Sicilian Fusilli with Spinach, Ricotta Cheese and Raisins

*Spinach, ricotta and raisins are a classic combination in Sicily and southern Italy.*

MAKES 4 SERVINGS

2 tablespoons golden raisins

2 cups fusilli

One 10-ounce box frozen chopped spinach, thawed

4 teaspoons olive oil

½ onion, chopped

¼ teaspoon salt

¼ cup grated Parmesan cheese

¼ cup part-skim ricotta cheese

¼ teaspoon ground white pepper

1. In a small bowl, soak the raisins in hot water to cover until soft and plumped, about 10 minutes. Drain, discarding the water.

2. Cook the fusilli according to package directions; drain and place in a serving bowl.

3. Meanwhile, cook the spinach according to package directions; drain, squeezing out the excess liquid.

4. In a medium nonstick skillet, heat the oil. Sauté the onion until softened, about 2 minutes. Reduce the heat and stir in the spinach and salt; cook until wilted, about 2 minutes. Add the spinach, raisins, Parmesan and ricotta to the fusilli; toss to combine, then sprinkle with the pepper.

**Per serving:** 302 Calories, 10 g Total Fat, 3 g Saturated Fat, 13 mg Total Cholesterol, 408 mg Sodium, 40 g Total Carbohydrate, 3 g Dietary Fiber, 14 g Protein, 280 mg Calcium. *POINTS* per serving: 6.

# Asian Beef Skewers

*For a different side dish, shred carrot and cabbage; top with a splash of rice or wine vinegar, a pinch of sugar and a sprinkling of poppy seeds.*

MAKES 4 SERVINGS

3 scallions, sliced

2 tablespoons reduced-sodium soy sauce

1 tablespoon minced peeled gingerroot

1 tablespoon rice-wine vinegar

2 teaspoons Asian sesame oil

1 teaspoon balsamic vinegar

½ teaspoon freshly ground pepper

1 garlic clove, minced

¾ pound lean beef loin, cut into 16 strips

¼ cup Chinese mustard

1. Preheat the grill. If you are using wooden skewers, soak in water 30 minutes.

2. In a gallon-size sealable plastic bag, combine the scallions, soy sauce, gingerroot, rice-wine vinegar, oil, balsamic vinegar, pepper and garlic; add the beef. Seal the bag, squeezing out the air. Marinate 15 minutes.

3. With tongs, remove the beef from the marinade; discard any remaining marinade. On each of sixteen 6" metal or wooden skewers, thread 1 beef strip, piercing the beef in several places. Grill until cooked through, about 5 minutes on each side. Serve with the mustard on the side.

**Per serving:** 141 Calories, 6 g Total Fat, 2 g Saturated Fat, 50 mg Cholesterol, 338 mg Sodium, 1 g Total Carbohydrate, 0 g Dietary Fiber, 18 g Protein, 11 mg Calcium. *POINTS* per serving: 3.

# Balsamic Glazed Veal Chops

*Veal chops make an elegant entrée for any occasion. Remember to brown the chops over high heat so they develop a nice crust before you baste them.*

MAKES 4 SERVINGS

¼ cup balsamic vinegar

3 tablespoons fresh lemon juice

1 tablespoon Worcestershire sauce

2 teaspoons honey

2 teaspoons Dijon mustard

2 teaspoons vegetable oil

Four 3-ounce veal loin chops

½ teaspoon salt

¼ teaspoon freshly ground pepper

1. To prepare the glaze, in a small bowl, combine the vinegar, lemon juice, Worcestershire sauce, honey and mustard.

2. In a medium nonstick skillet, heat the oil. Season the chops with salt and pepper, then cook over high heat until browned, about 2 minutes on each side. Reduce the heat; brush the chops with the glaze and cook until cooked through, 3–5 minutes on each side.

**Per serving:** 121 Calories, 4 g Total Fat, 1 g Saturated Fat, 60 mg Cholesterol, 433 mg Sodium, 5 g Total Carbohydrate, 0 g Dietary Fiber, 15 g Protein, 16 mg Calcium. *POINTS* per serving: 3.

# Greek Roast Chicken

*Roasting in a hot oven makes this chicken wonderfully juicy. It makes great leftovers, sliced in sandwiches or shredded into salads.*

MAKES 4 SERVINGS

One 3–3½-pound chicken, rinsed inside and out with cold water and patted dry

1 garlic clove, halved

1 lemon

1 cup cooked rice

1 egg

2 teaspoons dried oregano leaves, crumbled

2 tablespoons chopped parsley

¼ teaspoon cinnamon

Pinch nutmeg

Freshly ground pepper

1. Preheat the oven to 450° F. Line a roasting pan with foil. Rub the inner cavity of the chicken with the cut side of the garlic; discard any remaining garlic.

2. Cut 4 thin slices off the lemon, and chop the remaining lemon into ½" chunks (rind included). Slip 2 lemon slices under the skin on each chicken breast. Cover the breast with foil.

3. In a medium bowl, combine the rice, chopped lemon, egg, oregano, parsley, cinnamon and nutmeg; stuff the mixture into the chicken cavity. Tie the legs together and put the chicken in the roasting pan; sprinkle the chicken with the pepper.

4. Roast the chicken 20 minutes; reduce the oven temperature to 400° F, remove the foil and roast 20 minutes longer, basting with the pan juices every 5 minutes. Reduce the oven temperature to 350° F; continue roasting until cooked through and the juices run clear when the thigh is pierced in the thickest part with a fork, about 15 minutes. Let stand 10 minutes before carving. Remove the skin before eating.

**Per serving:** 257 Calories, 8 g Total Fat, 2 g Saturated Fat, 143 mg Cholesterol, 102 mg Sodium, 12 g Total Carbohydrate, 0 g Dietary Fiber, 32 g Protein, 40 mg Calcium. **POINTS** per serving: 6.

# Turkey Breast Peruvian

*If you're serving a crowd or need sandwich fixings for a week, consider roasting a turkey breast. One 3-pound bone-in breast will yield about a pound and a half of juicy lean meat with a piquant flavor.*

MAKES 12 SERVINGS

2 tablespoons red-wine vinegar

1 tablespoon olive oil

2 large garlic cloves, smashed

2 teaspoons paprika

1 teaspoon dried oregano leaves, crumbled

$\frac{1}{4}$ teaspoon ground cumin

Pinch freshly ground pepper

Pinch seasoned salt

One 3-pound turkey breast

1. To prepare the marinade, in a gallon-size sealable plastic bag, combine the vinegar, oil, garlic, paprika, oregano, cumin, pepper and salt; add the turkey. Seal the bag, squeezing out the air; turn to coat the turkey. Refrigerate, turning the bag occasionally, at least 3 hours or overnight.

2. Preheat the oven to 450° F; line a roasting pan with foil. Place the turkey in the roasting pan and drizzle with the remaining marinade. Roast, skin-side up, 15 minutes. Reduce the oven temperature to 325° F; continue roasting, basting occasionally with the pan juices, until cooked through and the juices run clear when the turkey is pierced with a fork, about 1 hour. Let stand 10 minutes before carving. Remove the skin before eating.

**Per serving:** 90 Calories, 2 g Total Fat, 0 g Saturated Fat, 47 mg Cholesterol, 38 mg Sodium, 1 g Total Carbohydrate, 0 g Dietary Fiber, 17 g Protein, 11 mg Calcium. *POINTS* per serving: 2.

# Southwestern Salmon

*Although we like this easy entrée with salmon steaks, try it with fillets as well—or tuna or swordfish steaks.*

MAKES 2 SERVINGS

$1\frac{1}{2}$ cups fresh cilantro leaves

1 tablespoon fresh lime juice

$\frac{1}{2}$ teaspoon ground cumin

$\frac{1}{4}$ teaspoon salt

Dash hot red pepper sauce

$\frac{1}{2}$–$\frac{3}{4}$-pound salmon steak

1 yellow bell pepper, seeded and sliced

1 red bell pepper, seeded and sliced

1. In a food processor, combine the cilantro, lime juice, cumin, salt, pepper sauce and $\frac{1}{4}$ cup water; puree. Transfer to a gallon-size sealable plastic bag; add the salmon. Seal the bag, squeezing out the air; turn to coat the salmon. Refrigerate, turning the bag occasionally, 1 hour.

2. Preheat the oven to 400° F; spray a 9" square baking dish with nonstick cooking spray. Arrange the peppers in a single layer in the pan. Bake, turning once, 20 minutes.

3. Drain the salmon; discard the marinade. Place the salmon on top of the peppers. Bake until the fish is just opaque in the center, 5–6 minutes on each side.

**Per serving:** 236 Calories, 12 g Total Fat, 3 g Saturated Fat, 75 mg Cholesterol, 198 mg Sodium, 7 g Total Carbohydrate, 1 g Dietary Fiber, 24 g Protein, 43 mg Calcium. *POINTS* per serving: 6.

# Chicken Picadillo

*Picadillo is a classic dish in Mexico, the Caribbean and Latin America. It's usually made with ground pork or beef but it's just as tasty with shredded chicken. Serve this with rice and beans, as they do in Mexico.*

MAKES 4 SERVINGS

2 teaspoons corn oil

2 onions, chopped

2 cups shredded cooked chicken breast

1 Granny Smith apple, peeled, cored and chopped

1 cup stewed tomatoes

¼ cup low-sodium chicken broth

2 tablespoons raisins

2 teaspoons cider vinegar

1 teaspoon pureed *chipotles en adobo*

⅛ teaspoon ground cinnamon

In a medium nonstick skillet, heat the oil. Sauté the onions until lightly browned, 8–10 minutes. Stir in the chicken, apple, tomatoes, broth, raisins, vinegar, *chipotles* and cinnamon; cook, stirring frequently, until the liquid is slightly reduced and the flavors are blended, about 10 minutes.

**Per serving:** 192 Calories, 7 g Total Fat, 2 g Saturated Fat, 50 mg Cholesterol, 241 mg Sodium, 16 g Total Carbohydrate, 3 g Dietary Fiber, 18 g Protein, 47 mg Calcium. **POINTS** per serving: 4.

# Easy Snapper with Corn Chutney

*Chutney's sweet-and-sour flavors are a perfect foil for rich snapper. Refrigerate any leftover chutney for up to 3 days in a glass container.*

MAKES 4 SERVINGS

1 cup cider vinegar

2 tablespoons sugar

One 10-ounce box frozen corn kernels, thawed

1 red onion, diced

¼ cup + 2 tablespoons raisins

¼ teaspoon cinnamon

¼ teaspoon ground cloves

½ cup drained canned crushed pineapple, with 2 tablespoons juice

1¼ pounds red snapper fillets, patted dry and cut into 4 pieces

1. To prepare the chutney, in a medium nonreactive saucepan, combine the vinegar and sugar, stirring until the sugar dissolves; bring to a boil. Reduce the heat; stir in the corn, onion, raisins, cinnamon and cloves. Simmer, uncovered, stirring frequently, until the liquid is slightly reduced, about 20 minutes. Increase the heat to high; stir in the pineapple and juice. Cook, stirring frequently, until the chutney is thickened and syrupy, about 10 minutes longer.

2. Meanwhile, preheat the grill or broiler. Grill or broil the snapper 5–6" from the heat until just opaque in the center, 2–3 minutes on each side. Serve with the chutney on the side.

**Per serving:** 322 Calories, 3 g Total Fat, 1 g Saturated Fat, 52 mg Cholesterol, 110 mg Sodium, 45 g Total Carbohydrate, 4 g Dietary Fiber, 33 g Protein, 77 mg Calcium. **POINTS** per serving: 6.

# Cod in Grape Leaves

*Like foil, grape leaves eliminate the problem of fish sticking to the grill; unlike foil, grape leaves are edible. Make these packets in the morning and refrigerate until grilling time. They are delicious cold, so you might want to grill a few extra.*

MAKES 4 SERVINGS

16 pickled grape leaves, drained

1¼ pounds boneless cod steaks, cut into 4 pieces

8 paper-thin lemon slices

½ teaspoon dried oregano leaves, crumbled

½ teaspoon freshly ground pepper

4 teaspoons olive oil

1. Preheat the oven to 400° F, or preheat the grill. Soak 4–5 feet of kitchen twine in water.

2. Bring 8 cups water to a rolling boil. Place the grape leaves in a colander in the sink; pour the boiling water over them. Immediately rinse with cold water and drain.

3. Place about 3 leaves, overlapping each other by half, on a work surface. Place a cod steak in the center. Top with 2 lemon slices, a pinch each of oregano and pepper, and 1 teaspoon of the olive oil. Wrap the fish in the leaves (use additional leaves, if needed, to enclose fish completely) and tie crosswise and lengthwise with twine. Repeat to make 4 packets. If you are baking, place the packets on a baking sheet. Bake or grill until the fish is opaque in the center, about 15 minutes; if you are grilling, turn often to avoid charring the leaves. Remove the twine before serving.

**Per serving:** 179 Calories, 5 g Total Fat, 1 g Saturated Fat, 61 mg Cholesterol, 877 mg Sodium, 1 g Total Carbohydrate, 0 g Dietary Fiber, 25 g Protein, 111 mg Calcium. **POINTS** per serving: 4.

# Whole Broiled Fish Moroccan Style

*Buying a whole fish rather than fillets saves money and makes it easier to judge freshness. Look for bright, clear bulging eyes and skin that is firm to the touch, and no fishy odor. Cooking it whole adds flavor. This easy seasoning mixture—known as* chermoula *in Morocco—has vivid flavors that won't overwhelm the fish. Try red snapper, striped bass or trout.*

MAKES 4 SERVINGS

1 onion, finely chopped

½ cup finely chopped flat-leaf parsley

½ cup finely chopped cilantro

¼ cup fresh lemon juice

4 teaspoons olive oil

2 garlic cloves, minced

1 teaspoon ground cumin

1 teaspoon paprika

¼ teaspoon turmeric

Pinch salt

2 small (2 pounds each) whole white-fleshed fish, gutted and scaled

1. To prepare the chermoula, in a medium bowl, whisk the onion, parsley, cilantro, lemon juice, oil, garlic, cumin, paprika, turmeric and salt.

2. Arrange the fish in a nonreactive roasting pan or large casserole. Pour the chermoula over the fish, spreading some in the inner cavity of each fish. Cover with plastic wrap and refrigerate, turning the fish once, at least 6 hours or overnight.

3. Line the broiler rack or grill rack with foil. Preheat the broiler or grill.

4. Brush the chermoula off the outside of the fish, leaving some in the inner cavity. Broil or grill the fish 5" from the heat, until the flesh is barely opaque when pierced with a knife, about 10 minutes on each side.

**Per serving:** 195 Calories, 7 g Total Fat, 1 g Saturated Fat, 47 mg Cholesterol, 103 mg Sodium, 6 g Total Carbohydrate, 1 g Dietary Fiber, 27 g Protein, 77 mg Calcium. **POINTS** per serving: 4.

# Lamb Shanks with Lentils

*Like hanger steak, lamb shanks are a lower-priced cut that has come into vogue lately. Long stewing makes the most of their flavor-rich bones and meltingly tender meat. Look for the meatier, larger shanks from the upper leg, and have the butcher slice them. If you can only find smaller, lower-leg shanks, keep them whole and have each shank serve two.*

## MAKES 6 SERVINGS

Two 1-pound lamb shanks, each cut into
3 pieces, or three 12-ounce lamb shanks

Freshly ground pepper

¼ cup dry vermouth

2 celery stalks, sliced

1 carrot, sliced

1 onion, diced

1 cup reduced-sodium chicken broth

3 sprigs flat-leaf parsley

2 garlic cloves

1 bay leaf

1 teaspoon dried thyme leaves, crumbled

10 black peppercorns

1 cup lentils

1. Sprinkle the shanks with pepper. Spray a large nonstick saucepan or Dutch oven with nonstick cooking spray; heat. Add the shanks and cook, turning as needed, until browned, about 10 minutes. Transfer the shanks to a plate and pour off any fat in the pan. Add the vermouth and cook, scraping up the browned bits from the bottom of the pan, until the liquid is reduced by half.

2. Add the celery, carrot and onion; sauté until the onion is translucent, about 3 minutes. Add the shanks, broth, parsley, garlic, bay leaf, thyme and peppercorns; bring to a boil. Reduce the heat and simmer, partially covered, until the meat is barely tender, about 1 hour. Add the lentils and simmer until they are tender, about 1 hour longer. Discard the parsley and bay leaf before serving.

**Per serving**: 268 Calories, 6 g Total Fat, 2 g Saturated Fat, 62 mg Cholesterol, 74 mg Sodium, 22 g Total Carbohydrate, 11 g Dietary Fiber, 30 g Protein, 44 mg Calcium. **POINTS** per serving: 4.

# Roast Pork Puertoricano

*Delicious hot or cold, this subtle spice combination makes the most of pork's leanest, most tender cut. Be careful to avoid overcooking, as it can dry out rapidly. Scrape the seeds out of the jalapeños if you prefer milder foods.*

MAKES 4 SERVINGS

Grated zest of 1 orange

¼ cup orange juice

4 teaspoons olive oil

1 jalapeño pepper, sliced (wear gloves to prevent irritation; scrape out the seeds if you don't like it spicy)

2 garlic cloves, sliced

1½ teaspoon ground cumin

½ teaspoon salt

½ teaspoon freshly ground pepper

One 1-pound pork tenderloin

1. To prepare the marinade, in a gallon-size sealable plastic bag, combine the orange zest, orange juice, oil, jalapeño, garlic, cumin, salt and pepper; add the pork. Seal the bag, squeezing out the air; turn to coat the pork. Refrigerate, turning the bag occasionally, at least 2 hours or overnight.

2. Preheat the oven to 450° F; line a roasting pan with foil and spray with nonstick cooking spray. Place the tenderloin in the pan; drizzle with the remaining marinade. Roast 5 minutes; reduce the oven temperature to 350° F and roast until an instant-read thermometer registers 165° F, 15–18 minutes. Let stand 5 minutes before slicing.

**Per serving**: 194 Calories, 9 g Total Fat, 2 g Saturated Fat, 65 mg Cholesterol, 340 mg Sodium, 4 g Total Carbohydrate, 1 g Dietary Fiber, 24 g Protein, 23 mg Calcium. *POINTS* per serving: 4.

## Tip

**Even moderately hot peppers like jalapeños have volatile oils that can irritate skin and mucous membranes. Wear gloves, or wash your hands *thoroughly*, after handling them.**

# Greek Meatballs (Keftedes)

*When it's spaghetti and meatball night, try this deliciously spiced variation. These are great over rice or pasta, or on a hero sandwich roll. Another option: Skip the tomatoes and shape the meatballs into one inch rounds; serve them as finger food at a party.*

MAKES 4 SERVINGS

5 ounces lean ground pork

5 ounces lean ground beef (10% or less fat)

1 onion, minced

1 small eggplant, peeled and finely diced (about 1 cup)

1 egg

3 tablespoons plain dried bread crumbs

¼ cup minced flat-leaf parsley

1 teaspoon dried oregano leaves, crumbled

½ teaspoon ground allspice

¼ teaspoon cinnamon

One 28-ounce can diced tomatoes

1. In a large bowl, lightly combine all the ingredients except the tomatoes. Shape the mixture into 16 meatballs, about 2" each.

2. Spray a large nonstick skillet with nonstick cooking spray; heat. Cook the meatballs, turning as needed, until well browned, 7–8 minutes. Add the tomatoes and bring to a boil, stirring occasionally. Reduce the heat and simmer, stirring occasionally, until the sauce thickens and the flavors are blended, about 20 minutes.

**Per serving:** 161 Calories, 6 g Total Fat, 2 g Saturated Fat, 95 mg Cholesterol, 147 mg Sodium, 10 g Total Carbohydrate, 2 g Dietary Fiber, 17 g Protein, 50 mg Calcium. *POINTS* per serving: 3.

## Got Leftovers?

If you've got extra meatball mixture, try combining it half and half with cooked rice or bulgur, and stuffing it into lightly steamed cabbage leaves; steam again until the cabbage is tender and the filling is cooked through.

# Chinese Pepper Steak Wraps

*This is so much better than take-out! The thinner you slice the beef, the better; freezing it for about 20 minutes first will make the job easier.*

MAKES 4 SERVINGS

1 tablespoon dry sherry

1 tablespoon reduced-sodium soy sauce

1 tablespoon cornstarch

4 teaspoons peanut oil

1 teaspoon sugar

½–1 teaspoon red chile paste*

10 ounces lean beef round steak, cut into paper-thin strips

1 green bell pepper, seeded and cut into 1" pieces

1 red green pepper, seeded and cut into 1" pieces

1 medium onion, coarsely chopped

Four 6" fat-free flour tortillas

1. To prepare the marinade, in a gallon-size sealable plastic bag, combine the sherry, soy sauce, cornstarch, 2 teaspoons of the oil, the sugar and chile paste; add the beef. Seal the bag, squeezing out air; turn to coat the beef. Refrigerate, turning the bag occasionally, at least 1 hour. Drain, reserving the marinade.

2. In a large nonstick skillet or wok, heat the remaining 2 teaspoons of oil. Add the beef and sauté until barely pink, 1–2 minutes. Transfer the beef to a plate.

3. In the skillet, sauté the peppers and onion until soft, about 10 minutes, adding the reserved marinade after 5 minutes and cooking until it evaporates. Return the beef to the pan and cook, stirring gently, until heated through.

4. To assemble the wraps, soften the tortillas according to package directions. Divide the beef and vegetables among the tortillas. Fold up the bottom edge of each tortilla, then the left and right sides to enclose the filling.

**Per serving:** 211 Calories, 7 g Total Fat, 2 g Saturated Fat, 34 mg Cholesterol, 318 mg Sodium, 20 g Total Carbohydrate, 7 g Dietary Fiber, 16 g Protein, 34 mg Calcium. **POINTS** per serving: 3.

*\* Made from mashed red hot chile peppers, vinegar and seasonings, this pungent condiment adds fiery zest to many dishes. Find it in Asian markets and gourmet grocery stores; if unavailable, substitute crushed red pepper flakes.*

# Thai Fish Curry Wraps

*What, no curry powder? This recipe uses the piquant green curry paste that gives so many Thai dishes their complex flavor. To save time, you can skip Step 1 and substitute 1–2 tablespoons of canned green curry paste, available at Asian grocery stores.*

MAKES 4 SERVINGS

### Curry Paste

1 small onion, coarsely chopped

6 sprigs cilantro

Grated zest of 1 lemon

1 tablespoon fish sauce* or soy sauce

1 garlic clove

One ¼" piece peeled gingerroot

¼ teaspoon ground coriander

¼ teaspoon chili powder

⅛ teaspoon ground cumin

Pinch crushed red pepper flakes

Pinch salt

### Fish Wraps

1¼ pounds firm, white-fleshed fish such as halibut or monkfish, cut into 1" pieces

¼ cup unsweetened coconut milk

¼ cup evaporated skimmed milk

One 10-ounce box frozen cut green beans, thawed

One 10-ounce box frozen sliced or diced carrots, thawed

¼ teaspoon coconut extract

Four 6" fat-free flour tortillas

1. To prepare the curry paste, in a blender or food processor, combine the curry paste ingredients; pulse to a coarse paste.

2. In a large saucepan or Dutch oven over medium heat, combine the fish, coconut milk and evaporated milk; bring to a simmer and cook, stirring gently, just until the fish turns opaque, 1–2 minutes. With a slotted spoon, transfer to a plate; keep warm.

3. Bring the liquid to a boil and cook until it is reduced by half. Stir in the green beans, carrots and curry paste; cook until the vegetables are heated through, about 3 minutes. Add the fish and coconut extract; cook, stirring gently, just until heated through, 2–3 minutes.

4. To assemble the wraps, soften the tortillas according to package directions. Divide the fish mixture among the tortillas. Fold up the bottom edge of each tortilla, then the left and right sides to enclose the filling.

**Per serving:** 310 Calories, 7 g Total Fat, 4 g Saturated Fat, 46 mg Cholesterol, 549 mg Sodium, 26 g Total Carbohydrate, 10 g Dietary Fiber, 35 g Protein, 214 mg Calcium. **POINTS** per serving: 5.

*\*Fish sauce (also called* nuoc cham *or* nuoc mam*), a thin brown sauce made from salted and fermented fish, is available in Asian groceries and some supermarkets.*

# Sicilian Tuna Wraps

*The combination of sweet raisins, sour vinegar and salty olives and capers produces a wonderful sensory experience. Try the sauce over fresh tuna or swordfish steaks, too.*

MAKES 4 SERVINGS

2 tablespoons raisins

2 teaspoons olive oil

4 celery stalks, chopped

1 red bell pepper, seeded and chopped

1 garlic clove, coarsely chopped

20 small green olives, halved crosswise and pitted

2 tablespoons red-wine vinegar

1 tablespoon capers, rinsed and drained

½ teaspoon crushed red pepper flakes

One 6-ounce can water-packed solid white tuna, drained

Four 6" fat-free flour tortillas

1. In a small bowl, soak the raisins in hot water to cover until soft and plumped, about 10 minutes. Drain, discarding the water.

2. In a large nonstick skillet, heat the oil. Sauté the celery, bell pepper and garlic until soft, 10–12 minutes. Add the raisins, olives, vinegar, capers and pepper flakes; simmer until the liquid evaporates, 2–3 minutes. Add the tuna and cook, stirring gently, until heated through, 2–3 minutes.

3. To assemble the wraps, soften the tortillas according to package directions. Divide the tuna mixture among the tortillas. Fold up the bottom edge of each tortilla, then the left and right sides to enclose the filling.

**Per serving:** 172 Calories, 5 g Total Fat, 1 g Saturated Fat, 18 mg Cholesterol, 710 mg Sodium, 18 g Total Carbohydrate, 7 g Dietary Fiber, 14 g Protein, 48 mg Calcium. *POINTS* per serving: 2.

# Chicken Quesadillas with Corn-Tomato Salad

*This out-of-the-ordinary salad adds a special richness to a popular Mexican dish. For the best texture, use thawed frozen corn—it's been cooked but isn't mushy.*

MAKES 4 SERVINGS

### Corn-Tomato Salad

1 cup thawed frozen corn kernels

½ green bell pepper, seeded and diced

½ tomato, seeded and diced

2 tablespoons chopped cilantro

2 teaspoons balsamic vinegar

¼ teaspoon salt

### Quesadillas

1½ cups diced cooked chicken breast

1 cup shredded iceberg lettuce

½ cup thick and chunky salsa

Six 8" flour tortillas

⅓ cup shredded sharp cheddar cheese

1. In a medium bowl, combine the salad ingredients; set aside.

2. To prepare the quesadillas, in another medium bowl, combine the chicken, lettuce and salsa; divide among 3 of the tortillas. Sprinkle with the cheese; top with the 3 remaining tortillas.

3. Spray a large nonstick skillet with nonstick cooking spray. One at a time, cook the quesadillas until lightly browned, 3 minutes on each side; turn carefully with wide spatula.

4. Cut the quesadillas into quarters; arrange 3 quarters on each of 4 plates. Serve with the salad on the side.

**Per serving**: 297 Calories, 11 g Total Fat, 4 g Saturated Fat, 49 mg Cholesterol, 712 mg Sodium, 31 g Total Carbohydrate, 3 g Dietary Fiber, 19 g Protein, 134 mg Calcium. *POINTS* per serving: 6.

*Chicken Quesadillas with Corn-Tomato Salad*

# Chicken Fajitas

*This Tex-Mex specialty started the wrap craze. For a variation, try it with skinless turkey breast or lean pork.*

MAKES 4 SERVINGS

2 tablespoons fresh lime juice

1 tablespoon reduced-sodium soy sauce

½ teaspoon chili powder

¼ teaspoon ground cumin

Pinch crushed red pepper flakes

10 ounces skinless boneless chicken breasts, cut into thin strips

4 teaspoons vegetable oil

1 green bell pepper, seeded and thinly sliced

1 red bell pepper, seeded and thinly sliced

1 onion, halved lengthwise and thinly sliced

Four 6" fat-free flour tortillas

½ cup salsa

¼ cup nonfat sour cream

Chopped cilantro, to garnish

1. To prepare the marinade, in a quart-size sealable plastic bag, combine the lime juice, soy sauce, chili powder, cumin and pepper flakes; add the chicken. Seal the bag, squeezing out the air; turn to coat the chicken. Refrigerate, turning the bag occasionally, at least 2 hours or overnight. Drain the chicken and set aside; discard the marinade.

2. In a large nonstick skillet, heat 2 teaspoons of the oil. Sauté the bell peppers and onion until softened, 8–10 minutes, adding a tablespoon or two of water if the mixture becomes too dry. Transfer to a plate and keep warm.

3. In the skillet, heat the remaining 2 teaspoons of oil. Sauté the chicken until cooked through, 3–5 minutes.

4. To assemble the fajitas, soften the tortillas according to package directions. Divide the chicken and sautéed vegetables among the tortillas; garnish with salsa, sour cream and cilantro. Fold up the bottom edge of each tortilla, then the left and right sides to enclose the filling.

**Per serving:** 226 Calories, 7 g Total Fat, 1 g Saturated Fat, 43 mg Cholesterol, 314 mg Sodium, 22 g Total Carbohydrate, 8 g Dietary Fiber, 19 g Protein, 58 mg Calcium. **POINTS** per serving: 4.

# Vietnamese Turkey in Lettuce Wraps

*Try this dish when you want to serve something fun and light; everyone will enjoy making their own bundles, seasoned to their taste, and dipping them in the piquant sauce. The result is an interplay of many textures and flavors—a real feast for the senses!*

MAKES 4 SERVINGS

3 tablespoons fish sauce*

2 tablespoons fresh lime juice

1 tablespoon sugar

¼–½ teaspoon red chile paste†

2 carrots, cut into matchstick-size pieces

1 cucumber, seeded and cut into matchstick-size pieces

2 tablespoons minced onion

2 tablespoons rice vinegar

2 teaspoons peanut oil

One 10-ounce skinless boneless turkey breast, cut into thin strips

2 cups hot cooked short-grain rice

2 large heads Boston lettuce, cleaned and separated into leaves

½ cup whole mint leaves

½ cup whole cilantro leaves

3 tablespoons unsalted dry-roasted peanuts, chopped

1. To prepare the dipping sauce, in a small serving bowl, whisk together 2 tablespoons of the fish sauce, the lime juice, sugar and chile paste with ¼ cup water; set aside.

2. In a medium nonreactive bowl, combine the carrots, cucumber, onion and vinegar; let stand 20 minutes. Drain, discarding the vinegar, and place in a medium serving bowl.

3. In a large nonstick skillet or wok, heat the oil. Sauté the turkey until no longer pink, 1–2 minutes. Sprinkle with the remaining tablespoon of fish sauce and place in another medium serving bowl.

4. To assemble a wrap, spoon about a tablespoon each of the rice, turkey and cucumber-carrot mixture into a lettuce leaf; top with 1–2 mint and cilantro leaves, sprinkle with peanuts and fold the lettuce leaf over to enclose the filling. Dip into the dipping sauce.

**Per serving**: 354 Calories, 7 g Total Fat, 1 g Saturated Fat, 59 mg Cholesterol, 740 mg Sodium, 44 g Total Carbohydrate, 4 g Dietary Fiber, 29 g Protein, 136 mg Calcium. **POINTS** per serving: 7.

*Fish sauce (also called nuoc cham or nuoc mam), a thin brown sauce made from salted and fermented fish, is available in Asian groceries and some supermarkets.*

*† Made from mashed red hot chile peppers, vinegar and seasonings, this pungent condiment adds fiery zest to many dishes. Find it in Asian markets and gourmet grocery stores; if unavailable, substitute crushed red pepper flakes.*

# Middle Eastern Salad Wraps

*Cool, crunchy and full of flavor, these wraps are a vegetarian version of gyros, the popular street fare throughout the Middle East.*

MAKES 4 SERVINGS

2 tablespoons tahini (sesame paste)

2 tablespoons plain nonfat yogurt

1 tablespoon fresh lemon juice

2½ teaspoons extra virgin olive oil

1 small garlic clove, minced

Pinch salt

2 tomatoes, cut into 8 wedges each

1 cucumber, halved lengthwise and thinly sliced

2 tablespoons chopped flat-leaf parsley

1 tablespoon chopped mint

¼ small onion, thinly sliced

Eight 6" fat-free flour tortillas

1. To prepare the dressing, in a small bowl, whisk the tahini, yogurt, lemon juice, oil, garlic and salt with 2 tablespoons water.

2. In a medium bowl, combine the tomatoes, cucumber, parsley, mint and onion. Drizzle with the dressing; toss to coat.

3. To assemble the wraps, soften the tortillas according to package directions. Divide the salad among the tortillas. Fold up the bottom edge of each tortilla, then the left and right sides to enclose the filling.

**Per serving:** 201 Calories, 8 g Total Fat, 0 g Saturated Fat, 0 mg Cholesterol, 319 mg Sodium, 27 g Total Carbohydrate, 10 g Dietary Fiber, 7 g Protein, 79 mg Calcium. **POINTS** per serving: 3.

# Garlicky Red Beans and Pork

*If you like, use canned beans—simmer about 15–20 minutes, just long enough to blend the flavors.*

MAKES 4 SERVINGS

4 teaspoons olive or vegetable oil

10 ounces lean boneless pork loin, cut into 1½" cubes

¼ teaspoon freshly ground pepper

2 red onions, chopped

6 garlic cloves, minced

2 tomatoes, coarsely chopped

1 cup dried red kidney beans, soaked overnight, rinsed and drained

¼ cup canned chopped green chiles, drained

½ teaspoon ground cumin

1. In a large saucepan, heat the oil. Add the pork and pepper; cook, stirring as needed, until the pork is cooked through and lightly browned, 8–10 minutes. Add the onions and garlic; cook, stirring as needed, until the onions are tender, about 8 minutes.

2. Stir in the tomatoes, beans, chiles, cumin and ½ cup water; bring to a boil. Reduce the heat and simmer, covered, until the beans are tender, 50–60 minutes.

**Per serving:** 328 Calories, 9 g Total Fat, 2 g Saturated Fat, 42 mg Cholesterol, 185 mg Sodium, 35 g Total Carbohydrate, 6 g Dietary Fiber, 27 g Protein, 102 mg Calcium. **POINTS** per serving: 6.

# Grilled Eggplant and Tomato

*Grilling gives vegetables a wonderful depth of flavor; served with rice or pasta, this makes a wonderful meal.*

MAKES 4 SERVINGS

½ yellow bell pepper, seeded and diced

¼ cup low-sodium chicken broth

4 teaspoons olive oil

1 tablespoon balsamic vinegar

2 garlic cloves, minced

¼ teaspoon salt

¼ teaspoon freshly ground pepper

1 medium (1-pound) eggplant, peeled and cut into ½" slices

1 tomato, cut into ½" slices

¾ cup crumbled goat cheese

¼ cup coarsely chopped basil

1. Preheat the grill. In a mini food processor or blender, combine the bell pepper, broth, oil, vinegar, garlic, salt and pepper; puree. Place the eggplant and tomato on a sheet of wax paper and brush on both sides with the broth mixture; discard any remaining broth mixture.

2. Grill the eggplant until lightly charred, about 4 minutes on each side. Grill the tomatoes about 2 minutes on each side.

3. Arrange the vegetables on a platter, alternating them and overlapping the slices. Sprinkle with the cheese and basil.

**Per serving:** 161 Calories, 11 g Total Fat, 5 g Saturated Fat, 17 mg, Cholesterol, 260 mg Sodium, 11 g Total Carbohydrate, 2 g Dietary Fiber, 7 g Protein, 124 mg Calcium. **POINTS** per serving: 4.

# Wild Rice–Mushroom Casserole

*Though we like the flavor of portobellos, you can use large white mushrooms if you prefer. This dish can be baked ahead and reheated at serving time.*

MAKES 6 SERVINGS

2–3 portobello mushrooms, or 6 large white mushrooms, stemmed

1 tablespoon olive oil

3 shallots, minced

2¾ cups reduced-sodium chicken or beef broth

1 cup wild rice

½ teaspoon dried thyme or rosemary leaves, crumbled

½ teaspoon freshly ground pepper

1 bay leaf

1. Preheat the broiler; line a baking sheet with foil. Place the mushrooms, stemmed-side down, on the baking sheet. Broil until lightly browned, about 4 minutes. Let cool slightly, then dice; transfer to a plate.

2. Reduce the oven temperature to 350° F. In a medium saucepan, heat the oil. Sauté the shallots until softened, about 4 minutes. Stir in the broth, the mushrooms with any juices, the rice, thyme, pepper and bay leaf. Transfer to a 1-quart casserole. Cover and bake until the liquid is absorbed and the rice is tender but still slightly chewy, about 1 hour. Discard the bay leaf.

**Per serving:** 145 Calories, 3 g Total Fat, 0 g Saturated Fat, 0 mg Cholesterol, 261 mg Sodium, 25 g Total Carbohydrate, 2 g Dietary Fiber, 6 g Protein, 16 mg Calcium. **POINTS** per serving: 3.

# Risotto Milanese

*Saffron and lemon zest give this risotto its regal quality and lovely color. Its traditional partner is the braised veal shank dish, Osso Buco.*

MAKES 4 SERVINGS

3½ cups low-sodium chicken broth

Pinch saffron threads

1 tablespoon olive oil

1 onion, chopped

1 cup Arborio rice

½ cup dry white wine

2 tablespoons grated Parmesan cheese

2 teaspoons reduced-calorie tub margarine

2 teaspoons grated lemon zest

Freshly ground black or white pepper, to taste

1. In a medium saucepan, bring the broth to a boil. Reduce the heat and simmer.

2. In a small bowl, dissolve the saffron in 1 cup of the broth.

3. In a large nonstick saucepan, heat the oil. Sauté the onion until softened, about 2 minutes. Add the rice; cook, stirring to coat, about 1 minute.

4. Add the wine and ½ cup of the broth; cook, stirring, until the liquid is absorbed. Continue adding the broth, alternating between plain broth and saffron broth, ½ cup at a time, stirring until the broth is absorbed before adding more, until the rice is just tender. The total cooking time should be 25–30 minutes. Stir in the cheese, margarine, lemon zest and pepper; serve at once.

**Per Serving:** 294 Calories, 9 g Total Fat, 2 g Saturated Fat, 4 mg Cholesterol, 216 mg Sodium, 43 g Total Carbohydrate, 1 g Dietary Fiber, 9 g Protein, 97 mg Calcium. **POINTS** per serving: 6.

# Roman Rice Frittata

*This is a perfect fallback recipe when you can't get out to the grocery store. If you don't happen to have figs on hand, use prunes instead.*

MAKES 4 SERVINGS

2 teaspoons olive oil

1 onion, finely chopped

1 garlic clove, minced

1 cup fat-free egg substitute

½ cup cooked white rice

2 large dried figs, finely chopped

2 tablespoons grated Parmesan

¼ teaspoon dried thyme leaves, crumbled

1. Place the broiler rack 5" from heat; preheat the broiler.

2. In a medium nonstick skillet with a heatproof handle, heat the oil. Sauté the onion and garlic until softened, about 2 minutes.

3. In a large bowl, beat the egg substitute until frothy; stir in the sautéed onion, rice, figs, cheese and thyme.

4. Wipe out the skillet with a paper towel. Spray the sides as well as the bottom of the skillet with nonstick cooking spray; heat. Pour in the egg substitute mixture, tilting to cover the bottom of the pan. Reduce the heat and cook until the underside is set, 10–12 minutes. Run the frittata under the broiler until the top is set and a light crust forms, 1–1½ minutes. Slide the frittata onto a large plate. Cut into 4 wedges.

**Per serving:** 145 Calories, 4 g Total Fat, 1 g Saturated Fat, 4 mg Cholesterol, 201 mg Sodium, 17 g Total Carbohydrate, 1 g Dietary Fiber, 9 g Protein, 118 mg Calcium. *POINTS* per serving: 3.

## Tip

**If your skillet's handle isn't heatproof (or if you aren't sure), wrap it in a few layers of foil, or leave the broiler door ajar and keep the handle sticking out.**

# Scrambled Eggs Mexican Style

*If you can't find chorizo, substitute any spicy cooked sausage—pepperoni is a good choice.*

## MAKES 4 SERVINGS

1 onion, minced

2 ounces cooked chorizo sausage, diced

1 tomato, finely chopped

1 poblano pepper, roasted and diced

1 cup egg substitute

2 eggs

Pinch salt

1. In a medium nonstick skillet, sauté the onion and sausage until the onion is golden brown and the sausage is cooked through, 10–12 minutes. Add the tomato and pepper; cook, stirring frequently, until most of the liquid evaporates, about 2 minutes.

2. In a small bowl, whisk the egg substitute, eggs and 1 tablespoon water. Add to the tomato mixture; cook, stirring gently and occasionally, to form large curds, 3–5 minutes (do not overcook); sprinkle with the salt.

**Per serving:** 137 Calories, 7 g Total Fat, 2 g Saturated Fat, 117 mg Cholesterol, 331 mg Sodium, 7 g Total Carbohydrate, 1 g Dietary Fiber, 13 g Protein, 48 mg Calcium. *POINTS* per serving: 3.

## How We Did It

To roast the poblano pepper, preheat the broiler. Line a baking sheet with foil; place pepper on baking sheet. Broil 4–6" from the heat, turning frequently with tongs, until the skin is lightly charred on all sides, about 10 minutes. Transfer to a paper bag; fold bag closed and steam 10 minutes. Peel, seed and devein pepper over bowl to catch juices.

# Spicy Shrimp with Papaya-Lime Salsa

*You'll love the spicy flavors of the shrimp and the beautiful color of the papaya in this recipe. If you like, thread the shrimp onto the skewers before grilling or broiling.*

## MAKES 4 SERVINGS

1½ teaspoons paprika

½ teaspoon dried thyme leaves, crumbled

½ teaspoon salt

½ teaspoon freshly ground black pepper

⅛–¼ teaspoon cayenne pepper

1¼ pounds large shrimp, peeled and deveined

2 cups cubed papaya

3 scallions, sliced

1 lime, peeled and diced

1. Preheat the grill or broiler. Spray a grill basket or the broiler rack with nonstick cooking spray. In a gallon-size sealable plastic bag, combine the paprika, thyme, salt, black pepper and cayenne; add the shrimp. Seal the bag, squeezing out the air; shake to coat.

2. Meanwhile, in a small bowl, combine the papaya, scallions and lime; set aside.

3. Grill the shrimp in the basket or broil them 6" from the heat until pink and cooked through, about 3 minutes on each side. Serve, with the salsa on the side.

**Per serving:** 150 Calories, 1 g Total Fat, 0 g Saturated Fat, 221 mg Cholesterol, 531 mg Sodium, 10 g Total Carbohydrate, 1 g Dietary Fiber, 25 g Protein, 79 mg Calcium. *POINTS* per serving: 3.

*Spicy Shrimp with Papaya-Lime Salsa*

# Spicy Shrimp with Black Bean Salsa

*Beans are a staple in Mexico and can be prepared in ways almost too numerous to count. Here, we've combined them with colorful vegetables and fiery jalapeño pepper to make a marvelous salsa for shrimp.*

MAKES 4 SERVINGS

One 15-ounce can black beans, rinsed and drained

1 yellow or green bell pepper, seeded and diced

½ red onion, chopped

¼ celery stalk, chopped

¼ cup chopped cilantro

1 jalapeño pepper, seeded, deveined and minced (wear gloves to prevent irritation)

2 tablespoons fresh lime juice

2 garlic cloves, crushed

4 teaspoons olive or vegetable oil

24 medium shrimp, peeled and deveined

1 tablespoon dry sherry

1½ teaspoons chili powder

1 garlic clove, crushed

½ teaspoon ground cumin

¼ teaspoon salt

2 teaspoons olive or vegetable oil

1. In a medium nonreactive bowl, combine the beans, bell pepper, onion, celery, cilantro, jalapeño, lime juice, half of the garlic and 2 teaspoons of the oil. Let stand, covered, until the flavors are blended, 1–2 hours.

2. To prepare the shrimp, in another medium bowl, combine the shrimp, sherry, chili powder, the remaining garlic, the cumin and salt; toss to coat.

3. In a large nonstick skillet, heat the remaining 2 teaspoons of oil. Add the shrimp and marinade; cook, stirring frequently, until the shrimp turn pink, about 4 minutes. Serve with the salsa on the side.

**Per serving:** 273 Calories, 7 g Total Fat, 1 g Saturated Fat, 129 mg Cholesterol, 282 mg Sodium, 27 g Total Carbohydrate, 3 g Dietary Fiber, 26 g Protein, 89 mg Calcium. **POINTS** per serving: 5.

# Scallops with Parsley-Brandy Pesto

*Scallops become tough and rubbery if they're over-cooked, so be sure to add them to the hot skillet a few at a time, and watch them carefully. Remove them from the heat just before they're thoroughly opaque, because they'll continue to cook when you remove them from the heat.*

MAKES 4 SERVINGS

¾ cup minced flat-leaf parsley

½ ounce goat cheese

1 tablespoon brandy

2 tablespoons walnuts, chopped

1 tablespoon fresh lemon juice

3 teaspoons olive oil

1 garlic clove, minced

1¼ pounds large sea scallops

1. To prepare the pesto, in a food processor, combine the parsley, cheese, brandy, walnuts, lemon juice, 1 teaspoon of the oil and the garlic; puree.

2. In a large nonstick skillet, heat the remaining 2 teaspoons of oil. Add the scallops in small batches and sauté until they are browned outside and still just slightly translucent in the center, 2–3 minutes on each side. Transfer to a medium bowl and toss with the pesto.

**Per serving:** 193 Calories, 7 g Total Fat, 1 g Saturated Fat, 50 mg Cholesterol, 251 mg Sodium, 5 g Total Carbohydrate, 1 g Dietary Fiber, 25 g Protein, 61 mg Calcium. **POINTS** per serving: 4.

# Teriyaki-Grilled Tuna with Water Chestnuts

*This dish is fast and easy, especially if you make the marinade ahead of time and store it in the refrigerator. If your grill is large enough, cook the tuna and water chestnuts at the same time.*

MAKES 4 SERVINGS

¼ cup reduced-sodium soy sauce

2 tablespoons rice-wine vinegar

2 tablespoons dry sherry

6 garlic cloves, minced

1 tablespoon minced peeled gingerroot

2 teaspoons honey

¼ teaspoon freshly ground pepper

One 8-ounce can whole water chestnuts, drained

1¼ pounds tuna steaks, cut into 4 pieces

1. Preheat the grill. If you are using wooden skewers, soak in water 30 minutes. In a small bowl, combine the soy sauce, vinegar, sherry, garlic, gingerroot, honey and pepper.

2. Thread the water chestnuts onto four 6" metal or wooden skewers, spacing them ⅛" apart; brush twice with the marinade. Grill, turning and brushing with the marinade occasionally, until heated through, 6–8 minutes.

3. Brush the tuna with the marinade. Grill, brushing constantly with remaining marinade, until just opaque in the center, about 5 minutes on each side. Serve, with the water chestnuts on the side.

**Per serving:** 269 Calories, 7 g Total Fat, 2 g Saturated Fat, 54 mg Cholesterol, 660 mg Sodium, 11 g Total Carbohydrate, 0 g Dietary Fiber, 35 g Protein, 12 mg Calcium. **POINTS** per serving: 6.

# Veal Pizzaiola

*Some Italian cooks dip the meat in bread crumbs before sautéing it; others insist on adding capers to the sauce. But most believe that less is more, and that it's the fresh oregano that really gives this dish its distinctive flavor.*

MAKES 4 SERVINGS

4 teaspoons olive oil

1 pound veal cutlets, pounded ¼" thick

One 14½-ounce can no-salt-added diced tomatoes

½ cup dry white wine

2 tablespoons minced oregano

2 garlic cloves, minced

¼ teaspoon salt

Freshly ground pepper, to taste

1. In a large nonstick skillet, heat the oil. Sauté the veal until browned, 2–3 minutes on each side. Transfer to a plate.

2. In the skillet, combine the tomatoes, wine, oregano, garlic, salt and pepper. Reduce the heat and cook until the tomatoes are slightly softened, about 5 minutes.

3. Return the veal and any accumulated juices to the skillet and spoon the sauce over it. Reduce the heat and simmer until the sauce is thickened and the veal is cooked through and very tender, 15–20 minutes.

**Per serving:** 201 Calories, 7 g Total Fat, 1 g Saturated Fat, 83 mg Cholesterol, 221 mg Sodium, 6 g Total Carbohydrate, 1 g Dietary Fiber, 24 g Protein, 52 mg Calcium. **POINTS** per serving: 4.

## Tip

**Depending on the size of your skillet and the cutlets, you may want to brown them in two batches, using half of the oil each time.**

# Tuscan White Bean Salad

*You won't go very far in Tuscany without encountering beans and sage. This salad is delicious as is, but if you like, enhance it with red onion, canned tuna or both.*

MAKES 4 SERVINGS

2 tablespoons minced fresh sage,
or 2 teaspoons dried

4 teaspoons extra virgin olive oil

1 tablespoon dry white wine

1 tablespoon white-wine vinegar

2 garlic cloves, minced

¼ teaspoon salt

Freshly ground pepper, to taste

One 16-ounce can cannellini beans, rinsed and drained

In a large bowl, whisk the sage, oil, wine, vinegar, garlic, salt and pepper. Add the beans; toss to coat. Let stand, covered, until the flavors are blended, 1–2 hours.

**Per serving:** 190 Calories, 5 g Total Fat, 1 g Saturated Fat, 0 mg Cholesterol, 138 mg Sodium, 27 g Total Carbohydrate, 4 g Dietary Fiber, 10 g Protein, 41 mg Calcium. *POINTS* per serving: 3.

# Swiss Chard with Potatoes

*Greens and potatoes are a classic combination in many culinary traditions—what varies are the seasonings: garlic and lemon are Italian, jalapeños and tomatoes are Mexican.*

MAKES 4 SERVINGS

2 teaspoons corn oil

2 onions, thinly sliced

1 jalapeño pepper, seeded, deveined and thinly sliced (wear gloves to prevent irritation)

1 cup stewed tomatoes

2 medium red potatoes, diced

½ cup low-sodium vegetable broth

10 cups lightly packed Swiss chard leaves, cleaned and cut crosswise into 1" strips

1. In a large saucepan, heat the oil; sauté the onions and pepper until the onions are golden brown, 10–12 minutes.

2. Add the tomatoes; bring to a boil. Cook, stirring constantly, until slightly reduced, about 2 minutes. Stir in the potatoes and broth; bring to a boil. Reduce the heat and simmer, covered, until the potatoes are tender and the liquid is reduced to about ⅓ cup, 10–12 minutes. Add the chard; cook, stirring, until wilted, about 3 minutes.

**Per serving:** 135 Calories, 3 g Total Fat, 0 g Saturated Fat, 0 mg Cholesterol, 536 mg Sodium, 26 g Total Carbohydrate, 3 g Dietary Fiber, 5 g Protein, 91 mg Calcium. *POINTS* per serving: 2.

# METRIC CONVERSIONS

• • •

If you are converting the recipes in this book to
metric measurements, use the following chart as a guide.

| VOLUME | | WEIGHT | | LENGTH | | OVEN TEMPERATURES | |
|---|---|---|---|---|---|---|---|
| ¼ teaspoon | 1 milliliter | 1 ounce | 30 grams | 1 inch | 25 millimeters | 250°F | 120°C |
| ½ teaspoon | 2 milliliters | ¼ pound | 120 grams | 1 inch | 2.5 centimeters | 275°F | 140°C |
| 1 teaspoon | 5 milliliters | ½ pound | 240 grams | | | 300°F | 150°C |
| 1 tablespoon | 15 milliliters | ¾ pound | 360 grams | | | 325°F | 160°C |
| 2 tablespoons | 30 milliliters | 1 pound | 480 grams | | | 350°F | 180°C |
| 3 tablespoons | 45 milliliters | | | | | 375°F | 190°C |
| ¼ cup | 50 milliliters | | | | | 400°F | 200°C |
| ⅓ cup | 75 milliliters | | | | | 425°F | 220°C |
| ½ cup | 125 milliliters | | | | | 450°F | 230°C |
| ⅔ cup | 150 milliliters | | | | | 475°F | 250°C |
| ¾ cup | 175 milliliters | | | | | 500°F | 260°C |
| 1 cup | 250 milliliters | | | | | 525°F | 270°C |
| 1 quart | 1 liter | | | | | | |

# Index

Page numbers in *italics* refer to photos.

435